WILEY
PATHWAYS

SMALL
BUSINESS
ACCOUNTING

WILEY
PATHWAYS

SMALL BUSINESS ACCOUNTING

LITA EPSTEIN, MBA

with
SUSAN MYERS

WILEY

John Wiley & Sons, Inc.
New York • Chichester • Weinheim • Brisbane • Toronto • Singapore

PUBLISHER	Anne Smith
PROJECT EDITOR	Beth Tripmacher
SENIOR EDITORIAL ASSISTANT	Tiara Kelly
PRODUCTION MANAGER	Micheline Frederick
PRODUCTION EDITOR	Kerry Weinstein
CREATIVE DIRECTOR	Harry Nolan
COVER DESIGNER	Hope Miller
COVER PHOTO	©Chemistry/Getty Images

This book was set in Times New Roman PS 10.5/13 pt by Aptara, Inc.® and printed and bound by R.R. Donnelley. The cover was printed by R.R. Donnelley.

To order books or for customer service, please call 1-800-CALL WILEY (225-5945).

ISBN-13 978-0-470-19863-6

Printed in the United States of America

10 9 8 7 6 5 4 3 2 1

PREFACE

Today's students have different goals, different life experiences, and different academic backgrounds, but they are all on the same path to success in the real world. This diversity, coupled with the reality that these learners often have jobs, families, and other commitments, requires a flexibility that our nation's higher education system is addressing. Distance learning, shorter course terms, new disciplines, evening courses, and certification programs are some of the approaches that colleges employ to reach as many students as possible and help them clarify and achieve their goals.

The *Wiley Pathways* program, a specially designed suite of services and content, helps you address this diversity and the need for flexibility. *Wiley Pathways* content puts a focus on the fundamentals to help students grasp the subject, bringing them all to the same basic understanding. Content from the *Wiley Pathways* program has an emphasis on teaching job-related skills and practical applications of concepts with clear and professional language. The core competencies and skills help students succeed in the classroom and beyond, whether in another course or in a professional setting. A variety of built-in learning resources allow the students to practice what they need to perform and help instructors and students gauge students' understanding of the content. These resources enable students to think critically about their new knowledge and apply their skills in any situation.

Our goal with *Wiley Pathways* is to celebrate the many students in your courses, respect their needs, and help you guide them on their way.

LEARNING SYSTEM

To meet the needs of working college students, *Wiley Pathways* uses a learning system based on Bloom's Taxonomy. Key topics in *Wiley Pathways Small Business Accounting* are presented in easy-to-follow chapters. The text then prompts analysis, evaluation, and creation with a variety of learning aids and assessment tools. Students move efficiently from reviewing what they have learned, to acquiring new information and skills, to applying their new knowledge and skills to real-life scenarios.

Using this learning system, students not only achieve academic mastery of small business accounting *topics*, but they master real-world *skills* related to that content. The learning system also helps students become independent learners, giving them a distinct advantage in the field, whether they are just starting out or seeking to advance in their careers.

ORGANIZATION, DEPTH, AND BREADTH OF THE TEXT

Modular Format

Research on college students shows that they access information from textbooks in a non-linear way. Instructors also often wish to reorder textbook content to suit the needs of a particular class. Therefore, although *Wiley Pathways* proceeds logically from the basics to increasingly more challenging material, chapters are further organized into sections that are self-contained for maximum teaching and learning flexibility.

Numeric System of Headings

Wiley Pathways uses a numeric system for headings (e.g., 2.3.4 identifies the fourth subsection of Section 3 of Chapter 2). With this system, students and teachers can quickly and easily pinpoint topics in the table of contents and the text, keeping class time and study sessions focused.

Core Content
Part I: The Foundation of Accounting

Chapter 1, Accounting for Your Business, demonstrates the four basic accounting principles and how to implement them. The chapter includes a brief analysis of the advantages and disadvantages of each legal form of business structure. The chapter ends with instructions on how to set up an accounting system.

Chapter 2, Mastering Debits and Credits, delineates the five main account types and how they are used. The chapter contrasts and compares the balance sheet with the income sheet. A chart of accounts is presented along with the necessary steps to build one.

Chapter 3, Beginning the Accounting Cycle, outlines the steps completed in an accounting period. The accounting cycle is discussed from a transaction to the closing of the books. The book of original entry is defined as is the book of final entry. Finally, the chapter explores the importance of creating an efficient filing system and how to determine what records need to be stored and for what length of time.

Part II: Accounting for a Service Business

Chapter 4, Journalizing Transactions, introduces readers to the concept of using journaling to organize transaction information. Recording sales and purchases is covered in detail including an examination of assets, liabilities, revenue, and expense. The chapter concludes with a discussion of the accounts payable and accounts receivable.

Chapter 5, Posting Transactions and Preparing a Trial Balance, outlines the steps for posting transactions in a manual accounting system. In addition, the computerized transactions are also reviewed. Finally, the chapter covers a method for finding errors in your books as well as how to produce a trial balance.

Chapter 6, Adjustments and the Worksheet, examines how to create and use a worksheet. The chapter profiles the reasons why a small businessperson would need adjustments to their worksheets. The chapter concludes with a detailed account of how to use a completed worksheet to compute the business's bottom line.

Chapter 7, Financial Statements and the Closing Process, compares an income statement with a statement of owner's equity, and a balance sheet. Each of these statements displays the financial health of a company from a different perspective. The necessary steps in preparing a balance sheet are also outlined. Finally, the chapter offers a discussion on why some accounts are closed out to zero and others stay open.

Part III: Basic Accounting Procedures

Chapter 8, Cash, Banking, and Internal Controls, provides an overview of the four types of internal fraud and how to guard against each one. Monitoring and protecting the cash that flows in and out of the business is covered. Finally, the chapter ends with a discussion on how to prevent the theft of any cash that one must have on hand to run the business.

Chapter 9, Employee Payroll and Deductions, explains what documents are legally required for hiring employees. The chapter offers an in-depth review of what taxes must be withheld from employees' paychecks. A discussion of how the company benefits, such as health insurance, affect employees' earnings concludes the chapter.

Chapter 10, Understanding Payroll Legalities, focuses on the responsibilities of business owners to keep an account of, file, and pay payroll taxes. The tax returns employers must file are covered in-depth. Creating a system for maintaining this information and for organizing employee records is covered. Finally, this chapter ends with an overview of how to find out the state's requirements for worker's compensation and the related taxes.

Chapter 11, Special Journals: Sales and Cash Receipts, is devoted to using a sales journal to organize transactions and to save time, especially for retail businesses. In addition, the concept of sales tax is discussed as well as the merchant's responsibilities to collect and remit the sales tax. This chapter concludes with ideas on how to keep track of accounts receivables and aging accounts.

Chapter 12, Special Journals: Purchases and Cash Disbursements, discusses how to use the purchase journal to record merchandise purchases on credit. In addition, how to calculate the principal and interest on monthly payments is reviewed. Finally, tools that manage vendor accounts are explained and demonstrated.

Part IV: Accounting for a Merchandising Business

Chapter 13, Merchandise Inventory, explains how to compute gross profit. The chapter also differentiates between two systems of inventory with a discussion on how to record initial cost using both systems of inventory. Evaluating costing methods for the business is also reviewed in detail. Finally, the chapter concludes with a discussion of the "lower of cost or market rule," an established accounting principle.

Chapter 14, Adjustments and the Worksheets for Merchandising Business, examines the matching principle and how to use it. In addition, general ledger accounts are examined and conclusions about the health of a business are drawn. How to estimate future bad debt and how to bring payroll expenses up to date are reviewed.

Chapter 15, Financial Statements and the Closing Process for a Merchandising Business, assesses how to compute the gross profit percentage. The principle of COGS, or cost of goods sold, is discussed along with an explanation of how to zero it out. The chapter concludes with an examination of the IRS paperwork needed to hire independent contractors as it differs from the paperwork needed to hire full-time employees.

PRE-READING LEARNING AIDS

Each chapter of *Wiley Pathways* features a number of learning and study aids, described in the following sections, to activate students' prior knowledge of the topics and orient them to the material.

Do You Already Know?

This bulleted list focuses on *subject matter* that will be taught. It tells students what they will be learning in this chapter and why it is significant for their careers. It also helps students understand why the chapter is important and how it relates to other chapters in the text.

The online assessment tool in multiple-choice format not only introduces chapter material, but it also helps students anticipate the chapter's learning outcomes. By focusing students' attention on what they do not know, the self-test provides students with a benchmark against which they can measure their own progress. The Pre Test is available online at www. wiley.com/college/epstein.

What You Will Find Out and *What You Will Be Able To Do*

This bulleted list emphasizes *capabilities* and *skills* students will learn as a result of reading the chapter and notes the sections in which they will be found. It prepares students to synthesize and evaluate the chapter material and relate it to the real world.

WITHIN-TEXT LEARNING AIDS

The following learning aids are designed to encourage analysis and synthesis of the material, support the learning process, and ensure success during the evaluation phase.

Introduction

This section orients the student by introducing the chapter and explaining its practical value and relevance to the book as a whole. Short summaries of chapter sections preview the topics to follow.

In the Real World

These boxes tie section content to real-world organizations, scenarios, and applications. Engaging stories of professionals and institutions—challenges they faced, successes they had, and their ultimate outcome.

Small Business Accounting in Action

These margin boxes point out places in the text where professional applications of a concept are demonstrated. An arrow in the box points to the section of the text and a description of the application is given in the box.

For Example

These margin boxes highlight documents and Web sites from real companies that further help students understand a key concept. The boxes can reference a figure or the Toolkit found at the end of each chapter.

Career Connection

Case studies of people in the field depicting the skills that helped them succeed in the professional world. Each profile ends with a list of "Tips from the Professional" that provide relevant advice and helpful tools.

Pathway to . . .

This boxed section provides how-to or step-by-step lists to help students perform specific tasks.

Summary

Each chapter concludes with a summary paragraph that reviews the major concepts in the chapter and links back to the "Do You Already Know" list.

Key Terms and Glossary

To help students develop a professional vocabulary, key terms are bolded when they first appear in the chapter and are also shown in the margin of page with their definitions. A complete list of key terms with brief definitions appears at the end of each chapter and again in a glossary at the end of the book. Knowledge of key terms is assessed by all assessment tools (see below).

Toolkit

An end-of-chapter appendix that contains relevant documents and examples from real companies.

EVALUATION AND ASSESSMENT TOOLS

The evaluation phase of the *Wiley Pathways* learning system consists of a variety of within-chapter and end-of-chapter assessment tools that test how well students have learned the material and their ability to apply it in the real world. These tools also encourage students to extend their learning into different scenarios and higher levels of understanding and thinking. The following assessment tools appear in every chapter of *Wiley Pathways*.

Self-Check

Related to the "Do You Already Know" bullets and found at the end of each section, this battery of short-answer questions emphasizes student understanding of concepts and mastery of section content. Though the questions may be either discussed in class or studied by students outside of class, students should not go on before they can answer all questions correctly.

Understand: What Have You Learned?

This online Post Test should be taken after students have completed the chapter. It includes all of the questions in the Pre Test so that students can see how their learning has progressed and improved. The Post Test is available online at www.wiley.com/college/holden.

Apply: What Would You Do?

These questions drive home key ideas by asking students to synthesize and apply chapter concepts to new, real-life situations and scenarios.

Be a Small Business Accountant

Found at the end of each chapter, "Be a . . ." questions are designed to extend students' thinking and are thus ideal for discussion or writing assignments. Using an open-ended format and sometimes based on Web sources, they encourage students to draw conclusions using chapter material applied to real-world situations, which fosters both mastery and independent learning.

INSTRUCTOR AND STUDENT PACKAGE

Wiley Pathways is available with the following teaching and learning supplements. All supplements are available online at the text's Book Companion Web site, located at www.wiley.com/college/epstein.

Instructor's Resource Guide

The Instructor's Resource Guide provides the following aids and supplements for teaching a small business accounting course:

- **Text summary aids:** For each chapter, these include a chapter summary, learning objectives, definitions of key terms, and answers to in-text question sets.
- **Teaching suggestions:** For each chapter, these include at least three suggestions for learning activities (such as ideas for speakers to invite, videos to show, and other projects), and suggestions for additional resources.

PowerPoints

Key information is summarized in ten to fifteen PowerPoints per chapter. Instructors may use these in class or choose to share them with students for class presentations or to provide additional study support.

Test Bank

The test bank features one test per chapter, as well as a mid-term and two finals—one cumulative and one non-cumulative. Each includes true/false, multiple-choice, and open-ended questions. Answers and page references are provided for the true/false and multiple-choice questions, and page references are given for the open-ended questions. Tests are available in Microsoft Word and computerized formats.

ACKNOWLEDGMENTS

Taken together, the content, pedagogy, and assessment elements of *Wiley Pathways Small Business Accounting* offer the career-oriented student the most important aspects of the small business accounting field as well as ways to develop the skills and capabilities that current and future employers seek in the individuals they hire and promote. Instructors will appreciate its practical focus, conciseness, and real-world emphasis.

Special thanks are extended to James Benedum of Milwaukee Area Technical College for acting as an academic advisor to the text. His careful review of the manuscript, significant contributions to the content, and assurance that the book reflects the most recent trends in small business accounting, were invaluable assets in our development of the manuscript. We'd also like to thank Denise Wooten of Erie Community College for her help in crafting the practice questions.

We would like to thank the reviewers for their feedback and suggestions during the text's development. Their advice on how to shape *Wiley Pathways Small Business Accounting* into a solid learning tool that meets both their needs and those of their students is deeply appreciated.

Joan Cook, Milwaukee Area Technical College
Jim DeLisa, Highline Community College

BRIEF CONTENTS

CONTENTS

**PART IV Accounting for
a Merchandising
Business**

**CHAPTER 13. MERCHANDISE
INVENTORY 319**

1

ACCOUNTING FOR YOUR BUSINESS
Knowing Your Options

- The four basic accounting concepts and how to implement them
- The advantages and disadvantages of each legal form of business structure
- How to set up a computerized accounting system

For additional questions to assess your current knowledge of making business accounting decisions, go to **www.wiley.com/college/epstein.**

What You Will Find Out	What You Will Be Able To Do
1.1 How basic accounting concepts help record, classify, and report information about a business's financial transactions	• Choose a time period for tracking business finances; determine whether a cash-basis accounting system or an accrual accounting system is best for your business
1.2 The types of business structures	• Evaluate business structures
1.3 How the various accounting software options serve a business	• Choose a computerized accounting program; set up a computerized accounting system

INTRODUCTION

Accounting is called "the language of business" because it is used to communicate financial information. Like any language, accounting has its own vocabulary and structure. This chapter explores the terms and concepts used in accounting for a small business.

1.1 BASIC ACCOUNTING CONCEPTS

Bookkeeping:
The methodical way in which businesses track their financial transactions.

Accounting:
The total structure of records and procedures used to record, classify, and report information about a business's financial transactions.

Bookkeeping is the methodical way in which businesses track their financial transactions. **Accounting** is the total structure of records and procedures used to record, classify, and report information about a business's financial transactions. Bookkeeping involves the recording of that financial information into the accounting system while maintaining adherence to solid accounting principles.

Accurate and complete bookkeeping is crucial to any business owner, but it's also important to others who are interested in the business, such as investors, financial institutions, and employees. People both inside (managers, owners, and employees) and outside the business (investors, lenders, and government agencies) depend on accurate recording of financial transactions.

Many small-business people who are just starting their businesses serve as their own bookkeepers until the business is large enough to hire someone dedicated to keeping the books. Few small businesses have accountants on staff; instead, they have bookkeepers on staff who serve as the outside accountant's eyes and ears. A bookkeeper is not required to be a certified public accountant (CPA). However, most businesses do require that the outside accountant has a CPA certification.

Whether you are the business owner, bookkeeper, or CPA, you will need to apply basic accounting concepts. These concepts include the following:

- Separate entity assumption.
- Accounting period assumption.
- Cash-basis accounting and accrual accounting.
- Internal controls.

1.1.1 Separate Entity Assumption

Separate entity assumption:
The concept that a business is an economic entity separate from its owner.

An *entity* is something that has an independent existence. You are an entity, and your business is a different entity. The **separate entity assumption** is the concept that a business is an economic entity separate from its owner.

You may already know that a corporation is a separate *legal* entity. The separate entity assumption applies to all forms of business, not just corporations. In practical terms, this means that the business's financial records must be kept separate from the owner's financial records.

IN THE REAL WORLD

Organizing Your Accounts

Some people would say it's a good problem to have. When Monica started working as an event planner, the word spread about her exceptional talent. She planned every detail of an event, yet could think on her feet and make adjustments seamlessly.

The problem was Monica's success. When she wasn't working an event, she was preparing for the next one. She never seemed to have time to set up an accounting system for her business. She used her personal bank account and did not have a separate file location for business papers. At tax time she had to hire an accountant to help her sort out the mess and file her income tax return. With the accountant, Monica set up a system that included a separate bank account for the business and a location for her work files.

Accounting period assumption:
The concept that income is reported in regular time periods.

Accounting period:
The time for which financial information is being tracked.

Annual report:
A year-end summary of the company's activities and financial results.

Fiscal year:
A 12-month accounting period.

1.1.2 Accounting Period Assumption

The **accounting period assumption** is the concept that income is reported in regular time periods. An **accounting period** is the time for which financial information is being tracked. Most businesses track their financial results on a monthly basis, so each accounting period equals one month. Some businesses choose to do financial reports on a quarterly basis, so the accounting periods are three months. Other businesses only look at their results on a yearly basis, so their accounting periods are 12 months. A business that tracks its financial activities monthly usually also creates quarterly reports and an **annual report** (a year-end summary of the company's activities and financial results).

A **fiscal year** is a consecutive 12-month accounting period. The fiscal year is not always the same as the calendar year (January 1–December 31).

Small Business Accounting in Action ➡
Choose a time period for tracking business finances.

1.1.3 Cash-Basis Accounting and Accrual Accounting

Before starting to record transactions, you must decide whether to use cash-basis accounting or accrual accounting. The key difference between these two accounting methods is the point at which you record sales and purchases in your books. Cash-basis accounting is used for service businesses only. If a business

**PATHWAY TO...
CHOOSING A FISCAL YEAR**

- The calendar year is usually easiest, especially since the IRS requires calendar-year tax reporting for most businesses.
- Choose a different fiscal year if your company's busiest season occurs at calendar year-end. Many retail stores operate on a fiscal year of February 1 to January 31.
- If your inventory levels are high at the end of December, schedule your fiscal year-end for when levels are lower. This makes the year-end inventory count easier.

has inventory, then it must use accrual accounting. This book concentrates on the accrual accounting method. If you choose to use cash-basis accounting, don't panic: You can still find most of the bookkeeping information here useful.

Cash-basis accounting:
A system in which transactions are recorded when cash changes hands.

Cash-Basis Accounting

Cash-basis accounting is a system in which you only record transactions when cash actually changes hands. You record a sale when a cash payment is received from the customer. You record a purchase when cash is paid out. Cash receipts or payments can be in the form of cash, check, credit card, electronic transfer, or other means used to pay for an item.

Cash-basis accounting can't be used if a store sells products on store credit and bills the customer at a later date. There is no provision to record and track money due from customers at some time in the future in the cash-basis accounting method.

That's also true for purchases. With the cash-basis accounting method, the owner only records the purchase of supplies or goods that will later be sold when he or she actually pays cash. If goods are bought on credit to be paid later, the transaction isn't recorded until the cash is actually paid out.

Depending on the size of your business, you may want to start out with cash-basis accounting. Many small businesses run by an individual or a small group of partners use cash-basis accounting because it's easy. But as the business grows, the business owners find it necessary to switch to accrual accounting in order to more accurately track revenue and expenses.

Accrual accounting:
A system in which transactions are recorded when completed, even if cash doesn't change hands.

Accrual Accounting

Accrual accounting is a system in which you record a transaction when it's completed, even if cash doesn't change hands. For example, if you sell on store credit, you record the transaction immediately.

Suppose your company buys products to sell from a vendor but doesn't actually pay for those products for 30 days. If you're using cash-basis accounting, you don't record the purchase until you actually lay out the cash to the vendor. If you're using accrual accounting, you record the purchase when you receive the products, and you also use an account called accounts payable to record the future debt.

Like cash-basis accounting, accrual accounting has its drawbacks. It does a good job of matching revenue and expenses, but it does a poor job of tracking cash. Because you record revenue when the transaction occurs and not when you collect the cash, you can show a high income even if you don't have cash in the bank. For example, suppose you're running a contracting company and completing jobs on a daily basis. You can record the revenue upon completion of the job even if you haven't yet collected the cash. If your customers are slow to pay, you may end up with lots of revenue but little cash.

Many companies that use the accrual accounting method monitor cash flow on a weekly basis to be sure they have enough cash on hand to operate the business. If your business is seasonal, such as a landscaping business with little to do during the winter months, you can establish short-term lines of credit through your bank to maintain cash flow through the lean times.

Small Business Accounting in Action ➡️
Determine whether a cash-basis accounting system or an accrual accounting system is best for a business.

Making the Switch to Accrual Accounting

Changing between the cash-basis and accrual methods of accounting may not be simple, and you should check with your accountant to be sure you do it right. You may even need to get permission from the IRS, which tests whether you're seeking an unfair tax advantage when making the switch.

Keep in mind that the following types of businesses should only use accrual accounting (and never cash-basis):

- Businesses that carry an inventory.
- Businesses that incorporated as a C corporation (more on incorporation in the next section).
- Businesses with gross annual sales that exceed $5 million.

1.1.4 Internal Controls

Internal controls:
Procedures that protect assets and provide reliable records.

Every business owner needs to be concerned with keeping tight controls on company cash and how it's used. **Internal controls** are critical procedures that carry out the following:

- Protect assets.
- Provide reliable records.

One way to institute internal controls is to place restrictions on who has the ability to enter information into your books and who has access to use that information.

You also need to carefully control who has the ability to accept cash receipts and who has the ability to disburse your business's cash. Separating duties appropriately helps you protect your business's assets from error, theft, and fraud. Chapter 8 goes into detail about controlling cash and protecting your financial records.

SELF-CHECK

1. Define the separate entity assumption.
2. List three examples of accounting periods.
3. Describe the key difference between cash-basis accounting and accrual accounting.
4. Define internal controls and list three examples.

Apply Your Knowledge You plan to start a Web site design business that caters to engineering firms. Using the four basic accounting concepts, create a "to-do" list of various items you will need to research before making decisions about your accounting system.

1.2 TYPES OF BUSINESSES

Businesses can by classified in two ways: by their type of operation and by their legal form of business structure.

1.2.1 Types of Business Operations

The term *business operation* refers to ways that businesses make money. There are three types of business operations:

- Service.
- Merchandising.
- Manufacturing.

Service business:
A business that sells services.

A **service business** is a business that sells services. Service businesses range from huge international accounting firms to walking the neighbors' dogs for a fee.

Merchandising business:
A business that buys inventory for resale.

Manufacturing business:
A business that sells goods it produces from raw materials.

A business that buys inventory for resale is a **merchandising business.** Wal-Mart Inc. is a merchandising business. So is your corner newsstand.

A **manufacturing business** is a business that sells goods it produces from raw materials. General Motors Corporation and a local bakery are examples of manufacturing businesses.

Some businesses have more than one type of operation. A styling salon is primarily a service business, but it can also sell merchandise such as specialty shampoos.

1.2.2 Legal Forms of Business Structure

Paying taxes and reporting income for your company are very important jobs, and the way in which you complete these tasks properly depends on your business's legal structure. This section discusses the main forms of legal structure:

- Sole proprietorship.
- Partnership.
- Corporation.
- Limited Liability Company (LLC).

> **FOR EXAMPLE**
> See Table 1-1 for a comparison of business structures.

Sole Proprietorship

Sole proprietorship:
A business that is owned by one person and is not separate from its owner for legal purposes.

The simplest legal structure for a business is the **sole proprietorship,** a business that's owned by one individual. Most new businesses with only one owner start out as sole proprietorships. In fact, about 75 percent of U.S. businesses do not have payroll. Most are self-employed persons who have unincorporated businesses. Although a sole proprietorship is a separate entity for business purposes, it is legally the same economic unit as the business owner. The business's profit is reported on the owner's individual income tax return.

Some sole proprietorships never change their status, but others grow by adding partners and becoming partnerships. Some add lots of staff and want to protect themselves from lawsuits, so they become Limited Liability Companies (LLCs). Those seeking the greatest protection from individual lawsuits, whether they have employees or are simply single-owner companies without employees, become corporations.

Partnership

Partnership:
A business that is owned by more than one person and is not separate from its owners for legal purposes.

A business owned by more than one person is a **partnership.** Like a sole proprietorship, a partnership is a separate *business* entity but not a separate *legal* entity. The business's profit "passes through" directly to the partners and is reported on each partner's individual tax return. The owner is also personally responsible for all business debts.

The partnership is the most flexible type of business structure involving more than one owner. Each partner in a partnership is personally liable for all the debts of the partnership. This structure is slightly more complicated than a sole proprietorship, and partners should work out certain key issues before the business opens its doors. These issues include the following:

- How the partners will divide the profits and losses.
- How each partner can sell his or her share of the business, if he or she so chooses.
- What will happen to each partner's share if a partner becomes sick or dies.
- How the partnership will be dissolved if one of the partners wants out.

General partner:
A partner who runs the day-to-day business in a partnership and has unlimited legal liability.

Limited partner:
A partner who is a passive owner of a partnership and has limited legal liability.

Partners in a partnership don't always have to share equal risks. A partnership may have two different types of partners: general and limited. The **general partner** runs the day-to-day business and is held personally responsible for all activities of the business, no matter how much he or she has personally invested in the business. **Limited partners,** on the other hand, are passive owners of the business and are not involved in its day-to-day operations. If a claim is filed against the business, the limited partners can only be held personally liable for the amount of money that matches how much they individually invested in the business.

Small Business Accounting in Action ➡
Evaluate business structures.

Corporation:
A separate legal entity, which protects an owner's personal assets from claims against the corporation.

Corporation

If your business faces a great risk of being sued, the safest business structure for you is the corporation. Courts in the United States have clearly determined that a **corporation** is a separate legal entity and that its owners' personal assets are protected from claims against the corporation. Essentially, an owner or shareholder in a corporation can't be sued or face collections because of actions taken by the corporation. This veil of protection is the reason many small-business owners choose to incorporate even though it involves a lot of expenses (lawyers and accountants) and government paperwork.

In a corporation, each share of stock represents a portion of ownership, and profits must be split based on stock ownership. You don't have to sell stock on the public stock markets in order to be a corporation, though. In fact, most corporations are private entities that sell their stock privately among friends and investors.

Corporations come in two varieties, *S corporations* and *C corporations*. As you may expect, each has unique tax requirements and practices. In fact, not even all corporations pay tax on the company's profits. Some smaller corporations are designated as S corporations and pass their earnings on to the stockholders, who report that income on their individual tax returns.

If you're a small-business owner who wants to incorporate, first you must form a board of directors. Boards can be made up of owners of the company as well as nonowners.

Corporations provide an umbrella of protection for company owners, but in order to maintain that protection, the owners must comply with many rules unique to corporations. The board of directors takes on the key role of complying with these rules, and it must maintain a record of meeting minutes that prove the board is following key operating procedures.

PATHWAY TO...
THE RESPONSIBILITIES OF
THE BOARD OF DIRECTORS

- Establishment of records of banking associations and any changes to those arrangements.
- Tracking of loans from stockholders or third parties.
- Selling or redeeming shares of stock.
- Payment of dividends.
- Authorization of salaries or bonuses for officers and key executives.
- Undertaking of any purchases, sales, or leases of corporate assets.
- Buying another company.
- Merging with another company.
- Making changes to the Articles of Incorporation or bylaws.
- Election of corporate officers and directors.

Corporate board minutes are considered official and must be available for review by the IRS, state taxing authorities, and the courts. If a company's owners want to invoke the veil of protection that corporate status provides, they must prove that the board has met its obligations and that the company operated as a corporation. In other words, you can't form a board and have no proof that it ever met and managed these key functions.

Check with your accountant to determine whether incorporating your business makes sense for you. Tax savings isn't the only issue you have to think about; operating a corporation also increases administrative, legal, and accounting costs. Be sure that you understand all the costs before incorporating.

IN THE REAL WORLD

Small Beginnings

You have probably used a FedEx Kinko's for your business, job, school projects, or personal life. Even before Kinko's became part of FedEx, the company had many stores that offered a wide variety of services.

Did you know that it all started in 1970 with a tiny storefront and a single copy machine? In addition to copy services, Paul Orfalea offered offset press, film processing, and school supplies. The space was too small to actually make copies; the copier had to be moved outside to the sidewalk.

The business expanded beyond its Santa Barbara, California, home and now has more than 1,500 locations worldwide. Kinko's remained a privately held corporation until it was acquired by FedEx in 2004.

Limited Liability Company (LLC)

Limited Liability Company (LLC):
A structure that provides a business owner with some protection from being held personally liable for their business's activities.

The **Limited Liability Company,** or LLC, is a structure that provides a business owner with some protection from being held personally liable for their business's activities. This business structure is somewhere between a sole proprietorship or partnership and a corporation. The business ownership and IRS tax rules are similar to those of a sole proprietorship or partnership, but like a corporation, if the business is sued, the owners aren't held personally liable.

LLCs are state entities, so the level of legal protection given to a company's owners depends upon the rules of the state in which the LLC was formed. Most states give LLC owners the same protection from lawsuits as the federal government gives corporation owners. However, these LLC protections haven't been fully tested in court to date, so no one knows for certain whether or not they hold up in the courtroom. An owner should seek legal and accounting advice before choosing this structure, as it has both tax benefits and limits.

LLCs are relatively new to the world of business structures. They were first established in the United States about 25 years ago, but didn't become popular until the mid-1990s, when most states approved the LLC as a business structure. They are still not adopted by all 50 states.

Many law firms and accounting firms are set up as LLCs. More and more small-business owners are choosing this structure rather than a corporation because the LLC is easier and cheaper to maintain (less government paperwork and lower legal and accounting fees), yet it still provides personal protection from legal entanglements.

Table 1-1 compares the characteristics of the different forms of business structure.

Table 1-1: Comparing Legal Forms of Business Structure

Characteristic	Sole Proprietorship	Partnership	S Corporation	C Corporation	LLC
Ease of formation and maintenance	Simple	Moderate	Complex	Complex	Moderate
Limited Liability	No	General Partner: No Limited Partner: Yes	Yes	Yes	Yes
Pass-through profits and losses	Yes	Yes	Yes	No[1]	Yes

[1] The C corporation pays taxes as a separate legal entity. If shareholders receive dividends, they also pay taxes at the individual level.

CAREER CONNECTION

Two friends form a knitting partnership with the hopes of making the world a more beautiful place—one row at a time.

When May Chao taught friend Jodi Toubes to knit in 2005, the two simply thought the hobby would be a way to take a break from their busy lives as mothers and working women in Los Angeles. Less than a year—and many scarves and blankets—later, Chao and Toubes were crafting uniquely styled tote bags for themselves, knitted in funky colors such as periwinkle and lime green. Soon after, they began taking orders from friends. It was clear to May and Jodi that they were onto something, and so "wabi-sabi knits" was born (www.wabisabiknits.biz).

Rooted in Japanese Shinto philosophy, wabi-sabi is an appreciation of beauty that is "imperfect, impermanent, and incomplete." This idea of simplicity and natural beauty is represented in the two's functional and environmentally friendly products. In forming a business partnership, Toubes and Chao wanted to focus on that same idea of simplicity. To do so, says Chao, "We agreed on a plan, because if we could agree on the 'big picture' and how to get there, there would be less room for misunderstanding or disagreements on the day-to-day running of the business." Part of their plan included dividing up the responsibilities of the business; they also set clear goals, budgets, and objectives for growing the business.

Chao, whose strengths lie in marketing and accounting, uses QuickBooks and Excel for the business's finances. "QuickBooks is an easy way to record sales and expenses and maintain a customer database," she says, "and Excel allows me to format the data for specific needs, like

(continued)

CAREER CONNECTION *(continued)*

annual sales tax reporting. It also serves as a backup to double-check that our numbers tie together." Toubes, who handles sales, merchandising, and inventory, appreciates the value of having an inventory database to help keep the business on track.

Although the two have been pleased with the gradual growth of the business, they hope their new Web site will be a useful tool for customers, who can now choose designs and colors over the Internet. "We're ready for the Web site to take us to the next level," says Toubes.

Tips from the Professionals

- Know what financial information you need to have first, and buy or create a system to keep track of it.
- Keep diligent records of all expenses and sales, and run monthly/quarterly reports to monitor how your business is performing.
- Reevaluate your business plan vs. performance each year to see where new opportunities lie, and find ways to continually improve (for example, cut costs, find new markets).

SELF-CHECK

1. Identify and define the three types of business operations.
2. List the legal forms of business structure.
3. Which legal form of business structure is the most simple to set up? Which is the most complicated?
4. Which business structures protect the owners' personal assets in lawsuits?

Apply Your Knowledge You and a coworker are striking out on your own to open a licensed day-care center. What type of business operation is this? What must you consider in choosing the legal form of structure for a day-care business? List the pros and cons of each business structure as it relates to your business.

1.3 ACCOUNTING SOFTWARE OPTIONS

Some small-business owners who have been around a while still do things the old-fashioned way—they keep their books using paper forms. However, in this age of technology and instant information, the majority of today's businesses computerize their books.

Not only is computerized bookkeeping easier, it also minimizes the chance of errors, because most of the work involves using on-screen forms to input data. The forms can be understood even by someone without training in accounting or bookkeeping. The person entering the information doesn't need to know whether something is a debit or credit (Chapter 2 explains the difference), because the computerized system takes care of everything.

In addition to increasing accuracy and cutting the time it takes to do your bookkeeping, computerized accounting also makes designing reports easier. These reports can then be used to help make business decisions. Your computerized accounting system stores detailed information about every transaction, so you can group that detail in any way that may assist your decision making.

1.3.1 Overview of Software Options

More than 50 different types of accounting software programs are on the market, and all are designed to computerize your bookkeeping. The more sophisticated ones target specific industry needs, such as food services or utilities, and can cost thousands of dollars. To check out those options, visit www.findaccountingsoftware.com, where you can browse for accounting software that's grouped by industry—29 to be exact, from accommodations and food services to utilities.

Luckily, as a small businessperson, you probably don't need all the bells and whistles offered by the top-of-the-line programs. Instead, three software programs reviewed in this section can meet the needs of most small-business people:

- Simply Accounting Pro.
- Peachtree Accounting.
- QuickBooks.

Using one of these three systems, you can get started with a modest initial investment. It may not be fancy, but basic computerized accounting software can do a fine job of helping you keep your books. And you can always upgrade to a more expensive program, if needed, as your business grows.

Accounting software packages are updated almost every year. That's because tax laws and laws involving many other aspects of operating a business change so often. In addition, computer software companies are always improving their products to make computerized accounting programs more user-friendly, so be sure that you always buy the most current version of an accounting software package.

Simply Accounting Pro

Simply Accounting Pro (www.simplyaccounting.com) is a cost-effective choice for bookkeeping software if you're just starting up and don't have sophisticated bookkeeping or accounting needs. For example, you can process credit-card transactions and electronic features from inside the other two accounting software programs discussed in this section, but Simply Accounting requires you to use an add-on tool. This program caters to the bookkeeping novice and even provides an option that lets you avoid accounting jargon. The program includes more than 100 accounting templates for things like sales orders, quotes, receipts, and other basic needs for a variety of industries, including medical/dental, real estate, property management, and retail firms. Simply Accounting Pro has an integrated feature that allows you to do Employee Direct Deposit for payroll.

If you're working with another software system to manage your business data and are interesting in switching to Simply Accounting Pro, you may be able to import that data directly into Simply Accounting. (Information about how to import data is included with the program.) You can import data from software such as Microsoft Excel (a spreadsheet program) or Access (a database program). If you're converting from QuickBooks or another accounting software program called MYOB, you can easily import your data to Simply Accounting. However, data from Microsoft Money and Intuit Quicken can't be imported.

Peachtree Accounting

Peachtree Accounting (www.peachtree.com) is an excellent software package for your bookkeeping and accounting needs, but it's definitely not recommended if you're a novice. You need to be familiar with accounting jargon to use the Peachtree system.

According to CNET (www.cnet.com), a company that offers reviews of computer software and hardware, Peachtree Accounting's inventory-management tools are the best in its class. The software automatically generates purchase orders when inventory reaches a level predetermined by the user. You can also export Peachtree Accounting's customer, vendor, or employee information into Microsoft Word and use the data with Word's mail-merge feature to send emails or letters.

Peachtree Accounting offers a utility that's easy to use to convert data from Intuit's QuickBooks. You can also import files from Quicken. There's no conversion tool for Microsoft Excel data, but you can import and export Excel files into the program without problems.

If you want to be able to integrate your shipping with UPS, have more than one user, control users by screen-level security, have advanced inventory or job costing capabilities, or have an audit trail of your work, you need to start with Peachtree Complete Accounting instead of Peachtree Accounting.

QuickBooks

Small Business Accounting in Action → Choose a computerized accounting program.

QuickBooks (www.quickbooks.intuit.com) offers the best of both worlds: an easy user interface (for the novice) and extensive bookkeeping and accounting features (for the experienced bookkeeper or accountant). More small-business owners today use QuickBooks than any other small-business accounting software package. Even CNET gives QuickBooks its highest rating for accounting software packages in this class. Many nonprofit organizations—schools, churches, and social agencies—also use QuickBooks for accounting purposes.

The QuickBooks learning center walks you through every type of key transaction with an interactive program that not only shows you how to do the function, but also explains the basics of bookkeeping. You don't have to use the tutorial, but the option pops up when you do a task for the first time, so the choice is always yours. You also can go back to the learning center to review at any time.

QuickBooks Basic can probably meet most of your bookkeeping and accounting needs. If you want to integrate your bookkeeping with a point-of-sale package, which integrates cash register sales, you need to get QuickBooks Pro. You also need QuickBooks Pro if you want to do inventory management, generate purchase orders from estimates or sales orders, do job costing and estimates, automatically create a budget, or integrate your data for use with Microsoft Word and Excel programs. This book uses QuickBooks Pro to demonstrate various bookkeeping functions.

QuickBooks is a versatile program and can share data with over 325 popular business software applications. Sales, customer, and financial data can be easily shared, so you don't have to enter that information twice.

IN THE REAL WORLD

Show Business

Donal wanted to combine his entrepreneurial ambition with his love of movies. Armed with a degree in accounting and knowledge from completing an internship the previous summer at a film studio, Donal launched a freelance career as a production accountant.

Donal's first job was working on the accounting team of a romantic comedy. He did not go on location to Prague and London, but he did have to deal with time differences and currency-exchange issues. He also learned about union regulations for cast and crew members. Although accounting systems such as QuickBooks were available, Donal's team chose and used accounting software that was developed for production accountants. Working with the software's industry-specific features, Donal developed a wider understanding of the film business.

1.3.2 Add-Ons and Fees

The three accounting programs discussed in this section offer add-ons and features you're likely to need, such as:

- **Tax updates:** If you have employees and want up-to-date tax information and forms to do your payroll using your accounting software, you need to buy an update each year.
- **Online credit-card processing and electronic bill paying:** Having the capabilities to perform these tasks means additional fees.
- **Point-of-sale software:** This add-on helps you integrate your sales at the cash register with your accounting software.

Before signing on for one of the add-ons, be sure you understand what the fees will be. Usually, you're advised of the additional costs whenever you try to do anything that incurs extra fees.

1.3.3 Setting Up Your Computerized Books

After you pick your software, the hard work is done because actually setting up the package will probably take you less time than researching your options and picking your software. The three packages discussed in this section have good start-up tutorials to help you set up the books.

A building block of any accounting system is the chart of accounts, which is a list of the accounts used in the business. Chapter 2 discusses the chart of accounts in more detail. Simply Accounting Pro, Peachtree Accounting, and QuickBooks all produce a number of sample charts of accounts that automatically appear after you choose the type of business you plan to run and upon which industry that business falls. Start with one of the charts offered by the software, like you see in Figure 1-1, and then tweak it to your business's needs.

Once your chart of accounts appears, all three programs ask you to enter a company name, address, and tax identification number to get started. If you're operating as a sole proprietor or if your business is based on a partnership and you don't have a federal tax ID for the business, you can use your Social Security number.

You then select an accounting period (see Figure 1-2). If the calendar year is your accounting period, you don't have to change anything. But if you operate your business based on another period of 12 months, such as September 1 to August 31, you must enter that information.

If you don't change your accounting period to match how you plan to develop your financial statements, then you have to delete the business from the system and start over.

Figure 1-1

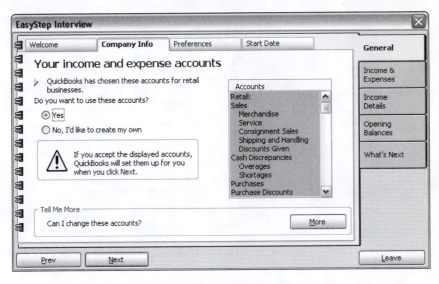

QuickBooks generates a chart of accounts based on the type of business you have.

Figure 1-2

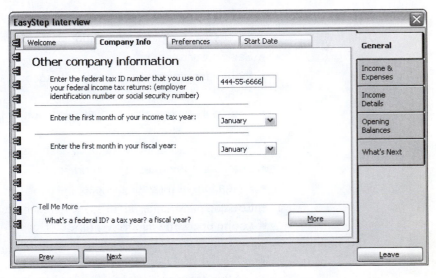

QuickBooks asks you to input your fiscal year.

This is also the time to input information about your bank accounts and other key financial data (see Figure 1-3). Your main business bank account is the one that should be used for Cash in Checking, the first account listed in your software's chart of accounts.

Figure 1-3

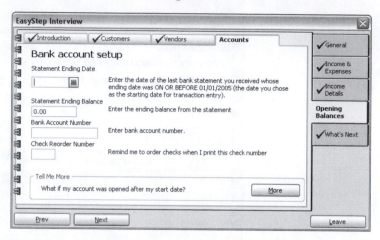

QuickBooks collects information about your bank accounts.

PATHWAY TO...
SETTING UP A COMPUTERIZED ACCOUNTING SYSTEM

- Create your chart of accounts.
- Enter your company name, address, and tax identification number.
- Select your accounting period.
- Input information about your bank accounts and other key financial data.
- Enter data unique to your business, such as budget information, vendors, and customers.
- Select your accounting method: cash-basis or accrual.
- Enter sales tax rates, if appropriate.
- Pick a format for your invoices.
- Set up payroll data.
- Define how you want to pay bills.

After entering your bank and other financial information, you enter data unique to your business. If you want to use the program's budgeting features, you enter your budget information before entering other data. Then you add your vendor and customer accounts so that when you start entering transactions, the information is already in the system. If you don't have any outstanding bills or customer payments due, you can wait and enter vendor and customer information as the need arises.

Small Business Accounting in Action → Set up a computerized accounting system.

Other information collected includes the type of accounting method you'll be using—either cash-basis or accrual accounting. You also need to enter information about whether or not you collect sales taxes from your customers and, if you do, the sales tax rates. Also, you can pick a format for your invoices, set up payroll data, and make arrangements for how you want to pay bills. The steps to set up your system are summarized in Section 1.3.3.

Don't worry about entering everything into your computerized system right away. All programs make it very easy to add customers, vendors, and employees at any time.

SELF-CHECK

1. Describe the advantages of using a computerized accounting system.
2. Identify three accounting software programs.
3. List the information you should have ready when you set up a computerized accounting system.

Apply Your Knowledge ▶ When you started your car-detailing business, most of your income was from providing services. Eighteen months later, you found that you were making a lot of profit from selling high-end vehicle accessories. Eventually, you opened a store and you spend most of your time managing the retail side of the business. Your employees perform the detailing work. Which software program is appropriate for each stage of your business? Explain why each program is best for a particular stage.

SUMMARY

Section 1.1
- Bookkeeping is the methodical way in which a business tracks financial transactions. Accounting is the total structure of records and procedures used to record, classify, and report information about a business's financial transactions.
- The four main accounting concepts are separate entity assumption, accounting period assumption, cash-basis and accrual accounting, and internal controls.

Section 1.2
- Businesses can be classified by their type of operation; the three forms of business operations are service, merchandising, and manufacturing.

- Small businesses are usually organized as one of the following legal forms of business structure: sole proprietorship, partnership, corporation, or Limited Liability Company.

Section 1.3
- Although some small-business owners still keep their books using paper forms, the majority of today's businesses computerize their books. In doing so, they save time and energy—and they minimize the risk of errors.
- Popular accounting software programs for small businesses include Simply Pro Accounting, Peachtree Accounting, and QuickBooks.

ASSESS YOUR UNDERSTANDING

UNDERSTAND: WHAT HAVE YOU LEARNED?

 Go to **www.wiley.com/college/epstein** to assess your knowledge of making business accounting decisions.

PRACTICE: WHAT WOULD YOU DO?

1. If you are starting a gardening business, what are three things you can do to make sure you comply with the separate entity assumption?

2. Your friend has a full-time job, but he plans to have a side-business teaching music lessons during the school year. He wants to take summers off from his music business. What would be the most useful fiscal year for his business?

3. Identify advantages and disadvantages of cash-basis accounting and accrual accounting.

4. You own a packaging business and employ three workers. What can you do to strengthen internal controls?

5. Think of a business you would like to open. Briefly describe the type of business operation. Which legal structure do you think would be best? Why?

6. Suppose you are starting a corporation. What qualities would you want in the people who serve on your board of directors? How would you go about choosing and recruiting board members?

7. Your business partner does not want to spend money on software and prefers to do the books manually. Prepare a list of talking points to convince your partner to invest in accounting software.

8. Which software features are most important to you as a potential small-business owner?

BE A SMALL BUSINESS ACCOUNTANT

You Be the Teacher

Prepare a three-minute lecture on one of the following topics. The focus of your lecture should be the needs of your audience.

- How to Be a Separate Entity
- How to Choose an Accounting Period
- Cash-Basis or Accrual: Which Is Best for Your Business?
- Do Your Internal Controls Work?

Research Legal Forms of Business Structure

On the Web site of the Small Business Administration (www.sba.gov), go to "SMALL BUSINESS PLANNER," "Start Your Business," "Choose a Structure," and "Forms of Ownership." What is the first step in determining how to structure your company? What factors should you consider in selecting the form of ownership? Which business structure requires that the owner be paid wages if he or she works for the company and it makes a profit? Would this wage requirement affect your decision about business structure? Why or why not?

Accounting Software Wish List

List the things you want your software to do, and the types of information you want from it. Based on what you have learned so far, can accounting software deliver what you want? Check over your list periodically and compare it to what you learn about accounting software.

KEY TERMS

Accounting	The total structure of records and procedures used to record, classify, and report information about a business's financial transactions.
Accounting period	The time for which financial information is being tracked.
Accounting period assumption	The concept that income is reported in regular time periods.
Accrual accounting	A system in which transactions are recorded when completed, even if cash doesn't change hands.
Annual report	A year-end summary of the company's activities and financial results.
Bookkeeping	The methodical way in which businesses track their financial transactions.
Cash-basis accounting	A system in which transactions are recorded when cash changes hands.
Corporation	A separate legal entity, which protects an owner's personal assets from claims against the corporation.
Fiscal year	A 12-month accounting period.
General partner	A partner who runs the day-to-day business in a partnership and has unlimited legal liability.
Internal controls	Procedures that protect assets and provide reliable records.
Limited Liability Company (LLC)	A structure that provides a business owner with some protection from being held personally liable for their business's activities.
Limited partner	A partner who is a passive owner of a partnership and has limited liability.
Manufacturing business	A business that sells goods it produces from raw materials.
Merchandising business	A business that buys inventory for resale.
Partnership	A business that is owned by more than one person and is not separate from its owners for legal purposes.
Separate entity assumption	The concept that a business is an economic entity separate from its owner.
Service business	A business that sells services.
Sole proprietorship	A business that is owned by one person and is not separate from its owner for legal purposes.

2

MASTERING DEBITS AND CREDITS
Building Useful Information

Do You Already Know?

- The five main account types and how they are used
- The balance sheet and income statement
- The chart of accounts and how to build one

For additional questions to assess your current knowledge of mastering debits and credits, go to **www.wiley.com/college/epstein.**

What You Will Find Out	What You Will Be Able To Do
2.1 How debits and credits differ, as well as the five types of accounts; how to analyze a transaction	Know when to use a debit or a credit; understand the difference between assets, liabilities, equity, revenue, and expenses; analyze a transaction
2.2 The types of basic financial statements	Interpret the balance sheet and income statement
2.3 The purpose of the chart of accounts	Create the accounts necessary for a business

INTRODUCTION

In accounting, you use a combination of *debits* and *credits*. You may think of a debit as a subtraction because you've found that debits usually mean a decrease in your bank balance. On the other hand, you've probably been happy to find unexpected credits that mean more money in your favor. Now forget all that you ever learned about debits or credits. In this chapter you will learn how to use debits and credits in accounting.

2.1 DIFFERENTIATING DEBITS AND CREDITS

Debit:
An entry on the left side of an account.

Credit:
An entry on the right side of an account.

Account:
A record that keeps track of increases and decreases in specific items.

Debit and *credit* are not value terms; they are directional terms only. Each one is neither good nor bad. The only definite thing about debits and credits in accounting is that a **debit** is an entry on the left side of an account and a **credit** is an entry on the right side of an account. The total debits should equal the total credits:

DEBITS (left) = CREDITS (right)

This fact is nothing new; during the Italian Renaissance, in the year 1494, Luca Pacioli gave this warning to accountants: "A person should not go to sleep at night until the debits equal the credits!"

An **account** is a record that keeps track of increases and decreases in a specific item. For example, you have an account to keep track of the cash you have in the bank. This is not the same as your actual bank account. It is an independent record that you maintain to keep track of your cash balance. You have another account for keeping track of how much you spend on office supplies. If you make your living as a graphic artist, you have an account to keep track of the earnings you make from your design fees.

2.1.1 Double-Entry Accounting

Double-entry accounting:
A system in which you record all transactions twice, using debits and credits.

Transaction:
An economic event that causes changes in accounts.

Businesses use **double-entry accounting,** a system in which you record all transactions twice, using debits and credits. A **transaction** is an economic event that causes changes in accounts. In each transaction, at least two accounts are affected.

TRANSACTION
You bought a desk, table, and chairs for $900, paying by check at the time of purchase.

In this example, you paid cash for office furniture. In accounting, the term *cash* includes the cash in your checking account. The Furniture account will increase $900 and the Cash in Checking account will decrease $900.

Increase in Furniture account = Decrease in Cash in Checking account

$$\$900 = \$900$$

When do you use a debit and when do you use a credit? The answer is "it depends." Debits and credits are used in the context of accounts.

Normal balance:
The increase side of an account.

Some accounts are increased by debits and some are increased by credits. It all depends on the account's normal balance. The **normal balance** is the increase side of an account. Table 2-1 shows the normal balance for the five main account types: assets, liabilities, equity, revenue, and expenses.

Small Business Accounting in Action ➡
Know when to use a debit or a credit.

Table 2-1: The Normal Balances of Accounts

Debit	Credit
Assets	Liabilities and equity
Expenses	Revenue

2.1.2 The Accounting Equation

Most accounts fall into these categories:

- Assets.
- Liabilities.
- Equity.
- Revenue.
- Expenses.

Some businesses use a sixth category called Cost of Goods Sold, which is the cost directly connected with the items sold. This category is similar to expenses in its debit and credit applications. While accounting software gives a service business the option to use Cost of Goods Sold, this book discusses Cost of Goods Sold as it relates to merchandising (Chapters 13 through 15).

Assets:
All the things a company owns.

Assets are all the things a company owns. Examples include cash, building, land, tools, equipment, vehicles, and furniture. Though this is sometimes difficult to ascertain, a business should also include the idea of assets' future value to a business.

Liabilities:
All the debts the company owes.

Liabilities are all the debts the company owes. These debts represent outside claims on the company's assets. An example of liabilities is a bill you have received but have not yet paid. Suppose you bought art supplies on credit for your graphic design business. Until you pay the bill, the art store has a claim on your assets. (You owe the store money.)

Equity:
The claim the owners have on the assets of the company.

Equity is the claim the owners have on the assets of the company. The **accounting equation** is the relationship among these three types of accounts:

Accounting equation:
The relationship among the balance sheet accounts:
Assets = Liabilities + Equity.

$$\text{Assets} = \text{Liabilities} + \text{Equity}$$

Revenue:
The money earned in the process of selling the company's goods or services.

Expenses:
The cost of everything used to operate the company, excluding costs directly related to the sale of merchandise.

Revenue is the money earned in the process of selling the company's goods or services. **Expenses** are the cost of everything used to operate the company, excluding costs directly related to the sale of merchandise. Expenses for operating a business include rent, salaries, advertising, and supplies.

How do revenue and expenses fit into the accounting equation? They are not separate elements of the equation, but instead are rolled up into the equity.

At the end of each accounting period, revenue and expenses accounts are closed and their balances are transferred to equity. An increase in revenue eventually increases equity, and an increase in expenses decreases equity. Table 2-2 shows that equity and revenue have the same normal balance. Equity and expenses have opposite normal balances.

IN THE REAL WORLD

No Debits? No Credits? No Problem!

Traci and her husband Allen took business courses before opening their vintage clothing shop. Traci liked accounting and enjoyed doing the store's books. She found that Excel spreadsheets were sufficient for her needs, and she knew her way around debits and credits.

Then things got interesting. Just as the business flourished due to Allen's knack for finding mint-condition items from the 1960s and 1970s, they learned they were expecting their first child. Time was becoming increasingly precious, and they knew they had to make changes.

They decided to a hire a high school student part-time to help with the bookkeeping. Traci bought an accounting software program that did the work behind the scenes. The user just entered data in the on-screen forms for each type of transaction. Traci was able to interpret the financial reports produced by the software, but she did not need to analyze every debit and credit.

Small Business Accounting in Action ➡
Understand the difference between assets, liabilities, equity, revenue, and expenses.

Table 2-2: Rules of Debit and Credit

Account Type	Normal Balance	Increase	Decrease
Assets	Debit	Debit	Credit
Liabilities	Credit	Credit	Debit
Equity	Credit	Credit	Debit
Revenue	Credit	Credit	Debit
Expenses	Debit	Debit	Credit

CAREER CONNECTION

For some entrepreneurs, being business-savvy means knowing where your weaknesses lie and when to bring in the experts to help.

Catherine DeVito is creative. She knows a lot about computers. She is a talented Web site designer. She is not, however, an accountant. This fact didn't seem like that much of a problem two years ago when she started CD Designs, her own Web design business. After all, she had just finished a successful stint with a large design firm and she had clients lined up to pay her for her designs. It didn't take long for Catherine's ideas to change.

As far as the clients went, Catherine spent an extraordinary amount of time working with them. She did so because she wanted to offer her personalized service, but because she hadn't bothered to set written guidelines for the contracted work, she found herself having to add content and do dozens of revisions. When it came time to collect payment, customers were surprised at the added costs of the extra work. To make matters worse, she was struggling with the basic accounting functions and was falling behind in sending out bills and following up on payments.

Though she considered going back to her old design job, Catherine instead chose to use an accountant to set up her accounting system and handle all the aspects of billing and taxes. In doing so, she had more time to focus on her design work and her client relations.

Tips from the Professional

- Hire an accountant from the very beginning.
- Go after the money that you've earned. Follow up with your clients—they may be happy with your services, but just not quick to respond with a check.
- Work with prewritten contracts so that both you and your clients have clear expectations; contracts should cover creative concepts as well as financial concepts—from deposits required to late payment fees.

2.1.3 The T-Account Tool

T account:
A visual tool used to represent actual accounts such as assets, liabilities, equity, revenue, and expenses.

Recall that the only definite thing about debits and credits is that a debit goes on the left side of a recorded transaction and a credit goes on the right side. T accounts provide a good way to show this. A **T account** is a visual tool used to represent actual accounts such as assets, liabilities, equity, revenue, and expenses. It helps you figure out the effects of a transaction. The T account has three parts:

- Title.
- Debit side (the left side).
- Credit side (the right side).

Figure 2-1

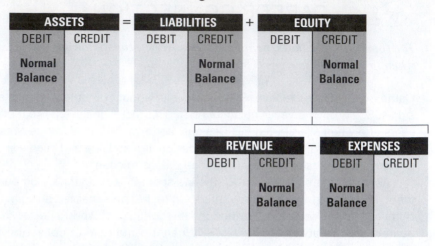

T accounts showing five main account types.

A T account is not part of the formal accounting system. It is more like scratch paper. Figure 2-1 shows the five types of accounts in T-account form. In this book, the T accounts have shading on the normal balance side.

2.1.4 Analyzing Transactions

Reexamine the furniture purchase.

TRANSACTION
You wrote a check for $900 to buy office furniture.

In this transaction, which account is debited and which is credited? You need to ask yourself a series of questions:

- Which accounts are affected? *(Furniture and Cash in Checking)*
- What type of account is Furniture? *(Assets)*
- What type of account is Cash in Checking? *(Assets)*
- What is the increase or decrease of each account? *(Furniture will increase $900. Cash in Checking will decrease $900.)*
- Which account is debited? *(Furniture. An increase to assets is a debit.)*
- Which account is credited? *(Cash in Checking. A decrease to assets is a credit.)*

The process to determine which accounts are debited and credited is summarized in the Pathway To . . . Analyzing Business Transactions sidebar. Table 2-3 applies this process to the furniture purchase.

PATHWAY TO...
ANALYZING BUSINESS TRANSACTIONS

1. Identify the accounts affected.
2. Classify the accounts affected.
3. Determine the increase or decrease for each account.
4. Apply the rules of debit and credit.

Table 2-3: Determining Which Accounts Are Debited and Credited

Step	Activity	Result	
1	Identify accounts.	Furniture	Cash in Checking
2	Classify accounts.	Assets	Assets
3	Determine the increase or decrease.	Increase 900	Decrease 900
4	Apply the rules of debit and credit.	Debit 900	Credit 900

You might want to use the T-account tool to help figure out the debits and credits. Figure 2-2 shows the furniture purchase in T-account form.

Notice that in Figure 2-2, the debit half is shown before the credit half. This is the standard way of showing transactions in accounting. Debits are shown first and appear on the left.

Remember that the T account is just a tool, not part of the accounting system. You use *journals* to record transactions into the system. Journals are covered in Chapters 3 and 4. It is also important to note that every entry into a record system must be supported by a source document (receipt, invoice, and so on).

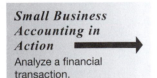

Small Business Accounting in Action

Analyze a financial transaction.

FOR EXAMPLE

See Table 2-3 for how to determine which accounts are credited and debited.

Figure 2-2

Furniture		Cash in Checking	
DEBIT	CREDIT	DEBIT	CREDIT
900			900

Increase Furniture with a debit and decrease Cash in Checking with a credit.

SELF-CHECK

1. Describe the difference between debit and credit.

2. What is meant by normal balance?

3. List five account types and give a brief description of each type. Include the normal balance in your description.

4. What is the accounting equation? Restate the accounting equation in your own words.

Apply Your Knowledge You went to the neighborhood newspaper office and wrote a check for an advertisement in the next weekend edition. Which account will be debited? Which account will be credited?

2.2 OVERVIEW OF FINANCIAL STATEMENTS

Financial statements:
Reports that summarize information about the financial performance and status of the business.

Using debits and credits, you can compute your financial results and communicate those results to others. At the end of the accounting period, the account balances are totaled and reported in financial statements. **Financial statements** are reports that summarize information about the financial performance and status of the business; this is the "output" of the system.

The three main financial statements are as follows:

• Balance sheet.

• Income statement.

• Statement of owner's equity.

These financial statements are standard reports that can go to people outside the company. For example, a bank will want to see your financial statements before granting a loan.

Some businesses prepare a fourth financial statement called the statement of cash flows. This chapter briefly touches on two financial statements: the balance sheet and the income statement. Chapter 7 goes into more detail about these two statements as well as the statement of owner's equity.

Balance sheet:
The financial statement that presents a snapshot of the company's financial position as of a particular date in time.

2.2.1 The Balance Sheet

The **balance sheet** is the financial statement that presents a snapshot of the company's financial position as of a particular date in time; as such, the title of a balance sheet shows the date of the snapshot. It's called a balance sheet because the things owned by the company (assets) must equal the claims against those assets (liabilities and equity):

$$\text{Assets} = \text{Liabilities} + \text{Equity}$$

The balance sheet has three sections:

- Assets.
- Liabilities.
- Equity.

See Figure 2-3 for an example of a balance sheet.

Figure 2-3

REVIS BOOKKEEPING SERVICE
Balance Sheet
As of May 31, 200X

Assets		
Cash in Checking	$ 5,200	
Computer Equipment	3,500	
Total Assets		$ 8,700

Liabilities		
Accounts Payable		$ 1,500

Equity		
Lonnie Revis, Capital		7,200
Total Liabilities and Equity		$ 8,700

The balance sheet reflects the accounting equation.

IN THE REAL WORLD

Ownership Matters

Robert's interior plantscape business began small—with him caring for the plants of a single office building. Now that his business is growing, he and two friends have decided to form a partnership. The company will now have a Capital account for each partner:

- Robert Drew, Capital
- Amy Cheung, Capital
- Joe Popo, Capital

(continued)

IN THE REAL WORLD   *(continued)*

Although the partners are satisfied with the current arrangement, if and when the business were to be incorporated, the balance sheet will show two equity accounts:

- Capital Stock.
- Retained Earnings.

Capital Stock is the total amount invested by shareholders. The Retained Earnings account contains accumulated profits kept in the corporation (not paid out to shareholders).

2.2.2 The Income Statement

Income statement:
The financial statement that presents a summary of the company's financial activity over a certain period of time.

The **income statement** is the financial statement that presents a summary of the company's financial activity over a certain period of time, such as a month, quarter, or year; the title of an income statement shows the period of time covered by the statement. The difference between the balance sheet and the income statement is like the difference between a snapshot and a video. One is a point in time; the other is a period of time.

The income statement has three sections:

- Revenue.
- Expenses.
- Net Income (or Net Loss).

Small Business Accounting in Action ➡

Interpret the balance sheet and income statement.

The income statement starts with revenue earned, subtracts the expenses, and ends with the bottom line—net income or loss. The income statement in Figure 2-4 shows a net income.

SELF-CHECK

1. What is a balance sheet? Why is it called a "balance sheet"?
2. Which debit accounts appear on the balance sheet? Which credit accounts?
3. What is an income statement? Which debit accounts are on the income statement? Which credit accounts?
4. What is the bottom line of an income statement?
5. How do the titles of a balance sheet and an income statement differ?

Apply Your Knowledge ▶ Suppose a potential investor wants to know about your business's finances. What would you do?

Figure 2-4

REVIS BOOKKEEPING SERVICE Income Statement For the Month Ended May 31, 200X		
Revenue		
Fees Income	$	5,200
Expenses		
Advertising	$	100
Office Supplies		300
Telephone		100
Total Expenses		500
Net Income	$	4,700

The income statement shows the results for an accounting period.

2.3 THE CHART OF ACCOUNTS

Chart of accounts:
A list of all the accounts of a business.

As you record transactions, you need a roadmap to help you determine which accounts to use. This roadmap is called the **chart of accounts,** which is a list of all the accounts your business has.

Every business creates its own chart of accounts based on how the business is operated and structured, so you're unlikely to find two businesses with identical charts of accounts. There's no secret to making your own chart—just make a list of the accounts that apply to your business.

Some basic characteristics are common to all charts of accounts. The organization and structure are designed around the balance sheet and the income statement.

2.3.1 Account Sections

The chart of accounts starts with the balance sheet accounts (assets, liabilities, and equity) and ends with income statement accounts (revenue and expenses).

Current assets:
Things the company owns and expects to use in the next 12 months.

Assets Section

Assets are classified as current or long-term. **Current assets** are things the company owns and expects to use in the next 12 months, such as cash and

Long-term assets:
Things that have a lifespan of more than 12 months.

accounts receivable (money expected from customers you have invoiced). **Long-term assets** are things that have a life span of more than 12 months, such as buildings, furniture, and equipment.

Liabilities Section

Current liabilities:
The debts the company must pay over the next 12 months.

Long-term liabilities:
Debts the company must pay over a period of time longer than 12 months.

Like assets, the liabilities are either current or long-term. **Current liabilities** are the debts the company must pay over the next 12 months, such as accounts payable (bills from vendors, contractors, and consultants) and credit cards payable. **Long-term liabilities** are debts the company must pay over a period of time longer than 12 months, such as mortgages or loans due more than one year in the future. In fact, it is often helpful to potential and present creditors and owners to compare a business's "current assets" to its "current liabilities" to assess the ability of the business to pay its bills on a timely basis.

Equity Section

The equity section includes the accounts that track owners of the company and their claims against the company's assets. For example, money invested or withdrawn by the owners is recorded in the equity accounts. An equity account is also used to record net income at the end of the accounting period by closing revenue and expenses accounts. (See Chapter 7 for information about the statement of owner's equity.)

Revenue Section

The revenue section contains accounts that track sales of goods and services.

Expenses Section

Small Business Accounting in Action ➡
Create the accounts needed for your business.

This section contains accounts that track expenses that aren't directly tied to the sale of merchandise.

Figure 2-5 is a partial chart of accounts created using QuickBooks. In this sample chart, you can see a few accounts that are unique to the business in Figure 2-5, such as Cooking Supplies, and other accounts that are common only to a retail business, such as Cash Discrepancies.

2.3.2 Account Numbers

Many companies assign numbers to the accounts. Computerized systems can automatically assign account numbers. Otherwise, you need to plan out your own numbering system. The most common number system is:

• Assets: 1000 to 1999.

• Liabilities: 2000 to 2999.

Figure 2-5

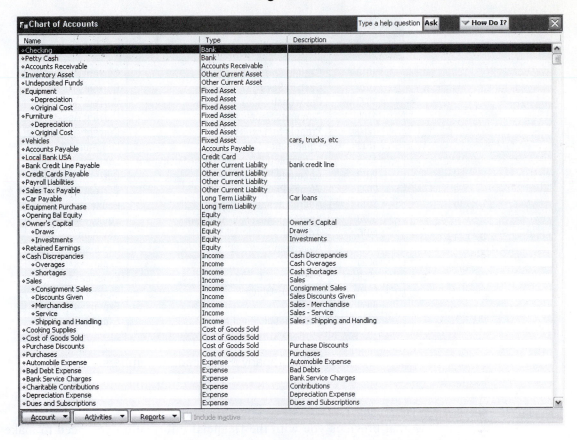

Name	Type	Description
Checking	Bank	
Petty Cash	Bank	
Accounts Receivable	Accounts Receivable	
Inventory Asset	Other Current Asset	
Undeposited Funds	Other Current Asset	
Equipment	Fixed Asset	
Depreciation	Fixed Asset	
Original Cost	Fixed Asset	
Furniture	Fixed Asset	
Depreciation	Fixed Asset	
Original Cost	Fixed Asset	
Vehicles	Fixed Asset	cars, trucks, etc
Accounts Payable	Accounts Payable	
Local Bank USA	Credit Card	
Bank Credit Line Payable	Other Current Liability	bank credit line
Credit Cards Payable	Other Current Liability	
Payroll Liabilities	Other Current Liability	
Sales Tax Payable	Other Current Liability	
Car Payable	Long Term Liability	Car loans
Equipment Purchase	Long Term Liability	
Opening Bal Equity	Equity	
Owner's Capital	Equity	Owner's Capital
Draws	Equity	Draws
Investments	Equity	Investments
Retained Earnings	Equity	
Cash Discrepancies	Income	Cash Discrepancies
Overages	Income	Cash Overages
Shortages	Income	Cash Shortages
Sales	Income	Sales
Consignment Sales	Income	Consignment Sales
Discounts Given	Income	Sales Discounts Given
Merchandise	Income	Sales - Merchandise
Service	Income	Sales - Service
Shipping and Handling	Income	Sales - Shipping and Handling
Cooking Supplies	Cost of Goods Sold	
Cost of Goods Sold	Cost of Goods Sold	
Purchase Discounts	Cost of Goods Sold	Purchase Discounts
Purchases	Cost of Goods Sold	Purchases
Automobile Expense	Expense	Automobile Expense
Bad Debt Expense	Expense	Bad Debts
Bank Service Charges	Expense	Bank Service Charges
Charitable Contributions	Expense	Contributions
Depreciation Expense	Expense	Depreciation Expense
Dues and Subscriptions	Expense	Dues and Subscriptions

A chart of accounts is customized for the individual business.

- Equity: 3000 to 3999.
- Revenue: 4000 to 4999.
- Expenses: 5000 to 5999.

The chart of accounts in Figure 2-6 uses this numbering system. Some accounts in Figure 2-6 are not discussed in this chapter. The Withdrawals accounts are covered in Chapter 7; Accumulated Depreciation, Prepaid Insurance, and Depreciation in Chapter 6; and Petty Cash in Chapter 8.

2.3.3 Managing an Efficient Chart of Accounts

The following tips will help keep your chart of accounts on track:

- **Help yourself:** The chart of accounts is a money management tool that helps you track your business transactions, so set it up in a way

Figure 2-6

Andréa's Artistic Visions		
Account No.	**Account Name**	**Classification**
1010	Cash in Checking	Current Assets
1020	Cash in Savings	Current Assets
1030	Petty Cash	Current Assets
1100	Accounts Receivable	Current Assets
1200	Prepaid Insurance	Current Assets
1510	Equipment	Long-term Assets
1515	Accumulated Depreciation--Equipment	Long-term Assets
2010	Accounts Payable	Current Liabilities
2020	Wages Payable	Current Liabilities
3010	Andréa Johnson, Capital	Equity
3020	Andréa Johnson, Withdrawals	Equity
4010	Art Fees	Revenue
6010	Advertising	Expenses
6020	Insurance	Expenses
6030	Supplies--Art	Expenses
6040	Supplies--Office	Expenses
6050	Wages	Expenses
6510	Depreciation--Equipment	Expenses

This company uses account numbers.

that provides you with the financial information you need to make smart business decisions.

- **Leave room:** Be sure to leave a lot of room between accounts to add new accounts. For example, number your Cash in Checking account 1000 and your accounts receivable account 1100. That leaves you plenty of room to add other accounts to track cash.

- **Find accounts:** The expenses accounts don't have to appear in any specific order, but most businesses list them alphabetically for convenience.

- **Add accounts:** Don't panic if you can't think of every type of account you may need for your business. It's very easy to add accounts at any time.

- **Delete accounts:** You might want to delete an account that you don't use. It's best not to delete accounts until the end of a 12-month reporting period.

- **Stay current:** Keep the chart of accounts updated and distribute it to any employees who record transactions into the accounting system. Employees who don't use the accounting system but code invoices or other transactions also need a copy of your chart of accounts.

IN THE REAL WORLD

Get Help from National Organizations

James moved to the New Orleans area after Hurricane Katrina to put his carpentry skills to good use. Though he was only 27, James had worked for his father's Boston-area contracting business since he was in high school, and he was now ready to start his own home-building business. During the process of establishing his company, James sought guidance from the National Association of Home Builders (www.nahb.org). The organization's Web site, which covers a wide array of business tools including tax strategies and tips for loan financing, goes as far as offering a number of sample charts of accounts. Because James was going to start small, he used the "Basic Accounts for Small Volume Builders" as the foundation for his accounting system.

SELF-CHECK

1. What is a chart of accounts?
2. How are the accounts organized in a chart of accounts?
3. What is the difference between current assets and long-term assets? Current liabilities and long-term liabilities?
4. Define *expenses account* and give three examples.

Apply Your Knowledge You work as a disc jockey at weddings, parties, and corporate events. List five accounts you would include in your chart of accounts (one account from each main category).

SUMMARY

Section 2.1

- A debit is an entry on the left side of an account and a credit is an entry on the right side of an account. The total debits should equal the total credits.
- Accounts with normal debit balances are assets and expenses.
- Accounts with normal credit balances are liabilities, equity, and revenue.

Section 2.2

- The three main financial statements are the balance sheet, income statement, and statement of owner's equity.

Section 2.3

- The chart of accounts is a list of all the accounts a business has; each business's chart of accounts will vary according to how the business is operated and structured.

ASSESS YOUR UNDERSTANDING

UNDERSTAND: WHAT HAVE YOU LEARNED?

 Go to **www.wiley.com/college/epstein** to assess your knowledge of mastering debits and credits.

APPLY: WHAT WOULD YOU DO?

1. Complete the chart below using the following information to fill in the blanks:

Type of Account = Assets, Liabilities, Owner's Equity, Revenue, Expenses
Effect of Debit = Increase or Decrease
Effect of Credit = Increase or Decrease
Normal Balance = Debit or Credit

Account	Type of Account	Debit	Credit	Normal Balance
Cash				
Advertising Expense	___	___	___	___
Accounts Payable	___	___	___	___
F. Fairway, Capital	___	___	___	___
Service Revenue	___	___	___	___
Computer	___	___	___	___
Income Tax Payable	___	___	___	___
Salary Expense	___	___	___	___
Accounts Receivable	___	___	___	___
W. Wedge, Withdrawals	___	___	___	___
Service Fees Earned	___	___	___	___
Office Supplies	___	___	___	___
Rent Expense	___	___	___	___
Office Equipment	___	___	___	___
Notes Payable	___	___	___	___

2. You are delegating the day-to-day bookkeeping tasks to a worker who will use an accounting software program. Because you feel a basic understanding of accounting is necessary, you decide to provide information about debits and credits. Prepare some brief notes on the subject.

3. Identify on which financial statement the following items would appear:
   a. Cash in Checking
   b. Equipment
   c. Rita Singh, Capital
   d. Styling Services Income
   e. Accounts Payable
   f. Sales—Hair Products
   g. Salaries Expenses
   h. Supplies—Shop

Questions 4–6: Express each of the following business transactions in T-account form:

4. **TRANSACTION:** Your company borrowed $3,000 from the bank.

5. **TRANSACTION:** You received a check for $4,000 for an interior decorating job.

6. **TRANSACTION:** You wrote a check for $45 for a six-month subscription to a professional journal.

7. For each account listed, identify the financial statement on which the account will appear:
   a. Computers
   b. Consulting Income
   c. Dues and Subscriptions
   d. Loan Payable
   e. Rafael Salas, Capital
   f. Sales—Software
   g. Car
   h. Utilities

Questions 8–9: On July 31, 200X, Critters Pet Care had the following account balances after one month of activity:

Cash in Checking	$2,800
Cash in Savings	8,000
Equipment	1,500
Accounts Payable	2,100
John Ross, Capital	10,200
Pet Grooming Income	4,000

Postage	50
Printing	200
Supplies—Office	70
Supplies—Pet	300
Telephone	80

8. Prepare the income statement for Critters Pet Care.

9. Prepare the balance sheet for Critters Pet Care.

10. You just opened the bank account for your landscaping business and are setting up your accounting system. What expenses accounts will you include in your chart of accounts?

11. Your business has a high volume of vendor invoices and you hired an accounts payable clerk to help with the coding and inputting. This person is new to your line of business. What advice would you give about using the chart of accounts?

BE A SMALL BUSINESS ACCOUNTANT

Research Double-entry Accounting

Using the library or the Internet, research the origin of double-entry accounting. Whose name is most linked with double-entry accounting? Why? Which aspects of the business environment supported the rise of double-entry accounting? How does the business environment of that time and place compare to today's business environment?

Scoring Free Advice

SCORE® Counselors to America's Small Business (www.score.org) is a volunteer organization that offers free advice. Go to the Web site's "How-To" section and click "Full Business Columnist archive." Choose the column titled "7 Steps to Small Business Success." What are the seven steps? Who should be on your team as you plan your business? What is the most basic system every business should have? Assess the article's relevance to your own plans for a small business.

Create a Chart of Accounts

Select a service industry that interests you and create a complete chart of accounts. Anticipate the accounts you will need and make the chart of accounts as detailed as possible.

KEY TERMS

Account	A record that keeps track of increases and decreases in specific items.
Accounting equation	The relationship among the balance sheet accounts: Assets = Liabilities + Equity.
Assets	All the things a company owns.
Balance sheet	The financial statement that presents a snapshot of the company's financial position as of a particular date in time.
Chart of accounts	A list of all the accounts of a business.
Credit	An entry on the right side of an account.
Current assets	Things the company owns and expects to use in the next 12 months.
Current liabilities	The debts the company must pay over the next 12 months.
Debit	An entry on the left side of an account.
Double-entry accounting	A system in which you record all transactions twice, using debits and credits.
Equity	The claim the owners have on the assets of the company.
Expenses	The cost of everything used to operate the company, excluding costs directly related to the sale of merchandise.
Financial statements	Reports that summarize information about the financial performance and status of the business.
Income statement	The financial statement that presents a summary of the company's financial activity over a certain period of time.
Liabilities	All the debts the company owes.
Long-term assets	Things that have a life span of more than 12 months.
Long-term liabilities	Debts the company must pay over a period of time longer than 12 months.
Normal balance	The increase side of an account.
Revenue	The money earned in the process of selling the company's goods or services.
T account	A visual tool used to represent actual accounts such as assets, liabilities, equity, revenue, and expenses.
Transaction	An economic event that causes changes in accounts.

CHAPTER 3

BEGINNING THE ACCOUNTING CYCLE
Using Your Accounting System

Do You Already Know?

- The journey from transactions to closing
- The book of original entry and the book of final entry
- Important documents and how to safeguard them

 For additional questions to assess your current knowledge on using an accounting system, go to **www.wiley.com/college/epstein.**

What You Will Find Out	What You Will Be Able To Do
3.1 What to do in an accounting period	Implement a systematic approach to maintaining and using financial information
3.2 How to use a journal to record daily transactions; how a ledger differs from a journal	Use a journal to chronologically record daily transactions; record transactions in a ledger, organized by account
3.3 How to manage paperwork so financial successes and failures can be tracked	Create an efficient filing system; determine what records to keep and for how long

INTRODUCTION

You are familiar with cycles of the moon or consumer spending cycles related to the seasons. Accounting also has a cycle. In this chapter you will learn about the accounting cycle and focus on its first three steps. You will also learn about managing your business's paperwork.

3.1 STEPS OF THE ACCOUNTING CYCLE

Accounting cycle:
A series of steps completed in an accounting period.

The **accounting cycle** is a series of steps completed in an accounting period. It's called a cycle because the workflow is circular: entering transactions, manipulating the transactions through the accounting cycle, closing the books at the end of the accounting period, and then starting the entire cycle again for the next accounting period. The accounting cycle has eight basic steps, as shown in Figure 3-1.

Figure 3-1

The Accounting Cycle

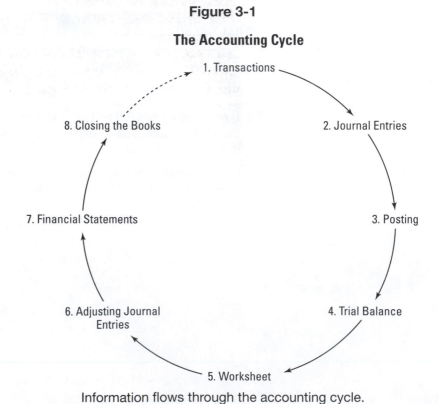

Information flows through the accounting cycle.

3.1.1 Transactions

As Step 1 of the accounting cycle, financial transactions start the process. A **source document** is evidence of a transaction. All transactions that are entered into the records should have some sort of evidence to prove that the transaction actually occurred. Examples of source documents are bills you receive from vendors and checks you receive from customers. A business can have many types of transactions:

- The owner's initial investment in the business.
- Additional amounts invested by the owner.
- Cash withdrawn by the owner.
- Purchase of a vehicle with a loan.
- Payoff of the vehicle loan.
- Sale of services on credit.
- Sale of a product on credit.
- Return of a product by a customer.
- Cash collected from a customer.
- Payment of wages to employees.
- Payment of payroll taxes to the government.
- Purchase of supplies for cash.
- Payment for a one-year lease on office space.
- Purchase of a new copy machine for cash.
- Sale of the old copy machine to a neighboring business.

Chapter 4 covers transactions in greater detail and discusses how to record the basics of business activities.

3.1.2 Journal Entries

The transactions, as shown in Section 3.1.3, are recorded in the appropriate journal, which is a chronological order of transactions. This is the point where information enters the accounting system.

Small Business Accounting in Action ➡
Implement a systematic approach to maintain and use financial information.

3.1.3 Posting

The transactions are posted to individual accounts in the general ledger. The general ledger is organized in the same order as the chart of accounts: assets, liabilities, equity, revenue, and expenses.

3.1.4 Trial Balance

At the end of the accounting period (which may be a month, quarter, or year depending on your business's practices), you prepare a trial balance.

3.1.5 Worksheet

The worksheet is a tool used to organize the adjustments to your accounts. For example, a large one-time payment (such as insurance) should be allocated on a monthly basis to more accurately match monthly expenses with monthly revenue.

3.1.6 Adjusting Journal Entries

You record any adjustments calculated on your worksheet into the accounting system. You don't need to make adjusting entries until the trial balance process is completed and all needed adjustments have been identified. After you record adjustments, you prepare another trial balance to be sure the accounts are still in balance.

3.1.7 Financial Statements

You prepare the financial statements, which summarize information about the performance and status of the business.

3.1.8 Closing

Income statement accounts are temporary and are closed—made to have a zero balance. In other words, you close the books for the revenue and expenses accounts and begin the entire cycle again with zero balances in those accounts.

As a businessperson, you want to be able to measure your profit or loss on month-by-month, quarter-by-quarter, and year-by-year bases. To do that, revenue and expenses accounts must start with a zero balance at the beginning of each accounting period.

In contrast, you carry over assets, liabilities, and equity account balances from cycle to cycle. The business doesn't start each cycle by getting rid of old assets and buying new assets, paying off and then taking on new debt, or paying out all claims to owners and then collecting the money again. So those accounts stay open.

IN THE REAL WORLD

Cycle Overlap

Month-end, quarter-end, and especially year-end can be hectic times for small-business owners, especially those who are handling all aspects of a business. For Tara, who creates personalized handbags for a small clientele, the December holidays are the most hectic. Unfortunately, she can't stop doing business just to take care of her financial statements and close the books. More often than not, Tara spends the first two weeks of January finishing up transactions and closing the books for December and the previous year.

SELF-CHECK

1. What is the accounting cycle?

2. Give four examples of source documents.

3. At what point does a transaction enter the accounting system?

4. Which accounts are closed at the end of an accounting period? Why?

Apply Your Knowledge   Your company loaned another business $5,000 at 7% annual interest for a three-month period ($5,000 × 0.07 × 3/12). At the end of the loan term, the other business handed over a check for $5,087.50. Describe which transactions, if any, occurred.

3.2 INTRODUCTION TO JOURNALS AND LEDGERS

Step 2 and Step 3 of the accounting cycle are journal entries and posting. This section is an overview of the parts of the accounting system used for these tasks:

- Journals (for journal entries).
- Ledgers (for posting).

3.2.1 Journals

Journal:
A chronological record of daily company transactions.

A **journal** is a chronological record of daily company transactions. It is known as the "book of original entry" because information first enters the accounting system in the journal. Each transaction goes in the appropriate journal in chronological order. The entry should include information about the date of the transaction, how the accounts are affected, and the source material used for developing the transaction.

Businesses use two types of journals:

- General journal.
- Special journals.

The following example shows the flow of information from the transaction (Step 1 of the accounting cycle) to the journal (Step 2 of the cycle).

FOR EXAMPLE

See the accompanying example, which illustrates the flow of information from a transaction to a journal.

TRANSACTION
On September 1, 200X, you wrote Check 889 to Sid's Book Shop for $150 to buy reference books for your business.

RECORDING IN THE JOURNAL

First: Use the source document (Check 889) to analyze the transaction into debit and credit parts:

1. Identify the accounts. (Identify Books Expense and Cash in Checking.)
2. Classify the accounts. (Books Expense are expenses and Cash in Checking is an asset.)
3. Determine the increase or decrease. (Books Expense will increase and Cash in Checking will decrease.)
4. Apply the rules of debit and credit. (Debit Books Expense and credit Cash in Checking.)

Then: Record information about the transaction into the journal:

Date of transaction:	September 1, 200X
Debit:	Books Expense $150
Credit:	Cash in Checking $150
Description:	Check 889, Sid's Book Shop, for reference books

Your actual journal entry won't look like the example above, but it will contain the same information. How your journal entry looks will depend on the type of journal you use. All journals record the same details about a transaction.

The General Journal

General journal:
A journal that can be used to record all types of transactions.

The **general journal** is a journal that can be used to record all types of transactions. Chapter 4 uses the general journal only. This is to focus attention on the nature of the transactions, rather than on filling out forms. In reality, a business usually has several other journals in addition to the general journal.

Special Journals

It's acceptable to keep one general journal for all your transactions, but one big journal can be hard to manage because you might have thousands of entries in that journal by the end of the year. Instead, most businesses employ a system of journals that includes a Cash Receipts journal for incoming cash and a Cash Disbursements journal for outgoing cash. Not all transactions involve cash, however, so the two most common non-cash journals are the Sales journal and the Purchases journal.

Small Business Accounting in Action
Use a journal to chronologically record daily transactions.

You decide which accounts you want to create journals for based on your business operation and your need for information about key financial transactions. Chapters 11 and 12 go into more detail about special journals.

3.2.2 Ledgers

Ledger:
A collection of all a business's accounts.

Recall that the journal is organized by time. If you wanted to use the journal to research all the transactions for a single account, such as Supplies Expense, you would have to look for every entry throughout the journal. Also, the journal does not keep a running total of the account balance. You would need to use a **ledger,** which is a collection of all the accounts.

Businesses use two types of ledgers:

* General ledger.
* Subsidiary ledgers.

Posting:
The step by which information is transferred from the journals to the ledger.

Information is transferred from the journals to the ledger by **posting.** Posting is Step 3 of the accounting cycle. The posting process "telegraphs" certain information to an account: the date, the amount, and whether it is a debit or credit. This flow of information is illustrated in Figure 3-2.

Figure 3-2

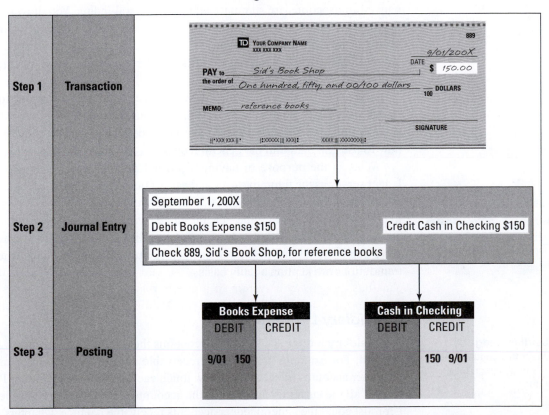

A transaction is posted to the ledger accounts in Step 3 of the accounting cycle.

IN THE REAL WORLD

One Step

Ki's least favorite part about running his own bike repair shop is dealing with his accounting system. Fortunately, he's discovered QuickBooks, which has made handling his accounts much more manageable. Quick-Books, like other computerized accounting systems, often combines steps of the accounting cycle. For example, QuickBooks both records (Step 2) and posts (Step 3) in the same operation. And when Ki is creating a customer invoice, QuickBooks will do Steps 1, 2, and 3 at the same time.

The General Ledger

General ledger:
A permanent record of all the accounts used in your business.

The **general ledger** is a permanent record of all the accounts used in your business. It is known as the "book of final entry." All your business's financial transactions are summarized in the general ledger. You draw upon the general ledger's account summaries to develop your financial reports on a monthly, quarterly, or annual basis. You can also use these account summaries to develop internal reports that help you make key business decisions.

The general ledger is the one place you need to go to find transactions that impact Cash, Accounts Receivable, Accounts Payable, and any other account included in your business's chart of accounts. Chapter 5 shows you how to use and maintain the general ledger.

Small Business Accounting in Action
Record transactions in a ledger, organized by account.

What is the purpose of having a journal *and* a ledger? The general ledger serves as the figurative eyes and ears of bookkeepers and accountants who want to know what financial transactions have taken place historically in a business. By reading the general ledger, you can see, account by account, every transaction that has taken place in the business. To uncover more details about those transactions, you can turn to your journals, where transactions are kept on a daily basis.

Subsidiary Ledgers

Subsidiary ledger:
A ledger that contains the details of a general ledger account.

A **subsidiary ledger** is a ledger that contains the details of a general ledger account. For example, an accounts receivable subsidiary ledger contains customer accounts (details about how much each customer owes you). The total of all the customer accounts in the accounts receivable subsidiary ledger must equal the general ledger accounts receivable balance. Chapters 11 and 12 cover subsidiary ledgers.

SELF-CHECK

1. Describe the difference between a journal and a ledger.

2. What types of transactions can be recorded in the general journal?

3. What is the general ledger and why is it considered the book of final entry?

4. If you wanted to find more information about a transaction in the general ledger, what would you do?

Apply Your Knowledge You receive a bill from a vendor. You decide to take advantage of the vendor's terms (30 days). Where do you get the information for the journal entry? Where do you get information for the posting?

3.3 KEEPING THE RIGHT PAPERWORK

Keeping the books is all about creating an accurate paper trail. You want to keep track of all your company's financial transactions so if a question comes up at a later date, you can turn to the books to figure out what went wrong.

An accurate paper trail is the only way to track your financial successes and review your financial failures, tasks that are vitally important in order to grow your business. You need to know what works successfully so you can repeat it in the future and build on your success. On the other hand, you need to know what failed so you can correct it and avoid making the same mistake again.

When it comes to handling cash, whether you're talking about the cash register, deposits into your checking accounts, or petty cash withdrawals, you can see that a lot of paper changes hands. In order to properly control the movement of cash into and out of your business, careful documentation is key. And don't forget about organization; whether on paper or on a computer, you need to be able to find that documentation if questions about cash flow arise later. It may be interesting to note that a 2005 survey revealed that, 10 years after the so-called paperless office revolution, one-half of all small businesses still use paper files.

Monitoring cash flow isn't the only reason you need to keep loads of paperwork. In order to do your taxes and write off business expenses, you have to have receipts for expenses. You also need details about the money you paid to employees and taxes collected for your employees in order to file the proper reports with government entities. Setting up a good filing system and knowing what to keep and for how long to keep it is very important for any small businessperson.

3.3.1 Creating a Filing System

To get started setting up your filing system, you need some supplies, specifically:

- **Filing cabinets:** This one's pretty self-explanatory—it's hard to have a filing system with nothing to keep the files in.

- **File folders:** Use these to set up separate files for each of your vendors, employees, and customers who buy on store credit, as well as files for backup information on each of your transactions. Many bookkeepers file transaction information by the date the transaction was added to their journal. If the transaction relates to a customer, vendor, or employee, they may add a duplicate copy of the transaction to the individual files as well. The idea is to make the records complete while at the same time keeping paperwork at a minimum.

- **Three-ring binders:** These binders are great for things like your chart of accounts (discussed in Chapter2), your system of journals (Chapter 4), and your general ledger (Chapter 5) because you'll be adding to these documents regularly and the binders make it easy to add additional pages. Be sure to number the pages as you add them to the binder, so you can quickly spot a missing page. How many binders you need depends on how many financial transactions you have each accounting period. You can keep everything in one binder, or you may want to set up a binder for the chart of accounts and general ledger and then a separate binder for each of your active journals. It's your decision based on what makes your job easier.

- **Expandable files:** These are the best way to keep track of current vendor activity and any bills that may be due.

  - **Alphabetical file:** Use this file to track all your outstanding purchase orders by vendor. After you fill the order, you can file all details about that order in the vendor's individual file in case questions about the order arise later.

  - **12-month file:** Use this file to keep track of bills that you need to pay. Simply place the bill in the slot for the month that it's due. Many companies also use a 30-day expandable file. At the beginning of the month, the bills are placed in the 30-day expandable file based on the dates that they need to be paid.

  - **Not needed:** If you're using a computerized accounting system, you likely don't need the 12-month file for bills because your accounting system can remind you when bills are due (as long as you added the information to the system when the bill arrived).

- **Blank computer disks or other storage media:** Use these to back up your computerized system on a daily basis. Keep the backup disks in a fire safe or some place that won't be affected if the business is destroyed by a fire. (A fire safe is a must for any business; it's the best way to keep critical financial data safe.)

CAREER CONNECTION

At 63, a retired math teacher sticks to tradition when handling the accounts of his small business.

It would make perfect sense for a math tutor to take advantage of the computing bells and whistles that come with accounting systems like Peachtree Accounting and QuickBooks. But Nathan Richardson thinks differently. Since his retirement in 2003, Richardson has tutored Bear, Delaware, high school students as they prepare for college entrance exams. He has an idea that computing tools have made it too easy for kids to really learn the math skills they need for higher education. So he practices what he preaches.

Richardson, who tutors at least 10 students a week, uses a general journal and ledger system to track his accounts. Aside from minimal teaching supplies and an occasional educational conference or lecture, his expenses are generally limited to his transportation and cell phone, which has been one of his few concessions to technology. Richardson finds the phone to be an invaluable tool for tracking down late clients or letting other clients know he's running a few minutes behind. Because he uses the phone strictly for business, Richardson is able to deduct the phone as an expense.

Meticulous about paperwork, Richardson uses a series of binders to file copies of any invoices and receipts. After each quarter, he generates a quarterly statement and stores those files in a file cabinet. In the event of a question regarding payment or taxes, Richardson simply pulls the appropriate file.

Tips from the Professional

- Use a system you're comfortable using.
- Err on the side of caution when it comes to keeping paperwork.
- Consult a tax accountant every five years (or when necessary) to double-check your taxes.

Small Business Accounting in Action →
Create an efficient filing system.

3.3.2 Figuring Out What to Keep and for How Long

As you can probably imagine, the pile of paperwork you need to hold on to can get very large very quickly. As they see their files getting thicker and thicker, most business people wonder what they can toss, what they really need to keep, and how long they need to keep it.

Always consult your CPA and attorney when creating your records retention policy. Businesses generally keep most transaction-related paperwork for as long as the IRS or other taxing authority requires. For most types of audits, that's three years after you file your return.

Some experts recommend that tax returns be kept indefinitely, and that other tax-related documents be retained at least seven years. Also, if a business failed to file taxes or filed taxes fraudulently, it may be questioned by the IRS at any time because there's no statute of limitations in these cases.

A tax audit isn't the only reason to keep records around longer than one year. You may need proof-of-purchase information for your insurance company if an asset is lost, stolen, or destroyed by fire or other accident. Also, you need to hang on to information regarding any business loan until it's paid off, just in case the bank questions how much you paid. After the loan's paid off, be sure to keep proof of payment indefinitely in case a question about the loan ever arises.

Information about real estate and other asset holdings also should be kept around for as long as you hold the asset and for at least three years after the asset is sold. Again, some experts recommend that you keep these records indefinitely.

The Department of Labor requires employers to keep information about employees for at least three years after the employee leaves. (If any legal action arises regarding that employee's job tenure after the employee leaves, the statute of limitations for legal action is at most three years.) The IRS requests that you keep information about payroll for four years after the payroll tax due date or actual date paid.

Laws are subject to change and court interpretation. Keep informed about legal record retention requirements and seek the advice of a professional.

FOR EXAMPLE

For the Small Business Administration's guidelines for record retention, go to http://www.sbaonline.sba.gov/gopher/Business-Development/Success-Series/Vol1/Prof/prof11.txt.

Small Business Accounting in Action

Determine which records to keep and for how long.

PATHWAY TO...
MANAGING RECORDS RETENTION

- **Stay informed:** Check with your lawyer and accountant to get their recommendations on what to keep and for how long.
- **Keep it handy:** Keep the current year's files easily accessible in a designated filing area and keep the most recent past year's files in accessible filing cabinets if you have room.
- **Make room for more:** Box up records when they hit the two-year-old mark, and put them in storage. Be sure to date your boxed records with information about what they are, when they were put into storage, and when it's okay to destroy them.
- **Hold on:** Generally, keep information about all transactions around for about three years. After that, make a list of things you want to hold on to longer for other reasons, such as asset holdings and loan information.

IN THE REAL WORLD

A Moving Experience

We often don't realize what we have until we want it gone.

The clients of Lori's consulting business had a policy of requesting bids, and the bids were usually quite detailed. For each deal, there was a lot of back-and-forth in hammering out the scope, specifications, and financial details of the project. Lori kept copies of the communications in file cabinets behind her desk.

Lori decided to move her office closer to her home. As she packed for the move, she was dismayed at the pounds of paper and the time it took to sort through and shred. She resolved to keep everything in electronic form, organized her computer file folders, and began scanning any documents that she had only in hardcopy.

Lori still has trouble letting go of paper, but she consoles herself with the knowledge that she is scrupulous about making backup copies of the electronic files.

SELF-CHECK

1. List four reasons for maintaining an accurate paper trail.
2. What do you need to create a filing system?
3. Whom should you consult about record retention?
4. Name two government agencies that have strict record retention policies for employers.

Apply Your Knowledge You are preparing to put a box of records in storage. What information do you need for the box?

SUMMARY

Section 3.1

- The accounting cycle is a circular workflow starting with transactions and ending with closing the books.
- The eight steps of the accounting cycle are transactions, journal entries, posting, trial balance, worksheet, adjusting journal entries, financial statements, and closing.

Section 3.2

- Transactions are recorded daily in journals; the general journal can be used for all transactions, but special journals are created for specific types of transactions such as cash disbursements.
- Historical account records are kept in ledgers, with transactions being posted from the journals to the ledgers.

- The general ledger is the permanent record of all the accounts used in your business.
- A subsidiary ledger can have a separate set of records, such as accounts receivable. However, the balance of the subsidiary ledger must always match the associated general ledger account.

Section 3.3

- An accurate paper trail is important for monitoring cash flow, keeping track of details, and meeting legal requirements.
- Seek advice from your CPA and attorney when creating your record retention policy.

ASSESS YOUR UNDERSTANDING

UNDERSTAND: WHAT HAVE YOU LEARNED?

 Go to **www.wiley.com/college/epstein** to assess your knowledge of using an accounting system.

APPLY: WHAT WOULD YOU DO?

1. List the first three steps of the accounting cycle. Create an imaginary transaction (be specific) and describe what happens to this transaction in the first three steps.

2. Describe five transactions that a janitorial service would have.

3. You are starting a catering business and are preparing to meet with a printer about ordering business forms. Which forms will you have printed?

4. You prepared an invoice for a customer and you want to enter it in the journal. What specific information will you copy from the invoice to the journal? What information is not on the invoice?

5. In a manual accounting system, would you ever post a transaction directly from a source document to the general ledger? Why or why not?

6. Which of the following accounts would be closed at the end of the accounting period?

   Cash in Checking
   Loan Payable
   Tom Gegich, Capital
   Sales—Hardware
   License Renewal Fees

7. Which of the following accounts would be carried forward at the end of the accounting period?

   Accounts Receivable
   Sales Tax Payable
   Diane Fratelli, Capital
   Floor Installation Income
   Truck Maintenance

8. How would an expandable file help with your accounts payable? Can you think of a reason why you would use an expandable file if you already have a computerized accounting system? Explain your answer.

9. How long do you think you should keep income tax returns? What about other income-tax-related documents? Why?

10. What is the suggested time frame for keeping files accessible? Do you think this is reasonable? Why or why not?

BE A SMALL BUSINESS ACCOUNTANT

Express Yourself

Select a business that interests you and design at least two source documents using computer application software or paper and pencil. Be sure to include the name, address, and phone number of the business (all imaginary). Consider creating a logo and/or slogan. Fill out each source document with details of a sample transaction.

Specializing

Choose a business that you are familiar with. Would you use any special journals or subsidiary ledgers in this business? Why or why not? If yes, which ones would you use?

Ask the Experts

Find three recent online articles about record retention from SCORE (www.score.org) or other organizations. Construct a five-point bullet list of the most important recommendations. Support your reasons for choosing these as the five most important points.

KEY TERMS

Accounting cycle	A series of steps completed in an accounting period.
General journal	A journal that can be used to record all types of transactions.
General ledger	A permanent record of all the accounts used in your business.
Journal	A chronological record of daily company transactions.
Ledger	A collection of all a business's accounts.
Posting	The step by which information is transferred from the journals to the ledger.
Source document	Evidence of a transaction.
Subsidiary ledger	A ledger that contains the details of a general ledger account.

JOURNALIZING TRANSACTIONS

Analyzing and Recording Economic Events

Do You Already Know?

- The parts of a general journal
- Store credit and how it is different from bank credit cards
- The transactions that affect accounts payable and accounts receivable

For additional questions to assess your current knowledge on journalizing transactions, go to **www.wiley.com/college/epstein.**

What You Will Find Out	What You Will Be Able To Do
4.1 How journalizing records transactions for a new business; how to use a general journal to record equity transactions	Use journalizing to organize transaction information; journalize changes in ownership interest
4.2 How to record sales and purchases	Record transactions involving assets, liabilities, revenue, and expenses
4.3 The role of accounts payable and accounts receivable	Record reduction in amounts you owe and amounts others owe you

INTRODUCTION

This chapter explores the transactions of a new business for one month. From the initial investment by the owner through sales to clients, many transactions enter the accounting system. Along the way you will learn how owners withdraw funds for personal use and how they account for sales and purchases on credit.

4.1 STARTING YOUR BUSINESS

Journalizing:
The process of recording transactions in a journal.

As discussed in Chapter 3, the accounting cycle starts with transactions, followed by journal entries. **Journalizing** is the process of recording transactions in a journal. The general journal can be used to journalize any transaction, but a typical business uses special journals. An example of a special journal is the cash disbursements journal, which records all the checks you write. The general journal is usually reserved for entries that don't fit into any of the special journals.

This chapter uses the general journal exclusively, not because that is how it's done in the real world, but because it allows a focus on the nature of each transaction. Even if you use a computerized accounting program, you need to understand what happens behind the scenes.

FOR EXAMPLE

See Figure 4-1, which illustrates how a general journal organizes transaction information.

4.1.1 Using the General Journal

Whether you use special journals or the general journal, each journal entry will contain the same information about a transaction:

- **Date:** The date of the transaction.
- **Debit:** The account debited in the transaction and the amount of the debit.
- **Credit:** The account credited in the transaction and the amount of the credit.
- **Description:** Brief information and a reference to the source document.

Figure 4-1 shows how the general journal organizes this information into columns.

The column titled "Post Ref." is left blank for now. You won't need the "Post Ref." column until the next step, which is posting (covered in Chapter 5).

Small Business Accounting in Action ➡
Use journalizing to organize transaction information.

In a general journal, transactions are entered on multiple lines because each transaction impacts at least two accounts (and sometimes more than two). Notice how the information is formatted in the Description column:

> All debit accounts are written at the left of the column.
>   All credit accounts are indented.
>   The description is further indented.

Figure 4-1

General Journal					Page 1
Date		Description	Post Ref.	Debit	Credit
Year Month	Day	Account Debited Account Credited Description		Amount	Amount
	Day	Account Debited Account Credited Description		Amount	Amount

The general journal.

PATHWAY TO . . .
MAKING A GENERAL JOURNAL ENTRY

1. **Date**
   - If you are starting a new page, write the year at the top of the page in the date column.
   - Write the month below the year.
   - Do not write the month again on the page unless the month changes while you are still using that page.
   - Write the day.

2. **Debit**
   - Write the name of the account debited in the Description column.
   - Write the amount of the debit in the Debit column.

3. **Credit**
   - Indent slightly so that your credit entry begins to the right of (and below) your debit entry.
   - Write the name of the account credited in the Description column.
   - Write the amount of the credit in the Credit column.

4. **Description**
   - Indent again so that your description begins to the right of (and below) your credit entry.
   - Write a brief description of the transaction.
   - Include source document numbers.

If you use a manual accounting system, be sure to number the pages of your general journal. You will need page numbers to post transactions and to research the details of any particular transaction.

4.1.2 Equity Transactions

Every business is owned by somebody. Equity accounts track owners' contributions to the business as well as their share of ownership. Small, unincorporated companies track equity using the Capital and Withdrawals accounts.

Capital:
The equity account that tracks owners' contributions to the business.

- **Capital:** This account reflects the amount of initial money the business owner contributed to the company as well as owner contributions made after initial start-up. The value of this account is based on cash contributions and other assets contributed by the business owner, such as equipment, vehicles, or buildings. If a small company has several different partners (or members in the case of an LLC), then each individual gets his or her own Capital account.

Withdrawals:
The equity account that tracks money that owners take out of the business.

- **Withdrawals:** This account tracks any money that a business owner takes out of the business. If a business has more than one owner, each owner gets his or her own Withdrawals account.

The Withdrawals account has a normal balance that seems to break the rules of debit and credit. It is an equity account, but a withdrawal *decreases* equity. Therefore its normal balance is a debit, the opposite of the Capital account. Table 4-1 shows the normal balances for all the main account types.

Like revenue and expenses, the Withdrawals balance is transferred to the Capital account at the end of the accounting period. If this seems confusing, don't worry. It makes perfect sense when you do the closing (Chapter 7). Just remember that Withdrawals has a normal debit balance.

Table 4-1: Normal Balances Including Withdrawals

Account Type		Normal Balance	Increase	Decrease
Assets		Debit	Debit	Credit
Liabilities		Credit	Credit	Debit
Equity	Capital account	Credit	Credit	Debit
	Withdrawals account	Debit	Debit	Credit
Revenue		Credit	Credit	Debit
Expenses		Debit	Debit	Credit

Owner's Initial Investment

Let's journalize the first transaction of a new business.

TRANSACTION

On January 2, 200X, Andrea Williams deposited $18,000 of her personal funds into the business checking account of her new business, Andrea's Artistic Visions. The source document consists of two pieces of paper: a photocopy of the check and Memo 1. ("Memo" is short for *memorandum,* an internal communication used in a company.)

First: Analyze the transaction.

1. Identify the accounts. (Cash in Checking and Andrea Williams, Capital.)
2. Classify the accounts. (Cash in Checking is an asset. Andrea Williams, Capital is an equity account with a normal credit balance.)
3. Determine the increase or decrease. (Andrea Williams, Capital will increase $18,000. Cash in Checking will also increase $18,000.)
4. Apply the rules of debit and credit. (Debit Cash in Checking for $18,000 and credit Andrea Williams, Capital for $18,000.)

In this transaction, both accounts will be increased. You might want to use the T- account tool to analyze transactions.

Cash in Checking		Andrea Williams, Capital	
DEBIT	CREDIT	DEBIT	CREDIT
18,000			18,000

Then: Do the journal entry.

General Journal			Page 1		
Date		Description	Post Ref.	Debit	Credit

200X Jan.	2	Cash in Checking
		  Andrea Williams, Capital
		  Initial Investment, Memo 1
				18,000	18,000

Note that the debit amount and credit amount are equal—$18,000 each. All journal entries must be balanced; that's the cardinal rule of double-entry bookkeeping.

Any additional investment by the owner is journalized the same as the owner's original investment.

CAREER CONNECTION

Many couples dream about starting their own business. With an idea and some clever financing, one Jersey Shore couple has taken the leap.

Heather and TJ Brustowicz don't exactly have a lot of free time. TJ works full-time in the recording industry, and Heather cares for their young children—Jack, 3, and Abby, 2. Still, when they had a free moment or two, the couple would toy with the idea of going into business for themselves. The two spent an "entrepreneurial evening" kicking around various business ideas in May 2007, coming up with the concept of rolling giant TVs into backyards for movie nights. They did some research and found a company that makes inflatable movie screens. More research, debate, and worry followed. Three months later Shore Flicks (www.shoreflicks.com) had its first paid event, showing a movie outdoors at their town's Community Day.

"One of the things that made us decide to take the plunge was the relatively low risk," says TJ. The majority of the investment was up front for the equipment. Rather than taking out a business loan, the couple used a chunk of their home equity line of credit and spread the balance across four 0% interest credit cards. "We have an aggressive goal of paying off the initial investment by the end of 2008," TJ says.

Although there are larger regional companies providing the same services, Shore Flicks has little competition in the area. In fact, Heather and TJ discovered that the local weekly outdoor movies were put on by a traveling company based in Massachusetts. The couple is determined to be "first and foremost, a local company," says Heather. "That is reflected in our name and logo, and it's stressed in everything we do."

So far, the majority of time the couple has dedicated to the business has been spent on marketing. Heather takes care of the books, via a journal/ledger system right now, but the two may look into QuickBooks or an outside service as the business grows.

Being a seasonal business, Heather and TJ view Shore Flicks as a part-time venture with full-time potential. "We don't see getting to the point of franchising, we just want it to be at a level where we can both work from home," says TJ. "Getting paid to watch movies isn't bad, either!"

Tips from the Professional

- Explore all your options when it comes to financing; don't be limited to the idea of traditional bank loans.
- Set ambitious but reasonable financial goals.
- Look at the competition and find a way to set your business apart from others.

Owner's Cash Withdrawal

Suppose that on January 9 Andrea needed to withdraw $500 from the business for personal expenses.

TRANSACTION

On January 9, 200X, Andrea's Artistic Visions wrote Check 101 in the amount of $500 to Andrea Williams.

First: Analyze the transaction.

1. Identify the accounts. (Cash in Checking and Andrea Williams, Withdrawals.)
2. Classify the accounts. (Cash in Checking is an asset. Andrea Williams, Withdrawals is an equity account with a normal debit balance.)
3. Determine the increase or decrease. (Andrea Williams, Withdrawals will increase $500. Cash in Checking will decrease $500.)
4. Apply the rules of debit and credit. (Debit Andrea Williams, Withdrawals $500 and credit Cash in Checking $500.)

When analyzing transactions involving cash, it helps to think of the cash side of the transaction first. You can quickly determine whether cash increases (debit) or decreases (credit). That makes it easier to figure out the other side of the transaction.

Andrea Williams, Withdrawals		Cash in Checking	
DEBIT	CREDIT	DEBIT	CREDIT
500			500

Then: Do the journal entry.

General Journal					Page 1
Date		Description	Post Ref.	Debit	Credit
200X Jan.					
	9	Andrea Williams, Withdrawals		500	
		Cash in Checking			500
		Check 101, Memo 2			

IN THE REAL WORLD

Avoiding Fraud—and Infamy

When a business owner records a transaction in which the owner directly pays for a personal item, such as the owner's personal utility bill, two important rules must be noted:

1. This transaction should be charged to the owner's withdrawal account.
2. It is against the law for the owner to charge it to a business account.

Leona Helmsley, a New York hotelier and real estate investor, is one of the best-known examples of someone who broke these rules—and later went to jail for doing so. She charged many personal items to hotel business accounts—bathroom remodeling in her Connecticut country home, clothing items, and so on—and was eventually convicted of federal income tax evasion and other crimes in 1989.

SELF-CHECK

1. In the real world, when does a business use the general journal?
2. Why are the pages of a journal numbered?
3. What is the purpose of the Withdrawals account?
4. What is the normal balance of the Withdrawals account? How does the Withdrawals account affect a person's ownership interest?

Apply Your Knowledge The following transactions occurred in a six-month period:

- Owner made an initial investment of $10,000.
- Owner withdrew $2,500.
- Owner made an additional investment of $3,000.
- Owner withdrew $1,000.
  a. What is the balance of the Capital account?
  b. What is the balance of the Withdrawals account?
  c. What is the total owner's equity?

4.2 BUYING AND SELLING

A new business needs equipment, supplies, or other items to start earning revenue. Any new enterprise expects to make a profit eventually. For profits, you need to have sufficient sales.

4.2.1 Buying for the Business

Expenses accounts often are the biggest section of the chart of accounts. Any money you spend on the business that can't be tied directly to the sale of an individual product falls under the expenses account category. For example, advertising a storewide sale isn't directly tied to the sale of any one product, so the costs associated with advertising fall under the expenses account category.

The most common expenses accounts include the following:

- Advertising.
- Bank Service Charges.
- Credit Card Processing Fees.
- Dues and Subscriptions.
- Equipment Rental.
- Insurance.
- Legal and Accounting.
- Office Expenses.
- Payroll Taxes.
- Postage.
- Rent.
- Salaries and Wages.
- Supplies.
- Telephone.
- Travel and Entertainment.
- Utilities.
- Vehicle Maintenance.

Buying Supplies for Cash

Andrea bought supplies at The Office Space, which has a huge semi-annual sale each July and January.

TRANSACTION
On January 10, 200X, Andrea's Artistic Visions wrote Check 102 in the amount of $850 for supplies.

Supplies are expenses, and expenses accounts have a normal debit balance. The transaction is shown below in T-account form and in the general journal.

Supplies—Office		Cash in Checking	
DEBIT	CREDIT	DEBIT	CREDIT
850			850

General Journal				Page 1
Date	Description	Post Ref.	Debit	Credit
200X Jan.				
10	Supplies—Office Cash in Checking The Office Space, Check 102		850	850

Buying Supplies on Credit

Some companies extend credit to their customers. This is not the same as a credit card such as Visa or MasterCard. This is a company's own credit system. The company can offer a charge card (like Target or J.C. Penney) or simply give you a bill.

When you make a purchase on store credit, it is a current liability because it is expected to be paid in the near future. (A long-term liability would be 12 months or longer.) The debt is recorded in one of the hardest-working liabilities accounts:

Accounts payable:
The current liability account that tracks money the company owes to vendors, contractors, and others.

• **Accounts payable:** This account tracks money the company owes to vendors, contractors, suppliers, and consultants that must be paid in less than a year. Most of these liabilities must be paid in 30 to 90 days from the initial billing, but some companies have shorter terms.

Andrea's Artistic Designs opened an account at Art World, a large art supply store where Andrea bought supplies and received a bill to be paid within 15 days.

TRANSACTION
On January 10, 200X, Andrea's Artistic Visions bought art supplies for $900 on credit from Art World and received Invoice 242.

Small Business Accounting in Action

Record transactions involving assets, liabilities, revenue, and expenses.

The T-account analysis and general journal are shown below. (You can always skip the T-account analysis if you don't need it.)

Supplies–Art		Accounts Payable	
DEBIT	CREDIT	DEBIT	CREDIT
900			900

General Journal					Page 1
Date	Description	Post Ref.	Debit	Credit	
200X Jan.					
10	Supplies—Art		900		
	Accounts Payable			900	
	Art World, Invoice 242				

Buying Assets with Cash and Credit

Businesses usually need assets to generate revenue. Chapter 2 divides assets into two categories: current and long-term. Current assets will be used up within 12 months. Long-term assets will be used for one year or longer. One of the most common long-term assets is:

Equipment:
The long-term assets account that is used to record equipment purchased for the business.

• **Equipment:** This account tracks equipment that was purchased for use for more than one year, such as computers, copiers, and cash registers.

Andrea had a busy day shopping. She bought computer equipment for $3,000, paying $500 in cash and receiving an invoice for the balance that was due in 30 days.

TRANSACTION
On January 10, 200X, Andrea's Artistic Visions purchased computer equipment for $3,000 from Tech Solutions. The $500 down payment was paid by Check 103, and Tech Solutions gave Invoice 3295 for $2,500 to Andrea.

Equipment		Cash in Checking		Accounts Payable	
DEBIT	CREDIT	DEBIT	CREDIT	DEBIT	CREDIT
3,000			500		2,500

Compound journal entry:
An entry that affects more than two accounts.

A transaction affecting more than two accounts requires a **compound journal entry.** In a compound journal entry, always record all the debits before recording the credits.

	General Journal				Page 1
Date	Description	Post Ref.	Debit	Credit	
200X Jan.					
10	Equipment		3,000		
	Cash in Checking			500	
	Accounts Payable			2,500	
	Tech Solutions, Check 103, Inv. 3295				

IN THE REAL WORLD

A More Perfect Union

John, an accounting professor at a community college, has served for the past 10 years as the chief financial officer of the school's teachers' union. When he first took office, the union's accounting system was essentially a "single-entry system" that employed "D-Base III" as the only software. It was quite embarrassing for John when he could not get the initial trial balance to balance, and it was clearly time for a change. The union has now switched to QuickBooks and has used it without problems to document the financial operations of the union. Like any business, a union is subject to auditing, and John was pleased to find that the union's auditors were also very familiar with QuickBooks.

4.2.2 Making the Sale

Companies can sell on cash or credit. Sales made on credit don't involve cash until the customer pays his or her bill. The amount of the credit sale becomes an asset of your business (something you have a claim to because the customer owes you money). You expect to get paid within a short time, so it is a current asset:

Accounts receivable:
The current asset account used to record money due from customers.

- **Accounts receivable:** The current asset account that tracks all money due from customers.

Cash Sale

Andrea completed a design job for Fab Ads Inc. and collected $2,000 in payment.

TRANSACTION

On January 15, 200X, Andrea's Artistic Visions completed design services for Fab Ads Inc., collected Check 308 for $2,000, and gave the customer Sales Slip 01 for the check.

Cash in Checking		Art Fees	
DEBIT	CREDIT	DEBIT	CREDIT
2,000			2,000

General Journal					Page 1
Date	Description	Post Ref.	Debit	Credit
200X Jan.				
15	Cash in Checking		2,000	
	Art Fees			2,000
	Fab Ads Inc., Ck. 308, Sales Slip 01			

Credit Sale

Andrea established a credit policy for her business and accepted Mega-Corp as a credit customer. She completed and billed a job on January 20.

TRANSACTION

On January 20, 200X, Andrea's Artistic Visions completed a design job for Mega-Corp and sent out Invoice 001 for $3,500.

Accounts Receivable		Art Fees	
DEBIT	CREDIT	DEBIT	CREDIT
3,500			3,500

General Journal					Page 1
Date		Description	Post Ref.	Debit	Credit
200X Jan.					
	20	Accounts Receivable 　　Art Fees 　　　Mega-Corp, Invoice 001		3,500	3,500

Small service-type businesses (and many nonprofit organizations) do not make this type of entry if they use cash-basis accounting.

SELF-CHECK

1. What type of account is Accounts Payable? What is it used for?

2. What is a compound entry? Describe how the debits and credits are listed in a compound entry.

3. What is the normal balance of Accounts Receivable? What type of account is this?

Apply Your Knowledge   The following transactions occurred in the first three months of a new business's operation:

• The business bought video and projection equipment for $5,000 on credit.

• The business paid cash for video supplies that cost $900.

• The business bought a computer for $1,200 and paid cash.

What is the balance of the Equipment account at the end of the accounting period?

4.3 OTHER TRANSACTIONS

A business can have many types of transactions. A merchandising business purchases goods and then sells them. A business can loan money, borrow money, and pay or collect interest. Two common transactions are payment of vendor invoices and cash collections from credit customers.

4.3.1 Accounts Payable and Accounts Receivable

The following examples show the entries for paying a vendor bill and receiving a customer payment.

Small Business Accounting in Action

Record reductions in amounts a business owes and amounts others owe a business.

Paying a Bill

TRANSACTION

On January 22, 200X, Andrea's Artistic Visions wrote Check 104 to pay Invoice 242 from Art World, $900.

IN THE REAL WORLD

Setting Up an Accounts Receivable Process

After his father passed away, Sean took over the family's appliance repair business, which had been a staple of their Syracuse-area community for nearly 50 years. It quickly became clear to Sean that the business was experiencing some cash-flow issues. Part of the problem was that the business was slow to generate customer invoices, and money was not coming in as quickly as it should. The other problem, though, had to do with the customers, who had grown accustomed to the friendly, neighborhood feeling of the business—and didn't feel any urgency to pay their balances when payments were due. Sean didn't want to alienate this customer base, but he knew he had to make some changes. He began by issuing invoices promptly; soon after, he introduced new credit policies such as credit limits and payment options. For those accounts that were past due, Sean later began charging interest.

Receiving a Payment

TRANSACTION

On January 29, 200X, Andrea's Artistic Visions deposited Mega-Corp's Check 795602, in payment of Invoice 002, $3,500.

4.3.2 The Completed General Journal

Figure 4-2 shows all the January transactions for Andrea's Artistic Visions in one journal. Some businesses use a modified journal called the *combined journal* that has columns for extra accounts.

Figure 4-2

General Journal					Page 1
Date		Description	Post Ref.	Debit	Credit
200X Jan.	2	Cash in Checking		18,000	
		Andrea Williams, Capital			18,000
		Initial Investment, Memo 1			
	9	Andrea Williams, Withdrawals		500	
		Cash in Checking			500
		Check 101, Memo 2			
	10	Supplies—Office		850	
		Cash in Checking			850
		The Office Space, Check 102			
	10	Supplies—Art		900	
		Accounts Payable			900
		Art World, Invoice 242			
	10	Equipment		3,000	
		Cash in Checking			500
		Accounts Payable			2,500
		Tech Solutions, Check 103, Inv. 3295			
	15	Cash in Checking		2,000	
		Art Fees			2,000
		Fab Ads Inc., Ck. 308, Sales Slip 01			
	20	Accounts Receivable		3,500	
		Art Fees			3,500
		Mega-Corp, Invoice 001			
	22	Accounts Payable		900	
		Cash in Checking			900
		Check 104, Art World, Invoice 242			
	29	Cash in Checking		3,500	
		Accounts Receivable			3,500
		Mega-Corp, Check 795602, Inv. 002			

The journal is a chronological record of transactions.

SELF-CHECK

1. List three transactions of your own creation that reflect the categories demonstrated in the chapter.

2. Which transaction decreases the Accounts Payable account? Is the account debited or credited?

3. Which transaction decreases the Accounts Receivable account? Is the account debited or credited?

4. How is the combined journal different from the general journal?

Apply Your Knowledge The following transactions occurred in the first three months of a new business's operation:

• The business had cash sales of $25,000.

• The business had credit sales of $67,000.

• The business collected $59,000 from credit customers.

   a. How much revenue did the business earn?

   b. What is the balance of the Accounts Receivable account at the end of the period?

SUMMARY

Section 4.1

• Journalizing is the process of recording transactions in a journal. Although the typical business uses special journals, the general journal can be used to journalize any transaction.

• Journal entries must be balanced: debits = credits.

• A journal entry includes the transaction date, the account debited and debit amount, the account credited and credit amount, and a description.

• The Capital account is an equity account that shows the balance of the owner's initial and subsequent contributions to the company.

• The Withdrawals account is an equity account that shows the amount the owner has taken out of the company for personal use. The Withdrawals account has a debit balance.

Section 4.2

• A new business needs equipment, supplies, or other items to start earning revenue.

• Expenses accounts often are the biggest section of the chart of accounts. Any money you spend on the business that can't be tied directly to the sale of an individual product falls under the expenses account category.

• When a business buys on credit, it increases the current liability Accounts Payable.

• In a compound journal entry, all debits are listed first.

Section 4.3

• A business can have many types of transactions; two common transactions are payment of vendor invoices and cash collections from credit customers.

ASSESS YOUR UNDERSTANDING

UNDERSTAND: WHAT HAVE YOU LEARNED?

 Go to **www.wiley.com/college/epstein** to assess your knowledge of journalizing transactions.

APPLY: WHAT WOULD YOU DO?

1. You have three business partners. How many equity accounts will your business have? Briefly describe the accounts.

2. Why do you think the owner's cash withdrawals are not recorded directly in the Capital account?

3. When would you credit the Withdrawals account?

4. The chapter shows an example of a compound journal entry. Give two more examples of compound journal entries.

5. If your company offered credit to customers, what payment terms would you have (the number of days before you require payment)? Why?

6. Journalize the following transactions:

   6/01/200X: Rafael Salas, owner of Creative Software, Invested $3,000 in the business, Memo 21.

   6/10/200X: Rafael Salas took $1,450 out of the business for personal living expenses, Check 3121.

   6/30/0X: Rafael Salas put $500 into the business, Memo 22.

7. Journalize the following transactions:

   7//01/200X: Beautiful Day Salon replaced the chairs at three styling stations, buying on credit at Specialty Fixtures, Invoice 912 for $1,900.

   7/02/200X: The salon purchased shampoo and conditioner to use when providing services to salon clients. The supplier was Wholesale Mart and the salon paid with Check 456, $300.

   7/25/200X: According to Specialty Fixtures' credit terms, 50 percent of the outstanding amount is due in 30 days and the remaining 50 percent is due in 60 days. Beautiful Day takes advantage of the terms and writes Check 457.

8. Journalize the following transaction:

   8/15/200X: Gegich Repair Service bought the following items at Wholesale Mart, Check 189:

Copier paper, $35

Motor oil for vans, $200

Hardware supplies including nails in bulk, $50

9. Journalize the following transaction:

9/15/200X: The owner of Solid Foundation Flooring went to Hal's Tech World and bought a computer system for $1,700. She also bought CD-ROMs and computer-cleaning supplies for $50, receiving Sales Slip 2010 for the total purchase.

She wrote Check 125 for $2,400. The check included payment of a Hal's Tech World invoice from the previous month (Invoice 1968 for $650).

10. Journalize the following transactions:

10/01/200X: John Ross transferred a van that he owned to his business, Critters Pet Care. According to the Kelley Blue Book, the van was worth $12,000. John wrote the details of the transfer in Memo 29.

10/05/200X: John went to an office-services center and paid $150 to print invoices and $25 for overnight delivery of a business package, Check 222.

10/10/200X: John signed an agreement with Commerce Bank for a short-term business loan of $3,000. The bank's check was number 00058936.

BE A SMALL BUSINESS ACCOUNTANT

Accounting Software

Choose a software program such as QuickBooks or Peachtree. Using the Internet, your school's computer resources, or other means, find the names of the modules or menus that you would access for the following functions:

- Recording owner investments and withdrawals.
- Writing a check for expenses.
- Inputting a vendor bill.
- Paying a vendor bill.
- Recording a cash sale.
- Recording a sale on credit.
- Recording a credit customer's payment.

Credit Card Fees

Research the fess that credit card companies charge merchants. Use the Internet, interview business people, or call the companies directly. Report on the range of fees and what factors go into the fee structure. Present a case in favor of (or against) accepting credit cards in your business.

Custom Journal

Design a journal with two extra columns for accounts that are used most often. Describe how you would use the journal to record transactions.

KEY TERMS

Accounts payable	The current liability account that tracks money the company owes to vendors, contractors, and others.
Accounts receivable	The current assets account used to record money due from customers.
Capital	The equity account that tracks owners' contributions to the business.
Compound journal entry	An entry that affects more than two accounts.
Equipment	The long-term asset account that is used to record equipment purchased for the business.
Journalizing	The process of recording transactions in a journal.
Withdrawals	The equity account that tracks money that owners take out of the business.

POSTING TRANSACTIONS AND PREPARING A TRIAL BALANCE
Putting Data into Categories

...w?

...osting transactions in a manual accounting

...ons are posted in computerized systems

...ng errors in your books

...ons to assess your current knowledge of post-
...paring a trial balance go to **www.wiley.com/**

... | What You Will Be Able To Do

...t	What You Will Be Able To Do
...ccounts	Update the general ledger in a manual system
...eneral	Examine and question account balances
...tem can ...iences	Use a computerized system to reduce workload
...es	Produce a trial balance

INTRODUCTION

Before you can use the information you collect regarding business transactions, the transactions must be posted to your accounts. If you forget to post a transaction to your books, your reports won't reflect that financial activity and that can be a serious problem. Or, if you post an incorrect transaction to your books, any reports that draw on the information will be wrong—again, a problem. This chapter explores Steps 3 and 4 of the accounting cycle: posting and the trial balance.

5.1 UPDATING LEDGER ACCOUNTS

Posting:
The process used to update accounts by transferring information from the journal to the ledger.

Ledger account:
An account in the general ledger.

Posting is the process used to update accounts by transferring information from the journal to the ledger. All journal entries are posted to the general ledger, where the company's accounts are summarized.

A **ledger account** is an account in the general ledger. The ledger is the place where all of the ledger accounts are contained. Your ledger accounts are the same as those in your chart of accounts. Ledger accounts are subdivisions of assets, liabilities, equity, expenses, and revenue. Examples of ledger accounts are Cash in Checking, Accounts Payable, and Office Supplies.

5.1.1 The Ledger Account Form

This section discusses posting in a manual accounting system. Using the manual system allows us to focus on what happens in the accounts when a transaction is posted. Computerized systems provide convenient methods, but we still need to know the basic concept behind the action.

Each ledger account has its own page in the general ledger. The page is a form used to keep track of changes in, and the balance of, that particular account. The ledger account forms are organized in the same sequence as the chart of accounts.

Figure 5-1 shows the structure of the ledger account form. The ledger account form includes:

- Account Name.
- Account Number.
- Date column.
- Description column.
- Posting Reference column.
- Debit column.

Figure 5-1

General Ledger							
Account Name							Account Number
						Balance	
Date	Description	Post Ref.	Debit	Credit	Debit	Credit	

Parts of a ledger account form.

- Credit column.
- Balance columns (a Debit column and a Credit column).

The Description column is usually left blank until you do adjusting entries (Chapter 6) and closing entries (Chapter 7).

Notice the column titled "Post Ref." This is the abbreviation for "Posting Reference." It is an important part of the **audit trail,** a chain of references that allows you to trace information back through the accounting system.

The posting reference shows where the transaction was originally entered into the books so you can find the details if a question arises later. For example, you may wonder what a number means, or an auditor (an outside accountant who checks your books for accuracy) could raise a question.

Whatever the reason someone is questioning an entry in the general ledger, you want to be able to find the point of original entry for every transaction in every account. The posting reference guides you to the original journal entry to answer any question that arises. If necessary, you can even go back to the source document.

Audit trail:
A chain of references that allows you to trace information back through the accounting system.

5.1.2 Posting from the General Journal to the General Ledger

Because each transaction affects at least two accounts, you will post the transaction to at least two accounts (one for the account debited and one for

Small Business Accounting in Action ➡ Update the general ledger in a manual system.

the account credited). Most of the posting occurs in the ledger. But you will circle back to the journal to add one final piece of information.

Step by step, each important piece of information is transferred from the journal entry to the ledger accounts. Figure 5-2 illustrates the posting of the debit part of a transaction.

Figure 5-2

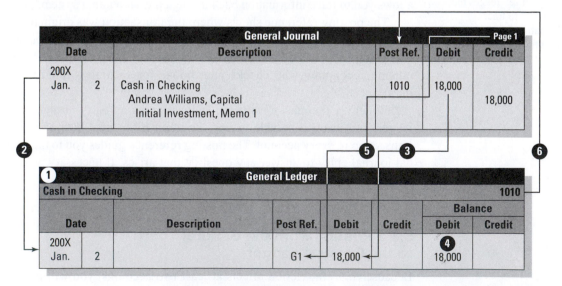

Posting the debit side of a transaction.

PATHWAY TO...
POSTING TO THE GENERAL LEDGER

- For the account debited:
  1. In the ledger, find the account to be debited.
  2. In the account, enter the date of the transaction in the Date column.
  3. In the account, enter the amount in the Debit column.
  4. In the account, calculate the balance and enter that amount in the appropriate Balance column (usually Debit).
  5. In the account, enter the journal page number in the Post Ref. column.
  6. In the journal, write the account number in the Post Ref. column.

- For the account credited:
  1. In the ledger, find the account to be credited.
  2. In the account, enter the date of the transaction in the Date column.
  3. In the account, enter the amount in the Credit column.
  4. In the account, calculate the balance and enter that amount in the appropriate Balance column (usually Credit).
  5. In the account, enter the journal page number in the Post Ref. column.
  6. In the journal, write the account number in the Post Ref. column.

In the ledger account, the posting reference tells which journal contains the transaction and the page number of the journal:

- G = general journal
- 1 = page 1

If a person wanted to find out more about this transaction, they would know to look for details on page 1 of the general journal.

The posting reference in the general journal refers to the account number of the account posted:

- 1010 = account number 1010, Cash in Checking

A person who looked at this posting reference would know two things: This part of the transaction has already been posted, and it was posted to account number 1010.

Figure 5-3 and Figure 5-4 show the general journal and general ledger after posting. It is still the beginning of the month, so the financial statements for January will likely reflect additional transactions.

FOR EXAMPLE

See Figures 5-3 and 5-4 for general journals and general ledgers after posting.

Figure 5-3

General Journal					Page 1
Date		Description	Post Ref.	Debit	Credit
200X Jan.	2	Cash in Checking	1010	18,000	
		Andrea Williams, Capital	3010		18,000
		Initial Investment, Memo 1			
	9	Andrea Williams, Withdrawals	3020	500	
		Cash in Checking	1010		500
		Check 101, Memo 2			
	10	Supplies--Office Expenses	6040	850	
		Cash in Checking	1010		850
		The Office Space, Check 102			
	10	Supplies--Art Expenses	6030	900	
		Accounts Payable	2010		900
		Art World, Invoice 242			
	10	Equipment	1510	3,000	
		Cash in Checking	1010		500
		Accounts Payable	2010		2,500
		Tech Solutions, Check 103, Inv. 3295			
	15	Cash in Checking	1010	2,000	
		Art Fees	4010		2,000
		Fab Ads Inc., Ck. 308, Sales Slip 01			
	20	Accounts Receivable	1100	3,500	
		Art Fees	4010		3,500
		Mega-Corp, Invoice 001			
	22	Accounts Payable	2010	900	
		Cash in Checking	1010		900
		Check 104, Art World, Invoice 242			
	29	Cash in Checking	1010	3,500	
		Accounts Receivable	1100		3,500
		Mega-Corp, Check 795602, Inv. 002			

The general journal after posting.

Figure 5-4

General Ledger							
Cash in Checking							**1010**
						Balance	
Date		**Description**	**Post Ref.**	**Debit**	**Credit**	**Debit**	**Credit**
200X							
Jan.	2		G1	18,000		18,000	
	9		G1		500	17,500	
	10		G1		850	16,650	
	10		G1		500	16,150	
	15		G1	2,000		18,150	
	22		G1		900	17,250	
	29		G1	3,500		20,750	

General Ledger							
Accounts Receivable							**1100**
						Balance	
Date		**Description**	**Post Ref.**	**Debit**	**Credit**	**Debit**	**Credit**
200X							
Jan.	20		G1	3,500		3,500	
	29		G1		3,500		

General Ledger							
Equipment							**1510**
						Balance	
Date		**Description**	**Post Ref.**	**Debit**	**Credit**	**Debit**	**Credit**
200X							
Jan.	10		G1	3,000		3,000	

General Ledger							
Accounts Payable							**2010**
						Balance	
Date		**Description**	**Post Ref.**	**Debit**	**Credit**	**Debit**	**Credit**
200X							
Jan.	10		G1		900		900
	10		G1		2,500		3,400
	22		G1	900			2,500

(continued)

Figure 5-4 *(continued)*

General Ledger							
Andrea Williams, Capital							3010
						Balance	
Date		Description	Post Ref.	Debit	Credit	Debit	Credit
200X Jan.	2		G1		18,000		18,000

General Ledger							
Andrea Williams, Withdrawals							3020
						Balance	
Date		Description	Post Ref.	Debit	Credit	Debit	Credit
200X Jan.	9		G1	500		500	

General Ledger							
Art Fees							4010
						Balance	
Date		Description	Post Ref.	Debit	Credit	Debit	Credit
200X Jan.	15		G1		2,000		2,000
	20		G1		3,500		5,500

General Ledger							
Supplies–Art							6030
						Balance	
Date		Description	Post Ref.	Debit	Credit	Debit	Credit
200X Jan.	10		G1	900		900	

General Ledger							
Supplies–Office Expenses							6040
						Balance	
Date		Description	Post Ref.	Debit	Credit	Debit	Credit
200X Jan.	10		G1	850		850	

The general ledger after posting.

SELF-CHECK

1. What is a ledger account? Give five examples.
2. Why is the audit trail necessary?
3. List the steps needed to post the credit side of a transaction.
4. How are the posting reference columns used?

Apply Your Knowledge You are questioned about an amount in the Meals and Entertainment account. How would you research this?

5.2 MAINTAINING THE GENERAL LEDGER

It is important to pay attention to your account balances as you update them. This allows you to address any unusual balances during the accounting period. Keep in mind that the normal balance of any account is always the same side as the increase for that account. When there is an "abnormal" balance in any account, it always signifies either an error or some unusual situation, for example a customer has overpaid his/her balance.

5.2.1 Calculating the Account Balances

The ledger accounts for Andrea's Artistic Visions did not have previous balances because this was a new business. In an ongoing business, certain accounts always show previous balances. The balance sheet accounts—assets, liabilities, and owners' Capital accounts—carry forward their balances into the new accounting period.

No matter which type of ledger account you are working with, you need to compute the new balance as part of the posting process. Table 5-1 shows how to calculate account balances in various scenarios.

Notice that the Cash in Checking account increases with debits and decreases with credits. Ideally, any Cash account always ends with a debit balance, which means there's still money in the account. A credit balance in a Cash account would indicate that the business is overdrawn, and you know what that means—checks are returned for non-payment.

The Accounts Receivable account also increases with debits and decreases with credits. The Accounts Receivable debit balance shows the amount still due from customers. If no money is due from customers, the account balance is zero. That isn't necessarily a bad thing if all customers have paid their bills. However, a zero balance may be a sign that your sales have slumped, which could be bad news.

Small Business Accounting in Action ➡ Examine and question account balances.

Table 5-1: Calculating Ledger Account Balances

IF the previous balance is	AND the column used is	AND the amount is	THEN the calculation is	AND the balance column used will be
0	Debit	any Debit amount	0 + Debit	Debit
a Debit balance	Debit	any Debit amount	Debit + Debit	Debit
a Credit balance	Debit	a Debit < the Credit balance	Credit – Debit	Credit
a Credit balance	Debit	a Debit > the Credit balance *	Debit – Credit	Debit
0	Credit	any Credit amount	0 + Credit	Credit
a Credit balance	Credit	any Credit amount	Credit + Credit	Credit
a Debit balance	Credit	a Credit < the Debit balance	Debit – Credit	Debit
a Debit balance	Credit	a Credit > the Debit balance*	Credit – Debit	Credit

* This is an unusual situation. It could mean three things: (1) the amount is wrong, (2) the previous balance was not the normal balance, or (3) the new balance is not the normal balance.

5.2.2 Correcting Errors in a Manual System

While posting transactions, you might find an error in the journal—the book of original entry. If the transaction has not been posted, simply cross out the incorrect data in the journal and then write the correct data above the crossed-out line. Suppose that you entered the wrong account name for a purchase of office supplies.

General Journal					Page 3
Date		**Description**	**Post Ref.**	**Debit**	**Credit**
200X May	5	Office Supplies Expenses ~~Radio Advertising Expenses~~ Cash in Checking Check 3169, Office Supply Mart		165	165

Correcting entry:
A journal entry that corrects a previous entry.

If you already posted incorrect data from the journal to the ledger, you will need to make a **correcting entry,** which is a journal entry that corrects a previous entry. You will then post the correcting entry to the general ledger.

General Journal					Page 3
Date		Description	Post Ref.	Debit	Credit
200X May	5	Radio Advertising Expenses	6015	165	
		Cash in Checking	1010		165
		Check 3169, Office Supply Mart			
	16	Office Supplies Expenses		165	
		Radio Advertising Expenses			165
		Correcting entry for Check 3169			

IN THE REAL WORLD

Taking Control of Corrections

An auto dealer who wants to increase profits must be armed with certain facts—sales figures, commissions, inventory numbers—essentially, who is selling what to whom and for how much. Jim Skeans, the president of Jim Skeans Consulting Group LLC and a 25-year veteran of the automobile business, believes that "the true purpose of the accounting department is to communicate information." When this information is accurate, it can tell a business owner useful things about the company; problems arise, however, when that information is inaccurate. Skeans points out that when erroneous data finds its way into the company's general ledger, it necessitates a correcting entry, and, he says, "Having to make a correcting entry costs you money to perform, and, more important, could cost you huge when not performed." For Skeans, "The value of the accounting department is not measured in how good it is at correcting transactions, but in how good it is at preventing correcting entries by helping operations get it right at the point of transaction."[1]

The purpose of this "extra work" is to preserve the audit trail. Note that erasures are never permitted in the journal or the ledger.

SELF-CHECK

1. If the ledger account has a debit balance and the account is then debited, in which column will the new balance appear?

2. If the ledger account has a $5,000 credit balance and the account is then debited for $700, which column will show the new balance? What is the new balance?

3. If your Cash ledger account shows a credit balance, what does this mean?

4. How do you correct an erroneous journal entry that has already been posted?

Apply Your Knowledge The general journal shows the following transaction:

Plumbing Services Expenses	1,170	
Cash		1,170

Check 798, Midland Plumbing

You know that the check was written for $170. This journal entry has not yet been posted. What would you do?

5.3 COMPUTERIZED POSTING

The process of recording transactions in a journal and then posting to the ledger can be a very time-consuming job. Luckily, most businesses today use computerized accounting software, so the same information doesn't need to be entered so many times. The computer does the work for you.

5.3.1 Several Tasks at the Same Time

Small Business Accounting in Action →
Use a computerized system to reduce workload.

Posting is done behind the scenes by your accounting software. You only have to enter a transaction once. Depending on which software you use, the program either posts the transaction automatically or prompts you to click a "Post" button on the screen. Either way, you do not need to enter information more than once.

When you record a credit sale (a customer buys your product or service on credit), you can automatically create an invoice for the sale. Figure 5-5 shows a customer invoice generated by QuickBooks. Adding the customer name in the box marked "Customer" automatically fills in all the necessary customer information. The date appears automatically, and the system assigns a customer invoice number. When the invoice is final, you can print it and send it off to the customer. You have just completed the first three steps of the accounting cycle for this sale:

1. Transaction.
2. Journal entry.
3. Posting.

5.3.2 Researching Transactions

You can view posted transactions by using two simple steps in QuickBooks. Other computerized accounting programs also allow you to view transactions

Figure 5-5

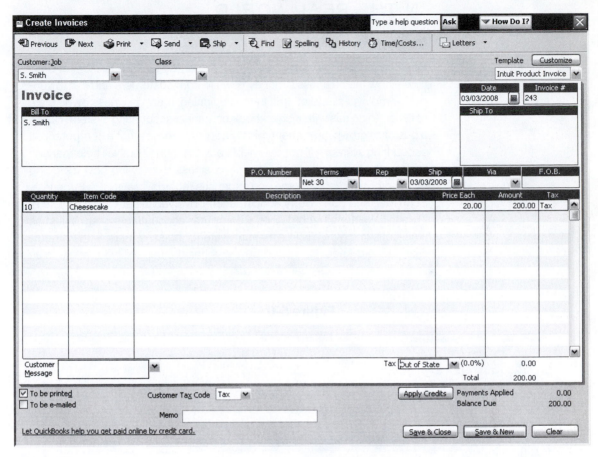

Customer invoice for a credit sale.

right on the screen. The examples throughout this book use QuickBooks because it is the most popular computerized accounting system.

1. Click the symbol for **Accnt** to pull up the Chart of Accounts (see Figure 5-6).

2. Click on the account for which you want more detail. In Figure 5-6, we chose Accounts Payable.

5.3.3 Correcting Transactions

If you need to correct a transaction, follow these steps:

1. Highlight the transaction.

2. Click Edit Transaction in the line below the account.

3. Make the necessary changes.

IN THE REAL WORLD

Making the Switch

One of a small-business owner's most important tasks is to monitor cash flow—how the business's money flows in from customers and out to vendors, employees, and others. In the beginning, many business owners are satisfied to do this with a checkbook or manual accounting system. But as a business grows, an owner typically begins to realize that a computerized accounting system will not only help track the money but will help manage the money. "The key to managing a business is knowing how it's doing by keeping accurate income and expenses records," says CPA Eugene A. Schnyder. And don't worry about the time involved in setting up a system. "The initial entry of records into a computer accounting system is just as time-consuming as it is in a manual system," he says. Plus, with computerized record-keeping, a small business has the capability for analysis as well as the quick retrieval of records.[2]

Figure 5-6

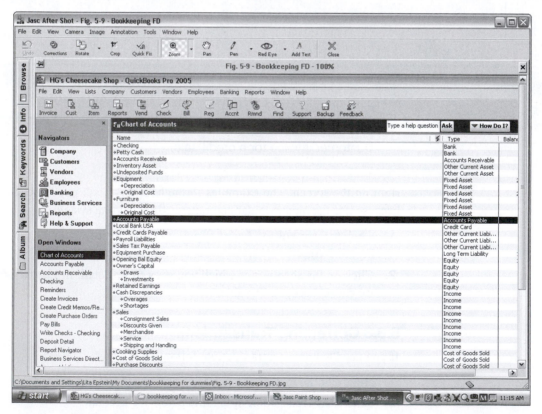

A Chart of Accounts with Accounts Payable selected.

What happened to the audit trail? You can see how easy it would be for someone to make changes in computerized records that alter your financial transactions and possibly cause serious harm to your business. Fortunately, you have tools to monitor and protect your accounting records.

- **Trail a transaction.** Use your software's audit trail to research any questionable transactions. The QuickBooks Audit Trail is a report that is available in the "Accountant and Taxes" reports section. It can provide valuable information, including what changes impacted the company's books and who made those changes.

- **Keep tabs daily.** Run an Audit Trail daily to have a complete record of everything that was entered into your accounting system. Keep the Audit Trail reports in a secure location to ensure confidentiality.

- **Get it in writing.** Establish a policy that any changes made to existing records (other than minor corrections) must be approved in writing in advance.

- **Be secure.** Be sure that you can trust whoever has access to your computerized system and that you have set up secure password access.

- **Strengthen internal controls.** Set up a series of checks and balances for managing your business's cash, other assets, and records. Chapter 8 covers safety and security measures in greater detail.

 ## SELF-CHECK

1. How does a computerized accounting program combine the first three steps of the accounting cycle? Provide two specific examples.

2. In a computerized accounting system, how would you research the details of amounts in the Paper Supplies account?

3. Is it easy or difficult to make changes to transactions in a computerized system? Explain your answer.

4. True or False? If you use accounting software, you give up the audit trail. Explain your answer.

Apply Your Knowledge Think of three transactions you might want to research. Provide the steps for researching each transaction in a computerized accounting system.

5.4 PREPARING THE TRIAL BALANCE

After you post all your transactions and reconcile your bank accounts (covered in Chapter 7, the time comes to test your work. Review the ledger accounts for any glaring errors, and then test whether or not they're in balance

Trial balance:
A list of all the ledger accounts and their balances.

by doing a trial balance. A **trial balance** is a list of all the ledger accounts and their balances at the end of an accounting period. The primary purpose of the trial balance is to prove that, at least mathematically, your debits and credits are equal. The trial balance does not go outside the company. It is a tool, not a formal financial statement.

Unfortunately, few people get their books to balance on the first try. And in some cases, the books balance, but errors still exist. This chapter explains how to do a trial balance of your books and gives tips on finding any errors that may be lurking.

5.4.1 Preparing a Manual Trial Balance

Small Business Accounting in Action ➡
Produce a trial balance.

If you've been entering transactions manually, you create a trial balance by listing all the accounts in the ledger that have balances. After preparing the list, you total both the Debit and Credit columns. If the totals at the bottom of the two columns are the same, the trial is a success, and your books are in balance.

Figure 5-7 shows the trial balance for Andrea's Artistic Visions as of January 31. Note that the Debit column and the Credit column both equal $28,500, making this a successful trial balance.

Figure 5-7

Andrea's Artistic Visions Trial Balance As of 1/31/200X			
Account Number	Account Name	Debit	Credit
1010	Cash in Checking	3,600	
1020	Cash in Savings	13,000	
1030	Petty Cash	100	
1100	Accounts Receivable	1,850	
1200	Prepaid Insurance	1,200	
1510	Equipment	3,000	
1515	Accumulated Depreciation--Equipment		-
2010	Accounts Payable		2,500
3010	Andrea Williams, Capital		18,000
3020	Andrea Williams, Withdrawals	3,500	-
4010	Art Fees		8,000
6010	Advertising Expenses	500	
6015	Bad Debt Expenses	-	
6020	Insurance Expenses	-	
6030	Supplies--Art Expenses	900	
6040	Supplies--Office Expenses	850	
6510	Depreciation--Equipment Expenses	-	
Totals		28,500	28,500

Trial balance for Andrea's Artistic Visions.

PATHWAY TO...
PREPARING A TRIAL BALANCE

The four basic steps to preparing a trial balance are as follows:

1. Prepare a worksheet with four columns: one for account numbers, one for account names, one for debits, and one for credits.
2. Fill in all the account numbers and names, and record their balances in the appropriate Debit or Credit column.
3. Total the Debit and Credit column.
4. Compare the column totals.

In Figure 5-7 you will notice some ledger accounts that we have not yet been discussed. Most are covered in Chapter 6 (Prepaid Insurance, Accumulated Depreciation, Bad Debt Expenses, Insurance, and Depreciation). Chapter 8 covers Petty Cash.

CAREER CONNECTION

To reduce the likelihood of serious bookkeeping errors, a reluctant accountant finds value in frequent trial balances.

When charitable donations to a small nonprofit arts center began to decrease, Vivian, the center's executive director, was disappointed, but not surprised. After all, when people are feeling a financial crunch, donations to charity are often the first to be cut from a family budget. To save costs on her end, Vivian was forced to lay off the center's part-time accountant. Vivian, who had done the books in the center's early years, felt confident that with some brushing up she'd be able to take over. Four months later, Vivian was left with an unbalanced year-end trial balance and an accounting nightmare. Not only had she posted several journal entries incorrectly to the general ledger, but she had miscalculated ledger account totals and written the wrong ledger account balances in the trial balance columns. Surely her methods would improve with time, but it had taken her hours and hours to find and correct her mistakes.

How could she avoid this in the future? By preparing a trial balance more frequently, Vivian would have fewer transactions to sort through, so the next time she has an error she would be able to find it more easily. Instead of waiting until the end of the year, Vivian now prepares a trial balance each month—and sometimes more often than that.

Tips from the Professional

- Don't wait until the end of an accounting period to prepare a trial balance.
- More frequent trial balances may save time and energy in the long-run.

5.4.2 What to Do If You're Out of Balance

If your trial balance isn't correct, you need to work backwards to find the error.

PATHWAY TO...
RESEARCHING TRIAL BALANCE ERRORS

1. **Check your math.** Add your columns again to be sure the error isn't just one of addition. That's the simplest kind of error to find. Correct the addition mistake and re-total your columns.

2. **Compare your balances.** Double-check the balances on the trial balance by comparing them to the account balances in the general ledger. Be sure you didn't make an error when transferring the account balances to the trial balance. Correcting this type of problem isn't very difficult or time-consuming. Simply correct the incorrect balances, and add up the trial balance columns again.

3. **Check your general ledger balances.** Double-check the math in all your ledger accounts, making sure that all totals are correct. Running this kind of a check is somewhat time-consuming, but it's still better than rechecking all your transactions. If you do find math errors in your general ledger, correct them, reenter the totals correctly, change the numbers on the trial balance to match your corrected totals, and retest your trial balance.

4. **Check your journal entries.** Unfortunately, if Steps 1, 2, and 3 fail to fix your problem, all that's left is to go back and check your original transaction entries in the journal.

5.4.3 Preparing a Trial Balance Using Software

If you use a computerized accounting system, your trial balance is automatically generated for you. Because the system allows you to enter only transactions that are in balance, the likelihood that your trial balance won't be successful is pretty slim. But that doesn't mean your accounts are guaranteed to be error free. The trial balance has its limitations, as discussed later in this chapter.

In QuickBooks, the trial balance is an option on the Report Navigator's Accountant & Taxes page. Although it doesn't match the trial balance done manually in Figure 5-8, a QuickBooks trial balance gives you an idea of what a computerized trial balance looks like.

Figure 5-8

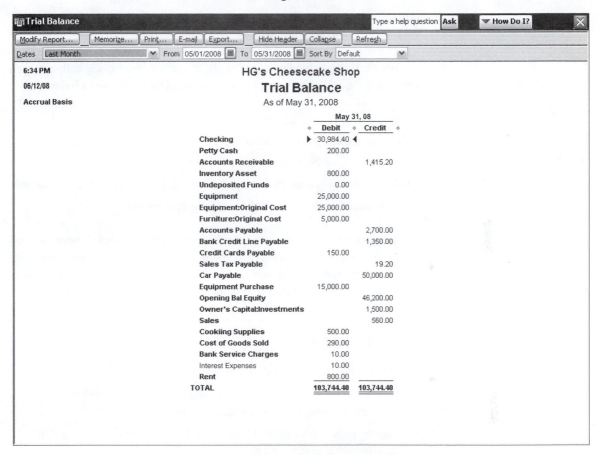

A sample trial balance produced by QuickBooks.

IN THE REAL WORLD

Save Time and Money

Julia's catering business had grown from a kitchen operation to a small but high-end alternative for Boston companies looking to bring in health-food catering for staff and meetings. When it came time for Julia to close the books at the end of the year, she was still managing just fine with her manual accounting methods. To get a better idea of how her business was really doing, however, Julia wanted to prepare more than one trial balance a year, or even a quarter. Certainly, a computerized method would simplify matters, but she simply did not want to make that type of investment yet. A quick Google search for "Excel trial balance template" led Julia to a number of free Excel templates, and using one has cut her preparation time by at least 50 percent.

5.4.4 Limitations of the Trial Balance

Remember the saying, "Garbage in, garbage out?" If you make a mistake when you enter transaction data into the system, even if the transactions are in balance, the information that comes out will be wrong.

Whether you do the books manually or you use accounting software, you could have the following errors in your accounts and still be in balance:

- You forgot to record a transaction.
- You forgot to post a transaction.
- You recorded or posted a transaction twice.
- You recorded or posted the wrong amount for both sides of the transaction.
- You recorded or posted using the wrong account(s).

If, by chance, the errors listed here slip through the cracks, there's a good chance that you will notice the discrepancy when the financial statements are prepared. Even with these potentially lurking errors, the trial balance is a useful tool and the essential first step in developing your financial statements.

 SELF-CHECK

1. What is the trial balance? What is its purpose?
2. List the four steps needed to prepare a manual trial balance.
3. How do you prepare a computerized trial balance?
4. True or False? If your trial balance debits and credits are equal, all your ledger accounts are correct. Explain your answer.

Apply Your Knowledge   Your manual trial balance columns don't match. You already checked the math in each column and it is correct. What would you do next?

SUMMARY

Section 5.1

- All journal entries are posted to the general ledger.
- In a manual system, each account is maintained on a ledger account form.
- Each part of a transaction is posted in six steps:
  1. Find the account in the ledger.
  2. Transfer the date from the journal to the ledger.

3. Transfer the amount to the appropriate column (Debit or Credit).
4. Write the new balance in the appropriate column (Balance Debit or Balance Credit).
5. Write the journal page number in the ledger's Post Ref. column.
6. Write the ledger account number in the journal's Post Ref. column.

Section 5.2

- By paying attention to your account balances as you update them, you can address any unusual balances during the accounting period and make any necessary corrections.

Section 5.3

- In some computerized systems, you can prepare a source document, journalize, and post in the same operation.

Section 5.4

- A trial balance tests if your total debits and total credits are equal.
- If your manual trial balance is not in balance, work backwards through the accounting records to find the error.
- A trial balance can't reveal all journalizing and posting errors.

ASSESS YOUR UNDERSTANDING

UNDERSTAND: WHAT HAVE YOU LEARNED?

 Go to **www.wiley.com/college/epstein** to assess your knowledge of posting transactions and preparing a trial balance.

PRACTICE: WHAT WOULD YOU DO?

1. Why do you think this chapter makes a point of defining ledger accounts? What other types of accounts might be in an accounting system?

2. In your own words, describe how you would calculate the new account balances as you post transactions manually.

3. From a security standpoint, what are the advantages and disadvantages of a manual accounting system? A computerized accounting system?

4. What are other possible uses of the trial balance (besides testing the equality of debits and credits)?

5. Your trial balance shows an usually high amount for Business Gifts Expenses. Describe the parts of the audit trail that you would use to research this amount.

6. Which of the following errors would not cause the trial balance to be "out of balance"?

   a. Math error in the Debit column.
   b. An amount transferred to the wrong trial balance column.
   c. Journal entry not posted.
   d. Math error in the general ledger.

Questions 7–8: Set up ledger account forms and post the following transactions. (For convenience, you can skip the step in which you enter the posting reference in the journal.) Assume that each account has a previous balance of $5,000.

7. Record the correcting entry for the following transaction.

   TRANSACTION: On October 2, 200X, Charisse Hunter started a house renovation business, depositing $10,000 of personal funds into the business checking account and transferring a truck she owned to the business. The truck was valued at $28,000 in Kelley Blue Book. Charisse described these contributions to her business in Memo No. 1.

General Journal					Page 6
Date		**Description**	**Post Ref.**	**Debit**	**Credit**
200X Nov.	3	Cash in Checking		5,000	
		Accounts Receivable			5,000
		Check 110, J. Brauner, Inv. 17			
	12	Accounts Receivable		6,500	
		Architectural Services			6,500
		Inv. 18, Builders Corp.			

General Journal					Page 8
Date		**Description**	**Post Ref.**	**Debit**	**Credit**
200X Dec.	5	Equipment		3,000	
		Accounts Payable			3,000
		Invoice 525, Specialty Fixtures			
	17	Accounts Payable		3,200	
		Cash in Checking			3,200
		Check 290, Discounts Plus, Inv. 1123			

General Journal					Page 4
Date		**Description**	**Post Ref.**	**Debit**	**Credit**
200X Oct.	2	Cash in Checking	1010	1,000	
		Truck	1620	28,000	
		Charisse Hunter, Capital	3010		29,000

8. On December 31, 200X, Tech Rescue had the following balances in the general ledger. All accounts have normal balances. Using this information, prepare a trial balance for Tech Rescue.

ACCOUNTS

101	Cash	$10,000
105	Petty Cash	100
110	Accounts Receivable	2,500
160	Computer Equipment	10,000
210	Accounts Payable	1,500
310	Henry Carmona, Capital	20,850
315	Henry Carmona, Withdrawals	8,500
410	Service Revenue	85,000

610	Advertising Expenses	4,000
615	Bank Fees Expenses	100
620	Gasoline Expenses	10,000
625	Insurance Expenses	2,500
630	Legal and Accounting Fees	4,500
635	Payroll Taxes Expenses	3,000
640	Salaries & Wages Expenses	24,500
645	Supplies Expenses	5,500
650	Telephone Expenses	13,900
655	Van Maintenance Expenses	5,000
660	Utilities Expenses	3,000
665	Web Site Expenses	250

BE A SMALL BUSINESS ACCOUNTANT

Hitting the Trails

Using the library, Internet, or other resources, find and write down five definitions of *audit trail*. Write a brief report discussing the similarities and differences in the definitions.

Here's How It Works

Table 5-1 shows how to calculate account balances. Is there a better way to communicate this concept? Explain the process in a different way, using any combination of words, diagrams, other visual tools, and multimedia if you want. Use your presentation to explain account balances to the class.

Electronic Security

Your team has been hired to do a review of the internal controls of a small business. Your task is to review and report on the security of the electronic accounting records. Write a list of questions you would ask each user of the accounting system. Then draft a general procedures manual that could apply to any business.

Less Than Perfect

Write a report explaining the limitations of the trial balance. Describe how you would address each limitation.

KEY TERMS

Audit trail	A chain of references that allows you to trace information back through the accounting system.
Correcting entry	A journal entry that corrects a previous entry.
Ledger account	An account in the general ledger.
Posting	The process used to update accounts by transferring information from the journal to the ledger.
Trial balance	A list of all the ledger accounts and their balances.

REFERENCES

1. "Measuring the Effectiveness of Your Accounting Department," Digital Dealer Magazine, December 2006, http://www.digitaldealer-magazine.com/index.asp?article=1155.
2. "It All Adds Up," Entrepreneur.com, http://www.entrepreneur.com/magazine/businessstartupsmagazine/1997/August/23098-1.html.

6

ADJUSTMENTS AND THE WORKSHEET
Timing Is Everything

Do You Already Know?

- How to create and use a worksheet
- Why you need adjustments
- The financial statement information available on a completed worksheet

For additional questions to assess your current knowledge of how to adjust journal entries and use worksheets, go to **www.wiley.com /college/epstein.**

What You Will Find Out	What You Will Be Able To Do
6.1 **The role and structure of a worksheet**	Set up a tool to organize information for financial statements
6.2 **How and why to make adjusting journal entries**	Record expenses that are not cash outlays
6.3 **How to determine net income or loss**	Use the completed worksheet to compute your business's bottom line

INTRODUCTION

Balancing your books at the end of the accounting period means you finally get to show what your company has accomplished financially. Before you can develop reports to present to others, you need to adjust the balances of certain accounts. These adjustments usually result from the passage of time or change in circumstances, not from any specific transactions with outside parties.

6.1 SETTING UP THE WORKSHEET

Worksheet:
An optional form used to gather the necessary information for the balance sheet and income statement.

After you produce a successful trial balance, you are closer to preparing the financial statements. You will use a worksheet, which is Step 5 of the accounting cycle. A **worksheet** is an optional form used to gather the necessary information for the balance sheet and income statement. It is an internal document and not part of the formal financial statements.

The worksheet has six sections:

Small Business Accounting in Action ➡
Set up a tool to organize information for financial statements.

- Account.
- Trial Balance.
- Adjustments.
- Adjusted Trial Balance.
- Income Statement.
- Balance Sheet.

The five dollar-amount sections each have two columns: one for debit amounts and one for credit amounts.

The first task in preparing a worksheet is transferring information from the trial balance to the worksheet:

- Transfer account names (and account numbers, if you use them) to the worksheet's Account section.
- Transfer debit balances to the worksheet's Trial Balance Debit column.

FOR EXAMPLE

See Figure 6-1 for an example of how information is transferred from a trial balance to a worksheet.

- Transfer credit balances to the worksheet's Trial Balance Credit column.

Figure 6-1 shows the worksheet for Andrea's Artistic Visions for the month ended January 31.

Figure 6-1

Andrea's Artistic Visions
Worksheet
For the Month Ended January 31, 200X

Account		Trial Balance Debit	Trial Balance Credit	Adjustments Debit	Adjustments Credit	Adjusted Trial Balance Debit	Adjusted Trial Balance Credit	Income Statement Debit	Income Statement Credit	Balance Sheet Debit	Balance Sheet Credit
1010	Cash in Checking	2,100									
1020	Cash in Savings	3,500									
1030	Petty Cash	100									
1100	Accounts Receivable	850									
1200	Prepaid Insurance	1,200									
1510	Equipment	3,000									
1515	Accumulated Depreciation--Equipment										
1520	Car	15,000									
1525	Accumulated Depreciaiton--Car										
2010	Accounts Payable		2,500								
2520	Loan Payable--Car		8,000								
3010	Andrea Williams, Capital		18,000								
3020	Andrea Williams, Withdrawals	8,500									
4010	Art Fees		8,000								
6010	Advertising	500									
6015	Bad Debt										
6020	Insurance										
6030	Supplies--Art	900									
6040	Supplies--Office	850									
6510	Depreciation--Equipment										
6520	Depreciation--Car										
		36,500	36,500								

Information is transferred from the trial balance to the worksheet.

SELF-CHECK

1. What is a worksheet?
2. What information is found in the three-line heading of a worksheet?
3. How many columns are in a worksheet? List the columns.
4. Where do you find the information for the first three columns?

Apply Your Knowledge It's the end of the month and you have already posted your daily transactions. What are the next three things you would do as you prepare a worksheet?

6.2 CALCULATING THE ADJUSTMENTS

During an accounting period, your bookkeeping duties focus on the business's day-to-day transactions. When it comes time to report those transactions in financial statements, you must make some adjustments to your books. Your financial statements are supposed to show your company's financial performance and status, so your books must reflect any significant change in the value of your assets, even if that change doesn't involve the exchange of cash.

Besides gathering the information for financial statements, the worksheet also helps you with Step 6, which is recording and posting the adjusting journal entries. An **adjusting journal entry** (also called an *adjustment*) is a journal entry that brings account balances up to date at the end of the accounting period.

Why do you need to bring the balances up to date? Doesn't the posting process already do that? The transactions posted in Chapter 5 are based on economic events involving parties outside the business. Some economic events occur within the business. For example, the following "non-cash transactions" decrease the value of certain assets:

Adjusting journal entry: A journal entry that brings account balances up to date at the end of the accounting period. Also called an *adjustment.*

• Your equipment ages and has wear-and-tear over time.
• You use up something that was paid for in advance, such as rent or insurance coverage.
• You discover and accept that a customer will not pay an amount due you.

If you use cash-basis accounting, these adjustments aren't necessary because you only record transactions when cash changes hands. This book uses accrual accounting, a system in which you record a transaction when it's completed, even if cash doesn't change hands. Chapter 1 goes into more detail about cash-basis accounting and accrual accounting.

Matching principle:
The concept that revenue earned in an accounting period is matched with expenses incurred in order to earn the revenue.

Accrual accounting is based on the **matching principle,** the concept that revenue earned in an accounting period is matched with expenses incurred in order to earn the revenue. Timing is an important factor in matching expenses with revenue. Using adjustments, you can apply the appropriate expenses to revenue earned in a specific accounting period.

Applying the matching principle can be difficult, and often requires estimates—for example pensions, warranties, and bad debts. Also, when applying the matching principle, keep in mind that you are trying to measure the activities of the business and ignore cash flows.

This chapter illustrates three adjustments:

• Prepaid expenses.

• Assets depreciation.

• Bad debts.

In each of these adjustments, an expense is increased and an asset is decreased. In another type of adjustment, the increase in expenses could increase liabilities. Other types of adjustments are covered in Chapter 14.

6.2.1 Prepaid Expenses

Most businesses have to pay certain expenses at the beginning of the year even though they will benefit from those expenses throughout the year. Insurance is a prime example of this type of expense. Most insurance companies require you to pay the premium annually at the start of the year even though the value of that insurance protects the company throughout the year. The benefit should be apportioned out against expenses for each month.

For example, suppose that Andrea's Artistic Visions paid an annual insurance premium of $1,200 at the beginning of the year. The premium paid in January maintains insurance coverage throughout the year. Showing the full cash expense of the insurance in the January financial statements would greatly reduce any profit that month and make the financial results look worse than they actually are.

Prepaid expense:
An asset that is paid up front and then allocated each month using an adjusting entry.

Instead, a large expense such as insurance or prepaid rent is recorded in the assets category called prepaid expenses. A **prepaid expense** is an asset that is paid up front and then allocated each month using an adjusting entry. It is often said that assets are expenses waiting to happen. You adjust the value of the asset to reflect that it's being expired, or used up.

The $1,200 annual insurance premium is actually valuable to the company for 12 months, so it is recorded in the assets account Prepaid Insurance. You calculate the actual expense for insurance by dividing $1,200 by 12 months, giving you $100 per month. At the end of each month, you record the use of that asset by preparing an adjusting entry that looks like this:

General Journal					Page 3
Date		**Description**	**Post Ref.**	**Debit**	**Credit**
200X Jan.	31	Depreciation--Car		225	
		Accumulated Depreciation--Car			225
		To record depreciation for Jan. 200x			

This entry increases insurance expenses on the income statement and decreases the assets Prepaid Insurance on the balance sheet. No cash changes hands in this entry because cash was laid out when the insurance bill was paid, and the assets account Prepaid Insurance was increased in value at the time the cash was paid.

6.2.2 Depreciation

Fixed assets:
Property used to generate revenue. Examples include buildings, factories, vehicles, equipment, and furniture.

Depreciation:
The systematic allocation of the cost of an asset to expense over the asset's useful life. It is also the name of the general ledger account used to record this expense.

The largest non-cash expense for most businesses is depreciation of fixed assets. The term **fixed assets** refers to property used to generate revenue; these assets will be useful to a business for more than one year. Examples are buildings, factories, vehicles, equipment, and furniture.

You are probably familiar with the concept of depreciation as it relates to personal vehicles. You might have heard that a new car "depreciates as soon as you drive it off the lot." In accounting, **depreciation** is the systematic allocation—not valuation—of the cost of an asset to expense over the asset's useful life. It is important to note that depreciation is an estimate; in fact, the two critical items used to calculate depreciation—estimated useful life and estimated salvage value—are both estimates.

What is the difference between cost and expense? *Cost* is the total amount paid or charged for something. *Expense* is the portion of cost that is associated with revenue earned in an accounting period. The cost of an asset is spread out over its useful life.

Depreciation reflects the use and aging of assets. Older assets need more maintenance and repair and also need to be replaced eventually. As the depreciation of an asset increases and the value of the asset dwindles, the need for more maintenance or replacement becomes apparent. For example, if you own a car, you know that each year you use the car its value is reduced (unless you own one of those classic cars that go up in value). Every fixed asset a business owns will age and eventually need replacement.

Straight-line method:
Used to calculate an amount to be depreciated that will be equal to each accounting period based on the anticipated useful life of an asset.

Straight-Line Method

Usually, you calculate depreciation for accounting purposes using the **straight-line method.** This method is used to calculate an amount to be depreciated that will be equal to each accounting period based on the anticipated useful life of the asset.

Suppose that Andrea's Artistic Visions bought a used car on January 2. Andrea paid $15,000 for the car. She anticipated that the car will have a useful life span of five years (60 months) and will have a salvage value of $1,500. **Salvage value** is an estimate of the amount that could be received by selling the asset at the end of its useful life. This example starts with the following values:

$$\text{Assets cost} = \$15,000$$
$$\text{Salvage value} = \$\ 1,500$$
$$\text{Accounting period} = 60 \text{ months}$$

The formula for calculating straight-line depreciation expense is:

$$(\text{Assets cost} - \text{Salvage value}) \div \text{Accounting periods}$$

In this example, the monthly depreciation expense is calculated as follows:

$$(\$15,000 - \$1,500) \div 60 \text{ months}$$
$$= \$13,500 \div 60 \text{ months}$$
$$= \$\ \ \ 225 \text{ per month (rounded)}$$

Using the straight-line depreciation method, you subtract $1,500 from the total car cost of $15,000 to find the cost of using the car during its 60-month useful life span ($13,500). Then, you divide $13,500 by 60 months to find your depreciation expense for the car ($225 per month).

Salvage value:
An estimate of the amount that could be received by selling an asset at the end of its useful life.

IN THE REAL WORLD

Accounting for Depreciation

Kyle bought a new computer for his digital photography business. The computer cost $5,000. He expects a salvage value of $200 when he disposes of it. Although accounting rules allow a maximum useful life of five years for computers, Kyle has typically upgraded his hardware every three years. Using that information, he can calculate the depreciation by taking the $5,000 purchase price and subtracting the $200 approximate salvage value. He then would divide that number by 3 (the years of estimated useful life), leaving him with a $1,600 depreciation charge his business would take annually.

Accumulated Depreciation

When adjusting the assets at the end of each month, your journal entry should look like this:

Andrea's Artistic Visions
Worksheet
For the Month Ended January 31, 200X

Account	Trial Balance Debit	Trial Balance Credit	Adjustments Debit	Adjustments Credit	Adjusted Trial Balance Debit	Adjusted Trial Balance Credit	Income Statement Debit	Income Statement Credit	Balance Sheet Debit	Balance Sheet Credit
1010 Cash in Checking	2,100				2,100					
1020 Cash in Savings	3,500				3,500					
1030 Petty Cash	100				100					
1100 Accounts Receivable	850			250	600					
1200 Prepaid Insurance	1,200			100	1,100					
1510 Equipment	3,000				3,000					
1515 Accumulated Depreciation--Equipment				125		125				
1520 Car	15,000				15,000					
1525 Accumulated Depreciation--Car				225		225				
2010 Accounts Payable		2,500				2,500				
2520 Loan Payable--Car		8,000				8,000				
3010 Andrea Williams, Capital		18,000				18,000				
3020 Andrea Williams, Withdrawals	8,500				8,500					
4010 Art Fees		8,000				8,000				
6010 Advertising	500				500					
6015 Bad Debt			250		250					
6020 Insurance			100		100					
6030 Supplies--Art	900				900					
6040 Supplies--Office	850				850					
6510 Depreciation--Equipment			125		125					
6520 Depreciation--Car			225		225					
Net Income	36,500	36,500	700	700	36,850	36,850				

Accumulated depreciation:
The contra asset account that tracks the cumulative amount of an asset's depreciation expense over its useful life span.

Contra account:
An account whose normal balance is the opposite of a related account's normal balance.

Contra asset account:
A contra account with a normal credit balance.

Small Business Accounting in Action ➡
Record expenses that are not cash outlays.

FOR EXAMPLE
See Table 6-2 for an example of a monthly increase in accumulated depreciation.

Book value:
The difference between the historical cost of an asset and its accumulated depreciation.

This entry increases depreciation expense, which appears on the income statement. The entry also increases **accumulated depreciation,** which is the account that tracks the cumulative amount of an asset's depreciation expense over its useful life span.

Accumulated Depreciation is a **contra account.** That means its normal balance is the opposite of a related account's normal balance. The related account is an asset (Car), so Accumulated Depreciation—Car is a **contra asset account.** As shown in Table 6-1, a contra asset account has a normal credit balance.

The Accumulated Depreciation account increases each month. Table 6-2 illustrates how the Accumulated Depreciation balance changes as the asset is depreciated over time.

Table 6-1: Normal Balance of a Contra Asset

Account Category	Example	Normal Balance	Financial Statement
Assets	Car	Debit	Balance Sheet
Contra Assets	Accumulated Depreciation—Car	Credit	Balance Sheet

Notice that the Car account is not touched. The historical cost of the assets remains on the books throughout its useful life. Instead, the book value of the asset is examined. **Book value** is the difference between the historical cost of an asset and its accumulated depreciation. The book value of the car at the end of April is calculated as follows:

$$\text{Historical Cost} - \text{Accumulated Depreciation} = \text{Book Value}$$
$$\$15,000 - \$1,500 = \$13,500$$

Readers of your financial statements can get a good idea of the health of your assets by reviewing your accumulated depreciation. If the reader sees that assets are close to being fully depreciated, he or she knows that you'll probably need to spend significant funds on replacing or repairing those assets sometime soon. The reader will take that future obligation into consideration before making a decision to loan money to the company or possibly invest in it.

Andrea's Artistic Visions purchased computer equipment in January for $3,000. Andrea anticipates that this equipment will have a useful life of two years and no salvage value. The formula to calculate depreciation is:

$$(\text{Assets Cost} - \text{Salvage Value}) \div \text{Accounting periods}$$
$$= (\$3,000 - \$0) \div 24 \text{ months}$$
$$= \$125 \text{ per month}$$

Table 6-2: Monthly Increase in Accumulated Depreciation Balance.

| | | | Adjusting Entry | | Accumulated |
| | Car Account | Car Account | | Accumulated | Depreciation—Car |
Month	Entry	Balance	Depreciation—Car	Depreciation—Car	Account Balance
January	15,000	15,000	225	225	225
February	0	15,000	225	225	450
March	0	15,000	225	225	675
April	0	15,000	225	225	900

The adjustment to record depreciation is as follows:

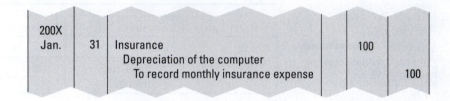

200X Jan.	31	Insurance	100	
		Depreciation of the computer		
		To record monthly insurance expense		100

If you use a computerized accounting system, as opposed to keeping your books manually, you may or may not need to make this adjustment at the end of an accounting period. If your system is set up with an asset management feature, depreciation is automatically calculated, and you don't have to worry about it. Check with your accountant (he or she is the one who would set up the asset management feature) before calculating and recording depreciation expenses.

You might end up using different depreciation methods for accounting purposes and income tax purposes. The IRS has strict rules about depreciation. Appendix A covers depreciation in more detail.

6.2.3 Bad Debts

No company likes to accept the fact that it will never see the money owed by some of its customers, but, in reality, that's what happens to most companies that sell products or services on credit. You may encounter a situation in which your business never gets paid by a customer, even after an aggressive collections process. In this case, you have no choice but to write off the amount due and accept the loss. **Bad debt** is the general ledger expenses account used to write off customer accounts that are determined to be uncollectible.

Bad debt:
The general ledger expenses account used to write off customer accounts that are determined to be uncollectible.

Selling on Credit

The decision to set up your own company credit system can depend on what your competition is doing. For example, if you run an office supply store and all other office supply stores allow store credit to make it easier for their customers to get supplies, you probably need to offer store credit to stay competitive.

If you want to allow your customers to buy on credit, however, you'll first need to make some decisions:

- How you plan to check a customer's credit history.
- What the customer's income level needs in order to be approved for credit.
- The length of time you give the customer to pay the bill before charging interest or late fees.

The harder you make it for customers to get credit and the stricter you make the bill-paying rules, the less chance you have of taking a loss. However, you may lose customers to a competitor with lighter credit rules. If you decide to loosen your qualification criteria and bill-paying requirements, you have to carefully monitor your customers' accounts to be sure they're not falling behind.

Writing Off Bad Debts

At the end of an accounting period, you should list all outstanding customer accounts in an aging report. (Chapter 12 covers the aging report in detail.) This report shows which customers owe how much and for how long. After a certain amount of time, you have to admit that some customers simply aren't going to pay. Each company sets its own determination of how long it wants to wait before tagging a customer account as a bad debt. For example, your company may decide that when a customer is six months late with a payment, you're unlikely to ever see the money.

After you determine that a customer account is a bad debt, you should no longer include its value as part of your assets in Accounts Receivable. Including its value doesn't paint a realistic picture of your situation for the readers of your financial statements. Because the bad debt is no longer an asset, you adjust the value of Accounts Receivable to reflect the loss of that asset.

You can use two methods to record bad debts:

Direct write-off method: A method of determining bad debts by identifying specific customer accounts to be written off.

- **Direct write-off method:** Some companies identify the specific customers whose accounts are bad debts and calculate the bad debt expense each accounting period based on specified customer accounts. This is the only method allowed for income tax expenses.

Allowance method:
A method of determining bad debts by applying percentages to sales amounts or the Accounts Receivable general ledger balance.

- **Allowance method:** Other companies look at their bad-debt histories and develop percentages that reflect those experiences. Instead of taking the time to identify each specific account that will be a bad debt, these companies record bad-debt expenses as a percentage of their sales or their Accounts Receivable. The allowance method adheres to the matching principle: Estimated bad-debt expenses are matched with revenue in the same accounting period. Chapter 14 covers the allowance method in detail.

Andrea's Artistic Visions uses the direct write-off method. Suppose Andrea identified a bad debt of $250 in January. (In reality, this would not occur in Andrea's first month of business. The company would attempt to collect on the invoice over a period of time. It is included here for purposes of illustration.)

The adjusting entry is as follows:

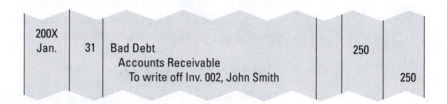

200X Jan.	31	Bad Debt	250	
		Accounts Receivable		250
		To write off Inv. 002, John Smith		

6.2.4 The Adjusted Trial Balance

After calculating the adjustments, you enter the amounts in the Adjustments section. In our examples, all the adjustments result in increased expenses. Since expenses have a normal debit balance, the increases are entered in the Debit column. Because the adjustments decreased assets (which also have a normal Debit balance), the assets amounts are entered in the Credit column. While the assets account Equipment remains unchanged, the decrease in the equipment's value is reflected in the contra asset account Accumulated Depreciation—Equipment.

Calculate the amounts for the Adjusted Trial Balance columns by combining the Adjustments column amounts with the original Trial Balance. Compute and enter the totals for the four columns. Make sure the debits equal the credits in the Adjusted Trial Balance. The worksheet in Figure 6-2 shows a worksheet with the Adjusted Trial Balance section completed.

Figure 6-2

Andrea's Artistic Visions
Worksheet
For the Month Ended January 31, 200X

Account	Trial Balance Debit	Trial Balance Credit	Adjustments Debit	Adjustments Credit	Adjusted Trial Balance Debit	Adjusted Trial Balance Credit	Income Statement Debit	Income Statement Credit	Balance Sheet Debit	Balance Sheet Credit
1010 Cash in Checking	3,600				3,600					
1020 Cash in Savings	13,000				13,000					
1030 Petty Cash	100				100					
1100 Accounts Receivable	1,850			250	1,600					
1200 Prepaid Insurance	1,200			100	1,100					
1510 Equipment	3,000				3,000					
1515 Accumulated Depreciation--Equipment				125		125				
2010 Accounts Payable		2,500				2,500				
3010 Andrea Williams, Capital		18,000				18,000				
3020 Andrea Williams, Withdrawals	3,500				3,500					
4010 Art Fees		8,000				8,000				
6010 Advertising	500				500					
6015 Bad Debt			250		250					
6020 Insurance			100		100					
6030 Supplies--Art	900				900					
6040 Supplies--Office	850				850					
6510 Depreciation--Equipment			125		125					
6520 Depreciation--Car										
	28,500	28,500	475	475	28,625	28,625				

The Adjusted Trial Balance shows ledger account balances after adjustments.

123

CAREER CONNECTION

After learning some costly lessons, a home renovation contractor understands the importance of doing the books himself.

Maxell Rush is the owner of Green Light Construction, a successful residential building and remodeling business in Portland, Oregon (www.glconstruction.com). He founded Green Light in 2004 as a way to focus on healthy home building, a growing trend in the Portland area. Although Rush has 20 years of experience behind him, he continues to find new ways to improve his business.

Over the years he has learned more about business and accounting than he ever expected. When he first started with a painting business in 1997, Rush operated as a sole proprietor. As he worked on bigger and bigger projects, he realized he was taking on too much personal risk. He formed a type C corporation in 2002 to limit his personal exposure to risk and take advantage of corporation tax benefits. He hired a lawyer and accountant, both of which proved too expensive for the volume of business he was then doing. In 2004, Rush changed over to a Limited Liability Corporation (LLC). "This has been the best fit for my needs as far as protection from personal risk and low operating cost," says Rush. "As an LLC I just have to file one tax return, and there is less paperwork and professional costs."

Rush has worked with three accountants (with some mixed results) along the way. His current accountant is affordable, happy to work with small businesses, and takes time to explain things. "He has helped me think about running the business and my future plans," says Rush. These days, Rush handles the daily bookkeeping himself and brings the reports to the accountant for discussion. Concerns about a computer disaster means that Rush does the books both on paper and on a computer. "First I record them in a journal and then I enter the journal into the computer," he says. "And I like to print reports out to paper so I can really see what is going on."

Tips from the Professional

- Set up a checking and a savings account. Put some of every check you get into savings; let that savings grow so that you can cover big expenses like insurance and taxes.
- Be careful with borrowed money. Use it carefully; it is always harder to pay it back than you imagine.
- Enjoy what you do. Feel good about talking to people about your current projects and your plans for the future.

SELF-CHECK

1. What is accrual accounting? Why are adjusting journal entries necessary if you use accrual accounting?

2. What is a contra account? Why is Accumulated Depreciation considered a contra account?

3. Why is the account category "prepaid expenses" considered an asset and not an expense?

4. True or False? The adjustment for bad debts will increase expenses and decrease assets.

Apply Your Knowledge   Which of the following situations would require an adjusting journal entry in March?

a. You paid the February rent on February 1.

b. You paid the February, March, and April rent in one lump sum on February 1.

c. You paid the March rent on March 1.

6.3   COMPLETING THE WORKSHEET

The numbers from the Adjusted Trial Balance section are transferred to the appropriate financial statement columns. For example, the Cash in Checking account, which is an asset, is shown in the Debit column of the Balance Sheet section. (Chapter 2 explains which accounts are used in the balance sheet and which are used in the income statement.)

6.3.1 Showing Net Income on the Worksheet

Small Business Accounting in Action

Use the completed worksheet to compute your business's bottom line.

After you transfer all the amounts to the appropriate Balance Sheet or Income Statement columns, you total the financial statement columns. Don't panic when you see that the totals at the bottom of your columns aren't equal—it's because the net income hasn't been "closed out" yet. The closing process is covered in Chapter 7. However, the difference between the debits and credits in both the Balance Sheet and the Income Statement totals should be the same. That amount represents the net income that will appear on the income statement.

Add a line titled "Net Income" in the Account section of the worksheet. Enter the amount of the difference in the Debit column of the Income Statement section. In the case of a net loss, the amount would be entered in the Income Statement Credit column.

This might not seem logical, but it makes more sense when you approach the Balance Sheet columns. Net income causes an increase in the owner's equity. In Figure 6-3, the $5,050 difference between the Balance Sheet columns is entered in the Balance Sheet Credit column. The profits for this accounting period will be transferred to the ledger account Andrea Williams, Capital. The Capital account has a normal credit balance, and it will be increased with a credit entry of $5,050. A net loss amount would be entered in the Balance Sheet Debit column, reflecting a decrease in owner's equity. After you enter the net income or net loss, compute the new totals for the Income Statement and Balance Sheet columns.

The steps used to prepare a worksheet are summarized in Pathway to . . . Preparing a Worksheet.

Figure 6-3

Andrea's Artistic Visions
Worksheet
For the Month Ended January 31, 200X

Account	Trial Balance Debit	Trial Balance Credit	Adjustments Debit	Adjustments Credit	Adjusted Trial Balance Debit	Adjusted Trial Balance Credit	Income Statement Debit	Income Statement Credit	Balance Sheet Debit	Balance Sheet Credit
1010 Cash in Checking	2,100				2,100				2,100	
1020 Cash in Savings	3,500				3,500				3,500	
1030 Petty Cash	100				100				100	
1100 Accounts Receivable	850			250	600				600	
1200 Prepaid Insurance	1,200			100	1,100				1,100	
1510 Equipment	3,000				3,000				3,000	
1515 Accumulated Depreciation--Equipment				125		125				125
1520 Car	15,000				15,000				15,000	
1525 Accumulated Depreciation--Car				225		225				225
2010 Accounts Payable		2,500				2,500				2,500
2520 Loan Payable--Car		8,000				8,000				8,000
3010 Andrea Williams, Capital		18,000				18,000				18,000
3020 Andrea Williams, Withdrawals	8,500				8,500				8,500	
4010 Art Fees		8,000				8,000		8,000		
6010 Advertising	500				500		500			
6015 Bad Debt			250		250		250			
6020 Insurance			100		100		100			
6030 Supplies--Art	900				900		900			
6040 Supplies--Office	850				850		850			
6510 Depreciation--Equipment			125		125		125			
6520 Depreciation--Car			225		225		225			
	36,500	36,500	700	700	36,850	36,850	2,950	8,000	33,900	28,850
Net Income							5,050			5,050
							8,000	8,000	33,900	33,900

The completed worksheet shows financial statement amounts including net income.

PATHWAY TO...
PREPARING A WORKSHEET

1. Transfer information from your trial balance to the Trial Balance section of the worksheet.
2. Calculate the adjustments and enter the amounts in the Adjustments section.
3. Combine the Adjustments section amounts with the Trial Balance section amounts and enter the totals in the Adjusted Trial Balance section.
4. Extend each Adjusted Trial Balance amount to the appropriate financial statement section (Balance Sheet or Income Statement).
5. Total the financial statement sections and determine the difference in each set of columns.
6. Add a "Net Income" line.
7. Enter the amount of net income or net loss on the worksheet.
   NET INCOME:
   - Income Statement Debit column.
   - Balance Sheet Credit column.
   NET LOSS:
   - Income Statement Credit column.
   - Balance Sheet Debit column.
8. Compute the new totals for the four financial statement columns.

IN THE REAL WORLD

Using a Trial Balance to Detect Errors

It was time for Max, a writer, to close the books of his freelance business for the year. He started by posting totals from his journals to his general ledger, then he calculated the general ledger accounts. In preparing the preliminary trial balance, using the balances from the general ledger accounts, the total debits were $450 more than the credits. To determine where he had made a mistake, Max began by checking that the numbers on the trial balance were the same as the numbers shown in the general ledger. He then went back to his general journal, where he found a debit that should have been classified as a credit.

6.3.2 Journalizing and Posting the Adjustments

After the worksheet is completed, the adjusting entries are journalized and posted. Figure 6-4 shows the adjustments for Andrea's Artistic

Figure 6-4

General Journal — Page 3

Date		Description	Post Ref.	Debit	Credit
200X Jan.	31	Depreciation--Car	6520	225	
		Accumulated Depreciation--Car	1525		225
		To record depreciation for Jan. 200x			
	31	Depreciation--Equipment	6510	125	
		Accumulated Depreciation--Equipment	1515		125
		To record depreciation for Jan. 200x			
	31	Bad Debt	6015	250	
		Accounts Receivable	1100		250
		To write off Inv. 002, John Smith			
	31	Insurance	6020	100	
		Prepaid Insurance	1200		100
		To record monthly insurance expense			

General Ledger

Accounts Receivable — 1100

Date		Description	Post Ref.	Debit	Credit	Balance Debit	Balance Credit
200X Jan.	20		G1	3,500		3,500	
	29		G1		3,500	–	
	30		G2	250		250	
	31		G2	600		850	
	31	Adjusting	G3		250	600	

General Ledger

Prepaid Insurance — 1200

Date		Description	Post Ref.	Debit	Credit	Balance Debit	Balance Credit
200X Jan.	2		G1	1,200		1,200	
	31	Adjusting	G3		100	1,100	

General Ledger

Acuumulated Depreciation--Equipment — 1515

Date		Description	Post Ref.	Debit	Credit	Balance Debit	Balance Credit
200X Jan.	31	Adjusting	G3		125		125

General Ledger

Acuumulated Depreciation--Car — 1525

Date		Description	Post Ref.	Debit	Credit	Balance Debit	Balance Credit
200X Jan.	31	Adjusting	G3		225		225

Adjustments are journalized and posted.

(continued)

Figure 6-4 *(continued)*

General Ledger							
Bad Debts							**6015**
						Balance	
Date		**Description**	**Post Ref.**	**Debit**	**Credit**	**Debit**	**Credit**
200X Jan.	31	Adjusting	G3	250		250	

General Ledger							
Insurance							**6020**
						Balance	
Date		**Description**	**Post Ref.**	**Debit**	**Credit**	**Debit**	**Credit**
200X Jan.	31	Adjusting	G3	100		100	

General Ledger							
Depreciation--Equipment							**6510**
						Balance	
Date		**Description**	**Post Ref.**	**Debit**	**Credit**	**Debit**	**Credit**
200X Jan.	31	Adjusting	G3	125		125	

General Ledger							
Depreciation--Car							**6520**
						Balance	
Date		**Description**	**Post Ref.**	**Debit**	**Credit**	**Debit**	**Credit**
200X Jan.	31	Adjusting	G3	225		225	

General Ledger							
Depreciation--Car							**6520**
						Balance	
Date		**Description**	**Post Ref.**	**Debit**	**Credit**	**Debit**	**Credit**
200X Jan.	31	Adjusting	G3	125		125	

Visions. The word "Adjusting" is entered in the Description column of the general ledger.

One of the primary advantages of the worksheet is that you can evaluate the adjusting entries *before* they are entered into the records, so you can evaluate if they are correct, if they look good, and if any required entries have been omitted. After that, they can be formally entered into the records.

6.3.3 Replacing Worksheets with Computerized Reports

If you use a computerized accounting system, you don't have to create a worksheet at all. In fact, computerized systems don't offer a worksheet report option. Instead, the system generates financial statements directly.

However, you still need to be aware of any accounts that need adjusting, and then enter the adjustments as general journal entries. It's a good idea to run your accounting program's trial balance report and use it to review your account balances.

SELF-CHECK

1. Name the financial statement sections of the worksheet. How many columns are in the financial statement sections?

2. How do you determine the amounts to be entered in the financial statement sections?

3. How do you use the worksheet to determine net income or net loss?

4. Does a computerized accounting system generate a worksheet? Why or why not?

Apply Your Knowledge Your Income Statement Debit column total is $35,000. The Income Statement Credit column total is $28,000. What was your total revenue? What were your total expenses? Did you have a net income or a net loss? What was the amount? Which worksheet columns will you use to enter this amount?

SUMMARY

Section 6.1

- The worksheet is an internal tool used to compute the adjusted trial balance as a preliminary step for the financial statements.

- The six sections of the worksheet are Account, Trial Balance, Adjustments, Adjusted Trial Balance, Income Statement, and Balance Sheet.

- To begin the worksheet, you transfer information from the trial balance to two worksheet sections: Account and Trial Balance.

Section 6.2

- Adjusting journal entries are used to record certain non-cash transactions at the end of the accounting period; adjustments often result in an increase in expenses and a decrease in assets.
- The adjusting journal entries follow the matching principle, which requires that expenses be matched with revenue in the correct accounting periods.
- Three common adjustments are assets depreciation, prepaid expenses, and bad debt.
- The decrease in a fixed asset's value is recorded in the Accumulated Depreciation account, which is a contra asset. The actual assets account remains unchanged.
- The amount depreciated over the asset's expected useful life is the asset's cost minus salvage value.
- The straight-line depreciation method spreads the amount evenly over the asset's expected useful life, resulting in the same depreciation expense in each accounting period.
- *Prepaid Expenses* are not expenses, despite the name. Prepaid expenses are assets. Payment for something that will be used up in future periods is recorded as an asset. This is because the payment buys a future claim to something. Common prepaid expenses include prepaid insurance and prepaid rent.
- As you consume the thing (use up the asset's utility or usefulness) that was previously paid for, it converts from an asset to an expense.
- When you accept that a customer won't pay your invoice, you record the expense as a bad debt and decrease the value of your accounts receivable.
- The allowance method applies an estimated percentage to sales or Accounts Receivable. One entry is made for all estimated bad debts in a single accounting period.

Section 6.3

- Determine net income or net loss (the difference between the Debit and Credit columns in both the Income Statement section and Balance Sheet section).
- If you have a net income, enter it in the Debit column of the Income Statement section and the Credit column of the Balance Sheet section. Do the opposite if you have a net loss.
- Computerized accounting systems provide a trial balance, but not a worksheet. The worksheet isn't necessary because the system generates financial statements without requiring this preliminary step. However, you still have to be mindful of any end-of-period adjustments that might be needed.

ASSESS YOUR UNDERSTANDING

UNDERSTAND: WHAT HAVE YOU LEARNED?

 Go to **www.wiley.com/college/epstein** to assess your knowledge of how to adjust journal entries and use worksheets.

APPLY: WHAT WOULD YOU DO?

1. Which of the following assets are depreciated? For each asset, state the reason why it is (or isn't) depreciated.

   a. Cash

   b. Cash Registers

   c. Prepaid Advertising

   d. Accounts Receivable

   e. Delivery Van

2. On a worksheet, why is the net income amount entered in the Debit column of the Income Statement section?

3. On July 1, 200X, Beautiful Day Salon bought chairs for styling stations. The chairs cost a total of $1,900 and the owner estimates she will use them for ten years, and then sell them for scrap for $100 total. She will use the straight-line method of depreciation.

   a. What is the expected useful life of the chairs?

   b. What is the cost?

   c. What is the salvage value?

   d. What amount will be depreciated over the useful life?

   e. How much is depreciated in the first month (July 200X)?

   f. What is the balance of the Accumulated Depreciation account after the July adjustment?

   g. How much is depreciated in the sixth month (December 200X)?

   h. What is the balance of the Accumulated Depreciation account after the December adjustment?

   i. Journalize the December adjustment for depreciation.

4. On September 19, 200X, Solid Foundation Flooring paid $2,640 for a color ad in a monthly magazine. The ad will run for two years and will begin in two weeks (the October issue).

a. Is an adjustment required on September 30? Why or why not?

b. Is an adjustment required on October 31? Why or why not?

c. After the December 31 adjustment in the first year, what is the balance of the Prepaid Advertising account?

d. Journalize the December 31 adjustment in the first year.

5. On 6/30/200X, the balance of Creative Software's Accounts Receivable account in the general ledger was $8,450. The following outstanding invoices made up the balance:

Date	Customer	Invoice	Amount
2/28/200X	Supply Warehouse	290	300.00
4/03/200X	Dewey Law Office	301	2,700.00
5/30/200X	Custom Designs	319	1,650.00
6/05/200X	Ontiveros Tax Consulting	322	800.00
6/22/200X	Midtown Taxi Service	327	3,000.00

Creative Software's policy is to write off specific customer accounts after 90 days if aggressive collection attempts do not succeed. So far Creative has not been able to collect on the outstanding accounts.

a. Journalize the adjustment for June 30, 200X.

b. Suppose that on June 30 the past-due customers made arrangements with Creative to pay the invoices over the next two months. Would you make an adjustment on June 30? Why or why not?

6. On December 31, 200X, Critters Pet Care had the following account balances in the general ledger for the month of December. All accounts have normal balances.

101 Cash in Checking	$ 2,750
105 Cash in Savings	4,000
110 Accounts Receivable	950
120 Prepaid Advertising	600
130 Prepaid Insurance	2,400
151 Equipment	2,112
152 Accumulated Depreciation—Equipment	440
161 Vehicle	15,600
162 Accumulated Depreciation—Vehicle	1,750
201 Accounts Payable	900

260 Loan Payable—Vehicle	9,900
301 John Ross, Capital	14,192
305 John Ross, Withdrawals	5,000
401 Pet Grooming Income	7,000
601 Advertising	0
605 Bad Debt	0
607 Gasoline	100
610 Insurance	0
615 Postage	60
620 Printing	80
625 Supplies—Office	50
630 Supplies—Pet	250
635 Telephone	80
640 Vehicle Maintenance	150
651 Depreciation—Equipment	0
661 Depreciation—Van	0

Prepare the first two sections of the worksheet for Critters Pet Care.

7. Using the information for Critters Pet Care and the following information, complete the Adjustments section and the Adjusted Trial Balance section of the Critters Pet Care worksheet.

   a. Critters Pet Care's equipment has zero salvage value and an expected useful life span of 24 months. The company uses the straight-line depreciation method for all its fixed assets.

   b. The vehicle has an expected useful life span of 36 months and an estimated salvage value of $3,000.

   c. On December 1, 200X, the company entered a six-month advertising contract to begin immediately and paid $600 to cover the entire six months.

   d. On December 1, 200X, the company bought an insurance policy and paid the entire premium of $2,400 for 12 months of coverage, effective immediately.

   e. A credit customer, Jane Jones, moved out of state with no forwarding address. The company has been unable to contact her. She has an outstanding invoice in the amount $75.00 (Invoice 155). The company uses the direct write-off method.

8. Using the information for Critters Pet Care, finish the worksheet, including the Net Income entries.

9. Using the information for Critters Pet Care, journalize the adjustments.

BE A SMALL BUSINESS ACCOUNTANT

Cash Only

Look at Question 5 in "Apply: What Would You Do?" Assume that Creative Software uses cash-basis accounting instead of accrual accounting.

1. What is the total amount owed to Creative Software by its customers?
2. How much revenue has the company recorded for these invoices?
3. On July 1, 200X, Creative Software receives Check 8911 from Midtown Taxi Service in the amount of $3,000. Journalize this transaction.
4. Discuss the benefits and drawbacks of cash-basis accounting for a small business.

Give Some Credit

Go to the Web site for the National Association of Credit Management (www.nacm.org). What is the purpose of the NACM? Find the "Current Credit Manager's Index Report." List the favorable and unfavorable factors that make up the Index. Which factor can the credit manager most easily control? What is the risk involved in exercising this control?

The Big Picture

The Balance Sheet columns in the worksheet have the following totals after a one-month period:

Debit column = $10,000
Credit column = $15,000

What is the company's bottom line? What factors would you consider when interpreting the bottom line?

KEY TERMS

Accumulated depreciation	The contra asset account that tracks the cumulative amount of an asset's depreciation expense over its useful life span.
Adjusting journal entry	A journal entry that brings account balances up to date at the end of the accounting period. Also called an adjustment.
Allowance method	A method of determining bad debts by applying percentages to sales amounts or the Accounts Receivable general ledger balance.
Bad debt	The general ledger expenses account used to write off customer accounts that are determined to be uncollectible.
Book value	The difference between the historical cost of an asset and its accumulated depreciation.
Contra account	An account whose normal balance is the opposite of a related account's normal balance.
Contra asset account	A contra account with a normal credit balance.
Depreciation	The systematic allocation of the cost of an asset to expense over the asset's useful life. It is also the name of the general ledger account used to record this expense.
Direct write-off method	A method of determining bad debts by identifying specific customer accounts to be written off.
Fixed assets	Property used to generate revenue. Examples include buildings, factories, vehicles, equipment, and furniture.
Matching principle	The concept that revenue earned in an accounting period is matched with expenses incurred in order to earn the revenue.
Prepaid expense	An asset that is paid up front and then allocated each month using an adjusting entry.
Salvage value	An estimate of the amount that could be received by selling an asset at the end of its useful life.
Straight-line method	Used to calculate an amount to be depreciated that will be equal to each accounting period based on the anticipated useful life of an asset.
Worksheet	An optional form used to gather the necessary information for the balance sheet and income statement.

CHAPTER

7

FINANCIAL STATEMENTS AND THE CLOSING PROCESS
Communicating Your Results

Do You Already Know?

- The uses of an income statement
- How the three financial statements relate to each other
- Why some accounts are closed out to zero and others stay open

 WWW For additional questions to assess your current knowledge of financial statements and the closing process, go to **www.wiley.com/college/epstein.**

What You Will Find Out	What You Will Be Able To Do
7.1 How to prepare an income statement	Summarize your financial results for people both inside and outside the company; analyze an income statement
7.2 How to prepare a statement of owner's equity and a balance sheet	Prepare a balance sheet; use the balance sheet to analyze your company's financial condition
7.3 How to "close the books"	Get ready for a new accounting cycle; prepare a postclosing trial balance

INTRODUCTION

This chapter shows how to use all the information you've collected throughout the accounting period to prepare financial statements that give investors, lenders, vendors, government agencies, and your employees a clear picture of how well your company performed during the month, the quarter, or the year. The chapter also covers the process of closing out the books and getting ready for the next accounting period.

7.1 THE INCOME STATEMENT

As discussed in Chapter 2, *financial statements* are reports that summarize information about the financial performance and status of a business. Preparation of financial statements is Step 7 of the accounting cycle. The three main financial statements are:

- Income statement.
- Balance sheet.
- Statement of owner's equity.

When presented to the outside world, financial statements are shown in the order listed above. However, they are actually prepared in this order:

1. Income statement.
2. Statement of owner's equity.
3. Balance sheet.

The statement of cash flows is a fourth kind of statement.

The income statement presents a summary of the company's financial activity over a period of time. Most businesses prepare income statements on a monthly basis, as well as quarterly and annually, in order to get periodic pictures of how well the business is doing financially. Analyzing the income statement and the details behind it can reveal lots of useful information to help you make decisions for improving your profits and business overall.

7.1.1 Preparing the Income Statement

The three key sections that make up an income statement for a service business are:

- Revenue.
- Expenses.
- Net Income or Net Loss.

A merchandising business also has a Cost of Goods Sold section.

If you are preparing the income statement manually, you will pick up the amounts from the Income Statement columns of the worksheet (Chapter 6). A computerized accounting system lets you skip this step; you just choose the income statement option from the Reports menu.

Revenue

The Revenue section shows the amount earned from selling the business's services. It is sometimes called the *Sales* section.

Expenses

The Expenses section of your income statement provides a summary of all the costs you incurred to earn revenue in this specific accounting period. Examples include administrative fees, salaries, advertising, utilities, and asset depreciation.

Net Income or Net Loss

Small Business Accounting in Action ➡ Summarize your financial results for people both inside and outside the company.

This section shows the bottom line: whether or not the business made a profit during the accounting period. If revenue exceeds expenses, you have a net income. If expenses are higher than revenue, you have a net loss. (It may be interesting to know that approximately 25 percent of sole proprietorships report a net loss; many of these businesses are in their first year of operation.) In the rare event that revenue and expenses are equal, the business is said to "break even."

Figure 7-1 shows the income statement for Andrea's Artistic Visions. The revenue and expenses amounts are taken directly from the worksheet in Chapter 6 (Figure 6-3).

Note that the income statement has a three-line heading:

- Name of company.
- Name of financial statement.
- Period of time reported.

7.1.2 Gaining Insight from an Income Statement

The income statement is a useful tool for business owners. The following guidelines are worth considering:

- **Most business owners prefer not to show all their operating detail to outsiders.** Remember, the more information you give to outsiders,

Figure 7-1

Andrea's Artistic Visions Income Statement For the Month Ended January 31, 200X		
Revenue		
Art Fees	$	8,000
Expenses		
Advertising	$ 500	
Bad Debt	250	
Insurance	100	
Supplies--Art	900	
Supplies--Office	850	
Depreciation--Equipment	125	
Depreciation--Car	225	
Total Expenses		2,950
Net Income		$ 5,050

The income statement summarizes the company's financial performance for a specific period of time.

the more they know about how your company operates and the easier it is for them to come up with strategies to compete with your business. Therefore, you should consider summarizing the Expenses section in income statements that are distributed externally. For external statements, many businesses group all advertising and promotions expenses into one line item and all administrative expenses into another line item.

- **If you notice a downward sales trend, it may be a sign that a competitor is successfully drawing customers away from your business.** It may also indicate that customers are dissatisfied with some aspect of the products or services you supply. Whatever the reason, preparing a monthly income statement gives you the ammunition you need to quickly find and fix a problem, thereby minimizing any negative hit to your yearly profits.

- **Business owners watch their expenses trends closely to be sure they don't creep upwards and lower the company's bottom lines.** Any cost-cutting you can do on the expenses side is guaranteed to increase your bottom-line profit.

CAREER CONNECTION

By staying up to date with financial statements, the new owner of a dance studio keeps her investors in the loop.

Ingrid had danced in ballet companies all over the world. Later, she taught at half a dozen dance studios in the Boston area, which perfectly suited Ingrid during the years in which her two daughters were young. However, having to follow the scheduling and administrative whims of her employers—the studio owners—began to wear thin, and by 2006 Ingrid was ready for a change.

After learning that a nearby studio owner was moving out of state, Ingrid formed a plan. She, along with a friend and a cousin who were looking for an investment opportunity, put together the money to buy the studio. Though the studio was well known, business had suffered in the past year after the owner had dropped many of the traditional ballet classes, replacing them with dance classes such as hip-hop.

Ingrid put together a comprehensive business plan, incorporating information from the owner's recent financial statements, which clearly indicated a loss of revenue, likely due to the number of other studios that already specialized in the new dance styles. "It can be a good idea to try new things, but not at the expense of the business," says Ingrid. To the great relief of her investors, Ingrid reinstated the more formal ballet classes, and enrollment gradually started to recover, all of which was reported in the business's monthly and quarterly income statements. One change that she did make, with little added expense, is to add a ballet fitness class for women. Ingrid plans to keep the class open for six months to see if the idea catches on and becomes profitable.

Tips from the Professional

- Stick with what you know.
- Take the time to prepare a business plan.
- Keep investors up to date with the business's finances.

7.1.3 Analyzing the Income Statement

Benchmarking:
The process of comparing your results to industry trends for similar businesses.

You may find it helpful to see how your income statement results compare to industry trends for similar businesses with similar revenue; this process is called **benchmarking.** By comparing results, you can find out if your revenue and expenses are reasonable for the type of business you operate, and you can identify areas with room to improve your profitability. You also may spot some red flags for line items upon which you spend much more than the national average.

To find industry trends for a business like yours with similar revenue, visit www.bizstats.com. To use the statistics tool on this Web site, select the industry that best matches the one your business operates in, such as Architectural Services or Home Health Care Services. (The site also includes merchandising and manufacturing industries.) Then enter your total

Quick ratio:
Another name for acid test ratio.

Return:
The percentage a business makes on a base amount.

Return on sales (ROS):
Ratio that indicates how efficiently a company runs its operations.

business revenue, click Compute, and review the resulting average profitability and expenses percentages for similar small businesses.

With a completed income statement, you can do a number of **quick ratio** tests to measure your return on your business. **Return** means the percentage you make on a base amount. Three common tests include the following:

- Return on sales.
- Return on assets.
- Return on equity.

To compute return on assets and return on equity, you need the balance sheet. These ratios are covered in Section 7.2. The **return on sales (ROS)** ratio tells you how efficiently your company runs its operations. Using the information on your income statement, you can measure how much profit your company produced per dollar of sales.

You calculate ROS by dividing net income before income taxes by sales:

$$\text{Net income before taxes} \div \text{Sales} = \text{Return on sales}$$

If your business isn't a C corporation, you don't have to consider income taxes because only C corporations pay income taxes. (Business income taxes are covered in Appendix B.)

Andrea's Artistic Visions had sales of $8,000 and net income of $5,050. The return on sales is calculated as shown here:

$$\$5,050 \div \$8,000 = 63.1\%$$

As you can see, the company made 63.1 cents profit on each dollar of sales. This is an exceptionally high return on sales, especially for a business in its first month of operation. An established and profitable business of this type would typically have a return on sales around 30 percent.

To determine whether your own return on sales calls for celebration, you need to find the ROS ratios for similar businesses. Check with your local Chamber of Commerce to see whether it has figures for local businesses, or order a report for your industry online at www.bizminer.com. (There is a fee for this online service.)

Small Business Accounting in Action ➡ Analyze an income statement.

7.1.4 Using the Income Statement Data

The income statement you produce for external use—for financial institutions and investors—may be very different from the one you produce for in-house use by your managers. Most business owners prefer to provide the minimum amount of detail necessary to satisfy external users of their financial statements, such as summaries of expenses instead of line-by-line expenses details.

Internally, the contents of the income statement are a different story. With more detail, your managers are better able to make accurate business decisions. Most businesses develop detailed reports based on the data

IN THE REAL WORLD

Retailer Return on Sales

Claire's Stores, Inc., is a leading specialty retailer of value-priced jewelry and accessories for girls and young women. The company, which operates two different types of store concepts, Claire's (North America and Europe) and Icing, was sold to another company in May 2007. The company has sought to expand internationally, with more than 859 stores in Europe alone. The company's European stores are typically smaller than North American stores, but account for more than twice the sales per square foot of their North American counterparts. As a result, the company's plans for expansion in Europe are more aggressive than in North America.

According to the financial information on the company's Web site (http://www.clairestores.com/phoenix.zhtml?c=68915&p=irol-company), the fiscal year 2007 return on sales (pre-tax) was 18%, down 1% from fiscal year 2006.

collected to develop the income statement. Items are commonly pulled out of income statements and broken down into more detail.

For example, many businesses design a report that looks at month-to-month trends in revenue, expenses, and income. Companies also design reports that compare actual spending to the budget. If you were reviewing this report, you'd flag any line item that's considerably higher or lower than expected and then research it to find a reason for the difference.

SELF-CHECK

1. In what order are the financial statements prepared?
2. Explain why a company would prepare more than one version of its income statement.
3. What is the formula for determining the bottom line?
4. What is benchmarking? What are the benefits of benchmarking?

Apply Your Knowledge In one month your business had the following transaction totals:

Sales	$12,500
Expenses	9,300
Withdrawals	1,500

a. What is the net income or net loss for the month?
b. What is the return on sales for the month?

7.2 THE BALANCE SHEET

After completing the income statement, you prepare a statement of owner's equity and a balance sheet. Small-business computerized accounting systems often combine both financial statements into one report titled "Balance Sheet."

7.2.1 The Statement of Owner's Equity

Statement of owner's equity:
Statement that shows the changes to equity in an accounting period.

The **statement of owner's equity** shows the changes to equity in an accounting period. It includes investments, withdrawals, and the results of business operations.

Preparing the Statement of Owner's Equity

The information for the statement of owner's equity comes from three sources:

• The worksheet.
• The income statement.
• The Capital account in the general ledger.

FOR EXAMPLE

See Figure 7-2 for how the statement of owner's equity provides details about the increases and decreases in equity during the accounting period.

Of course, if you are using a computerized system, there is no need to find the information for the statement of owner's equity. You just choose the appropriate report option in your program.

PATHWAY TO... PREPARING A STATEMENT OF OWNER'S EQUITY

If you are using a manual accounting system, follow these steps:

1. Enter the three-line heading:
   • Company name.
   • Financial statement name.
   • Time period covered by the statement.
2. Go to the general ledger and get the balance of the Capital account at the beginning of the accounting period. Enter this opening balance on the statement of owner's equity.
3. From the Capital general ledger account, compute the sum of additional investments by the owner and enter the total on the statement of owner's equity.

4. Enter the net income or net loss from the income statement.

5. Compute the subtotal of beginning capital, owner investments, and net income (or net loss).

6. Enter the balance of the Withdrawals account from the worksheet's Balance Sheet section. You can also use the general ledger to look up the Withdrawals balance.

7. Subtract the Withdrawals balance from the subtotal.

8. The result is the Capital account balance at the end of the accounting period.

Figure 7-2 shows the statement of owner's equity for Andrea's Artistic Visions.

Different Legal Forms of Business Structure

The line items, and even the name, of this statement can vary depending on the form of business structure. Chapter 1 discusses the various forms of business structure.

The business in Figure 7-2 is a sole proprietorship. If this company were a C corporation, the "Withdrawals" line item would be replaced by "Dividends" and "Capital" would be replaced by two components: "Capital Stock" and "Retained Earnings." The Capital Stock account tracks portions of ownership in the corporation, purchased as investments by company

Figure 7-2

Andrea's Artistic Visions Statement of Owner's Equity For the Month Ended January 31, 200X		
Andrea Williams, Capital January 1, 200X		$ 0
Investments by Andrea Williams	$ 18,000	
Net income	5,050	23,050
Subtotal		$ 23,050
Andrea Williams, Withdrawals		8,500
Andrea Williams, Capital January 31, 200X		$ 14,550

The statement of owner's equity provides details about the increases and decreases in equity during the accounting period.

Table 7-1: Reporting the Equity for Different Forms of Ownership

	Sole Proprietorship	*Partnership*	*C Corporation*	*S Corporation*	*Limited Liability Company*
Financial statement	Statement of Owner's Equity	Statement of Partners' Equity	Statement of Stockholders' Equity	Statement of Stockholders' Equity	Statement of Owner's Equity
Opening balance	Capital	Capital	Capital Stock + Retained Earnings	Capital Stock + Retained Earnings	Capital
Additional investments	Investments	Investments	Capital Stock	Capital Stock	Investments
Net income	Net income	Net income	Net income	Net income	Net Income
Payments to owner(s)	Withdrawals	Withdrawals	Dividends	Distributions	Withdrawals
Ending balance	Capital	Capital	Capital Stock + Retained Earnings	Capital Stock + Retained Earnings	Capital

owners. The Retained Earnings account holds all profits that have been re-invested in the company.

Table 7-1 shows the characteristics of equity reporting for the five main legal forms of business structure.

7.2.2 Preparing the Balance Sheet

The balance sheet is a snapshot of your business's financial condition as of a specific date. The three sections of the balance sheet are:

- Assets.
- Liabilities.
- Equity.

A manually prepared balance sheet is based on two sources of information:

- The worksheet.
- The statement of owner's equity.

Assets

The first step in developing the Assets section is dividing your assets into two categories: current assets and long-term assets. As defined in

Chapter 2, *current assets* are things the company expects to use, or benefit from, within the next 12 months. Examples are cash, accounts receivable, prepaid rent, and marketable securities (stocks, bonds, and other types of securities). Inventory is a current asset for merchandising businesses

Long-term assets have a life span of 12 months or longer. This category includes fixed assets such as buildings and vehicles. A manufacturing company that has a lot of tools, dies, or molds created specifically for its manufacturing processes would have a line item called Tools, Dies, and Molds in the Long-term Assets section of the balance sheet.

One type of long-term asset is the *intangible asset.* Intangible assets are not physical objects. Common examples are patents, copyrights, and trademarks (all of which are granted by the government).

Liabilities

Like assets, the liabilities are divided into current and long-term categories. *Current liabilities* are all bills and debts that are due within the next 12 months.

If you have a *long-term liability* (longer than 12 months), the current portion appears in the Current Liabilities section of the balance sheet. For example, Andrea's Artistic Visions has a five-year car loan. One-fifth of the loan ($8,000 \times 1/5 = $1,600$) is due within 12 months and is therefore classified as a current liability. The remaining amount is shown as a long-term liability. No adjusting journal entry is needed; it is just broken out on the balance sheet into current and long-term portions.

The balance sheet in Figure 7-3 shows both current and long-term liabilities. Most businesses try to minimize their current liabilities because the interest rates on short-term loans, such as credit cards, are usually much higher than those on loans with longer terms.

Equity

Small Business Accounting in Action ➡ Prepare a balance sheet.

The Equity section picks up the ending balance from the statement of owner's equity. Figure 7-3 shows the completed balance sheet for Andrea's Artistic Visions. Notice that the three-line heading includes a single date, not a period of time.

Small Business Accounting in Action ➡ Use the balance sheet to analyze your company's financial condition.

7.2.3 Analyzing the Balance Sheet

With a complete balance sheet in your hands, you can analyze the numbers to check your cash status and track your debt. Because these are the types of tests financial institutions and potential investors use to determine

Figure 7-3

Andrea's Artistic Visions
Balance Sheet
As of January 31, 200X

Current Assets:

Cash in Checking	$ 2,100	
Cash in Savings	3,500	
Petty Cash	100	
Accounts Receivable	600	
Prepaid Insurance	1,100	
Total Current Assets		$ 7,400

Long-term Assets:

Equipment	$ 3,000		
Less Accumulated Depreciation	125	$ 2,875	
Car	$ 15,000		
Less Accumulated Depreciation	225	14,775	
Total Long-term Assets			17,650
Total Assets			$ 25,050

Current Liabilities:

Accounts Payable	$ 2,500	
Current Portion of Loan Payable--Car	1,600	
Total Current Liabilities		$ 4,100

Long-term Liabilities:

Loan Payable--Car	6,400

Equity:

Andrea Williams, Capital	14,550
Total Liabilities and Equity	$ 25,050

The balance sheet shows the financial status of a business at a single point in time.

FOR EXAMPLE

Go to http://www.microsoft.com/msft/ar04/nonflash/10k_fr_bs.html to see an example of a balance sheet from Microsoft.

whether or not to loan money to or invest in your company, it's a good idea to run these tests yourself before seeking loans or investors.

Measures of Profitability

Two profitability ratios require numbers from both the balance sheet and the income statement:

IN THE REAL WORLD

Keeping Tabs on a Town Balance Sheet

Residents of Erie, Colorado, have access to the town's financial reports and statements through the town's Web site. Included in the monthly budget updates and financial information are monthly balance sheets (go to http://www.erieco.gov/index.cfm?objectid=0926CB87-65BD-D40A-FB24AB7E578EA1A5). The documents help provide residents of this growing suburb of Denver with a picture of the town's financial position as of a particular date.

- Return on assets (ROA).
- Return on equity (ROE).

Return on assets (ROA):
A measure of profitability that tests how well you're using your company's assets to generate profits.

The **return on assets (ROA)** ratio tests how well you're using your company's assets to generate profits. If your company's ROA is the same as or higher than that of similar companies, you're doing a good job of managing your assets. To calculate ROA, divide net income by total assets:

$$\text{Net income} \div \text{Total assets} = \text{Return on assets}$$

For Andrea's Artistic Visions, the calculation is:

$$\$5,050 \div \$25,050 = 20.1\%$$

The company made 20.1 cents on each dollar of assets it held. The ROA can vary significantly depending on the type of industry in which you operate. For example, if your business requires you to maintain lots of expensive equipment, such as with a manufacturing firm, your ROA will be much lower than a service business that doesn't need as many assets. ROA can range from below 5 percent for manufacturing companies and factories that require a large investment in machinery to as high as 20 percent or even higher for service companies with few assets.

Return on equity (ROE):
A measure of profitability that tests how well the company earns money on owner investments.

To measure how successful your company was in earning money for the owners or investors, calculate the **return on equity (ROE)** ratio. This ratio often looks better than return on assets because it doesn't take debt into consideration. To calculate ROE, you divide net income by owner's equity:

$$\text{Net income} \div \text{Owner's equity} = \text{Return on equity}$$

For Andrea's Artistic Visions, the calculation is:

$$\$5,050 \div \$14,550 = 34.7\%$$

Measures of Liquidity

Liquidity:
The ease with which an asset can be converted to cash.

The term **liquidity** refers to the ease with which an asset can be converted to cash. A company's liquidity indicates its ability to pay its bills when they become due. Cash is the ultimate liquid asset. If you see "Cash" as a single line item on a balance sheet, that amount includes contents of the cash registers as well as any bank accounts, money market accounts, and certificates of deposit. Common liquidity measurements are:

- Working capital.
- Current ratio.
- Acid test ratio.

Working capital:
A measure of liquidity that shows whether or not a company has the assets on hand to meet its obligations in the short-term (current assets – current liabilities).

Working capital is a quick test to see whether or not a company has the assets on hand to meet its short-term obligations. It is calculated by subtracting current liabilities from current assets:

Current assets − Current liabilities = Working capital

For Andrea's Artistic Visions, the calculation is:

$7,400 − $4,100 = $3,300

Current ratio:
A measure of liquidity that provides a quick glimpse of your company's ability to pay its bills (current assets ÷ current liabilities).

When you approach a bank or other financial institution for a loan, you can expect the lender to use one of two ratios to test your liquidity: the current ratio or the acid test ratio. The **current ratio** compares your current assets to your current liabilities and provides a quick glimpse of your company's ability to pay its bills. The formula for calculating the current ratio is:

Current assets ÷ Current liabilities = Current ratio

For Andrea's Artistic Visions, the calculation is:

$7,400 ÷ $4,100 = 1.8

Acid test ratio (quick ratio):
A measure of liquidity that uses only the most liquid assets ([cash + accounts receivable + marketable securities] ÷ current liabilities).

The **acid test ratio** (also called the **quick ratio**) only uses the most liquid assets: cash, accounts receivable, and marketable securities. This ratio is a stricter test of your company's ability to pay bills. The formula for calculating the acid test ratio is:

(Cash + Accounts receivable + Marketable securities) ÷ Current liabilities = Acid test ratio

For Andrea's Artistic Visions, the calculation is:

($2,100 + $3,500 + $100 + $600) ÷ $4,100 = 1.5

Looking at Liquidity

All businesses have two goals: profitability and liquidity. In managing the balance sheet, these two goals are in conflict. Keeping current assets high and current liabilities low supports liquidity but hurts profitability. Keeping current assets low and current liabilities high supports profitability and hurts liquidity. Thus, managers find themselves with a dilemma—safety (for example liquidity) v. profitability—and the ratios will often indicate the personal inclinations of the manager. Consider the following ways that lenders examine a business's liquidity:

- Because of its strictness, many lenders prefer the acid test ratio when determining whether or not to give you a loan.

- Lenders consider a company with an acid test ratio around 1.0 to be in good condition. An acid test ratio less than 1.0 indicates that the company may have to sell some of its marketable securities or take on additional debt.

- Lenders usually look for current ratios of 1.2 to 2.0. A current ratio less than 1.0 is considered a danger sign because it indicates the company doesn't have enough cash to pay its current bills.

- A current ratio higher than 2.0 may indicate that your company isn't investing its assets well and may be able to make better use of its current assets. For example, if your company is holding a lot of cash, you may want to invest that money in some long-term assets, such as additional equipment, that you need to help grow the business.

Measure of Financial Strength

Debt to equity ratio:
A measure of financial strength that compares the proportion of the company that is financed by creditors to that proportion financed by the owner (total liabilities ÷ owner's equity).

Before you consider taking on additional debt, you should always check out your debt condition. One common ratio that you can use to assess your company's debt position is the **debt to equity ratio.** This ratio compares the proportion of the company that is financed by creditors to the proportion financed by the owner(s):

Total liabilities ÷ Owner's equity = Debt to equity ratio

For Andrea's Artistic Visions, the calculation is:

$$(\$4,100 + \$6,400) \div \$14,550 = 0.72$$

Lenders like to see a debt to equity ratio close to 1.0 because it indicates that the amount of debt is equal to the amount of equity. Most business owners put in a lot of cash up front to get a business started, so it's fairly common to see a business whose liabilities and equity are split close to 50 percent each, resulting in a debt to equity ratio of 1.0. With a debt to equity ratio of 0.72, this company could probably obtain a bank loan without any trouble.

SELF-CHECK

1. What does the statement of owner's equity communicate? What similar statement would be issued by a corporation?
2. Which profitability ratios require both the income statement and the balance sheet?
3. What is liquidity? Name three measures of liquidity.
4. What does a debt to equity ratio of 1.5 indicate?

Apply Your Knowledge At the end of the accounting period, you have the following account balances:

Cash	$3,500	(checking account)
Accounts Receivable	4,000	(5 outstanding invoices)
Accounts Payable	800	(2 outstanding vendor bills)
Note Payable	3,200	(6 months, lump sum balance due at end of term)
Bank Loan Payable	6,000	(36 months, to be paid in equal monthly payments)

a. What are your current assets and current liabilities?
b. What is your working capital?
c. What is your current ratio?

7.3 THE CLOSING PROCESS

Small Business Accounting in Action

Get ready for a new accounting cycle.

The final step of the accounting cycle (Step 8) is closing the books. At the end of every accounting period, certain accounts need to be closed while others remain open. After closing the accounts, you prepare a trial balance of the remaining accounts to make sure that your debits and credits are still equal.

Permanent accounts: Accounts whose balances are carried forward to the new accounting period (assets, liabilities, and Capital).

Temporary accounts: Accounts whose balances are closed—zeroed out—at the end of the accounting period (revenue, expenses, and Withdrawals).

7.3.1 Permanent and Temporary Accounts

Permanent accounts always remain open. Their balances are carried forward to the new accounting period. The permanent accounts are assets, liabilities, and the owner's Capital account.

Temporary accounts are zeroed out after the financial statements are finalized. They start the new accounting period with zero balances. The temporary accounts are revenue, expenses, and the owner's Withdrawals account. Table 7-2 shows the differences between permanent accounts and temporary accounts.

Table 7-2: Permanent Accounts and Temporary Accounts

Account Type	Accounts	Accounts Closed?	Ending Balance
Permanent	Assets Liabilities Owner's Capital	No	Carried forward
Temporary	Revenue Expenses Owner's Withdrawals	Yes	Zero

7.3.2 Closing the Temporary Accounts

Income Summary account:
A temporary equity account that is used to close out revenue and expenses at the end of the accounting period.

The revenue accounts and expenses accounts are closed in order to transfer net income or net loss to owner's equity. Their balances are first transferred to the **Income Summary account,** which is a temporary equity account. Income Summary does not have a normal balance. In fact, its balance is zero throughout the accounting period. It is used in the closing process, and then it is zeroed out again.

Unlike revenue and expenses, the owner's Withdrawals account is not closed to Income Summary. Withdrawals are not related to net income or net loss, so they are not treated the same as expenses. The Withdrawals account is closed directly to Capital.

PATHWAY TO...
CLOSING THE TEMPORARY ACCOUNTS

1. Transfer the balances of revenue accounts to Income Summary.
2. Transfer the balances of expenses accounts to Income Summary.
3. Transfer the balance of Income Summary to the owner's Capital account.
4. Transfer the balance of the Withdrawals account to the owner's Capital account.

If you use a computerized accounting system, you may not actually have to zero out the temporary accounts. For example, QuickBooks adjusts your temporary accounts at cycle-end to zero them out, but it maintains the data in an archive so you're always able to access it.

Figure 7-4

General Journal					Page 4
Date		Description	Post Ref.	Debit	Credit
Year Month	Day	Revenue Account		Amount	
		Revenue Account		Amount	
		Income Summary			Amount
		To close revenue accounts			
	Day	Income Summary		Amount	
		Expenses Account			Amount
		Expenses Account			Amount
		To close expenses accounts			

The income statement accounts are closed to Income Summary.

Zeroing Out Revenue and Expenses

Because the income statement reflects the activities of an accounting period, the revenue and expenses accounts always start with a zero balance at the beginning of a new accounting cycle. Figure 7-4 shows the closing entries for the revenue and expenses accounts.

Zeroing Out the Income Summary Account

After the revenue and expenses accounts are closed, the balance in Income Summary is the same as the net income or net loss. This balance is transferred to the owner's Capital account, leaving the Income Summary account with a zero balance. Figure 7-5 illustrates this transaction.

Zeroing Out the Withdrawals Account

The owner's withdrawals are reported over a period of time in the statement of owner's equity. Therefore, the Withdrawals account is closed out so it can

Figure 7-5

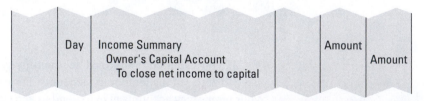

	Day	Income Summary		Amount	
		Owner's Capital Account			Amount
		To close net income to capital			

The Income Summary account is closed to Capital.

Figure 7-6

Day	Owner's Capital Account		Amount	
	Owner's Withdrawals Account			Amount
	To close withdrawals to capital			

The Withdrawals account is closed to Capital.

start the new accounting period with a zero balance. Figure 7-6 shows how the Withdrawals account is zeroed out.

After journalizing the closing entries, you bring the general ledger up to date by posting the entries. The general journal and general ledger in Figure 7-7 show the posted entries.

Figure 7-7

		General Journal			Page 4
Date		**Description**	**Post Ref.**	**Debit**	**Credit**
200X					
Jan.	31	Art Fees	4010	8,000	
		Income Summary	3030		8,000
		To close revenue for January 200X			
	31	Income Summary	3030	2,950	
		Advertising	6010		500
		Bad Debt	6015		250
		Insurance	6020		100
		Supplies--Art	6030		900
		Supplies--Office	6040		850
		Depreciation--Equipment	6510		125
		Depreciation--Car	6520		225
		To close expenses for January 200X			
	31	Income Summary	3030	5,050	
		Andrea Williams, Capital	3010		5,050
		To close net income to capital			
	31	Andrea Williams, Capital	3010	8,500	
		Andrea Williams, Withdrawals	3020		8,500
		To close withdrawals to capital			

(continued)

Figure 7-7 *(continued)*

General Ledger							
Andrea Williams, Capital							**3010**
						Balance	
Date		**Description**	**Post Ref.**	**Debit**	**Credit**	**Debit**	**Credit**
200X							
Jan.	2		G1		18,000		18,000
	31	Closing	G4		5,050		23,050
	31	Closing	G4	8,500			14,550

General Ledger							
Andrea Williams, Withdrawals							**3020**
						Balance	
Date		**Description**	**Post Ref.**	**Debit**	**Credit**	**Debit**	**Credit**
200X							
Jan.	9		G1	500		500	
	30		G2	8,000		8,500	
	31	Closing	G4		8,500		

General Ledger							
Income Summary							**3030**
						Balance	
Date		**Description**	**Post Ref.**	**Debit**	**Credit**	**Debit**	**Credit**
200X							
Jan.	31	Closing	G4		8,000		8,000
	31	Closing	G4	2,950			5,050
	31	Closing	G4	5,050			

General Ledger							
Art Fees							**4010**
						Balance	
Date		**Description**	**Post Ref.**	**Debit**	**Credit**	**Debit**	**Credit**
200X							
Jan.	15		G1		2,000		2,000
	20		G1		3,500		5,500
	30		G2		2,500		8,000
	31	Closing	G4	8,000			

General Ledger							
Advertising							**6010**
						Balance	
Date		**Description**	**Post Ref.**	**Debit**	**Credit**	**Debit**	**Credit**
200X							
Jan.	30		G2	500		500	
	31	Closing	G4		500		

Section 7.3: The Closing Process

General Ledger						
Bad Debt						**6015**
Date		Description	Post Ref.	Debit	Credit	Balance
						Debit	Credit
200X Jan.	31	Adjusting	G3	250		250	
	31	Closing			250		

General Ledger						
Insurance						**6020**
Date		Description	Post Ref.	Debit	Credit	Balance
						Debit	Credit
200X Jan.	31	Adjusting	G3	100		100	
	31	Closing	G4		100		

General Ledger						
Supplies--Art						**6030**
Date		Description	Post Ref.	Debit	Credit	Balance
						Debit	Credit
200X Jan.	10		G1	900		900	
	31	Closing	G4		900		

General Ledger						
Supplies--Office						**6040**
Date		Description	Post Ref.	Debit	Credit	Balance
						Debit	Credit
200X Jan.	10		G1	850		850	
	31	Closing	G4		850		

General Ledger						
Depreciation--Equipment						**6510**
Date		Description	Post Ref.	Debit	Credit	Balance
						Debit	Credit
200X Jan.	31	Adjusting	G3	125		125	
	31	Closing	G4		125		

(continued)

Figure 7-7 *(continued)*

General Ledger							
Depreciation--Equipment							**6510**
						Balance	
Date		**Description**	**Post Ref.**	**Debit**	**Credit**	**Debit**	**Credit**
200X Jan.	31	Adjusting	G3	125		125	
	31	Closing	G4		125		

The closing entries are journalized and posted.

7.3.3 Preparing a Postclosing Trial Balance

The **postclosing trial balance** is exactly what it sounds like: a trial balance prepared after the closing entries are completed. The postclosing trial balance is necessary only if you use a manual accounting system. This report lets you confirm that:

Small Business Accounting in Action ➡
Prepare a postclosing trial balance.

• The debits and credits are equal.
• The temporary accounts have zero balances.

The postclosing trial balance for Andrea's Artistic Visions is shown in Figure 7-8.

Figure 7-8

Andrea's Artistic Visions Postclosing Trial Balance As of 1/31/200X			
Account Number	**Account Name**	**Debit**	**Credit**
1010	Cash in Checking	2,100	
1020	Cash in Savings	3,500	
1030	Petty Cash	100	
1100	Accounts Receivable	600	
1200	Prepaid Insurance	1,100	
1510	Equipment	3,000	
1515	Accumulated Depreciation--Equipment		125
1520	Car	15,000	
1525	Accumulated Depreciation--Car		225
2010	Accounts Payable		2,500
2520	Loan Payable--Car		8,000
3010	Andrea Williams, Capital		14,550
Totals		25,400	25,400

Only the permanent accounts appear on the postclosing trial balance.

IN THE REAL WORLD

Year-End Trial Balance

After Joanne closes the books of her family's small travel agency in December each year, she generates a postclosing trial balance to check that the debits and credits in the general ledger are equal. She enters each account number that has a balance after the closing entries are posted in the general ledger, then enters the account title and the account balance in the appropriate columns. She then totals up each column and enters those numbers in the respective columns. Fortunately, as with the following balance sheet from December 31, 2007, the balances are equal about 80% of the time.

December 31, 2007

Account Number	Account Name	Debit Balance	Credit Balance
101	Cash	16,300	
108	Accounts Receivable – The Big M Market	300	
112	Accounts Receivable – Smiths Co.	750	
122	Computer Equipment	1,500	
134	Office Equipment	250	
206	Accounts Payable – Tri-City News		750
210	Accounts Payable – Homestead Office Supplies		250
320	Ted Freeman, Capital		18,100
	Totals	$19,100	$19,100

 SELF-CHECK

1. What is a permanent account? List three specific examples of permanent accounts.

2. What is a temporary account? List three specific examples.

3. Why are certain accounts closed at the end of the accounting period?

4. What is the purpose of a postclosing trial balance? Do you need a postclosing trial balance in a computerized accounting system? Why or why not?

Apply Your Knowledge Your income statement shows revenue of $25,000 and expenses of $18,000. What is the balance of the Income Summary account after you close revenue and expenses? What is the balance of Income Summary after you complete all the closing entries?

SUMMARY

Section 7.1

- The three main financial statements are the balance sheet, income statement, and statement of owner's equity.

- Most businesses provide minimum detail on their external income statements and prepare detailed income statements for internal use.

- Benchmarking allows you to compare your results to those of similar companies. One popular benchmark developed from the income statement is the return on sales.

Section 7.2

- Sole proprietorships and LLCs prepare a statement of owner's equity. Corporations prepare a statement of stockholders' equity. Partnerships prepare a statement of partners' equity.

- The balance sheet, which is a snapshot of the company's financial condition, can be used to analyze your business.

- Profitability measures that use both the balance sheet and income statement are return on assets (net income ÷ total assets) and return on equity (net income ÷ owner's equity).

- Liquidity measures include working capital, current ratio, and acid test ratio.

- The debt to equity ratio measures financial strength.

Section 7.3

- In the closing process, the temporary accounts are zeroed out.

- Revenue and expenses are zeroed out to Income Summary, which is then closed to Capital.

- The Withdrawals account is closed directly to Capital.

- The balances of the permanent accounts are listed on a postclosing trial balance.

ASSESS YOUR UNDERSTANDING

UNDERSTAND: WHAT HAVE YOU LEARNED?

 Go to **www.wiley.com/college/epstein** to assess your knowledge of financial statements and the closing process.

APPLY: WHAT WOULD YOU DO?

1. How would you use the information developed for your income statement to improve your business operations? Give three specific examples.

2. Prepare the statement of owner's equity for Company XYZ for the month ended June 30, 200X, based on the following information:

Pamela Page, Capital beginning balance	$20,000
Pamela Page, Withdrawals	3,500
Net loss	2,000

3. What is liquidity? Which financial statement provides information about liquidity?

4. In an S corporation, which account do you think is used to close out the net income or net loss at the period-end close?

The following information applies to Questions 5–10.

   On February 28, 200X, Critters Pet Care had the following balances in the Worksheet:

		Income Statement		Balance Sheet	
	Account	**Debit**	**Credit**	**Debit**	**Credit**
101	Cash in Checking			2,000	
105	Cash in Savings			4,000	
110	Accounts Receivable			300	
120	Prepaid Advertising			300	
130	Prepaid Insurance			1,800	
151	Equipment			2,112	
152	Accumulated Depreciation--Equipment				704
161	Vehicle			15,600	

**Critters Pet Care
Partial Worksheet
For the Month Ended February 28, 200X**

(continued)

(continued)

162	Accumulated Depreciation--Vehicle				2,800
201	Accounts Payable				2,100
260	Loan Payable--Vehicle				9,900
301	John Ross, Capital				15,528
305	John Ross, Withdrawals			3,000	
401	Pet Grooming Income		5,718		
601	Advertising	100			
605	Bad Debt	-			
606	Charitable Contributions	100			
607	Gasoline	150			
610	Insurance	200			
615	Postage	100			
620	Printing	200			
625	Supplies--Office	130			
630	Supplies--Pet	1,800			
635	Telephone	80			
640	Vehicle Maintenance	500			
651	Depreciation--Equipment	88			
652	Depreciation--Vehicle	350			
		3,798	5,718	29,112	31,032
Net Income		1,920			1,920
		5,718	5,718	29,112	32,952

The balance of the owner's capital account on February 1, 200X, was $15,528.

The vehicle loan has 34 months left of its term, and payments are made monthly.

5. Prepare the income statement.

6. Prepare the statement of owner's equity.

7. Prepare the balance sheet.

8. Compute the following measurements:

   a. Return on sales.

   b. Return on assets.

   c. Return on equity.

   d. Working capital.

   e. Current ratio.

   f. Quick ratio.

   g. Debt to equity ratio.

9. Journalize the closing entries.

10. Prepare the postclosing trial balance.

BE A SMALL BUSINESS ACCOUNTANT

The Business Landscape

Go to the Web site for the research company BizStats.com (www.bizstats.com). Scroll down to the section titled "National Business Statistics." Choose three selections that are the most interesting to you. Why do you find these particular statistics most interesting? Explore each of your three sets of statistics, and identify a specific fact in each set that you did not already know.

Statement of Stockholders' Equity

An S corporation with two stockholders had the following balances at the end of December. The corporation did not issue any additional stock during the month. The closing entries have not yet been journalized.

Capital Stock	$ 5,000
Retained Earnings	10,000
Cash distributed to Stockholder A	1,500
Cash distributed to Stockholder B	1,500
Revenue	20,000
Expenses	14,000

Compute the ending balances of the permanent accounts that will appear on the statement of stockholders' equity for the month ended December 31, 200X.

Case Closed?

Do you agree with the practice of closing out the accounts? Defend your position.

KEY TERMS

Acid test ratio	A measure of liquidity that uses only the most liquid assets ([cash + accounts receivable + marketable securities] ÷ current liabilities).
Benchmarking	The process of comparing your results to industry trends for similar businesses.
Current ratio	A measure of liquidity that provides a quick glimpse of your company's ability to pay its bills (current assets ÷ current liabilities).
Debt to equity ratio	A measure of financial strength that compares the proportion of the company that is financed by creditors to that proportion financed by the owner (total liabilities ÷ owner's equity).
Income Summary account	A temporary equity account that is used to close out revenue and expenses at the end of the accounting period.
Liquidity	The ease with which an asset can be converted to cash.
Permanent accounts	Accounts whose balances are carried forward to the new accounting period (assets, liabilities, and Capital).
Postclosing trial balance	A list of all the permanent accounts and their balances; it is prepared after the end-of-period closing.
Quick ratio	Another name for acid test ratio.
Return	The percentage you make on a base amount.
Return on assets (ROA)	A measure of profitability that tests how well you're using your company's assets to generate profits.
Return on equity (ROE)	A measure of profitability that tests how well the company earns money on owner investments.
Return on sales (ROS)	Ratio that indicates how efficiently a company runs its operations.
Statement of owner's equity	Statement that shows the changes to equity in an accounting period.
Temporary accounts	Accounts whose balances are closed—zeroed out—at the end of the accounting period (revenue, expenses, and Withdrawals).
Working capital	A measure of liquidity that shows whether or not a company has the assets on hand to meet its obligations in the short-term (current assets − current liabilities).

CASH, BANKING, AND INTERNAL CONTROLS
Protecting Your Business Assets

Do You Already Know?

- The four basic types of internal fraud
- The main tool for protecting cash flow
- How to prevent the theft of any cash you must keep on hand

 For additional questions to assess your current knowledge of how to protect business assets, go to **www.wiley.com/college/epstein.**

What You Will Find Out	What You Will Be Able To Do
8.1 How and why businesses have internal controls	Design procedures to protect a business's assets
8.2 How to make a checking account work for a business	Monitor and protect the cash that flows into and out of a business
8.3 How to work with cash registers and petty cash	Safeguard what cash is on hand

INTRODUCTION

Think about how careful you are with your personal cash. You find various ways to protect how you carry it around, you dole it out carefully to your family members, and you may even hide cash in a safe place just in case you need it for unexpected purposes. If you're that protective of your cash when you're the only one who handles it, consider the vulnerability of business cash if you have employees. In this chapter you will learn how to protect cash and other business assets.

8.1 PROTECTING AGAINST INTERNAL FRAUD

Many business people start their operations by carefully hiring people they can trust, thinking "We're family—they'll never steal from me." Unfortunately, those who have learned the truth are the ones who put too much trust in just one employee.

Too often a business owner finds out too late that an employee may steal from the company if the opportunity arises and the temptation becomes too great—or if the employee becomes caught up in a serious personal financial dilemma and needs fast cash. In fact, according to the American Management Association, at least 20 percent of all business failures are the direct result of employee theft.

Businesses protect themselves by setting up internal controls. As defined in Chapter 1, *internal controls* are procedures that protect assets and provide reliable records. Given the importance of these twin goals of internal control, consider the following:

- **Safeguard assets:** To achieve this goal means more than simply keeping assets from being stolen; it also includes the idea of using assets well and not wasting them.
- **Provide reliable records:** This goal is related to the simple definition of accounting as an information system: Input → Process → Output. The output does not have utility if it is not accurate. For example, if John prepares an accounting report and says, "Well, this report is about 80 percent accurate," then that report has little credibility.

8.1.1 Types of Internal Fraud

The four basic types of internal fraud are:

- Embezzlement.
- Internal theft.

- Payoffs and kickbacks.
- Skimming.

Embezzlement:
The illegal use of funds by a person who controls those funds.

Internal theft:
Stealing of company assets (such as inventory) by employees.

Payoffs:
A payment made before the fact to an employee who will provide a supplier with access to the company's business, often to the detriment of the employer.

Kickback:
A payment made after the fact to an employee who provided a supplier with access to the company's business, often to the detriment of the employer.

Skimming:
Taking money from customers and not recording revenue on the books.

Embezzlement is the illegal use of funds by a person who controls those funds. For example, a bookkeeper may use company money for his or her own personal needs. To put it another way, embezzlement is the wrongful use, for one's own selfish needs, of the property of another when that property has been legally entrusted to one.

Internal theft is the stealing of company assets by employees, such as taking office supplies or products the company sells without paying for them. Internal theft is often the culprit behind inventory shrinkage.

Payoffs and **kickbacks** are situations in which employees accept cash or other benefits in exchange for access to the company's business. A payoff is paid before the sale is made, essentially saying "please." A kickback is paid after the sale is made, essentially saying "thank you." In these situations the company that the employee works for often pays more for the goods or services than necessary. The extra money finds its way into the pocket of the employee who facilitated the access.

For example, say Widget Wholesale wants to sell its products to The Chain Store. An employee in The Chain Store helps Widget Wholesale get in the door. Widget Wholesale prices its product a bit higher and gives the employee of The Chain Store that extra profit in the form of a kickback for helping it out. In reality, payoffs and kickbacks are a form of bribery.

Skimming occurs when employees take money from customers and don't record the revenue on the books.

Although any of these financial crimes can happen in a small business, the one that hits small businesses the hardest is embezzlement. Embezzlement happens most frequently in small businesses when one person has access or control over most of the company's financial activities. For example, a bookkeeper may write checks, make deposits, and balance the monthly bank statement—talk about having your fingers in a very big cookie jar.

IN THE REAL WORLD

Criminal Words of Wisdom

Sam E. Antar is a convicted criminal and the former Chief Financial Officer of Crazy Eddie, the notorious New York City–area consumer electronics chain of the 1970s and 1980s. Sam E. Antar, the cousin of the real "Crazy Eddie" Antar, was convicted of crimes associated with the financial scandal, which cost investors about $145 million and involved frauds such as receipt skimming and money laundering. These days,

(continued)

IN THE REAL WORLD (continued)

Sam E. Antar is making a second career out of teaching others how to spot fraud in public companies, acknowledging that he "helped mastermind the fraud by giving advice to Eddie Antar on accounting aspects of the fraud." He speaks to law-enforcement, accounting, and student groups about Crazy Eddie and what it can tell them about spotting accounting fraud. He tells his audiences that most accountants "don't even get any training in fraud," and that one way to safeguard against accounting fraud is to train auditors better.

8.1.2 Dividing Staff Responsibilities

Your primary protection against internal fraud is properly separating staff responsibilities when the flow of cash is involved. Basically, you should never have one person handle more than one of the following tasks:

Small Business Accounting in Action ➡ Design procedures to protect your business assets.

• Bookkeeping.

• Authorization.

• Money-handling.

• Financial report preparation and analysis.

Bookkeeping

Bookkeeping involves reviewing and entering all transactions into the company's books. The bookkeeper makes sure that transactions are accurate, valid, appropriate, and have the proper authorization. For example, if a transaction requires paying a vendor, the bookkeeper makes sure the charges are accurate and that someone with proper authority has approved the payment.

The bookkeeper can review documentation of cash receipts and the overnight deposits taken to the bank, but he or she shouldn't be the person who actually makes the deposit. Also, if the bookkeeper is responsible for handling payments from external parties, such as customers or vendors, he or she shouldn't be the one to enter those transactions in the books.

Authorization

Each manager usually has the authority to approve expenditures for his or her department. You may decide that transactions over a certain amount must have two or more authorizations before the checks can be issued.

Authorization levels should be clearly spelled out and followed by all, even the owner or president of the company. (Remember, the owner sets the tone for how the rest of the office operates. If the owner takes shortcuts, it sets a bad example and undermines the system.)

Money-Handling

Money-handling involves direct contact with incoming cash or revenue, whether by check, credit card, or store credit transactions, as well as outgoing cash flow. The person who handles money directly, such as a cashier, shouldn't be the one who prepares and makes bank deposits.

Likewise, the person writing checks to pay company bills shouldn't be authorized to sign those checks. To be safe, one person should prepare the checks based on authorized documentation, and a second person should sign those checks after reviewing the authorized documentation.

Financial Report Preparation and Analysis

Financial reports should be prepared and analyzed by employees who are not involved in the day-to-day entering of transactions in the books. For many small businesses, the bookkeeper turns over the raw reports from the computerized accounting system to an outside accountant who reviews the materials and prepares the financial statements. The outside accountant also does a financial analysis of the business activity results for the previous accounting period.

If you're just starting up a small business, you might not have enough staff to separate the financial duties. Until you do have that capability, be sure to stay heavily involved in the inflow and outflow of cash in your business:

- **Sign all checks yourself.** As the business grows, you'll probably find that you need to delegate check-signing responsibilities to someone else, especially if your business requires you to travel frequently. Many small-business owners set up check-signing procedures that allow one or two of their staff people to sign checks up to a designated amount, such as $5,000.

- **Open your business's bank statements every month, and keep a close watch on the transactions.** Someone else can reconcile the bank statement to the books, but you should still keep an eye on the transactions listed.

- **Keep track of check numbers.** Periodically look at your blank check stock to be sure there aren't missing checks. A bookkeeper who knows that you keep track of checks is less likely to find an opportunity for theft or embezzlement. If you find that checks are missing, act quickly to find out if the checks were used legitimately. If you can't find the answer, call your bank and put a stop on the missing checks.

- **Periodically observe money-handling procedures by your cashiers and managers to be sure they're following the rules you've established.** It's known as *management by walking around*—the more often you're out there, the less likely you are to be a victim of employee theft and fraud.

When setting up your systems for cash inflow and outflow, try to think like an embezzler. Figure out ways someone could take advantage of a system, and address each potential threat.

Talk to your staff both before and after instituting the controls to see how the controls are working and to check for any unforeseen problems. Be willing and able to adjust your controls to balance the business needs of selling your products, managing the cash flow, and making a profit.

8.1.3 Insuring Your Cash through Employee Bonding

Fidelity bonds:
Insurance to protect your business against theft and reduce your risk of loss.

If you have employees who handle a lot of cash, insuring your business against theft is an absolute must. This insurance, called **fidelity bonds,** helps you protect yourself against theft and reduce your risk of loss. Employee bonding is a common part of an overall business insurance package.

If you carry a fidelity bond on your cash handlers, you're covered for losses sustained by any employee who's bonded. You also have coverage if an employee's act causes losses to a client of your business. For example, if you're a financial consultant and your bookkeeper embezzles a client's cash, you're protected for the loss.

You can buy fidelity bonds through the company that handles your business insurance policies. The cost varies greatly depending on the type of business you operate and the amount of cash or other assets that are handled by the employees you want to bond. If an employee steals cash or other property from you or from one of your customers, the insurance covers the loss.

8.1.4 Balancing Control Costs

As a small-business person, you'll always be trying to balance the cost of protecting your cash and assets with the cost of adequately separating those duties. It can be a big mistake to put in too many controls that end up costing you money. In other words, don't overlook the cost-benefit principle that the cost of a control should not exceed the benefits it provides.

For example, you may put in inventory controls that require salespeople to contact one particular person who has the key to your product warehouse. This kind of control may prevent employee theft, but it also may result in lost sales because salespeople can't find the key-holder when they're dealing with an interested customer. In the end, the customer gets frustrated, and you lose the sale.

The same is true for supplies. Don't go overboard to protect office supplies by forcing your staff to sit around waiting for hours to access needed supplies while you and a manager are at a meeting away from the office.

When you finish putting together the internal control rules, be sure to document why you decided to implement each rule and the information you collected in developing it. After a rule has been in place for a while, test your assumptions. Be sure you're in fact detecting the errors, theft, fraud, or embezzlement that you expected to detect.

Check the costs of keeping the rule in place by looking at cash outlay, employee time and morale, and the impact on customer service. If you find any problems with your internal controls, take the time to fix them and change the rule, again documenting the process. With detailed documentation, if two or three years down the road someone questions why he or she has to do something, you'll have the answers and be able to determine if the problem is still a valid one and if the rule is still necessary or needs to be changed.

SELF-CHECK

1. Define internal controls.
2. List and define the four basic types of internal fraud.
3. Describe the primary protection against internal fraud. If it is not possible for your business to implement this protection, what can you personally do to reduce the risk of internal fraud?
4. What is a fidelity bond? Name three specific protections a fidelity bond could provide.

Apply Your Knowledge   Your new company is very small and you have just one employee. This employee helps you with the bookkeeping. Write a procedure for processing vendor bills.

8.2 CASH IN THE BANK

All assets need proper control, but the nature of cash makes it most susceptible to improper use or diversion. If you were around to watch every transaction in which cash enters your business, you wouldn't have time to do the things you need to do to grow your business. If your business is small enough, you can maintain control of cash going out by signing all checks, but as soon as the business grows, you may not have time for that either. You could worry about all this cash flow, but the truth is that just putting in place the proper controls can help protect your business's cash.

8.2.1 Checking Accounts

Your checking account is your main tool for protecting your cash flow. When used properly, a checking account provides a written record of the flow of cash through a business. Almost every dime that comes into your business flows through your business's checking account (at least that's what should happen). Whether it's cash collected at your cash registers, payments received in the mail, cash used to fill the cash registers, petty cash you keep on hand, payments sent out to pay business obligations, or any other cash need, this cash enters and exits your checking account.

Choosing the Right Bank

Finding the right bank to help you set up your checking account and the controls that limit access to that account is crucial. When evaluating your banking options, ask yourself the following questions:

* Does this bank have a branch that's conveniently located to my business?
* Does this bank operate at times when I need it most?
* Does this bank offer secure ways to deposit cash even when the bank is closed?

   Most banks have secure drop boxes for cash so you can deposit cash receipts as quickly as possible at the end of the business day rather than secure the cash overnight yourself.

   Visit local bank branches yourself, and check out the type of business services each bank offers. Pay particular attention to:

* **How the bank handles your questions.** Is the bank responsive to your business's needs?
* **The type of personal attention you can expect to receive.** Some banks require business account holders to call a centralized line for assistance rather than depend on local branches. Some banks are even adding charges if you use a teller rather than an ATM (Automated Teller Machine).
* **Any charges that may be tacked on.** Some banks charge for every transaction, whether it's making a deposit or withdrawal, or cashing a check. Many have charges that differ for business accounts, and most have charges for printing checks.
* **Services and fees for credit-card processing.** If you plan to accept credit cards in your business, you need to explore your banking options for this service.

Deciding on Types of Checks

After you choose your bank, you need to consider what type of checks you want to use in your business. You need different checks depending upon whether you handwrite each check or print checks from your computerized accounting system.

If you plan to handwrite your checks, you'll most likely use manual checks in a three-ring binder. This type of check consists of a check stub on the left and a check on the right. The check stub has a place to keep a running total of your balance.

If you plan to print checks from your computerized accounting system, you'll need to order checks that match that system's programming. Each computer software program has a unique template for printing checks.

IN THE REAL WORLD

Keeping Tabs on Nonprofits

Nonprofits are not immune from internal fraud. Even PTAs have found themselves in the midst of serious legal trouble over issues of theft and embezzlement. In 2007, a Fairfax County, Virginia, woman who was formerly president of the parent-teacher association at her children's elementary school was charged with embezzling $180,000 from the group. It is believed that the PTA funds were embezzled during a five-year period. After the incident, the current president assured parents that it had adopted new financial controls to prevent future problems.

Making Deposits

Of course, you aren't just withdrawing from your business's checking account. You also need to deposit money into that account, and you want to be sure your deposit slips contain all the needed detail as well as documentation to back up the deposit information. Banks provide printed deposit slips with all the necessary detail to be sure the money is deposited in the appropriate account.

Endorsement:
A signature or stamp on the back of a check that transfers ownership of the check.

Restrictive endorsement:
An endorsement that transfers ownership of a check to a specific party for a specific purpose.

Banks also provide you with an endorsement stamp. An **endorsement** is a signature or stamp on the back of a check that transfers ownership of the check. For control purposes, the safest endorsement is the **restrictive endorsement,** one that transfers ownership of the check to a specific party for a specific purpose. Using the restrictive endorsement "for deposit only" with your company's name and bank account number ensures that your check can't be cashed; it can only be deposited into your business's bank account.

Whoever opens your business mail should be instructed to use the endorsement stamp immediately on the back of any check received in the mail. Even if the check will not be deposited right away, it should be endorsed as soon as it is received.

PATHWAY TO...
MAKING A BANK DEPOSIT

To properly make deposits to your business's bank account, follow these steps:

1. **Prepare the deposit slip.** List the amount of each check as well as the total currency (paper money) and total amount in coins. Some banks ask that you list the American Bankers Association (ABA) transit number for each check. The ABA transit number is the top part of the fraction that appears in the upper-right corner of a check.

2. **Make photocopies.** Copy all checks being deposited so that you have a record in case something gets lost or misplaced at the bank.

3. **Finish the documentation.** After you make the deposit, attach the photocopies of the checks to the deposit receipt and add any detail regarding the source of the deposited currency and coins.

4. **File everything.** File the documentation in your Cash Receipts folder.

Lock box:
A place, run by a bank, that receives payments for businesses.

To secure incoming cash even more carefully, some businesses set up a "lock box." A **lock box** is a place, run by a bank, that receives payments for businesses. Customers or others making payments to the business mail the checks to a post office box number that goes directly to the bank. A bank employee opens and deposits the checks right into the business's account.

8.2.2 Savings Accounts

Small Business Accounting in Action ➞
Monitor and protect the cash that flows into and out of your business.

Some businesses find they have more cash than they need to meet their immediate needs. Rather than keep that extra cash in a non-interest-bearing account, many businesses open a savings account to store the extra cash.

If you're a small-business owner with few employees, you'll probably be the one to control the flow of money into and out of your savings account. As your business grows and you find that you need to delegate the responsibility for the business's savings, be sure to think carefully about who gets access and how you will document the flow of funds into and out of the savings account.

8.2.3 Bank Reconciliations

Before you can begin to test whether the books are right by doing a trial balance, you need to know if your books have captured what's happened to your company's cash and if the amount of cash shown in your books actually

Bank reconciliation:
The process of explaining the differences between the bank statement balance and the general ledger Cash account balance.

FOR EXAMPLE

See Figure 8-1 for an example of a bank reconciliation.

Chargeback:
The reversal of a charge on a customer's credit card.

matches the amount of cash you have in the bank. The **bank reconciliation** is the process of explaining the differences between the bank statement balance and the general ledger Cash account balance.

Before you tackle reconciling your accounts with the bank's records, it's important to be sure that you've made all necessary corrections to your books. When you make corrections to your Cash accounts, you identify and correct any cash transactions that may not have been properly recorded.

In addition to corrections, you also make journal entries for certain adjustments. The Cash general ledger account adjustments include interest income, bank fees, and credit-card chargebacks. A **chargeback** is the reversal of a charge on a customer's credit card. (The customer gets a refund.)

You've probably reconciled your personal checking account at least a few times over the years. You'll be happy to learn that reconciling business accounts is a similar process.

PATHWAY TO...
RECONCILING A BANK ACCOUNT

The bank reconciliation has two sections:

Bank Balance Section

- Enter the ending balance from the bank statement.

- Compare the deposits in your Cash general ledger account with the bank statement deposits. Enter any **deposits in transit** (deposits that are recorded in your Cash account, but have not yet cleared the bank). The term **cleared** means that the transaction has been received and processed by the bank.

- List the outstanding checks. **Outstanding** is the opposite of cleared; it means a transaction has *not* been processed by the bank yet.

- Compute the adjusted bank balance:

beginning bank balance + deposits in transit − outstanding checks = adjusted bank balance

Book Balance Section

- Enter the balance of the Cash general ledger account.
- Enter any corrections or adjustments not already recorded.
- Compute the adjusted book balance.

Be sure to journalize any corrections or adjustments that you discover in the bank reconciliation. Figure 8-1 shows one common format for reconciling your bank account.

Deposits in transit:
A deposit recorded in the Cash ledger account that has not yet cleared the bank.

Cleared:
The term describing a transaction that has been received and processed by the bank.

Outstanding:
The opposite of cleared; it means a transaction has *not* been processed by the bank yet.

Figure 8-1

Krizinski Company Bank Reconciliation March 31, 200X		
Bank Balance 3/31/200X		$ 3,300
Add Deposits in Transit 3/31/200X		1,000
Deduct: Outstanding Checks		
170	$ 1,321	
172	105	
173	406	
174	95	
175	200	
176	60	$ 2,187
Adjusted Bank Balance		$ 2,113
Book Balance 3/31/200X		$ 2,113
Corrections or Adjustments		0
Adjusted Book Balance		$ 2,113

The bank reconciliation explains the differences between your balance and the bank's balance.

Tracking Down Errors

Ideally, the book balance and the adjusted bank balance should match. If they don't, you need to find out why.

PATHWAY TO...
TRACKING DOWN ERRORS

1. **Check your math in your bank reconciliation.**
2. **If the bank balance is higher than your balance,** make sure that all the deposits listed by the bank appear in the Cash account in your books. If you find that the bank lists a deposit that you don't have, or lists a deposit for a different amount, you need to do some detective work and correct your accounting records as needed.

Also, confirm that all checks shown as cleared in your records have actually cleared the bank. Your records may erroneously show a check as cleared when it is still outstanding.

3. **If the bank balance is lower than your balance,** make sure that all checks listed by the bank are recorded in your Cash account, and that they are recorded for the same amount as the bank shows. You may have missed one or two checks that were written but not properly recorded.

   You also may have missed a deposit in transit. If you notice that a deposit is missing from the bank statement, be sure you have your proof of the deposit, and contact the bank to be sure the cash gets into your account.

4. **If all deposits and checks are correct but you still see a difference,** you need to look for other bank activity that is not yet recorded in your books (such as service charges or interest earned).

Sometimes, you have to decide whether rooting out every little difference is really worth the time it takes. If it's just a matter of pennies, you probably don't need to waste your time trying to find the error, and you can just adjust the balance in your books. But if the difference is a significant amount for your business, you should try to track it down. You never know exactly which accounts are impacted by an error or how that difference may impact your profit or loss.

Using a Computerized System

FOR EXAMPLE

See Figure 8-2 for a look at how QuickBooks handles the reconciliation process.

If you use a computerized accounting system, reconciliation should be much easier than if you keep your books manually. In QuickBooks, for example, when you start the reconciliation process, a screen pops up in which you can add the ending bank statement balance and any bank fees or interest earned. Figure 8-2 illustrates that screen. In this example, the user input $30,000 as the ending bank balance and $10 in bank fees. (The bank fees that you input are automatically posted to the Bank Fees general ledger account.)

After you click Continue, you get a screen that lists all checks written since the last reconciliation as well as all deposits. You put a check mark next to the checks and deposits that have cleared on the bank statement, and then click Reconcile Now.

QuickBooks automatically reconciles the accounts and provides reports that indicate any differences. It also provides a **reconciliation summary,** which includes the beginning balance, the balance after all cleared transactions have been recorded, a list of all transactions that have not cleared, and the ending balance. Other computerized systems are effective as well; some appreciate the Excel system, which provides a list of outstanding checks.

Reconciliation summary: Report that includes the beginning balance, the balance after all cleared transactions have been recorded, a list of all transactions that have not cleared, and the ending balance.

Figure 8-2

Begin Reconciliation	Type a help question [Ask]	▼ How Do I?	☒

Select an account to reconcile, and then enter the ending balance from your account statement.

Account [Checking ▼]

Statement Date [05/31/2008 ▦]

Beginning Balance   1,000.00   What if my beginning balance doesn't match my statement?

Ending Balance [30000]

Enter any service charge or interest earned.

Service Charge	Date	Account	Class
[10.00]	[05/31/2008 ▦]	[Bank Service Charges ▼]	[▼]

Interest Earned	Date	Account	Class
[0.00]	[05/31/2008 ▦]	[▼]	[▼]

[Locate Discrepancies]   [Continue]   [Cancel]   [Help]

QuickBooks prompts you to enter the ending bank balance, service charge, and interest income.

SELF-CHECK

1. What is your main tool for protecting cash flow? Why?
2. What documentation should you keep for each bank deposit?
3. What is a lock box? What kinds of businesses would benefit most from having a lock box?
4. What is the bank reconciliation? List five reasons the bank reconciliation might be "out of balance."

Apply Your Knowledge   You are ready to open a checking account for your new pet supplies boutique. Before you shop for banks, create a list of questions that you will ask each bank representative.

8.3 CASH ON HAND

Although all your cash receipts are ultimately deposited in your business checking account, some business transactions involve only cash. This section discusses two types of cash-only transactions:

- Petty cash.
- Cash sales at cash registers.

8.3.1 Petty Cash

Every business needs unexpected cash on almost a weekly basis. Whether it's money to pay the mail carrier for a letter or package COD, money to buy a few emergency stamps to get the mail out, or money for some office supplies needed before the next delivery, businesses need to keep some cash on hand, called **petty cash,** for unexpected expenses.

Petty cash:
A small amount of cash kept on hand for unexpected expenses; also the name of the general ledger account used to establish this fund (Petty Cash).

In most cases, when an employee buys something for the business, he or she turns in an expense report and then gets reimbursed by check. If the expense is small enough, you can instead use the petty cash fund to reimburse the employee. Petty cash usually is used for minor expenses of $10 or less.

You certainly don't want to have a lot of cash sitting around in the office, but you should keep $50 to $100 in a locked petty cash box. If you find that you're faced with cash expenses more or less often than you initially expected, you can adjust the amount kept in petty cash accordingly.

To record the creation of a petty cash fund, you debit Petty Cash and credit Cash in Checking:

Date		Description	Post Ref.	Debit	Credit
200X Feb.	5	Petty Cash		50.00	
		Cash in Checking			50.00
		Establish petty cash fund, Check 146			

General Journal — Page 2

This is the only time you use the Petty Cash ledger account, unless you later decide to increase or decrease the amount of petty cash on hand. As petty cash is spent and you replenish the fund (to restore the amount to its original level), you do not use the Petty Cash account. You instead debit the individual expenses accounts.

No matter how much you keep in petty cash, be sure you set up a good control system that requires anyone who uses the cash to write a voucher that specifies how much was used and why. You should also ask that a sales slip from the store or post office, for example, be attached to the voucher in order to justify the cash expenditure. A **sales slip** is a proof of cash payment. It is often called a *receipt*.

Sales slip:
Proof of cash payment; often called a *receipt*.

The best control for petty cash is to pick one person in the office to manage the petty cash. The fund naturally gets depleted over time. The control person gathers the documentation for the expenditures and prepares a **petty cash requisition** like the one in Figure 8-3 to replenish the petty cash fund. The petty cash requisition shows how the petty cash was spent.

Petty cash requisition:
Required to replenish the petty cash fund; shows how the petty cash was spent.

Figure 8-3

	Krizinski Company			
	Petty Cash Requisition			
	For the Period 3/01/200X - 3/31/200X			

Date	Petty Cash Voucher	Description	General Ledger Account	Amount
200X				
March 1	59	COD package	Postage	$ 5.50
3	60	Office supplies	Supplies--Office	8.00
15	61	Emergency copying	Printing and Reproduction	11.00
30	62	COD package	Postage	4.50
Total expenditures				$ 29.00
Cash balance on hand				21.00
Total petty cash fund				$ 50.00

Expenditures Summary:

Postage	$ 10.00
Supplies--Office	8.00
Printing and Reproduction	11.00
Total	$ 29.00

Prepared by: _____

Approved by: _____

A petty cash requisition.

Small Business Accounting in Action ➡ Safeguard your cash on hand.

After the petty cash requisition and supporting documentation are approved, a check is written to replenish the petty cash fund:

March 31	Postage	10.00	
	Supplies--Office	8.00	
	Printing and Reproduction	11.00	
	Cash in Checking		29.00
	Replenish petty cash fund, Check 171		

Notice that the Petty Cash account is not used when you replenish the petty cash fund.

8.3.2 Cash Registers

Have you ever gone into a business and tried to pay with a large bill only to find out the cashier can't make change? It's frustrating, but it happens in many businesses, especially when they don't carefully monitor the money in their cash registers. Most businesses empty cash registers each night and put any cash not being deposited in the bank that night into a safe. However, many businesses instruct their cashiers to periodically deposit their cash in a company safe throughout the day and get a paper voucher to show the cash deposited. These daytime deposits minimize the cash held in the cash drawer in case the store is the victim of a robbery.

All these types of controls are necessary parts of business operations, but they can have consequences that might frustrate customers. Most customers will just walk out the door and not come back if they can't buy what they want using the bills they have on hand. That is why businesses carefully manage the **change fund,** which is the money used to make change in cash transactions.

Change fund:
The money used to make change in cash transactions; also the name of the general ledger account used to establish this fund (Change Fund).

When you first establish the change fund, you make the following journal entry:

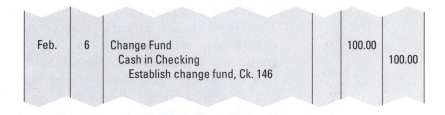

Feb.	6	Change Fund	100.00	
		Cash in Checking		100.00
		Establish change fund, Ck. 146		

This is the only time you use the Change Fund general ledger account, unless you later decide to increase or decrease the amount of cash you keep on hand in the cash registers.

Proving Out the Cash Register

Proving out the cash register:
The process of showing that the register has the right amount of cash.

To ensure that cashiers don't pocket a business's cash, at the end of each day, cashiers must prove out the cash register. **Proving out the cash register** is the process of showing that the register has the right amount of cash based on the following documents:

- The cash register summary.
- Actual cash in the drawer.
- Checks in the drawer.
- Bank credit-card charges.
- Store credit charges.

The cashier prepares a cash-out form like this example:

Cash-Out for Cash Register No. 1: M. Munro		4/25/200X
Activity	*Amount*	
Sales		
Cash Sales (cash)	$275	
Cash Sales (checks)	425	
Store Credit Sales	100	
Credit Card Sales	600	
Total Sales		$1,400
Cash Reconciliation		
Beginning Balance	$100	
Cash Sales (cash)	275	$ 375
Cash in Drawer		375
Cash Over or Short		$ 0

A store manager reviews the cash register summary (produced by the actual register) and compares it to the cash-out form. If the cash remaining in the register at the end of the day doesn't match the cash-out form, the cashier and the manager try to pinpoint the mistake. If they can't find a mistake, they fill out a cash-overage or cash-shortage form. Some businesses charge the cashier directly for any shortages, while others take the position that the cashier is fired after a certain number of shortages of a certain dollar amount (say, three shortages of more than $10).

Cash Over or Short:
The general ledger account used to record discrepancies between cash sales recorded in the cash register and the amount of cash in the drawer.

The amount of the shortage or overage is recorded in the **Cash Over or Short** account. This account does not have a normal balance. At the end of the accounting period, it is either revenue or expenses. It is revenue if it has an ending credit balance (the overages exceeded the shortages). However, if "cash short" is more than "cash over" for the period, the Cash Over or Short account is treated as an expenses.

The journal entry to record a cash overage for a single day is as follows:

Feb.	7	Cash in Checking	355.00	
		Sales		350.00
		Cash Over or Short		5.00
		Cash Register No. 1 Summary		

IN THE REAL WORLD

Petty Cash Procedure

By having an official petty cash policy in place, a business can do a great deal to reduce the chance of petty cash fraud. The College of Charleston, a public liberal arts and sciences university located in Charleston, South Carolina, posts its petty cash policy along with the controller's information on its Web site (http://controller.cofc.edu/BUSF4p1.html). The policy outlines the strict order of procedure that must be followed, including the following points:

- The petty cash custodian's supervisor "will ensure that the custodian understands the written procedures for processing petty cash transactions and knows that he/she is responsible for the amount of the petty cash fund."
- "The custodian's other regular duties may not include the receipt or disbursement of cash nor the recording of charges or credits to customer's or vendor's accounts."
- "Responsibility for the fund may not be shared between two or more people."
- "The fund is subject to surprise audit at all times."

The policy also includes a sample petty cash summary report, which is to be used for all petty cash transactions.

If the account has a credit balance at the end of the period, the closing entry debits Cash Over or Short and credits Income Summary:

Feb.	28	Cash Over or Short	33.00	
		Income Summary		33.00
		To close revenue for February 200x		

The corresponding journal entries for cash shortages follow:

Feb.	8	Cash in Checking	500.00	
		Cash Over or Short	9.00	
		Sales		509.00
		Cash Register No. 1 Summary		
	28	Income Summary	29.00	
		Cash Over or Short		29.00
		To close expenses for February 200x		

CAREER CONNECTION

A no-nonsense knack for numbers helps one professional keep the books in line for four different businesses.

Though she did not particularly set her path toward accounting, friends will attest that Janine Mincieli has always been good with money. Going back to her college days, Mincieli was the one who'd have to take charge and dole out everyone's money on spring break vacations—a walking, talking budget, so to speak. Today, Mincieli wears her bookkeeping hat for four very different businesses in central New Jersey: a motel, two on-premise catering facilities, and a mechanical contracting company.

Mincieli, now 43, has been involved with the food and beverage industry since beginning her career in the Atlantic City casinos. Though the food and beverage side is fulfilling (she is also an events planner for the catering businesses), these days Mincieli prefers the accounting side because "everything is black and white," she says. "Numbers do not lie, so if you follow the correct process your bottom line should always tie into certain numbers."

Thanks to annual upgrades, Mincieli has been able to use her most prized bookkeeping tool, QuickBooks, to manage the books for all four businesses. "All the information I need is at my fingertips," says Mincieli. Though it is far from "paperless" (as one boss promised when he hired her 14 years ago), the computerized system means that Mincieli prints far fewer year-end forms and reports than she used to.

(continued)

For her system of internal controls, Mincieli is clear about maintaining a division of financial responsibilities. Because she is the one entering checks into the systems, she did not want to have check-signing privileges. "I didn't want to be questioned about who gave the approval for a certain expenditure," she says. She also has the person who signs the checks reconcile the bank accounts. That way, the signer sees where the money went and to whom. "Since this person is the one who is signing the checks, anything without his signature would stick out like a sore thumb," she says. "It keeps me out of the gray area of being questioned for anything that might seem unethical."

Tips from the Professional

- Decide on the type of accounting system you would like to use and never look back.
- Devise a system of internal controls to help prevent errors and misunderstandings.

Cash Register Control

In addition to having the proper amount of cash in the register necessary to give customers the change they need, you also must make sure that your cashiers are giving the right amount of change and actually recording all sales on their cash registers. Keeping an eye on cashier activities is good business practice, but it's also a way to protect cash theft by your employees. There are three ways cashiers can pocket some extra cash:

- **They don't record the sale in the cash register and instead pocket the cash.** This is a form of skimming. The best deterrent to this type of theft is supervision. You can decrease the likelihood of theft through unrecorded sales by printing up sales tickets that the cashier must use to enter a sale in the cash register and open the cash drawer. If the recorded cash register transactions don't match the contents of the drawer, then the cashier must show a voided transaction for the missing ticket or explain why the cash drawer was opened without a ticket.

- **They don't provide a sales receipt and instead pocket the cash.** This is another form of skimming. In this scenario the cashier neglects to give a sales slip (receipt) to one customer in line. The cashier gives the next customer the unused sales receipt but doesn't actually record the second transaction in the cash register. Instead, he or she just pockets the cash. In the company's books, the second sale never took place.

    The customer whose sale wasn't recorded has a valid receipt though it may not exactly match the purchase, so the customer likely won't notice any problem unless he or she wants to return something later. Your best defense against this type of deception is to post a sign reminding all customers that they should get a receipt for all purchases and that the receipt is required to get a refund or exchange. Providing numbered sales receipts that include a duplicate copy can also help prevent this problem; cashiers need to produce the duplicates at the end of the day when proving the amount of cash flow that passed through their registers.

- **They record a false credit voucher and keep the cash for themselves.** In this case the cashier writes up a credit voucher for a nonexistent customer and then pockets the cash. Most stores control this problem by using a numbered credit voucher system, so each credit can be carefully monitored with some detail that proves it's based on a previous customer purchase, such as a sales receipt. Also, stores usually require that a manager reviews the reason for the credit voucher, whether a return or exchange, and approves the transaction before cash or credit is given. When the bookkeeper records the sales return in the books, the number for the credit voucher is recorded with the transaction so that he or she can easily find the detail about that credit voucher if a question is raised later about the transaction.

Even if cashiers don't deliberately pocket cash, they can inadvertently give a customer the wrong change. If you run a retail outlet, training and supervising your cashiers is a critical task that you must either handle yourself or hand over to a trusted employee.

SELF-CHECK

1. What is the purpose of petty cash? How do you document petty cash expenditures?
2. What is a change fund?
3. How do you use the cash register summary to prove out the cash register?
4. Describe two situations in which you would debit the Cash Over or Short account.

Apply Your Knowledge You decide to keep $75 cash in your office for unexpected expenses, and you write Check 818 for this purpose. Journalize the transaction.

SUMMARY

Section 8.1

- Internal controls are procedures that protect assets and provide reliable records.
- The four basic types of internal fraud are embezzlement, internal theft, payoffs and kickbacks, and skimming.

- Your primary protection against internal fraud is properly separating staff responsibilities when the flow of cash is involved; if you don't have enough staff to divide responsibilities, you need to stay heavily involved in the inflow and outflow of cash.

- With fidelity bonds, you can insure your business against employee theft.

Section 8.2

- Your checking account is your main tool for protecting your cash flow.
- Research different banks' services and fees before choosing a bank.
- Retain all documents relating to a bank deposit, including photocopies of the checks.
- After completing the bank reconciliation, you should be able to account for the difference between the bank balance and the book balance.

Section 8.3

- The petty cash fund is replenished after the person controlling the fund prepares a petty cash requisition with documentation for all expenditures.
- When cash is first made available for the cashiers to make change, the amount is debited to the Change Fund.
- The cashiers prove out the cash register daily, comparing the cash register summary to the contents of the cash drawer.
- Businesses use internal controls to prevent cashiers from skimming and issuing false credit vouchers.

ASSESS YOUR UNDERSTANDING

UNDERSTAND: WHAT HAVE YOU LEARNED?

 Go to **www.wiley.com/college/epstein** to assess your knowledge of how to protect business assets.

APPLY: WHAT WOULD YOU DO?

1. True or False? A small business is more vulnerable to internal fraud than a large business. Explain your answer.

2. Describe the controls you would put in place to prevent an employee from receiving customers' checks and then depositing the money into his or her own bank account.

3. What are the possible consequences of not reconciling the bank statements in a timely manner?

4. Suppose you have a small manufacturing business. What are some expenses you might need petty cash for? How much petty cash would you keep on hand? How often would you need to replenish the petty cash?

5. Your retail store does a large cash business. Develop a policy to safeguard the cash you take in during the day.

6. For Items a–k, identify whether:

   - It is an adjustment to the bank balance.
   - It is an adjustment to the book balance.
   - It is not a bank reconciliation adjustment.
   - It requires a journal entry.

   (Be aware that an item can have more than one answer.)

   a. Check 352 not cleared.
   b. Monthly bank fee that has been journalized.
   c. Interest income.
   d. Deposit in transit.
   e. A $300 deposit recorded in the Cash ledger account as $30.
   f. Check 353 cleared.
   g. Check-printing fee.
   h. Credit-card chargeback that has been journalized.
   i. Credit-card processing fee.
   j. Check 354 outstanding.
   k. Deposit cleared.

The following information applies to Questions 7–8:

Custom Doors & Windows received a bank statement dated 4/30/200X that showed an ending balance of $12,420. The balance of the Cash ledger account on this date was $13,192. A review of the bank statement and the Cash ledger account revealed the following:

a. The bank statement showed an $8 monthly fee, which had already been journalized as an automatic monthly entry.

b. The credit-card processing fees listed on the bank statement totaled $15.

c. Check 554 (for $1,418), Check 555 (for $425), and Check 556 (for $624) are outstanding.

d. Check 555 was written for $293 and cleared the bank. The amount recorded in the Cash account for Check 555 was $239.

e. A $3,200 deposit made on April 30 did not appear on the bank statement.

7. Prepare the bank reconciliation for Custom Doors & Windows.

8. Prepare any journal entries that are needed.

9. Journalize the following transactions:

| June 4, 200X | Established a petty cash fund for $50, Check 101. |
| June 28, 200X | Replenished the petty cash fund for the following expenditures with Check 131: |

Stamps	$ 4.20
COD on packages	6.00
Copier paper	6.50
Reimbursement for parking	5.00
Printer toner	28.00

June 30, 200X   Increased the petty cash fund to $100, Check 135.

10. Proving out the cash register during July 200X revealed the following cash discrepancies:

July 5	Cash register summary =	$1,095.00
	Cash in drawer =	1,090.50
July 10	Cash register summary =	1,555.75
	Cash in drawer =	1,560.00
July 29	Cash register summary =	998.00
	Cash in drawer =	990.00

Make all necessary journal entries for the Cash Over or Short account for July 200X.

BE A SMALL BUSINESS ACCOUNTANT

Separation of Duties

You own a small print shop with two employees. One employee has technical expertise in printing and also helps you at the front counter. The other employee is a part-time bookkeeper. Develop an internal control policy to prevent and detect financial fraud. For each inflow or outflow of cash, describe the steps in the process and who will be responsible for each step.

Too Much Money—Is There Such a Thing?

Suppose your business checking account usually has about $10,000 more than is needed for business operations. Develop a written plan for this extra cash. Include where you would keep the cash and the procedure for adding to it (or dipping into it if you needed it for business expenses). What documentation and journal entries are needed as you manage this extra cash?

E-Commerce

Suppose you are setting up a business that is entirely online. What special internal control needs will you have? Using your favorite search engine, enter the terms "e-commerce" and "internal control" (or "internal controls"). Identify the specific internal control needs and solutions available for an online business. Write a brief report and cite your online sources of information.

Who Are the Bad Guys?

It's not always easy to spot a criminal. In the case of embezzlement, small businesses and nonprofit organizations are often hit the hardest. One sees headlines like "Church Bookkeeper Gets Four Years"; Little League Volunteers Accused of Embezzlement." Using the Internet, find an article about embezzlement and prepare to discuss how you can spot embezzlement in your professional life.

KEY TERMS

Bank reconciliation	The process of explaining the differences between the bank statement balance and the general ledger Cash account balance.
Cash Over or Short	The general ledger account used to record discrepancies between cash sales recorded in the cash register and the amount of cash in the drawer.
Change fund	The money used to make change in cash transactions; also the name of the general ledger account used to establish this fund (Change Fund).
Chargeback	The reversal of a charge on a customer's credit-card.
Cleared	The term describing a transaction that has been received and processed by the bank.
Deposit in transit	A deposit recorded in the Cash ledger account that has not yet cleared the bank.
Embezzlement	The illegal use of funds by a person who controls those funds.
Endorsement	A signature or stamp on the back of a check that transfers ownership of the check.
Fidelity bonds	Insurance to protect your business against theft and reduce your risk of loss.
Internal theft	Stealing of company assets (such as inventory) by employees.
Kickback	A payment made after the fact to an employee who provided a supplier with access to the company's business, often to the detriment of the employer.
Lock box	A place, run by a bank, that receives payments for businesses.
Outstanding	The opposite of cleared; it means a transaction has *not* been processed by the bank yet.
Payoffs	A payment made before the fact to an employee who will provide a supplier with access to the company's business, often to the detriment of the employer.
Petty cash	A small amount of cash kept on hand for unexpected expenses; also the name of the general ledger account used to establish this fund (Petty Cash).
Petty cash requisition	Required to replenish the petty cash fund; shows how the petty cash was spent.

Proving out the cash register	The process of showing whether or not the cash register has the right amount of cash.
Reconciliation Summary	Report that includes the beginning balance, the balance after all cleared transactions have been recorded, a list of all transactions that have not cleared, and the ending balance.
Restrictive endorsement	An endorsement that transfers ownership of a check to a specific party for a specific purpose.
Sales slip	Proof of cash payment; also called a receipt.
Skimming	Taking money from customers and not recording revenue on the books.

EMPLOYEE PAYROLL AND DEMUCTIONS

Paying Your Team

Do You Already Know?

- The documents legally required for hiring employees
- The amounts that must be withheld from your employees' earnings
- How the benefits you offer employees can impact their income taxes

For additional questions to assess your current knowledge of managing employee payroll and deductions, go to **www.wiley.com/college/ epstein.**

What You Will Find Out	What You Will Be Able To Do
9.1 How to hire new employees	• Properly complete government forms for new hires; determine wage and salary types
9.2 How to withhold taxes from employees' earnings	• Calculate the amounts of taxes to be withheld from earnings
9.3 How employees' taxable income is affected by the benefits you provide	• Determine whether employee benefits will change the amount of taxable income and by how much
9.4 How to account for payroll expenses	• Record your total cost of payroll expenses and the resulting liabilities you incur

INTRODUCTION

It's a fact of business that you must pay employees to get them to stay around. No matter how much you beg, few people want to work for nothing. As an employer, you hire people, pay them, offer benefits, and manage a payroll. This chapter explores the processes and rules that you need to know in order to pay employees.

9.1 STAFFING YOUR BUSINESS

Responsibilities for hiring and paying employees are usually shared between the human resources staff and the accounting staff. Since this is an accounting book, the focus is on the tasks that are managed by your accounting staff (or by you, the owner).

9.1.1 Completing Government Forms

Even before you sign your first employee, you need to start filing government forms related to hiring. Additionally, when you hire employees, those individuals must also complete certain forms.

Employer Identification Number (EIN)

Employer identification number (EIN):
A number issued by the Internal Revenue Service to identify the tax account of a business that pays one or more employees.

Form SS-4, Application for Employer Identification Number:
An IRS form used by employers to apply for an EIN.

If you plan to hire staff, you must first apply for an employer identification number. The **employer identification number (EIN)** is used to identify the tax account of a business that employs one or more people. Government entities use this number to track the money you pay employees and the taxes collected and paid on their behalf.

Every company must have an EIN to hire employees. If your company is incorporated, which means you've filed paperwork with the state and become a separate legal entity, you already have an EIN. (Chapter 1 discusses corporations and other legal forms of business structure.) Otherwise, to get an EIN you must complete and submit **Form SS-4, Application for Employer Identification Number.** Form SS-4 is shown in Figure 9-1.

Luckily, the U.S. Internal Revenue Service offers four ways to submit the necessary information and obtain an EIN. The fastest way is to call the IRS's Business & Specialty Tax Line at 800-829-4933 and complete the form by telephone. IRS officials assign your EIN over the telephone. You can also apply online at www.irs.gov, or you can download Form SS-4 at www.irs.gov/pub/irs-pdf/fss4.pdf and submit it by fax or by mail.

Figure 9-1

Form **SS-4**	**Application for Employer Identification Number**	OMB No. 1545-0003
(Rev. July 2007)	(For use by employers, corporations, partnerships, trusts, estates, churches, government agencies, Indian tribal entities, certain individuals, and others.)	**EIN**
Department of the Treasury Internal Revenue Service	► See separate instructions for each line. ► Keep a copy for your records.	

Type or print clearly.

1 Legal name of entity (or individual) for whom the EIN is being requested

2 Trade name of business (if different from name on line 1)	**3** Executor, administrator, trustee, "care of" name

4a Mailing address (room, apt., suite no. and street, or P.O. box)	**5a** Street address (if different) (Do not enter a P.O. box.)
4b City, state, and ZIP code (if foreign, see instructions)	**5b** City, state, and ZIP code (if foreign, see instructions)

6 County and state where principal business is located

7a Name of principal officer, general partner, grantor, owner, or trustor	**7b** SSN, ITIN, or EIN

8a Is this application for a limited liability company (LLC) (or a foreign equivalent)? . . . . ☐ **Yes** ☐ **No**   **8b** If 8a is "Yes," enter the number of LLC members . . . . . ►

8c If 8a is "Yes," was the LLC organized in the United States? . . . . ☐ **Yes** ☐ **No**

9a **Type of entity** (check only one box). **Caution.** If 8a is "Yes," see the instructions for the correct box to check.

☐ Sole proprietor (SSN) _____
☐ Partnership
☐ Corporation (enter form number to be filed) ► _____
☐ Personal service corporation
☐ Church or church-controlled organization
☐ Other nonprofit organization (specify) ► _____
☐ Other (specify) ►

☐ Estate (SSN of decedent) _____
☐ Plan administrator (TIN) _____
☐ Trust (TIN of grantor) _____
☐ National Guard   ☐ State/local government
☐ Farmers' cooperative   ☐ Federal government/military
☐ REMIC   ☐ Indian tribal governments/enterprises
Group Exemption Number (GEN) if any ►

9b If a corporation, name the state or foreign country (if applicable) where incorporated	State	Foreign country

10 **Reason for applying** (check only one box)

☐ Started new business (specify type) ► _____
☐ Hired employees (Check the box and see line 13.)
☐ Compliance with IRS withholding regulations
☐ Other (specify) ►

☐ Banking purpose (specify purpose) ► _____
☐ Changed type of organization (specify new type) ► _____
☐ Purchased going business
☐ Created a trust (specify type) ► _____
☐ Created a pension plan (specify type) ► _____

11 Date business started or acquired (month, day, year). See instructions.	**12** Closing month of accounting year

13 Highest number of employees expected in the next 12 months (enter -0- if none).

Agricultural	Household	Other

14 Do you expect your employment tax liability to be $1,000 or less in a full calendar year? ☐ **Yes** ☐ **No** (If you expect to pay $4,000 or less in total wages in a full calendar year, you can mark "Yes.")

15 First date wages or annuities were paid (month, day, year). **Note.** If applicant is a withholding agent, enter date income will first be paid to nonresident alien (month, day, year) . . . . ►

16 Check **one** box that best describes the principal activity of your business.

☐ Construction   ☐ Rental & leasing   ☐ Transportation & warehousing   ☐ Health care & social assistance   ☐ Wholesale-agent/broker
☐ Real estate   ☐ Manufacturing   ☐ Finance & insurance   ☐ Accommodation & food service   ☐ Wholesale-other   ☐ Retail
☐ Other (specify)

17 Indicate principal line of merchandise sold, specific construction work done, products produced, or services provided.

18 Has the applicant entity shown on line 1 ever applied for and received an EIN? ☐ **Yes** ☐ **No**
If "Yes," write previous EIN here ►

Third Party Designee	Complete this section **only** if you want to authorize the named individual to receive the entity's EIN and answer questions about the completion of this form.	
	Designee's name	Designee's telephone number (include area code) ( )
	Address and ZIP code	Designee's fax number (include area code) ( )

Under penalties of perjury, I declare that I have examined this application, and to the best of my knowledge and belief, it is true, correct, and complete.

Name and title (type or print clearly) ►   Applicant's telephone number (include area code) ( )

Signature ►   Date ►   Applicant's fax number (include area code) ( )

For Privacy Act and Paperwork Reduction Act Notice, see separate instructions.   Cat. No. 16055N   Form **SS-4** (Rev. 7-2007)

You must file IRS Form SS-4 to get an employer identification number before hiring employees.

The state governments also issue identification numbers to employers. Contact your state for more information about this requirement.

Forms for New Hires

Before employees start working for you, they must fill out certain forms:

FOR EXAMPLE

See Figures 9-2, 9-3, and 9-4 to view the forms required for new hires.

- Form W-4 (for withholding taxes).
- Form I-9 (for confirming eligibility to work in the United States).
- Form W-5 (for employees eligible for the earned income credit).

Form W-4, Employee's Withholding Allowance Certificate:
An IRS form on which employees provide information used to determine the amounts of income taxes withheld from their pay.

Every person you hire must fill out **Form W-4, Employee's Withholding Allowance Certificate.** This form, shown in Figure 9-2, tells you how much to take out of your employees' paychecks in income taxes. You've probably filled out a Form W-4 at least once in your life, if you've ever worked for someone else. You can download this form at www.irs.gov/pub/irs-pdf/fw4.pdf and make copies for your employees.

On Form W-4, employees indicate whether they're married or single. They can also claim additional allowances if they have children or other major deductions that can reduce their tax bills. The amount of income taxes you need to take out of each employee's check depends on the information he or she provides on Form W-4.

It's a good idea to ask an employee to fill out Form W-4 immediately, but you can allow the person to take the form home to discuss allowances with his or her spouse or personal accountant. If an employee doesn't complete Form W-4, you must withhold the highest possible amount of income taxes for that person. Form W-4 is shown in Figure 9-2.

An employee can always fill out a new Form W-4 to reflect life changes that impact the tax withholding. For example, if the employee was single when hired and gets married later, he or she can fill out a new Form W-4 and claim the spouse, lowering the amount of taxes that must be deducted from the check. Another common life change that can reduce an employee's tax withholding is the birth or adoption of a child.

Form I-9, Employee Eligibility Verification:
A U.S. Citizenship and Immigration Services (USCIS) form used to verify an employee's eligibility to work in the United States.

A new employee must also fill out **Form I-9, Employee Eligibility Verification.** All employers in the United States must verify that any person they intend to hire is a U.S. citizen or has the right to work in the United States. As an employer, you verify this information by completing and keeping on file Form I-9 from the U.S. Citizenship and Immigration Services (USCIS). The new hire fills out Section 1 of the form by providing name, address, date of birth, social security number, and information about citizenship or residency status.

Figure 9-2

- - - - - Cut here and give Form W-4 to your employer. Keep the top part for your records. - - - - -

Form **W-4**	**Employee's Withholding Allowance Certificate**	OMB No. 1545-0074
Department of the Treasury Internal Revenue Service	▶ **Whether you are entitled to claim a certain number of allowances or exemption from withholding is subject to review by the IRS. Your employer may be required to send a copy of this form to the IRS.**	**2007**

1 Type or print your first name and middle initial.	Last name	**2** Your social security number

Home address (number and street or rural route)

City or town, state, and ZIP code

3 ☐ Single   ☐ Married   ☐ Married, but withhold at higher Single rate.
Note. If married, but legally separated, or spouse is a nonresident alien, check the "Single" box.

4 If your last name differs from that shown on your social security card,
check here. You must call 1-800-772-1213 for a replacement card. ▶ ☐

5	Total number of allowances you are claiming (from line **H** above **or** from the applicable worksheet on page 2)	**5**
6	Additional amount, if any, you want withheld from each paycheck	**6** $
7	I claim exemption from withholding for 2007, and I certify that I meet **both** of the following conditions for exemption.	

- Last year I had a right to a refund of **all** federal income tax withheld because I had **no** tax liability **and**
- This year I expect a refund of **all** federal income tax withheld because I expect to have **no** tax liability.

If you meet both conditions, write "Exempt" here . . . . ▶ | **7** |

Under penalties of perjury, I declare that I have examined this certificate and to the best of my knowledge and belief, it is true, correct, and complete.

Employee's signature
(Form is not valid
unless you sign it.) ▶   **Date** ▶

8 Employer's name and address (Employer: Complete lines 8 and 10 only if sending to the IRS.)	**9** Office code (optional)	**10** Employer identification number (EIN)

For Privacy Act and Paperwork Reduction Act Notice, see page 2.   Cat. No. 10220Q   Form **W-4** (2007)

IRS Form W-4 should be completed by all employees when they're hired so that you know how much to take out of their paychecks for taxes.

You then fill out Section 2, which requires you to check for and copy documents that establish identity and prove employment eligibility. For a new hire who is a U.S. citizen, you make a copy of one picture ID (usually a driver's license, but may be a military ID, student ID, or other state ID) and an ID that proves work eligibility, such as a social security card, birth certificate, or citizen ID card. A U.S. passport can serve as both a picture ID and proof of employment eligibility. Instructions provided with the form list all acceptable documents you can use to verify work eligibility.

Figure 9-3 shows Form I-9. You can download the form and its instructions from the U.S. Citizenship and Immigration Services Web site at www.uscis.gov.

Form W-5, Earned Income Credit Advance Payment Certificate:
An IRS form used by employees to request that the employer advance the EIC amount in paychecks.

Earned income credit (EIC):
A tax credit that refunds some of the money an employee would otherwise pay in social security or Medicare taxes.

Form W-5, Earned Income Credit Advance Payment Certificate, is completed by employees who are eligible for the earned income credit. The **earned income credit (EIC)** is a tax credit that refunds some of the money the employee would otherwise pay in social security or Medicare taxes. In order to get this credit, the employee must have a child and meet other income qualifications that are detailed on the form's instructions.

The government started the EIC tax credit, which reduces the amount of tax owed, to help lower-income people offset increases in living expenses and social security taxes. Having an employee complete Form W-5, shown in Figure 9-4, allows you to advance the expected savings of the EIC to the employee on his or her paycheck each pay period rather than make him or her wait to get the money back at the end of the year after filing tax forms. The advance amount isn't considered income, so you don't need to take taxes out on this amount.

As an employer, you aren't required to verify an employee's eligibility for the EIC tax credit. The eligible employee must complete Form W-5 each year to indicate that he or she still qualifies for the credit. If the employee does not file the form with you, you can't advance any money to the employee. You can download this form and its instructions at www.irs.gov/pub/irs-pdf/fw5.pdf.

If an employee claims the EIC on Form W-5, you calculate the paycheck the same as you would any other employee's paycheck, deducting all necessary taxes to get the employee's net pay. Then you add back the EIC advance credit that's allowed.

Any EIC advance money you pay to the employee can be subtracted from the employee taxes you owe to the government. For example, if you've taken out $10,000 from employees' checks to pay their income, social security, and Medicare taxes and then returned $500 to employees who qualified for the EIC, you subtract that $500 from the $10,000 and pay the government only $9,500 for the withheld taxes.

Small Business Accounting in Action ➡️
Properly complete government forms for new hires.

Figure 9-3

Department of Homeland Security
U.S. Citizenship and Immigration Services

OMB No. 1615-0047; Expires 03/31/07
Employment Eligibility Verification

Please read instructions carefully before completing this form. The instructions must be available during completion of this form. **ANTI-DISCRIMINATION NOTICE:** It is illegal to discriminate against work eligible individuals. Employers CANNOT specify which document(s) they will accept from an employee. The refusal to hire an individual because of a future expiration date may also constitute illegal discrimination.

Section 1. Employee Information and Verification. To be completed and signed by employee at the time employment begins.

Print Name: Last	First	Middle Initial	Maiden Name

Address (Street Name and Number)		Apt. #	Date of Birth (month/day/year)

City	State	Zip Code	Social Security #

I am aware that federal law provides for imprisonment and/or fines for false statements or use of false documents in connection with the completion of this form.

I attest, under penalty of perjury, that I am (check one of the following):

☐ A citizen or national of the United States
☐ A Lawful Permanent Resident (Alien #) A _____
☐ An alien authorized to work until _____

(Alien # or Admission #) _____

Employee's Signature	Date (month/day/year)

Preparer and/or Translator Certification. (To be completed and signed if Section 1 is prepared by a person other than the employee.) I attest, under penalty of perjury, that I have assisted in the completion of this form and that to the best of my knowledge the information is true and correct.

Preparer's/Translator's Signature	Print Name

Address (Street Name and Number, City, State, Zip Code)	Date (month/day/year)

Section 2. Employer Review and Verification. To be completed and signed by employer. Examine one document from List A OR examine one document from List B and one from List C, as listed on the reverse of this form, and record the title, number and expiration date, if any, of the document(s).

	List A	OR	List B	AND	List C
Document title:					
Issuing authority:					
Document #:					
Expiration Date (if any):					
Document #:					
Expiration Date (if any):					

CERTIFICATION - I attest, under penalty of perjury, that I have examined the document(s) presented by the above-named employee, that the above-listed document(s) appear to be genuine and to relate to the employee named, that the employee began employment on (month/day/year) _____ **and that to the best of my knowledge the employee is eligible to work in the United States. (State employment agencies may omit the date the employee began employment.)**

Signature of Employer or Authorized Representative	Print Name	Title

Business or Organization Name	Address (Street Name and Number, City, State, Zip Code)	Date (month/day/year)

Section 3. Updating and Reverification. To be completed and signed by employer.

A. New Name (if applicable)	B. Date of Rehire (month/day/year) (if applicable)

C. If employee's previous grant of work authorization has expired, provide the information below for the document that establishes current employment eligibility.

Document Title:	Document #:	Expiration Date (if any):

I attest, under penalty of perjury, that to the best of my knowledge, this employee is eligible to work in the United States, and if the employee presented document(s), the document(s) I have examined appear to be genuine and to relate to the individual.

Signature of Employer or Authorized Representative	Date (month/day/year)

NOTE: This is the 1991 edition of the Form I-9 that has been rebranded with a current printing date to reflect the recent transition from the INS to DHS and its components.

Form I-9 (Rev. 05/31/05)Y Page 2

U.S. employers must verify a new hire's eligibility to work in the United States by completing Form I-9.

Figure 9-4

▶ Give the bottom part to your employer; keep the top part for your records.

------------ Detach here ------------ ▶

Form **W-5**	**Earned Income Credit Advance Payment Certificate**	OMB No. 1545-0074
Department of the Treasury Internal Revenue Service	▶ Use the current year's certificate only. ▶ Give this certificate to your employer. ▶ This certificate expires on December 31, 2007.	**2007**

Print or type your full name	Your social security number
	___ ___

Note. *If you get advance payments of the earned income credit for 2007, you **must** file a 2007 federal income tax return. To get advance payments, you **must** have a qualifying child and your filing status must be any status **except** married filing a separate return.*

1   I expect to have a qualifying child and be able to claim the earned income credit for 2007 using that child. I do not have another Form W-5 in effect with any other current employer, and I choose to get advance EIC payments   .   .   .   .   ☐ **Yes**   ☐ **No**

2   Check the box that shows your expected filing status for 2007:
    ☐ Single, head of household, or qualifying widow(er)   ☐ Married filing jointly

3   If you are married, does your spouse have a Form W-5 in effect for 2007 with any employer?   .   .   .   .   ☐ **Yes**   ☐ **No**

Under penalties of perjury, I declare that the information I have furnished above is, to the best of my knowledge, true, correct, and complete.

Signature ▶ _____   **Date** ▶ _____

Cat. No. 10227P

Form W-5 is completed by employees who qualify for the earned income credit.

IN THE REAL WORLD

Handling New Hires

Deborah Salk owns a small landscape design business in Providence, Rhode Island. Though she operates year-round, the nature of the business requires that more than half of her 15 employees work seasonally. Whether they work for two weeks, two months, or two years, Brown sees to it that all employees fill out and submit the proper employment and tax forms; by doing so she protects both the employees and the business. To simplify matters, each employee is issued a new hire packet as soon as a position is offered and accepted. The packet includes an employment agreement; a W-4 (Employee Withholding Allowance) form, which she uses to calculate the taxes to be withheld from an employee's paychecks; an I-9 (Employment Eligibility Verification) form and copies of the necessary forms of identification; and an employee identification sheet, which includes emergency contact information. After an employee's paperwork has been completed, Brown stores it in the new employee's file.

9.1.2 Picking Pay Periods

Deciding how frequently you'll pay employees is an important point to work out before hiring staff. Most businesses choose one or more of these four pay periods:

- **Weekly:** Employees are paid every week, and payroll must be done 52 times a year.
- **Biweekly:** Employees are paid every two weeks, and payroll must be done 26 times a year.
- **Semimonthly:** Employees are paid twice a month, commonly on the 15th and last day of the month, and payroll must be done 24 times a year.
- **Monthly:** Employees are paid once a month, and payroll must be done 12 times a year.

You can choose to use any of these pay periods, and you may even decide to use more than one type. For example, some companies will pay hourly employees (employees paid by the hour) weekly or biweekly and pay salaried employees (employees paid by a set salary regardless of how many hours they work) semimonthly or monthly. Whatever your choice, decide on a consistent pay period policy and be sure to make it clear to employees when they're hired.

For each employee who's paid hourly, you need to have some sort of time sheet to keep track of work hours. These time sheets are usually completed by the employees and approved by their managers. Completed and approved time sheets are then sent to the bookkeeper so that payroll can be calculated based on the exact number of hours worked.

9.1.3 Determining Wage and Salary Types

Small Business Accounting in Action ➜
Determine wage and salary types.

You have a lot of leeway regarding the level of wages and salary you pay your employees, but you still have to follow the rules laid out by the U.S. Department of Labor. When deciding on wages and salaries, you have to first categorize your employees.

Nonexempt and Exempt

Employees fall into one of two categories:

Nonexempt employees: Employees who are covered by the FLSA; that is, they are paid overtime.

Fair Labor Standards Act (FLSA): The federal law that sets rules for minimum wage and overtime pay, among other things.

Exempt employees: Employees who are exempt from the FLSA; that is, they are not paid overtime.

• **Nonexempt employees** must be hired according to the rules of the **Fair Labor Standards Act (FLSA),** which sets rules for minimum wage and overtime pay, among other things. This means that companies must pay these employees a minimum wage. Also, any nonexempt employee who works over 40 hours in a seven-day period must be paid time and one-half for the additional hours.

• **Exempt employees** are exempt from the FLSA. They're normally paid a certain amount per pay period with no connection to the number of hours worked. Often, exempt employees work well over 40 hours per week without extra pay. Prior to new rules from the Department of Labor effective in 2004, only high-paid employees fell in this category. Today, however, employees making a weekly salary as low as $455 can be placed in the exempt category. The salary is only one test for determining exemption. Job duties also determine whether or not an employee is exempt.

You're probably wondering how to determine whether to hire exempt or nonexempt employees. Of course, most businesses would prefer to exempt all their employees from the overtime laws. You don't have a choice if your employees earn a salary of $455 or less per week. These employees are nonexempt—in other words, they are not exempt from the Fair Labor Practices Act and must be paid overtime.

You have more flexibility with employees earning more than $455 per week. You can classify employees who are executive, administrative, professional, and outside sales personnel as exempt. You can also treat certain computer employees as exempt. Keep in mind it is job duties, as well as the $455 salary test, that help define whether a position is exempt or nonexempt. It doesn't matter what the job *title* is; the government looks at job *duties*.

Employees who perform office or nonmanual work earning over $100,000 per year can be exempt. Blue-collar workers in manual labor positions cannot be exempt employees and must be paid overtime. Also police, fire fighters, paramedics, and other first responders cannot be exempt employees and must be paid overtime.

For more details about who can be designated an exempt employee, visit the U.S. Department of Labor's Web site at www.dol.gov/esa/regs/compliance/whd/fairpay/main.htm.

Minimum Wage

Minimum wage:
The lowest wage permitted under the FLSA.

A major provision of the FLSA is the minimum wage requirement. The **minimum wage** is the lowest wage permitted under the FLSA. As of this writing, the minimum wage is as follows:

- $5.85 per hour beginning July 24, 2007
- $6.55 per hour beginning July 24, 2008
- $7.25 per hour beginning July 24, 2009

For new employees who are under the age of 20 and need training, an employer can pay as little as $4.25 per hour for the first 90 days.

Certain companies do not need to meet the minimum wage requirement. However, the rules are strict and employers should check with the U.S. Department of Labor (www.dol.gov).

Some states decided that the federal minimum wage was too low and subsequently passed higher minimum wage laws, so be sure to check with your state department of labor to be certain you're meeting state wage guidelines.

Child Labor Laws

If you plan to hire employees who are under the age of 18, you must pay attention to child labor laws. Federal and state laws restrict what kind of work children can do, when they can do it, and how old they have to be to do it, so be sure you become familiar with the laws before hiring employees who are younger than 18. For minors below the age of 16, work restrictions are even tighter than for teens aged 16 and 17. You can hire your own child without worrying about age restrictions if you are the sole owner and operator, and the business is not mining, manufacturing, or any other occupation declared hazardous by the Secretary of Labor.

For more information, go to the Department of Labor Web site at www.youthrules.dol.gov.

SELF-CHECK

1. What is an employer identification number? How do you obtain one?

2. Which two forms must be filled out by all new hires? Which of these forms must the employer also fill out?

3. What is the purpose of the Fair Labor Standards Act? Do all employees fall under all provisions of the act? If not, what are the exceptions?

4. True or False? The minimum wage in all states is the same as that set by the federal government.

Apply Your Knowledge You have three employees and are trying to determine whether or not they are exempt. Which factors would you consider? Where would you go for more help in making this determination?

9.2 PAYROLL TAX WITHHOLDINGS

Various taxes are deducted from the employee's pay before the paycheck is issued. These taxes include social security; Medicare; and federal, state, and local income taxes. All amounts withheld from employees' pay constitute current liabilities for the employer.

9.2.1 Social Security Tax

Social security tax:
A federal tax collected to provide retirement and disability benefits to workers.

Social security tax is a federal tax collected to provide retirement and disability benefits to workers. Employers and employees share the social security tax equally. Each must pay 6.2 percent (0.062) of the employee's salary.

For social security tax purposes, the cap on salary is $97,500 per year (as of this writing). After an employee earns $97,500, no additional social security taxes are taken out for the rest of the year. The federal government adjusts the cap each year based on salary level changes in the marketplace. Essentially, the cap gradually increases as salaries increase.

The calculation for social security tax is relatively simple. For example, for an employee who makes $1,000 per pay period, you calculate social security tax this way:

$$\$1,000 \times 0.062 = \$62.00$$

The bookkeeper deducts $62.00 from this employee's gross earnings, and the company pays the employer's share of $62.00. Thus, the total amount remitted to the government in social security taxes for this employee is $124.00.

9.2.2 Medicare Tax

Medicare tax:
A federal tax collected to provide some medical insurance to people who are on social security and meet other requirements.

Medicare tax is a federal tax collected to provide some medical insurance to people who are on social security and meet other requirements. Employees and employers also pay the Medicare tax, which is 1.45 percent of the employee's salary (2.90 percent total). However, unlike social security tax, the Medicare tax has no salary cap. So even if someone makes $1 million per year, 1.45 percent is calculated for each pay period and that amount is paid by the employee and the also by the employer. Here's an example of how you calculate the Medicare tax for an employee who makes $1,000 per pay period:

$$\$1,000 \times 0.0145 = \$14.50$$

The bookkeeper deducts $14.50 from this employee's gross earnings, and the company pays the employer's share of $14.50. Thus, the total amount remitted in Medicare taxes for this employee is $29.00.

9.2.3 Federal Income Tax

Income tax:
A tax based on the amount of earnings that is considered taxable.

Income tax is based on the amount of earnings that is considered taxable. The government requires a "pay as you go" process. That is, the income tax is withheld from earnings throughout the year and then reported in an annual tax return.

Deducting federal income tax is a more complex task than deducting social security or Medicare tax. This is where Form W-4 comes in handy.

Under the tax rates in effect as of this writing, the first $7,825 of a single person's income (the first $15,650 for a married couple filing a joint income tax return) is taxed at 10 percent. Other tax rates depending on income are 15 percent, 25 percent, 28 percent, 33 percent, and 35 percent.

Trying to figure out taxes separately for each employee based on his or her tax rate and number of allowances would be an extremely time-consuming task, but luckily, you don't have to do that. The IRS publishes tax tables in Publication 15, *Employer's Tax Guide*, that let you just look up an employee's tax obligation based on the taxable salary and withholdings. You can access the *Employer's Tax Guide* online at www.irs.gov/pub/irs.pd/p15.pdf.

The IRS's tax tables give you detailed numbers for up to ten withholding allowances. Table 9-1 shows a sample tax table with only seven allowances because of space limitations. But even with seven allowances, you get the idea—just match the employee's wage range with the number of allowances he or she claims, and the box where they meet contains the amount of that employee's tax obligation. For example, suppose you're preparing a paycheck for an employee whose taxable income is $1,000. The employee claims three withholding allowances—one for

Table 9-1: Portion of an IRS Tax Table for Employers

If Wages Are:		And the Number of Allowances Claimed Is:						
At Least	But Less Than	1	2	3	4	5	6	7
1,000	1,010	178	163	148	133	118	103	88
1,010	1,020	180	165	150	135	120	105	91
1,020	1,030	183	168	153	138	123	107	93

self, one for spouse, and one for a child. Using the tax table, you learn that the amount of federal income taxes you deduct from the employee's pay is $148.

Small Business Accounting in Action ⟶ Calculate the amounts of taxes to be withheld from earnings.

9.2.4 State and Local Income Taxes

In addition to the federal government, most states have income taxes, and some cities even have local income taxes. You can find information about state tax forms at www.payroll-taxes.com. If your state or city has income taxes, the amounts need to be taken out of each employee's paycheck.

IN THE REAL WORLD

Schooled in Payroll Policies

George Washington University offers detailed information to its faculty, staff, and student employees on its Payroll Services Web site (www.gwu.edu/~payroll/index.html). The site contains information related to payroll cycles, payroll processing deadlines, time reporting, tax withholding, and other payroll issues.

The Web site details the University's policies related to individual tax withholding, stating "The University is responsible for withholding federal and state taxes from all employees' wages and reporting all taxable wages and taxes withheld to the Internal Revenue Service (Social Security Administration) and to the appropriate state. The University and each employee have responsibilities in this process." For their part, employees are responsible for completing Form W-4, as well as for notifying the payroll department when there are changes in their tax status.

The University also includes a feature that allows individuals a way to review personal payroll and benefit information online.

SELF-CHECK

1. List the taxes that are withheld from an employee's earnings.
2. Is the entire amount of an employee's pay subject to social security tax? To Medicare tax? Explain your answers.
3. Which withheld taxes does the employer match?
4. How do you determine the amount to withhold for federal income tax?

Apply Your Knowledge You have two employees whose payroll so far this year is $20,000 and $30,000, respectively. How much did you withhold for social security and Medicare? What is the total amount you remitted to the federal government for social security and Medicare?

9.3 EMPLOYEE BENEFITS

Benefits include programs that you provide employees to better their lives, such as health insurance and retirement savings opportunities. Some benefit costs are shared by the employee. For example, employees usually pay a portion of the premiums for health insurance coverage. Their share of the premium cost is deducted from their paychecks each pay period. Other benefits are paid for only by the employer. The premiums for group term life insurance are often paid exclusively by the employer.

Many benefits are tax-exempt, which means that the employee isn't taxed for them; small businesses and their employees often like tax-exempt benefits because, while the employer receives a current deduction, the employees do not have to include the benefit amounts in current income. However, some benefits are taxable.

9.3.1 Tax-Exempt Benefits

Tax-exempt benefits:
Benefits on which the employee does not pay taxes.

Most employer-paid benefits are **tax-exempt benefits,** which means the employee does not have to pay income tax on them. Some employee-paid benefits are also tax-exempt. If the employee pays for tax-exempt benefits, it effectively reduces the employee's taxable income.

Tax-Exempt Benefits Paid by the Employee

For example, in some cases an employee can set up a flexible spending account (FSA) to cover future medical expenses. The amounts set aside for this FSA are tax-exempt. If an employee sets aside $50 per pay period, and he or she makes $1,000 per pay period, the employee's taxable income is actually $1,000 minus the $50 FSA withholding, or $950. As the bookkeeper, you calculate taxes in this situation on $950 rather than $1,000.

The money that an employee contributes to certain retirement plans you might offer is tax deductible, too. For example, if an employee contributes $50 per pay period to your company's 401(k) retirement plan, that $50 can also be subtracted from the employee's gross earnings before you calculate taxable earnings.

Suppose an employee has $50 withheld for an FSA and $50 withheld for a 401(k). The $1,000 taxable pay is reduced to only $900 taxable pay. According to the tax table for that pay level and three allowances, the federal withholding taxes are only $123, a savings of $25 over a taxable income of $1,000. The employee recoups 25 percent of the medical and retirement costs in tax savings. Not bad!

Tax-Exempt Benefits Paid by the Employer

You can offer myriad employer-paid, the tax-exempt benefits to employees, including:

- **Adoption assistance:** You can provide up to $10,160 per child that an employee plans to adopt without having to include that amount in gross income for the purposes of calculating federal withholding taxes. However, the value of this benefit must be included when calculating social security and Medicare taxes.

- **Athletic facilities:** You can offer your employees the use of a gym on the premises your company owns or leases without having to include the value of the gym facilities in gross earnings. In order for this benefit to qualify as tax-exempt, the facility must be operated by the company primarily for the use of employees, their spouses, and their dependent children.

- **Dependent care assistance:** You can help your employees with dependent care expenses, which can include expenses for children and elderly parents, provided you offer the benefit in order to make it possible for the employee to work.

- **Education assistance:** You can pay employees' educational expenses up to $5,250 per year without having to include that payment in the employees' gross income.

- **Employee discounts:** You can offer employees discounts on the company's products without including the value of the discounts in their gross earnings, provided the discount is not more than 20 percent less than what's charged to customers. If you only offer this discount to high-paid employees, then the value of these discounts must be included in gross earnings of those employees.

- **Group term life insurance:** You can provide group term life insurance up to a coverage level of $50,000 to your employees without including the value of this insurance in their gross earnings. Premiums for coverage above $50,000 must be added to calculations for social security and Medicare taxes.

- **Health insurance:** The portion you pay for health insurance premiums is not considered income to your employees.

- **Meals:** Meals that have little value (such as coffee and doughnuts) don't have to be reported as taxable income. Also, occasional meals brought in so employees can work late also don't have to be reported in employees' income.

- **Moving expenses reimbursements:** If you pay moving expenses for employees, you don't have to report these reimbursements as employee income as long as the reimbursements are for items that would qualify as tax-deductible moving expenses on an employee's individual tax return. Employees who have been reimbursed by their employers can't deduct the moving expenses for which the employer paid.

Taxable benefits:
Benefits on which the employee pays taxes.

Small Business Accounting in Action ➡ Determine whether employee benefits will change the amount of taxable income and by how much.

9.3.2 Taxable Benefits

You may decide to provide some benefits that are **taxable benefits,** which means the employee has to pay taxes on the money or on the value of the benefits. These include the personal use of a company vehicle and benefits that exceed allowable maximums. For example, if you pay $10,250 toward an employee's education expenses, then $5,000 of that amount must be reported as income because the federal government's cap is $5,250.

IN THE REAL WORLD

Benefits Boost

Dental coverage and a solid 401(k) plan may not be enough to attract top talent to a small business. These days, alternative benefits such as volunteer programs are getting attention from small and large businesses alike. According to the Corporation for National and Community Service, volunteering continues to grow in popularity, recently reaching a 30-year high. Osprey Packs, a Colorado outdoor company specializing in technical packs and travel gear, gives each employee one day a year to spend volunteering with a charity of their choice. The program, which is managed by human resources staff, had 100 percent participation in 2007, totally 160 community hours—a benefit to both employees and the community. [1]

SELF-CHECK

1. Are benefits always paid for by the employer only? Explain your answer.

2. How do employee-paid, tax-exempt benefits reduce the amount of income tax an individual pays?

3. List three examples of employer-paid, tax-exempt benefits.

4. List three examples of employer-paid, taxable benefits.

Apply Your Knowledge You have one employee and you paid the following amounts for employee benefits in one calendar year: $6,000 for tuition reimbursement and $2,400 for health insurance premiums. What amount of these benefits is included in the employee's income that you report to the IRS?

9.4 PAYDAY

After you figure out all the necessary deductions to be taken from an employee's paycheck, you can calculate the check amount and pay the employee. You need to record this payment in the accounting records, along with the amounts you withheld and will pay to the taxing authorities or benefits providers.

9.4.1 Calculating Gross Earnings

Gross earnings:
The amount of an employee's earnings before any deductions.

Gross earnings are the amount of an employee's earnings before any deductions for taxes or benefits. How you calculate gross earnings depends on which type of pay structure you use:

• Hourly.

• Salaried.

• Commission.

Calculating Payroll for Hourly Employees

When you're ready to prepare payroll for nonexempt employees, the first thing you need to do is collect time records from each person being paid by the hour. Some companies use time clocks and some use time sheets to produce the required time records, but whatever the method used, usually the manager of each department reviews the time records for each employee he or she supervises and then sends those time records to the accountant for processing.

With time records in hand, the accountant has to calculate gross earnings for each employee. For example, if a nonexempt employee worked 45 hours and is paid $12 an hour, gross earnings are calculated like so:

$$40 \text{ regular hours} \times \$12 \text{ per hour} = \$480$$
$$5 \text{ overtime hours} \times \$12 \text{ per hour} \times 1.5 \text{ overtime rate} = \$\ 90$$
$$\$480 + \$90 = \$570$$

In this case, because the employee isn't exempt from the FLSA (see "Determining Wage and Salary Types" earlier in this chapter), overtime must be paid for any hours worked over 40 in a seven-day workweek. This employee worked 5 hours more than the 40 hours allowed.

Calculating Payroll for Salaried Employees

In addition to paying hourly employees, the acccountant must prepare payroll for salaried employees. Paychecks for salaried employees are relatively easy to calculate—all you need to know are their base salaries and their pay periods. For example, if a salaried employee makes $30,000 per year and is paid twice a month (totaling 24 pay periods), that employee's gross earnings are $1,250 for each pay period.

Calculating Commission Checks

Computing gross earnings for employees paid on commission can involve the most complex calculations. This section shows various scenarios to calculate a commission check for a salesperson who sells $60,000 worth of products during one month.

If the salesperson is on a straight commission of 10 percent, you calculate pay using this formula:

$$\text{Total amount sold} \times \text{Commission percentage} = \text{Gross earnings}$$
$$\$60,000 \times 0.10 = \$6,000$$

If the salesperson has a guaranteed base salary of $2,000 plus an additional 5 percent commission on all products sold, you calculate pay using this formula:

$$\text{Base salary} + (\text{Total amount sold} \times \text{Commission percentage})$$
$$= \text{Gross earnings}$$
$$\$2,000 + (\$60,000 \times 0.05) = \$5,000$$

Although this employee may be happier having a base salary to count on each month, the amount of gross earnings is actually less with a base salary because the commission rate is so much lower. By selling $60,000 worth of products, the salesperson made only $3,000 in commission at 5 percent. Without the base pay, the commission would have been 10 percent on the $60,000 ($60,000 $\times$ 0.10 = $6,000), so the earnings are actually $1,000 lower with a base pay structure that includes a lower commission rate.

If the salesperson has a slow sales month of just $30,000 worth of products sold, the gross earnings would be:

$$\$30,000 \times 0.10 = \$3,000 \text{ on straight commission of 10 percent,}$$
$$\text{or}$$
$$\$2,000 + (\$30,000 \times 0.05) = \$3,500 \text{ on base pay of \$2,000 and commission}$$
$$\text{of 5 percent}$$

In a slow month, the salesperson would make more money with the base salary rather than with the higher commission rate.

There are many other ways to calculate commissions. One common way is to offer higher commissions on higher levels of sales. Using the figures in this example, this type of pay system encourages salespeople to keep their sales levels over $30,000 to get the best commission rate.

With a graduated commission scale, a salesperson might make a straight commission of 5 percent on the first $10,000 in sales, then 7 percent on the next $20,000, and finally 10 percent on anything over $30,000. Here's what the gross earnings calculation looks like using this commission pay scale:

$$(\$10,000 \times 0.05) + (\$20,000 \times 0.07)$$
$$+ (\$30,000 \times 0.10) = \$4,900 \text{ Gross earnings}$$

One other type of commission pay system involves a base salary plus tips. This method is common in restaurant settings. Businesses that pay less than minimum wage must prove that their employees make at least minimum wage when tips are accounted for. Today, that's relatively easy to prove because most people pay their bills with credit cards and include tips on their bills. Businesses can then come up with an average tip rate using that credit-card data.

Employees must report tips to their employers on IRS Form 4070, *Employee's Report of Tips to Employer,* which is part of IRS Publication 1244, *Employee's Daily Record of Tips and Report to Employer.* If your employees receive tips and you want to supply the necessary paperwork, you can download it at www.irs.gov/pub/irs-pdf/p1244.pdf. The publication provides details about what the IRS expects you and your employees to do in an environment where tipping is common.

9.4.2 Calculating Net Pay

Net pay:
The amount an employee is paid after subtracting all deductions.

Net pay is the amount a person is paid after subtracting all tax and benefit deductions. Here's the equation and an example of how you calculate the net pay amount:

Gross earnings − (social security tax withholding + Medicare tax withholding + federal income tax withholding + state income tax withholding + local income tax withholding) = Net pay
$$\$1,000.00 - (\$62.00 + \$14.50 + \$148.00 + \$45.00 + \$0.00) = \$730.50$$

This net pay calculation doesn't include any deductions for benefits. Many businesses offer their employees health, retirement, and other benefits but expect the employees to share a portion of those costs. The fact that some of these benefits are tax-exempt and some are not makes a difference when you calculate the income tax withholding.

If an employee's benefits are tax-exempt and taken out of the check *before* federal income tax withholding is calculated, the federal tax rate may be lower than if the benefits were deducted *after* calculating federal withholding taxes. Many states follow the federal government's lead on tax-exempt benefits, so the amount deducted for state taxes will be lower as well.

9.4.3 Recording the Payroll

After calculating paychecks for all your employees, you prepare the payroll, make up the checks, and post the payroll to the books.

The Payroll Register

Payroll register:
A record of the payroll activity for all employees in a specific payroll period.

Before recording the payroll expense, you prepare a **payroll register,** which is a record of the payroll activity for all employees in a specific payroll period. The payroll register in Figure 9-5 contains information about each employee:

- Name: Employee name.
- Allow.:   Marital status and allowances information from Form W-4.
- Cumulative: The year-to-date earnings before the current payroll period.
  Earnings
- Hours: The hours worked in the current payroll period.
- Rate: The rate of pay.
- Earnings: The amount of money earned in the current payroll period.
- Cumulative: The cumulative earnings after the current payroll period.
  Earnings
- Taxable: The current earnings subject to three types of federal taxes.
  Earnings   (The FUTA tax is covered in Chapter 10.)
- Deductions: The amounts deducted from the current gross earnings.
- Net Pay/
  CK. NO: The amount of net pay and the check number.

The Employee Earnings Record

Employee earnings record:
A record that contains the payroll history for a single employee.

In addition to keeping records by payroll period, you also keep records by employee. The **employee earnings record** in Figure 9-6 contains the complete payroll history for one employee, Cleavant Burgess.

Figure 9-5

PAYROLL REGISTER															WEEK ENDING: August 4, 200X							PAY DATE August 10, 200X
			Hours				Earnings				Taxable Earnings					Deductions					
Name	Allow.	Cumulative Earnings	Reg.	OT	TOT.	Rate	Reg.	OT	Gross	Cumulative Earnings	Social Security	Medicare	FUTA	Social Security	Medicare	FED. Income Tax	State Income Tax	Health Insurance	Total Deductions	Net Pay	CK. NO
Benitez, Rosa	S 1	9,000.00	31.5	–	31.5	9.00	283.50	–	283.50	16,449.00	283.50	283.50	–	17.58	4.11	22.00	10.00	21.50	75.19	208.31	114
Burgess, Cleavant	M 2	2,488.25	40.0	–	40.0	9.25	370.00	–	370.00	2,858.25	370.00	370.00	370.00	22.94	5.36	26.00	11.50	40.00	105.80	264.20	115
Gallagher, Frank	S 3	6,800.00	40.0	2.0	42.0	8.50	340.00	25.50	365.50	7,165.50	365.50	365.50	200.00	22.66	5.30	25.00	10.75	40.00	103.71	261.79	116
		18,288.25					993.50	25.50	1,019.00	26,472.75	1,019.00	1,019.00	570.00	63.18	14.77	73.00	32.25	101.50	284.70	734.30	

The payroll register contains information organized by payroll period.

Figure 9-6

| EMPLOYEE EARNINGS RECORD FOR | 200X | | | | | | | | | | | | | | | |

NAME	Burgess, Cleavant					SOCIAL SECURITY NO.	XXXX		
ADDRESS	XXXX					RATE	$9.25/hour		
PHONE	XXXX					MARITAL STATUS	M		
DATE OF BIRTH	XXXX					ALLOWANCES	2		
EMPLOYMENT STARTED	6/12/200X					EMPLOYMENT ENDED	6/12/200X		

| | | | Hours | | Earnings | | | | | Deductions | | | | | |
Week	Week End.	Pay Date	Reg.	OT	Reg.	OT	Gross	Cumulative	Social Security	Medicare	FED. Income Tax	State Income Tax	Health Insurance	Net Pay
24	6/16	6/22	29	–	268.25	–	268.25	268.25	16.63	3.89	19.00	8.00	–	220.73
25	6/23	6/29	40	–	370.00	–	370.00	638.25	22.94	5.36	26.00	11.50	40.00	264.20
26	6/30	7/06	40	–	370.00	–	370.00	1,008.25	22.94	5.36	26.00	11.50	40.00	264.20
Quarter Totals					1,008.25	–	1,008.25	1,008.25	62.51	14.61	71.00	31.00	80.00	749.13
Yearly Totals					1,008.25	–	1,008.25	1,008.25	62.51	14.61	71.00	31.00	80.00	749.13
27	7/07	7/13	40	–	370.00	–	370.00	1,378.25	22.94	5.36	26.00	11.50	40.00	264.20
28	7/14	7/20	40	–	370.00	–	370.00	1,748.25	22.94	5.36	26.00	11.50	40.00	264.20
29	7/21	7/27	40	–	370.00	–	370.00	2,118.25	22.94	5.36	26.00	11.50	40.00	264.20
30	7/28	8/03	40	–	370.00	–	370.00	2,488.25	22.94	5.36	26.00	11.50	40.00	264.20
31	8/04	8/10	40	–	370.00	–	370.00	2,858.25	22.94	5.36	26.00	11.50	40.00	264.20

The employee earnings record contains information for a single employee.

Salaries and Wages:
The general ledger account used to record the employer's expense for employee gross earnings.

Payroll Taxes:
The general ledger account used to record the employer's payroll tax expenses.

Social Security Tax Payable:
The general ledger account used to record the liability for both the social security tax withheld from gross earnings and the employer's matching portion.

Medicare Tax Payable:
The general ledger account used to record the liability for both the Medicare tax withheld from gross earnings and the employer's matching portion.

Federal Withholding Payable:
The general ledger account used to record the liability for amounts withheld from gross earnings for federal income taxes.

The Payroll Journal Entry

The information for the payroll journal entry comes from the payroll register. In addition to Cash, many accounts are impacted by payroll:

- **Salaries and Wages,** the expense account used to record the amount of employees' gross earnings.
- **Payroll Taxes,** the expense account used to record the employer's portion of social security tax and Medicare tax, as well as some additional taxes discussed in Chapter 10.
- **Social Security Tax Payable,** the current liability account used to record the amounts withheld from gross earnings for social security taxes, and also the employer's matching share.
- **Medicare Tax Payable,** the current liability account used to record the amounts withheld from gross earnings for Medicare taxes, and also the employer's matching share.
- **Federal Withholding Payable,** the current liability account used to record the amounts withheld from gross earnings for federal income taxes.
- **State Withholding Payable,** the current liability account used to record the amounts withheld from gross earnings for state income taxes.
- **Employee Medical Insurance Payable,** the current liability account used to record the amounts withheld from gross earnings for medical insurance premiums.

The journal entry for the payroll shown in Figure 9-5 would look like this:

Date		Description	Post Ref.	Debit	Credit
General Journal					**Page 10**
200x Aug.	10	Salaries and Wages		1,019.00	
		Payroll Taxes		77.95	
		Social Security Tax Payable			126.36
		Medicare Tax Payable			29.54
		Federal Withholding Payable			73.00
		State Withholding Payable			32.25
		Health Insurance Payable			101.50
		Cash in Checking			734.30
		Payroll register for pay date 8/10/200x			

State Withholding Payable:
The general ledger account used to record the liability for amounts withheld from gross earnings for state income taxes.

Notice that you record the entire liability for social security and Medicare taxes, not just the amount that was withheld from gross earnings. The employer's share is recorded in the Payroll Taxes expense account. The payroll tax is an additional expense for the employer (above and beyond the salaries and wages).

IN THE REAL WORLD

Payroll Oversight

It can be good business to rely on others to help run a company when it gets to be too much for one person. However, business owners should think very carefully about where they put their trust. When Nalia's window-cleaning business grew to the point where she had 20 employees on job sites all over her service area in Wilmington, North Carolina, she hired a site supervisor to help her meet with clients and oversee the many jobs in progress. Nalia concentrated on marketing and bookkeeping. Little did she know that the supervisor had been padding his hours and those of two other employees. In effect, Nalia was paying them for not working. When Nalia discovered the discrepancies, she fired the three employees. Since then Nalia has hired a part-time bookkeeper, allowing her to split her time between the office and the job sites in order to keep a watchful eye on all involved.

Employee Medical Insurance Payable:
The general ledger account used to record the liability for amounts withheld from gross earnings for medical insurance premiums.

Small Business Accounting in Action ➡
Record your total cost of payroll expenses and the resulting liabilities you incur.

9.4.4 Depositing Payroll Taxes

Any taxes collected on behalf of employees must be deposited in a financial institution authorized to collect those payments for the government. You must also deposit the employer portion of social security and Medicare taxes.

Deposits must be made according to a strict schedule, or you can face large penalties. Payroll tax deposits are covered in Chapter 10.

9.4.5 Outsourcing Payroll and Benefits Work

Given all that's required of you to prepare payroll, you may think that it's a good idea for your small company to outsource the work of payroll and benefits. Many companies outsource the work because it's such a specialized area and requires extensive software to manage both payroll and benefits.

SELF-CHECK

1. Define gross earnings.
2. How do you calculate net pay?
3. Name the account(s) debited in the payroll journal entry. Name the account(s) credited.

Apply Your Knowledge ▸ Your nonexempt employee worked 48 hours in a seven-day workweek. The employee's pay rate is $8.50 per hour. Calculate the gross earnings for the week.

CAREER CONNECTION

Using a bookkeeper and an accountant, a busy chiropractor creates a finely tuned system of checks and balances to manage his company's finances.

Dr. Thomas Dandrea's chiropractic business has experienced remarkable growth since he began treating patients in 1998 at his practice in Red Bank, New Jersey. Today—thanks to his years of dedication and proven results—about 250 patients are cared for each week at Monmouth Spine and Rehabilitation Center (www.monmouthspine.com)—so many that Dandrea has recently doubled the size of his office space.

Though the health and overall well-being of his patients is clearly at the forefront, as president of his company, Dandrea must also care for his business's fiscal health. Between Dandrea and his bookkeeper, the two spend about seven hours a week on accounting. On top of that, Dandrea works with an accountant. "It's important to have an accountant hold a bookkeeper accountable by checking the bookkeeper's work quarterly for mistakes," he says. Dandrea realizes that internal theft is, unfortunately, quite common in small businesses, so this system of checks and balances helps prevent such problems.

When it comes to payroll for the business's 16 employees, Dandrea relies on a payroll company, largely because of complicated tax issues. To streamline matters, employees submit hours to Dandrea, who checks and approves them; he then forward the hours to his bookkeeper, who submits them to their payroll company. He and the bookkeeper meet with the accountant each quarter to discuss payroll and all other accounting issues.

Tips from the Professional

- The president of the company must sign all checks (no signature stamps!); no one else should be allowed to do this.
- Use a payroll company.
- Whenever possible, have a bookkeeper be the liaison with the payroll company.

SUMMARY

Section 9.1

- An employer must have an employer identification number (EIN) for payroll tax reporting purposes.
- New employees must complete a Form W-4 and a Form I-9.
- If an employee claims an advance of the earned income credit (EIC), he or she must complete a Form W-5.
- Pay periods include weekly, biweekly, semi-monthly, and monthly.

- The Fair Labor Standards Act (FLSA) sets employment rules including those relating to minimum wage and overtime.
- Certain employees can be exempt from FLSA requirements.

Section 9.2

- Payroll tax withholdings are made for social security (6.2%), Medicare (1.45%), and income.
- The salary cap for the social security tax at this writing is $97,500, and it increases each year.

- Medicare tax does not have a salary cap; all earnings are subject to Medicare tax.
- The employer matches the amounts withheld for social security and Medicare.

Section 9.3

- Employee benefits can be either taxable or tax-exempt.

Section 9.4

- Net pay is determined by subtracting deductions from gross earnings.

- Payroll details are recorded in the payroll register and the employee earnings records.
- The payroll journal entry debits expenses, and it credits liabilities and cash.
- Taxes withheld from employees' gross earnings must be deposited according to a strict schedule.
- Many companies outsource payroll and benefits work.

ASSESS YOUR UNDERSTANDING

UNDERSTAND: WHAT HAVE YOU LEARNED?

 Go to **www.wiley.com/college/epstein** to assess your knowledge of managing payroll and deductions.

PRACTICE: WHAT WOULD YOU DO?

1. Complete the table below using the data provided. Each employee must be paid according to the Fair Labor Standards Act with all hours worked over 40 in a 7-day period paid at a time and a half rate.

Employee Name	Hours Worked	Hourly Rate	Regular Pay	Overtime Pay	Total Gross Pay
J. Smith	45	15			
M. Jack	50	12			
T. Phelps	38.5	10			
P. Gordon	40	16			

2. Determine the amount of Medicare tax for each employee listed below.

Employee Name	Gross Pay	Medicare Tax
Will Larson	1,000	
Jonathan Ross	850	
Ernestine Brown	700	

3. Maxine Sanders is a single employee who claims one allowance. Prior to the current pay period, her year-to-date total earnings were $75,000. Her pay for the current pay period is $3,000. Calculate Maxine's social security payroll deduction for the current period.

4. Determine the amount of federal income tax for an employee that earns $1,025 per pay period and claims five withholding allowances.

5. Complete the chart shown below.

Employee Name	Current Pay	Year to Date Earnings	Social Security	Medicare
C. Jones	1,030	98,000		
S. Christian	1,000	80,000		
M. Wallace	1,015	76,000		

6. Joseph Smith is a salaried employee who is paid biweekly. His yearly salary is $52,000. Calculate his gross biweekly salary.

7. Refer to question 6. Suppose Joseph is paid semimonthly. Calculate his semimonthly salary.

8. An employer uses a commission process to determine his employee's gross pay. The employee is given his choice of two methods.

   a. 10% commission on all sales
   b. $500 base guaranteed salary & 5 percent commission on all sales

   Determine which method would yield the highest gross pay if the employee sold $15,000 of merchandise.

9. A married employee who claims two allowances earned $1,030 during the current pay period. The employee's year to date pay prior to this pay period is $54,000. The employee is not taxed at the state or local level. Calculate each of the following for the current pay period:

   a. Social Security Tax Withholding
   b. Medicare Tax Withholding
   c. Federal Income Tax Withholding
   d. Net Pay

10. The Allias Agency had the following payroll information:

Employee Name	Taxable Earnings	Allowances Claimed
Jeffrey Harrison	1,020	3
Sevana Reed	1,000	1
Nicole Evans	1,010	5
Robert Homes	1,030	2
Total	**4,060**	

Assuming no employee has earned more than $97,500 this year (including the current pay period), determine the Allias Agency's payroll taxes.

11. Refer to question 10. Give the journal entry to record the payroll taxes.

BE A SMALL BUSINESS ACCOUNTANT

Outsourcing Payroll

A budding entrepreneur is expected to open a new service entity in about six months. This business is expected to employ about 20 people, both professional and nonprofessional. The owner was advised to outsource the payroll. Research the various payroll servicing firms and prepare a listing of the pros and cons that come along with outsourcing. Determine if this owner should house his payroll department or outsource it.

Commission or Salary Payroll

An owner must determine if he can optimize his profits and reduce his expenses. He is currently looking at ways to reduce his payroll. He thinks that paying his salespeople using a straight commission basis would greatly reduce the cost of his payroll. However, he is concerned that many of his better salespeople would leave and find a job with a different pay scale. He feels as though all of his employees are valuable and he does not want to lose any. Is there any way he can reduce the cost of payroll and make the new procedure attractive enough to keep all of his current employees?

KEY TERMS

Earned income credit (EIC)	A tax credit that refunds some of the money an employee would otherwise pay in social security or Medicare taxes.
Employee earnings record	A record that contains the payroll history for a single employee.
Employee Medical Insurance Payable	The general ledger account used to record the liability for amounts withheld from gross earnings for medical insurance premiums.
Employer identification number (EIN)	A number issued by the Internal Revenue Service to identify the tax account of a business that pays one or more employees.
Exempt employees	Employees who are exempt from the FLSA; that is, they are not paid overtime.
Fair Labor Standards Act (FLSA)	The federal law that sets rules for minimum wage and overtime pay, among other things.
Federal Withholding Payable	The general ledger account used to record the liability for amounts withheld from gross earnings for federal income taxes.
Form I-9	Employee Eligibility Verification, a U.S. Citizenship and Immigration Services (USCIS) form used to verify an employee's eligibility to work in the United States.
Form SS-4	Application for Employer Identification Number, an IRS form used by employers to apply for an EIN.
Form W-4	Employee's Withholding Allowance Certificate, an IRS form on which employees provide information used to determine the amounts of income taxes withheld from their pay.
Form W-5	Earned Income Credit Advance Payment Certificate, an IRS form used by employees to request that the employer advance the EIC amount in paychecks.
Gross earnings	The amount of an employee's earnings before any deductions.
Income tax	A tax based on the amount of earnings that are considered taxable.
Medicare tax	A federal tax collected to provide some medical insurance to people who are on social security and meet other requirements.
Medicare Tax Payable	The general ledger account used to record the liability for both the Medicare tax withheld from gross earnings and the employer's matching portion.

Minimum wage	The lowest wage permitted under the FLSA.
Net pay	The amount an employee is paid after subtracting all deductions.
Nonexempt employees	Employees who are covered by the FLSA; that is, they are paid overtime.
Payroll register	A record of the payroll activity for all employees in a specific payroll period.
Payroll Taxes	The general ledger account used to record the employer's payroll tax expenses.
Salaries and Wages	The general ledger account used to record the employer's expense for employee gross earnings.
Social security tax	A federal tax collected to provide retirement and disability benefits to workers.
Social Security Tax Payable	The general ledger account used to record the liability for both the social security tax withheld from gross earnings and the employer's matching portion.
State Withholding Payable	The general ledger account used to record the liability for amounts withheld from gross earnings for state income taxes.
Taxable benefits	Benefits on which the employee pays taxes.
Tax-exempt benefits	Benefits on which the employee does not pay taxes.

REFERENCES

1. Edelhauser Chessman, Kristin. "Volunteering as a Benefit," Entrepreneur.com, December 27, 2007, www.entrepreneur.com/humanresources/compensationandbenefits/article188360.html.

10

UNDERSTANDING PAYROLL LEGALITIES
Knowing the Taxes and Laws

Do You Already Know?

- How and when to pay the payroll taxes
- Which tax returns you must file as an employer
- How to find out your state's requirements for workers' compensation

For additional questions to assess your current knowledge of the legal implications of employer payroll responsibilities, go to **www.wiley. com/college/epstein.**

What You Will Find Out	What You Will Be Able To Do
10.1 Tax deposit requirements	• Calculate, report, and pay the mandated tax amounts on time
10.2 Employer payroll tax returns	• File payroll tax returns quarterly and yearly
10.3 How to file W-2 forms	• Prepare and send wage and tax statements
10.4 How to meet workers' compensation obligations	• Understand and implement workers' compensation rules
10.5 Which records you must retain	• Create a system for maintaining employee records

INTRODUCTION

You may think that employees will make your job as a business owner easier, but it's really a mixed bag. While employees help you keep your business operating and enable your business to grow, they also add a lot of government paperwork. This chapter reviews the federal, state, and local government reporting requirements for employers, as well as the records you must keep in order to complete these reports. You will also find out about workers' compensation insurance requirements.

10.1 PAYROLL TAX DEPOSITS

There are specific rules that define what constitutes a timely payment of withheld taxes and employer taxes (for income tax, social security, and Medicare) as well as the employer matching amounts for social security and Medicare. Most major banks are authorized to collect tax deposits; check with your bank to see if it's authorized or to get a recommendation of a bank you can use.

10.1.1 When to Deposit Taxes

If your federal payroll tax liability is less than $2,500 in a calendar quarter, you can make the payment with your Form 941 payroll tax return. This quarterly form is covered in Section 10.2. Otherwise, you follow a monthly or semiweekly tax deposit schedule.

Monthly or Semiweekly

During the first calendar year as an employer, the company will have to make monthly deposits of employee taxes. Monthly deposits must be made by the 15th day of the month following when the taxes were collected. For example, taxes collected from employees in August must be paid by September 15. If the date the deposit is due falls on a weekend or bank holiday, the payment is due on the next day the banks are open.

Lookback period:
The 12-month period ending June 30 of the previous calendar year.

After the first calendar year, your deposit schedule is determined by your lookback period. The **lookback period** is the 12-month period ending June 30 of the previous calendar year. If your total payroll taxes were $50,000 or less in the lookback period, you continue as a monthly schedule depositor. But if your taxes were more than $50,000, you become a semiweekly schedule depositor.

A semiweekly payer must deposit taxes on Wednesday or Friday, depending on the pay date:

- **If you pay employees on Wednesday, Thursday, and/or Friday,** you must deposit the taxes due by the next Wednesday.

- **If you pay employees on Saturday, Sunday, Monday, and/or Tuesday,** you must deposit the taxes due by the next Friday.

The $100,000 Next Day Rule

Employers whose businesses accumulate $100,000 or more in taxes due on any day during a deposit period must deposit those taxes on the next banking day. If you hit $100,000 due when you're a monthly depositor, you must start paying taxes semiweekly for at least the remainder of the current tax year.

Consequences of Late Payment

Whatever schedule you are on, the one thing you definitely don't want to do is underpay. Interest and penalty charges for late payment can make your tax bite even higher.

If you are a monthly depositor and find it hard to accurately estimate your quarterly tax liability, your best bet is to deposit a slightly higher amount in the first and second months of a quarter. Then, if you've paid a bit more than needed, you can cut back the payment for the third month of

IN THE REAL WORLD

Payroll Implications of Incorporations

An accountant helped a friend who was a high school teacher prepare his business return when he decided to work over the summer doing what he teaches during the school year—HVAC. He began as a sole proprietorship. During that period, it was very easy for him to take money out of the business; he simply wrote himself a check. After an attorney advised him to incorporate—for protection from possible lawsuits—he had only two options for taking money out: 1) Pay a salary to himself—which entailed payroll withholding, monthly, quarterly, and annual payroll reports, and appropriate deposits of withheld amounts and payroll taxes, and 2) Treat the amount withdrawn as a dividend. It took him a long while to understand that he could no longer just write himself a check for $100 if he wanted to take the family out for dinner on Saturday night.

the quarter. This strategy lets you avoid the possibility of underpaying in the first two months of a quarter and risking interest and penalty charges. It is important to note that a business also runs the risk of the government taking more drastic action if amounts owed are not current.

10.1.2 How to Deposit Taxes

The federal government provides two ways to make tax deposits:

Electronic Federal Tax Payment System (EFTPS):
The federal government's system to receive payroll tax payments by electronic funds transfer.

- Electronic Federal Tax Payment System (EFTPS).
- Form 8109, Federal Tax Deposit Coupon.

You can make employee tax payments electronically using the **Electronic Federal Tax Payment System (EFTPS).** Employers with annual tax payments of more than $200,000 must deposit these taxes electronically using EFTPS. Otherwise, use of the electronic system is voluntary. For more information on EFTPS, go to www.eftps.gov.

Form 8109 Federal Tax Deposit Coupon:
A preprinted coupon used to deposit various taxes including payroll taxes and unemployment taxes.

If you don't use EFTPS, you must use Form 8109. Figure 10-1 shows a copy of Form 8109-B, which the IRS provides for informational use only. The actual **Form 8109 Federal Tax Deposit Coupon** is provided by the IRS and is preprinted with your company information. If you don't have the preprinted Form 8109, contact the IRS for **Form 8109-B** and fill in your EIN and other company information. You can't get a copy of these forms online; they are only provided when you contact the IRS directly.

Form 8109-B:
A Federal Tax Deposit Coupon that is not preprinted; you fill in your company information.

You might be required to make deposits to your state taxing authority. Contact your state for further information.

10.1.3 Accounting for Tax Deposits

When you make the tax deposit, you debit the tax liability accounts and credit the Cash account. Suppose your company is a monthly depositor and incurred the following federal payroll tax liabilities during the month of August:

Social Security	$1,240.00
Medicare	145.00
Income Tax Withholding	1,300.50

Small Business Accounting in Action ➡
Calculate, report, and pay the mandated tax amounts on time.

As discussed in Chapter 9, the tax liability is recorded at the time the employees are paid. In this example, the liabilities were recorded in the month of August. The journal entry to record payment of the tax deposit follows:

200X Sept.	10	Social Security Tax Payable	1,240.00	
		Medicare Tax Payable	145.00	
		Federal Withholding Payable	1,300.50	
		Cash in Checking		2,685.50
		Ck. 152, City Bank, federal tax deposit		

SELF-CHECK

1. What is the lookback period? How is it used in determining a company's payroll tax deposit schedule?

2. What schedule for making timely deposits does a new company use?

3. What are the two methods available for depositing payroll taxes? When must you use a specific method? Describe the circumstances in which you can only use one specific method.

4. When you make a tax deposit, which accounts are debited and credited?

Apply Your Knowledge Your company is on a monthly deposit schedule. On July 14, the balance of your undeposited federal payroll tax is $95,000. On the next pay date, Tuesday, July 21, the federal payroll tax liability is increased by $40,000. When must you make your next payroll tax deposit? What is the amount of this tax deposit? Can you continue to use the monthly deposit schedule? Why or why not?

10.2 PAYROLL TAX RETURNS

The federal government requires two payroll tax returns:

- Form 941.
- Form 940.

Form 941, Employer's Quarterly Federal Tax Return:
A form filed by employers at the end of each calendar quarter.

10.2.1 Filing Form 941

Each quarter you must file federal **Form 941, Employer's Quarterly Federal Tax Return,** which details the number of employees that received wages, tips, or other compensation for the quarter. Figure 10-2 shows Form 941.

Figure 10-1

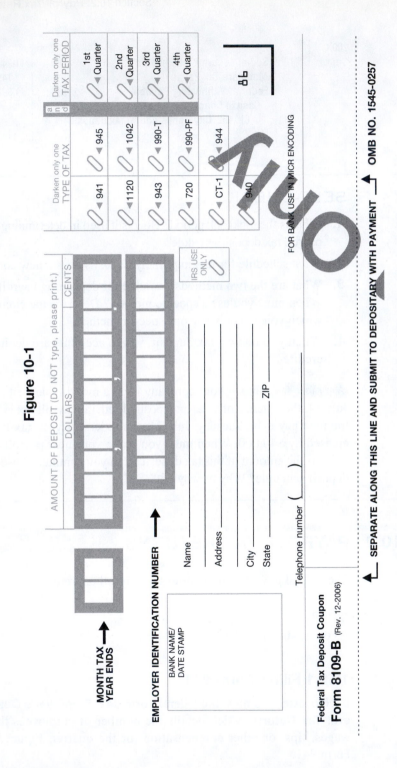

Federal Tax Deposit Coupon
Form 8109-B (Rev. 12-2006)

Employers who don't file electronically use the Federal Deposit Tax Coupon.

Figure 10-2

Form 941 for 2007: Employer's QUARTERLY Federal Tax Return

(Rev. January 2007)
Department of the Treasury — Internal Revenue Service

990107

OMB No. 1545-0029

(EIN)
Employer identification number ☐☐ — ☐☐☐☐☐☐☐

Name *(not your trade name)*

Trade name *(if any)*

Address
Number   Street   Suite or room number

City   State   ZIP code

Report for this Quarter of 2007
(Check one.)

☐ **1:** January, February, March
☐ **2:** April, May, June
☐ **3:** July, August, September
☐ **4:** October, November, December

Read the separate instructions before you fill out this form. Please type or print within the boxes.

Part 1: Answer these questions for this quarter.

1 Number of employees who received wages, tips, or other compensation for the pay period including: *Mar. 12 (Quarter 1), June 12 (Quarter 2), Sept. 12 (Quarter 3), Dec. 12 (Quarter 4)* **1** ☐

2 Wages, tips, and other compensation . . . . **2** ☐

3 Total income tax withheld from wages, tips, and other compensation . . . . **3** ☐

4 If no wages, tips, and other compensation are subject to social security or Medicare tax . . ☐ Check and go to line 6.

5 Taxable social security and Medicare wages and tips:

	Column 1		Column 2
5a Taxable social security wages	☐	× .124 =	☐
5b Taxable social security tips	☐	× .124 =	☐
5c Taxable Medicare wages & tips	☐	× .029 =	☐

5d Total social security and Medicare taxes (*Column 2,* lines 5a + 5b + 5c = line 5d) . . **5d** ☐

6 Total taxes before adjustments (lines 3 + 5d = line 6) . . . . . . **6** ☐

7 TAX ADJUSTMENTS (Read the instructions for line 7 before completing lines 7a through 7h.):

7a Current quarter's fractions of cents . . . . ☐

7b Current quarter's sick pay . . . . ☐

7c Current quarter's adjustments for tips and group-term life insurance ☐

7d Current year's income tax withholding (attach Form 941c) . . ☐

7e Prior quarters' social security and Medicare taxes (attach Form 941c) ☐

7f Special additions to federal income tax (attach Form 941c) . . ☐

7g Special additions to social security and Medicare (attach Form 941c) ☐

7h TOTAL ADJUSTMENTS (Combine all amounts: lines 7a through 7g.) . . . . . . **7h** ☐

8 Total taxes after adjustments (Combine lines 6 and 7h.) . . . . . . **8** ☐

9 Advance earned income credit (EIC) payments made to employees . . . . . **9** ☐

10 Total taxes after adjustment for advance EIC (line 8 – line 9 = line 10) . . . . . . **10** ☐

11 Total deposits for this quarter, including overpayment applied from a prior quarter . . . **11** ☐

12 Balance due (If line 10 is more than line 11, write the difference here.) . . . . **12** ☐
Follow the Instructions for Form 941-V, Payment Voucher.

13 Overpayment (If line 11 is more than line 10, write the difference here.) ☐ Check one ☐ Apply to next return.
☐ Send a refund.

▶ You **MUST** fill out both pages of this form and **SIGN** it.

Next ➡

For Privacy Act and Paperwork Reduction Act Notice, see the back of the Payment Voucher.   Cat. No. 17001Z   Form **941** (Rev. 1-2007)

(continued)

Figure 10-2 *(continued)*

990207

Name *(not your trade name)*	Employer identification number (EIN)

Part 2: Tell us about your deposit schedule and tax liability for this quarter.

If you are unsure about whether you are a monthly schedule depositor or a semiweekly schedule depositor, see *Pub. 15 (Circular E),* section 11.

14 ☐☐ Write the state abbreviation for the state where you made your deposits OR write "MU" if you made your deposits in *multiple* states.

15 Check one: ☐ Line 10 is less than $2,500. Go to Part 3.

☐ You were a monthly schedule depositor for the entire quarter. Fill out your tax liability for each month. Then go to Part 3.

Tax liability: Month 1 ☐ .

Month 2 ☐ .

Month 3 ☐ .

Total liability for quarter ☐ . Total must equal line 10.

☐ You were a semiweekly schedule depositor for any part of this quarter. Fill out *Schedule B (Form 941): Report of Tax Liability for Semiweekly Schedule Depositors,* and attach it to this form.

Part 3: Tell us about your business. If a question does NOT apply to your business, leave it blank.

16 If your business has closed or you stopped paying wages . . . . ☐ Check here, and

enter the final date you paid wages ☐ / / .

17 If you are a seasonal employer and you do not have to file a return for every quarter of the year . . ☐ Check here.

Part 4: May we speak with your third-party designee?

Do you want to allow an employee, a paid tax preparer, or another person to discuss this return with the IRS? (See the instructions for details.)

☐ Yes. Designee's name ☐

Select a 5-digit Personal Identification Number (PIN) to use when talking to IRS. ☐☐☐☐☐

☐ No.

Part 5: Sign here. You MUST fill out both pages of this form and SIGN it.

Under penalties of perjury, I declare that I have examined this return, including accompanying schedules and statements, and to the best of my knowledge and belief, it is true, correct, and complete.

X **Sign your name here** ☐

Print your name here ☐

Print your title here ☐

Date ☐ / /

Best daytime phone ( ) –

Part 6: For paid preparers only *(optional)*

Paid Preparer's Signature	
Firm's name	
Address	EIN
	ZIP code
Date / / Phone ( ) –	SSN/PTIN

☐ Check if you are self-employed.

Form **941** (Rev. 1-2007)

IRS Form 941 reports wages and taxes.

The following key information must be included on Form 941:

- Number of employees who received wages, tips, or other compensation in the pay period.
- Total of wages, tips, and other compensation paid to employees.
- Total tax withheld from wages, tips, and other compensation.
- Taxable social security and Medicare wages.
- Total amount paid out to employees in sick pay.
- Adjustments for tips and group term life insurance.
- Amount of income tax withholding.
- Advance earned income credit payments made to employees (see Chapter 9 for an explanation).
- Amount of tax liability per month.

The due dates for Form 941 are shown in Table 10-1.

Table 10-1: Filing Requirements for Form 941

Months in Quarter	Report Due Date
January, February, March	On or before April 30
April, May, June	On or before July 31
July, August, September	On or before October 31
October, November, December	On or before January 31

10.2.2 Filing Form 940

Form 940, Employer's Annual Federal Unemployment (FUTA) Tax Return:
A form filed by employers at the end of the calendar year.

Federal Unemployment Tax Fund (FUTA):
The federal unemployment fund.

State Unemployment Insurance (SUI):
Taxes collected by states for unemployment funds.

Each year, an employer must file IRS **Form 940, Employer's Annual Federal Unemployment (FUTA) Tax Return.** If you ever faced unemployment, you were probably relieved to get a weekly check while you looked for a job—meager as it may have been. Did you realize that unemployment compensation was partially paid by your employer? In fact, an employer pays his or her share of unemployment compensation based on the company's record of firing or laying off employees.

The fund that used to be known simply as Unemployment is now known as the **Federal Unemployment Tax Fund,** or **FUTA** (named after the Federal Unemployment Tax Act). States also collect taxes for unemployment funds. These taxes are referred to as **State Unemployment Insurance (SUI).**

For FUTA, employers pay a federal rate of 6.2 percent on the first $7,000 that each employee earns. Luckily, you don't just have to add

IN THE REAL WORLD

Wanted: Payroll Backup

Terri had quite capably handled the payroll of her brother Dan's printing company in Boulder, Colorado, for more than five years. She met all filing deadlines and had never experienced any major problems. That is until she took off the first week of 2008 to go skiing. A fall left her with a badly herniated disc, which required surgery. Terri would not be able to return to work until the end of February, clearly not in time to meet the January 31 deadline for filing the company's Form 941—not to mention handle the year-end financial reports. Although Terri's payroll system was organized enough that she was able to guide her other sister through the process, Dan has now determined that two employees need to be capable of both understanding and handling the payroll functions.

the state SUI rate on top of that; the federal government allows you to subtract up to 5.4 percent of the first $7,000 per employee, if that amount is paid to the state. Essentially, the amount you pay to the state can serve as a credit toward the amount you must pay to the federal government.

Each state sets its own unemployment tax rate. Many states also charge additional fees for administrative costs and job-training programs. You can check out the full charges for your state at payroll-taxes.com, but to give you an idea of how taxes vary from state to state as of this writing, check out the sampling shown in Table 10-2.

Table 10-2: Sampling of Unemployment Tax Rates by State

State	Percentage Range	For a Salary Up To	New Employer Percentage
California	1.5 to 6.2	$ 7,000	3.4
Florida	0.12 to 6.4	$ 7,000	2.7
Nevada	0.25 to 5.4	$24,600	2.95
New York	0.5 to 8.5	$ 8,500	4.1
Rhode Island	1.69 to 9.79	$14,000	2.62

The rate an employer pays for SUI isn't a set amount but instead a range. The percentage range is based on the company's employment history and how frequently its employees collect unemployment. The employee income amount upon which this percentage is charged also varies from state to state.

How States Calculate the Unemployment Tax Rate

States use four different methods to calculate how much you may need to pay in SUI taxes:

- **Benefit ratio formula:** The state looks at the ratio of benefits collected by former employees to your company's total payroll over the past three years. States also adjust your rate depending upon the overall balance in the state unemployment insurance fund.

- **Benefit wage formula:** The state looks at the proportion of your company's payroll that's paid to workers who become unemployed and receive benefits, and then divides that number by your company's total taxable wages.

- **Payroll decline ratio formula:** The state looks at the decline in your company's payrolls from year to year or from quarter to quarter.

- **Reserve ratio formula:** The state keeps track of your company's balance in the **unemployment reserve account,** which gives a cumulative representation of its use by your former employees that were laid off and received unemployment. This record-keeping dates back from the date you were first subject to the state unemployment rate. The reserve account is calculated by adding up all your contributions to the account and then subtracting total benefits paid. This amount is then divided by your company's total payroll. The higher the reserve ratio is, the lower the required contribution rate.

Unemployment reserve account:
A cumulative representation of its use by former employees that were laid off and received unemployment.

These formulas can be very complicated, so your best bet is to meet with your state's unemployment office to review how your company's unemployment rate will be set.

Calculating FUTA Tax

After you know what your SUI rate is, calculating the actual unemployment taxes you owe isn't difficult. As an example, consider a new company that's just getting started in the state of Florida; it has ten employees, and each employee makes more than $7,000 per year. For SUI taxes, I use Florida's new employer rate of 2.7 percent on the first $7,000 of income. The federal FUTA is the same for all employers—6.2 percent. The calculations for this company's unemployment taxes appear below.

FOR EXAMPLE
See Figure 10-3 for a sample of how employers report FUTA tax on IRS Form 940.

State unemployment taxes (SUI):

$$\$7,000 \times .027 = \$189 \text{ per employee}$$
$$\$189 \times 10 \text{ employees} = \$1,890$$

Federal unemployment taxes (FUTA):

$$\$7,000 \times 0.062 = \$434$$
$$\$434 \times 10 \text{ employees} = \$4,340$$

The company doesn't have to pay the full federal amount because it can take up to a 5.4 percent credit for state taxes paid ($7,000 × 0.054 = $378). Because, in this example, state taxes in Florida are only 2.7 percent of $7,000, this employer can subtract the full amount of Florida unemployment taxes from the federal FUTA tax:

$$\$4,340 - \$1,890 = \$2,450$$

So this company only needs to pay $2,450 to the federal government in FUTA taxes. A company can only take a credit of SUI tax against FUTA tax for no more than $78 per employee. So, every employer pays at least $56 per employee into the Federal FUTA pool.

The unemployment tax return, Form 940, is filed at the end of each year. Figure 10-3 shows Form 940. You can find Form 940 online at www.irs. gov/pub/irs-pdf/f940.pdf.

Depositing FUTA Tax

If your FUTA tax exceeds $500 for the year, you must make at least one quarterly deposit using the same method you use for Form 941 tax deposits (either EFTPS or Form 8109). If you use the Form 8109 coupon, do not combine it with the Form 941 tax deposit; use separate coupons. Do not use Form 8109 if you are an EFTPS filer; you will incur a 10 percent penalty. Make the quarterly deposit check payable to the financial institution that collects your tax deposits. A point to remember is that the deposit rules covering amounts for FUTA are the same as for the FICA plus income tax withheld.

Filing and Paying Unemployment Taxes to State Governments

States collect their unemployment taxes on a quarterly basis, and many states allow you to pay your unemployment taxes online. Check with your state to find out how to file and make unemployment tax payments.

Unfortunately, the filing requirements for state unemployment taxes are more difficult to complete than those for federal taxes. States require you to detail each employee by name and social security number because that's how unemployment records are managed at the state level. The state must know how much an employee was paid each quarter in order to determine his or her unemployment benefit, if the need arises. Some states also require you to report the number of weeks an employee worked in each quarter because the employee's unemployment benefits are calculated based on the number of weeks worked.

Figure 10-3

Form **940 for 2006:** Employer's Annual Federal Unemployment (FUTA) Tax Return

850106

Department of the Treasury — Internal Revenue Service

OMB No. 1545-0028

(EIN)
Employer identification number ☐☐ — ☐☐☐☐☐☐☐

Name *(not your trade name)*

Trade name *(if any)*

Address

Number   Street   Suite or room number

City   State   ZIP code

Type of Return
(Check all that apply.)

☐ **a.** Amended

☐ **b.** Successor employer

☐ **c.** No payments to employees in 2006

☐ **d.** Final: Business closed or stopped paying wages

Read the separate instructions before you fill out this form. Please type or print within the boxes.

Part 1: Tell us about your return. If any line does NOT apply, leave it blank.

1 If you were required to pay your state unemployment tax in ...

    1a One state only, write the state abbreviation . . . . . **1a** ☐ ☐
    - OR -
    1b More than one state (You are a multi-state employer) . . . . **1b** ☐ Check here. Fill out Schedule A.

2

Part 2: Determine your FUTA tax before adjustments for 2006. If any line does NOT apply, leave it blank.

3 Total payments to all employees . . . . **3** ☐

4 Payments exempt from FUTA tax . . . . **4** ☐

    Check all that apply: **4a** ☐ Fringe benefits **4c** ☐ Retirement/Pension **4e** ☐ Other
    4b ☐ Group term life insurance **4d** ☐ Dependent care

5 Total of payments made to each employee in excess of $7,000 . . . . **5** ☐

6 **Subtotal** (line 4 + line 5 = line 6) . . . . **6** ☐

7 **Total taxable FUTA wages** (line 3 – line 6 = line 7) . . . . **7** ☐

8 **FUTA tax before adjustments** (line 7 × .008 = line 8) . . . . **8** ☐

Part 3: Determine your adjustments. If any line does NOT apply, leave it blank.

9 If ALL of the taxable FUTA wages you paid were excluded from state unemployment tax, multiply line 7 by **.054** (line 7 × .054 = line 9). Then go to line 12 . . . . **9** ☐

10 If SOME of the taxable FUTA wages you paid were excluded from state unemployment tax, OR you paid ANY state unemployment tax late (after the due date for filing Form 940), fill out the worksheet in the instructions. Enter the amount from line 7 of the worksheet onto line 10 . **10** ☐

11

Employers report FUTA tax on IRS Form 940.

Each state has its own form and filing requirements. Some states require a detailed report as part of your quarterly wage and income tax reports. Other states allow a simple form for state income tax and a more detailed report with your unemployment tax payment. To give you an idea of what a state form looks like, Figure 10-4 shows the Florida Department of Revenue Employer's Quarterly Report Form UCT-6. Florida doesn't have an income tax, so only unemployment information needs to be filed. Eight other states—Alaska, Nevada, New Hampshire, South Dakota, Tennessee, Texas, Washington, and Wyoming—have no income tax on wages. (New Hampshire and Tennessee do have a state income tax on dividends and interest, however.)

Small Business Accounting in Action ➡

File payroll tax returns quarterly and yearly.

Accounting for Tax Payments

When you pay unemployment tax, you debit the Payroll Taxes expense account and credit the Cash account.

200X Jan.	25	Payroll Taxes	1,890.00	
		Cash in Checking		1,890.00
		Check 226, Florida U.C. Fund, SUI		
	25	Payroll Taxes	4,340.00	
		Cash in Checking		4,340.00
		Check 227, IRS, Form 940, FUTA		

SELF-CHECK

1. What is the difference between Form 940 and Form 941? When is each form filed?

2. Define FUTA and SUI.

3. How do you determine your FUTA rate? What is the maximum combined unemployment rate an employer will pay? What is the employee salary cap?

4. Which accounts are debited and credited when you pay the unemployment tax with the FUTA tax return?

Apply Your Knowledge   You have two employees. In the first quarter of the calendar year, their gross earnings are $6,500 and $7,500, respectively. Your state unemployment agency has assigned you a rate of 3.5 percent, and the salary cap for state purposes is $8,500. What is your SUI tax liability? What is your FUTA liability?

Figure 10-4

Florida Department of Revenue Employer's Quarterly Report
Employers are required to file quarterly tax/wage reports regardless of employment activity or whether any taxes are due.

UCT-6
R. 07/07

Use black ink. Example A - Handwritten Example B - Typed

0123456789 0123456789

| QUARTER ENDING | DUE DATE | PENALTY AFTER DATE | TAX RATE | UT ACCOUNT NUMBER |

☐☐/☐☐/☐☐☐☐

910009999999006805403175009999999900004

Do not make any changes to the pre-printed information on this form. If changes are needed, request and complete an *Employer Account Change Form* (UCS-3).

If you do not have an account number you are required to register (see instructions).

F.E.I. NUMBER

FOR OFFICIAL USE ONLY POSTMARK DATE

UCT-6

Name
Mailing Address
City/St/ZIP

Location Address
City/St/ZIP

1. Enter the total number of full-time and part-time covered workers who performed services during or received pay for the payroll period including the 12th of the month.

1st Month
2nd Month
3rd Month

If you are filing as a sole proprietor, is this for domestic (household) employment only? ☐ Yes ☐ No

US Dollars | Cents

2. Gross wages paid this quarter (Must total all pages)
3. Wages paid this quarter in excess of $7,000. (Only the first $7,000 paid to each employee per calendar year is subject to Florida Unemployment Tax.)
4. Taxable wages for this quarter (Line 2 minus Line 3)
5. Tax due (Multiply Line 4 by Tax Rate)
6. Penalty due (See instructions)
7. Interest due (See instructions)
8. **Total amount due** (Line 5 + Line 6 + Line 7) Make check payable to: Florida U.C. Fund

Reverse Side Must be Completed

Under penalties of perjury, I declare that I have read this return and the facts stated in it are true (sections 443.171(5) and 443.141(2) Florida Statutes).

Sign here: Signature of officer / Date
Title
Phone ( )   Fax ( )

Paid preparers only
Preparer's signature
Firm's name (or yours if self-employed) and address / Date
Preparer check if self-employed ☐
Preparer's SSN or PTIN
FEIN
ZIP
Preparer's phone number ( )

DO NOT DETACH

Employer's Quarterly Report Payment Coupon
UCT-6
R. 07/07

Florida Department of Revenue

COMPLETE and MAIL with your REPORT/PAYMENT. Please write your ACCOUNT NUMBER on check. Be sure to SIGN YOUR CHECK. Make check payable to: **Florida U.C. Fund**

UT ACCOUNT NO.
F.E.I. NUMBER

No number? (See instructions.)

DOR USE ONLY
☐☐/☐☐/☐☐
POSTMARK OR HAND DELIVERY DATE

Name
Mailing Address
City/St/ZIP

UCT-6

U.S. Dollars | Cents

AMOUNT ENCLOSED (if less than $1.00 no remittance is necessary)

PAYMENT FOR QTR/YR

☐ Check here if you transmitted funds electronically.

9100 0 99999999 0068054031 7 5009999999 0000 4

(continued)

Figure 10-4 *(continued)*

Florida Department of Revenue Employer's Quarterly Report

UCT-6
R. 07/07

Employers are required to file quarterly tax/wage reports regardless of employment activity or whether any taxes are due.

QUARTER ENDING

EMPLOYER'S NAME

UT ACCOUNT NUMBER

9. EMPLOYEE'S SOCIAL SECURITY NUMBER

10. EMPLOYEE'S NAME (please print first twelve characters of last name and first eight characters of first name in boxes)

Last Name
First Name / Middle Initial

11. EMPLOYEE'S GROSS WAGES PAID THIS QUARTER

U.S. Dollars | Cents

12. Total Gross Wages This Page (include in Line 2 on Page 1)

DO NOT DETACH

FLORIDA DEPARTMENT OF REVENUE
e Services

Hate paperwork? We can help!

File and pay your Florida unemployment tax **online**.

It's fast, easy, accurate and secure.

Internet Address: **www.myflorida.com/dor/eservices**
Call 800-482-8293 for assistance.

Mail Reply To:
Unemployment Tax
Florida Department of Revenue
5050 W Tennessee St
Tallahassee FL 32399-0180

Like all states, Florida requires employers to list detailed employee information.

10.3 YEAR-END REPORTING

Even though you've diligently filed all your quarterly reports with government agencies, you still have a lot of paperwork to complete at the end of the year.

10.3.1 Filing the W-2 Forms

Form W-2, Wage and Tax Statement:
A form prepared by employers and sent to employees and the federal government.

Although the federal government doesn't require that you prepare a separate wage and tax statement for each employee during the year, it's something you have to do at the end of the year for each employee. The employee form is called the **Form W-2, Wage and Tax Statement.** If you worked for anyone prior to setting up your own company, you surely got at least one of these. The W-2 is the form employers use to report payments made to employees.

When preparing the form through QuickBooks, click on Process Payroll Forms. You get a pop-up screen asking you to select a form; choose Annual Form W-2—Wage and Tax Statement. (Note that you can also generate Forms 940 and 941, which are covered in Section 10.2.)

When you were an employee, you probably noticed that every company you ever worked for waited until the last possible day to provide you with your W-2s. As you prepare these documents for your employees, you gain a better understanding of your previous employers' delay—it takes time to put W-2s together. Preparing these forms can be a very time-consuming task, especially if you want to make sure they're correct.

If you use a computerized accounting system's payroll software package to prepare your W-2s, there's no doubt that the task is much easier, but it still takes time to run the reports and review them to be sure everything is accurate before printing the final forms. Although you can send out corrected W-2s if necessary, filing the additional forms is just a lot of extra work, so you want to avoid correcting a W-2 whenever possible. The best way to eliminate the need for corrections is to be very careful in checking all information on the forms before distributing them to your employees.

Your company may be required to pay penalties if your W-2 forms are prepared incorrectly or aren't filed on time with your employees or with the government. The three levels of penalties for W-2s that are filed incorrectly or late are:

1. $15 for each Form W-2 that you file late or need to correct, provided that late filing is done within 30 days of the due date. The maximum penalty at this level for a company is $75,000. Small companies with average annual gross revenues of $5 million or less face only a $25,000 maximum penalty.

2. $30 for each Form W-2 that you file late or need to correct more than 30 days after the due date but by August 1. The maximum penalty at

this level for large companies is $150,000, and smaller companies face a $50,000 maximum penalty.

3. $50 for each Form W-2 that you file after August 1 or fail to prepare altogether. The maximum penalties at this level are $250,000 for large companies and $100,000 for small businesses.

You can avoid these penalties if you can prove to the federal government that your failure to file W-2s on time was the result of an event beyond your control, such as a fire that destroyed all your records, and not the product of neglect. You must also indicate the steps you took to avoid filing late. You can also avoid penalties if incorrect information on a W-2 wasn't significant or didn't hinder the work of the IRS or the Social Security Administration in processing the W-2 information.

You can be hit with a suit for civil damages if you fraudulently file a W-2 claiming you paid someone wages you didn't actually pay. The person may sue you for damages.

Most of the information required to put together an employee's W-2 should be kept as part of your payroll records and therefore be easy to pull together. When filling out the W-2, which you can see in Figure 10-5, you must supply information for the following boxes:

- **Box 1: Wages, tips, other compensation.** The total in this box should also include the value of any employee bonuses, prizes, awards, or non-cash payments that aren't exempt or excluded from taxes.

- **Box 2:** Federal income tax withheld.

- **Box 3:** Social security wages. Some benefits are exempt from wages for the purposes of federal income tax, but aren't exempt from social security (see Chapter 9 for details).

- **Box 4:** Social security tax withheld.

- **Box 5:** Medicare wages and tips. This amount is likely to be the same as the amount in Box 3, social security wages.

- **Box 6:** Medicare tax withheld.

- **Box 7:** Social security tips. Any tips your employees reported to you should be reported here.

- **Box 8:** Allocated tips. Use this box if you allocate tips among employees.

- **Box 9:** Advance EIC payment. If you paid employees advances on their earned income credit, record the value of those advances in this box.

- **Box 10:** Dependent care benefits. If you provide dependent care benefits to an employee, report the provided amount in this box.

- **Box 11:** Nonqualified plans. In this box, you report any distribution of assets from nonqualified retirement plans, which are plans that don't

Figure 10-5

22222	Void ☐	**a** Employee's social security number	For Official Use Only ▶ OMB No. 1545-0008	

b Employer identification number (EIN)			**1** Wages, tips, other compensation	**2** Federal income tax withheld
c Employer's name, address, and ZIP code			**3** Social security wages	**4** Social security tax withheld
			5 Medicare wages and tips	**6** Medicare tax withheld
			7 Social security tips	**8** Allocated tips
d Control number			**9** Advance EIC payment	**10** Dependent care benefits
e Employee's first name and initial	Last name	Suff.	**11** Nonqualified plans	**12a** See instructions for box 12
			13 Statutory employee ☐ Retirement plan ☐ Third-party sick pay ☐	**12b**
			14 Other	**12c**
				12d
f Employee's address and ZIP code				

15 State	Employer's state ID number	**16** State wages, tips, etc.	**17** State income tax	**18** Local wages, tips, etc.	**19** Local income tax	**20** Locality name

Form **W-2** Wage and Tax Statement   **2007**   Department of the Treasury—Internal Revenue Service

For Privacy Act and Paperwork Reduction Act Notice, see back of Copy D.

Copy A For Social Security Administration — Send this entire page with Form W-3 to the Social Security Administration; photocopies are **not** acceptable.

Cat. No. 10134D

Do Not Cut, Fold, or Staple Forms on This Page — Do Not Cut, Fold, or Staple Forms on This Page

Prepare a Form W-2 for each employee who was paid $600 or more in the year.

meet the requirements for tax-favored status. (Distributions from qualified plans such as 401(k)s are reported on Form 1099-R.)

- **Box 12:** The box contains sections for you to enter codes A through Z, AA, and BB. Each code is for reporting a different type of income. For example, code A is for uncollected social security tax on tips, and code J is for nontaxable sick pay. You can get a complete list of these codes in the IRS publication *Instructions for Forms W-2 and W-3,* available by mail or by visiting www.irs.gov/pub/irs-pdf/iw2w3.pdf.

- **Box 13:** This box contains three checkboxes that you mark according to what applies to the employee:

  - Check the first box, labeled "Statutory employee," for statutory employees whose earnings are subject to social security and Medicare taxes but not subject to federal income tax withholding. An example of a statutory employee is a full-time insurance salesperson that has a business selling for a single insurance company.

- Check the second box, labeled "Retirement plan," if the employee was covered by a qualified retirement plan.

- Check the third box, labeled "Third-party sick pay," if you provide payment as a third party for an employee's sick pay, or if you are an employer reporting sick payments made by a third party. This box is usually used if a third party is paying an employee's workers' compensation. (Workers' compensation is covered in Section 10.4.)

- **Box 14:** Other. This is the place for information you want to share with the employee, such as details about fringe benefits that were included in the total for Box 1.

- **Boxes 15–20:** In these boxes, you report payroll details for state and local tax information.

Usually, you give each employee four copies of his or her Form W-2:

- One for the employee's records.
- One to be filed with federal tax forms.
- One to be filed with state tax forms.
- One to be filed with local tax forms (which aren't always necessary).

You also need to make one copy for your company files and one copy to send to the Social Security Administration.

W-2s for the previous year must be delivered to employees by January 31. However, if you are mailing the W-2s instead of personally delivering them, they can be mailed on or before January 31. If for some reason you can't meet the January 31 deadline, you must file for an extension with the IRS by sending a letter to:

IRS – Enterprise Computing Center – Martinsburg
Information Reporting Program
Attn: Extension of Time Coordinator
240 Murall Drive
Kearneysville, WV 25430

Your letter must include:

- Your business name and address.
- Your employer identification number (EIN).
- A statement indicating that you're requesting an extension to furnish W-2 forms to employees.
- The reason for the delay.
- Your signature or the signature of your authorized agent.

IN THE REAL WORLD

Online Tax Benefits

As the owner of his own painting company, Warren understands the importance of reporting his employees' wage and tax statements on time. Warren had always met the appropriate February deadline for filing Limited Liability Company W-2 and W-3 forms. This year, for the first time, Warren filed electronically. He started by printing the forms off the IRS Web site. Because his records were fairly organized, he then was able to gather the necessary information for each W-2 form. He carefully completed the forms, with the employees' social security number, wages, and social security and Medicare withholdings. He then filled out the W-3 form, totalling the wages earned and taxes withheld for all the W-2 forms. At that point, it didn't take much to file the forms with the Social Security Administration. Not only did the online system save time for Warren, those who file electronically have until March 31 to do so.

If you don't get an extension and can't show reasonable cause, you'll be penalized based on the amounts discussed earlier in this section. The penalty from the IRS can be even stiffer if it determines that your failure to provide W-2 forms on time was an "intentional disregard of payee statement requirements." If your failure is judged as intentional, the fine is $100 per W-2 with no maximum penalty.

10.3.2 Filing the W-3 Form

Form W-3, Transmittal of Wage and Tax Statements:
A cover sheet for the W-2 forms that are sent to the federal government.

After you complete your W-2s and distribute them to employees, you still haven't seen the last of government paperwork. At this point, you total the numbers and fill out another form that looks very much like the W-2—the **Form W-3, Transmittal of Wage and Tax Statements.** Figure 10-6 shows a sample Form W-3.

The Form W-3 is essentially the cover sheet for the information you send to the Social Security Administration. This form is your last chance to reconcile your numbers before actually filing them with the government. The Form W-3 numbers should match the totals shown on the Form 941 payroll tax returns that you submitted to the federal government quarterly throughout the year.

Form W-3 and government copies of W-2s must be filed with the Social Security Administration by February 28 (February 29 in a leap year). As a

Figure 10-6

DO NOT STAPLE

33333	a Control number	For Official Use Only ▶ OMB No. 1545-0008	
b Kind of Payer ▶ 941 ☐ Military ☐ 943 ☐ 944 ☐ CT-1 ☐ Hshld. emp. ☐ Medicare govt. emp. ☐ Third-party sick pay ☐		1 Wages, tips, other compensation	2 Federal income tax withheld
		3 Social security wages	4 Social security tax withheld
c Total number of Forms W-2	d Establishment number	5 Medicare wages and tips	6 Medicare tax withheld
e Employer identification number (EIN)		7 Social security tips	8 Allocated tips
f Employer's name		9 Advance EIC payments	10 Dependent care benefits
		11 Nonqualified plans	12 Deferred compensation
		13 For third-party sick pay use only	
		14 Income tax withheld by payer of third-party sick pay	
g Employer's address and ZIP code			
h Other EIN used this year			
15 State Employer's state ID number		16 State wages, tips, etc.	17 State income tax
		18 Local wages, tips, etc.	19 Local income tax
Contact person		Telephone number ( )	For Official Use Only
Email address		Fax number ( )	

Under penalties of perjury, I declare that I have examined this return and accompanying documents, and, to the best of my knowledge and belief, they are true, correct, and complete.

Signature ▶   Title ▶   Date ▶

Form **W-3** Transmittal of Wage and Tax Statements   **2007**   Department of the Treasury
Internal Revenue Service

Send this entire page with the entire Copy A page of Form(s) W-2 to the Social Security Administration. Photocopies are not acceptable.

Do not send any payment (cash, checks, money orders, etc.) with Forms W-2 and W-3.

What's New

Relocation of form ID on Form W-3. For consistency with the revisions to Form W-2, we relocated the form ID number ("33333") to the top left corner of Form W-3.

Reminder

Separate instructions. See the 2007 Instructions for Forms W-2 and W-3 for information on completing this form.

Purpose of Form

Use Form W-3 to transmit Copy A of Form(s) W-2, Wage and Tax Statement. Make a copy of Form W-3 and keep it with Copy D (For Employer) of Form(s) W-2 for your records. Use Form W-3 for the correct year. **File Form W-3 even if only one Form W-2 is being filed.** If you are filing Form(s) W-2 electronically, **do not** file Form W-3.

When To File

File Form W-3 with Copy A of Form(s) W-2 by February 29, 2008.

Where To File

Send this entire page with the entire Copy A page of Form(s) W-2 to:

**Social Security Administration
Data Operations Center
Wilkes-Barre, PA 18769-0001**

Note. If you use "Certified Mail" to file, change the ZIP code to "18769-0002." If you use an IRS-approved private delivery service, add "ATTN: W-2 Process, 1150 E. Mountain Dr." to the address and change the ZIP code to "18702-7997." See Publication 15 (Circular E), Employer's Tax Guide, for a list of IRS-approved private delivery services.

For Privacy Act and Paperwork Reduction Act Notice, see the back of Copy D of Form W-2.

Cat. No. 10159Y

Form W-3 is a cover sheet for your W-2 forms.

small businessperson, you can mail Form W-3 and the copies of the W-2s to the Social Security Administration at:

> Social Security Administration
> Data Operations Center
> Wilkes-Barre, PA 18769-0001

Small companies have the option to file the forms online through the Social Security Administration Web site at www.ssa.gov/bso/bsowelcome. htm. Large companies with 250 or more employees must file their W-3s and W-2s electronically. Any business filing electronically can wait until March 31 to file.

If your company reports tips, you need to complete an additional form called Form 8027, *Employer's Annual Information Return of Tip Income and Allocated Tips*. The deadlines for filing Form 8027 are the same as for the W-3—February 28 for regular filings and March 31 for electronic filings.

Small Business Accounting in Action →
Prepare and send Wage and Tax Statements.

SELF-CHECK

1. Define Form W-2 and Form W-3.

2. List five important pieces of information that appear on Form W-2.

3. What are the due dates for Form W-2?

4. Who receives Form W-3? What are the due dates for this form?

Apply Your Knowledge You own a small boutique, and became overwhelmed with the holiday rush. As a result, you filed a late W-2 form. What penalties will you face?

10.4 WORKERS' COMPENSATION INSURANCE

Workers' compensation insurance:
Insurance coverage for employees in case they are injured on the job.

Taxes aren't the only thing you need to worry about when figuring out your state obligations after hiring employees. Every state (except Texas) requires employers to carry **workers' compensation insurance**, which covers your employees in case they're injured on the job. Texas doesn't require this insurance but permits employees injured on the job to sue their employers in civil court to recoup the costs of injuries.

If an employee gets hurt on the job, workers' compensation covers costs of lost income, medical expenses, vocational rehabilitation, and, if applicable, death benefits. Each state sets its own rules regarding how much medical coverage you must provide. If the injury also causes the employee to miss work, the state determines the percentage of the employee's salary you must pay and how long you pay that amount.

The state also decides who gets to pick the physician that will care for the injured employee; options are the employer, the employee, the state agency, or a combination of these folks. Most states allow either the employer or the injured employee to choose the physician.

Each state makes up its own rules about how a company must insure itself against employee injuries on the job. Some states create state-based workers' compensation funds to which all employers must contribute. Other states allow you the option of participating in a state-run insurance program or buying insurance from a private company. A number of states permit employers to use HMOs, PPOs, or other managed-care providers to handle workers' claims. If your state doesn't have a mandatory state pool, you'll find that shopping around for the best private rates doesn't help you much. States set the requirements for coverage, and premiums are established by either a national rating bureau called the National Council on Compensation Insurance, Inc. (NCCI) or a state rating bureau. For information about NCCI and workers' compensation insurance, visit www. ncci.com.

You may find lower rates over the long term if your state allows you to buy private workers' compensation insurance. Many private insurers give discounts to companies with good safety standards in place and few past claims. So the best way to keep your workers' compensation rates low is to encourage safety and minimize your company's claims.

Your company's rates are calculated based on risks identified in two areas:

- **Classification of the business:** These classifications are based on historic rates of risk in different industries. For example, if you operate a business in an industry that historically has a high rate of employee injury, such as a construction business, your base rate for workers' compensation insurance is higher than that of a company in an industry without a history of frequent employee injury, such as an office that sells insurance.

- **Classification of the employees:** The NCCI publishes classifications of over 700 jobs in a book called the *Scopes Manual*. Most states use this manual to develop the basis for their classification schedules. For example, businesses that employ most workers at desk jobs pay less in workers' compensation than businesses with a majority of employees

---

FOR EXAMPLE

The Business Owner's Toolkit Web site features an interactive U.S. map with information about each state's workers' compensation requirements: www.toolkit.com/small_business_guide/sbg.aspx?nid=P05_4403.

Small Business Accounting in Action ➡️
Understand and implement workers' compensation rules.

operating heavy machinery because more workers' are hurt operating heavy machinery than working at desks.

Be careful how you classify your employees. Many small businesses pay more than needed for workers' compensation insurance because they misclassify employees. Be sure you understand the classification system and properly classify your employee positions before applying for workers' compensation insurance.

When computing insurance premiums for a company, the insurer (whether the state or a private firm) looks at employee classifications and the rate of pay for each employee. For example, consider the position of an office worker who earns $25,000 per year. If that job classification is rated at 29 cents per $100 of income, the workers' compensation premium for that worker is $72.50.

Deductible:
The amount that must be paid before an insurance company pays anything.

Most states allow you to exclude any overtime paid when calculating workers' compensation premiums. You may also be able to lower your premiums by paying a deductible on claims. A **deductible** is the amount you would have to pay before the insurance company pays anything. Deductibles can lower your premium by as much as 25 percent, so consider that as well to keep your upfront costs low.

IN THE REAL WORLD

Caring for the Flock and the Finances

The Good Shepherd Nursing Home of Wheeling, West Virginia, is an example of how a company can both protect its workers and lower its workers' compensation expenses. The long-term health care facility has worked with the Occupational Safety and Health Administration for a decade to reduce its worker injuries, typically caused by heavy lifting. The facility purchased a mechanical lifting device to make it easier for employees to move residents from their beds to their chairs. The company also implemented a comprehensive safety program, which resulted in a 62 percent decrease in work-related injuries in its first year. As a result, staffers were able to work more efficiently and safely, reducing the company's exposure to liability and keeping insurance premiums low. Donald Kirsch, the nursing home's administrator, reported that between the years 2000 and 2005, Good Shepherd's workers' compensation insurance premiums were reduced in excess of $800,000, a substantial savings.[1]

SELF-CHECK

1. What is workers' compensation insurance?
2. Who sets the rules regarding workers' compensation insurance?
3. What are the main factors that determine a company's workers' compensation rates?
4. How can you decrease your company's workers' compensation premiums?

Apply Your Knowledge Employee A is in a job classification that is rated 22 cents per $100 of income, and Employee B is in a classification rated 31 cents per $100 of income. Employee A earns $22,500 per year. Employee B's annual earnings are $31,000. What is the total workers' compensation premium for these employees?

10.5 MAINTAINING EMPLOYEE RECORDS

One thing that's clear when you consider all the state and federal filing requirements for employee taxes is that you must keep good employee records. The best way to track employee information using a manual bookkeeping system is to set up an employee ledger and create a separate employee earnings record for each person. Chapter 9 shows a simplified employee earnings record for the purposes of recording payroll. The complete employee earnings record should contain this basic information, most of which is collected or determined as part of the hiring process:

- Name, address, phone number, and social security number.
- Department or division within the company.
- Start date with the company.
- Pay rate.
- Pay period (weekly, biweekly, semimonthly, or monthly).
- Whether hourly or salaried.
- Whether exempt or nonexempt.
- W-4 withholding allowances.
- Benefits information.
- Payroll deductions.
- All payroll activity.

Small Business Accounting in Action ➡ Create a system for maintaining employee records.

You may want to add other columns to your employee earnings records to keep track of things such as sick time, vacation time, and nontaxable wages such as the amount of a 401(k) deduction from gross earnings.

If an employee changes his or her withholding allowances by filing a new W-4 or asks for benefits changes, the employee earnings record must be updated to reflect the changes. Employee earnings records can get very lengthy very quickly. That's why many small businesses use computerized accounting systems to monitor both payroll and employee records.

As discussed in Chapter 3 (Section 3.3.2), certain government agencies have rules about how long you must keep employee information. Check with the U.S. Department of Labor, the Internal Revenue Service, and your state agencies for the current regulations.

CAREER CONNECTION

By enlisting the services of a payroll company, a volunteer organization is better able to serve those in need.

The Lowcountry Food Bank (LCFB), a cooperative of local volunteer organizations, is very good at what it does: it helps feed the poor and hungry in coastal South Carolina. Since it was founded in 1983, LCFB has educated the public about the problems of domestic hunger, excelling in distributing millions of pounds of donated food. The organization has its own internal distribution problem, however—that of getting paychecks to the LCFB's 24 employees in three different locations.

Liz Holt, the LCFB's bookkeeper, knew that the delay in delivering paychecks was creating unhappy employees. "With three locations, we had difficulty getting paychecks out to our employees in a timely manner," says Holt. "Not only did we lose time from the back-and-forth travel out to our branches, but we may have lost a paycheck along the way." It seemed clear that a direct deposit option would help matters, so the LCFB launched a search for the best way to implement the change. Holt looked into different software packages, but was not satisfied with the level of customer service offered until she found the perfect match: Peachtree's direct deposit system. The Lowcountry Food Bank had used other Peachtree software with good results, so the choice made sense. It also made for an easy transition. Holt enrolled and was easily able to set up the direct deposit within the company's existing Peachtree accounting system.

Using the direct deposit system has improved efficiency, reduced paperwork (by 75 percent), and improved employee morale. Now employees have timely deposits as well as the choice of distributing their paychecks in as many as four different accounts. "We no longer have to worry about an outstanding paycheck or if our employees' paychecks will be lost, stolen, or damaged," says Holt.[2]

Tips from the Professional

- Research all of your payroll options.
- Don't compromise on customer service.

SELF-CHECK

1. Describe a method for maintaining employee records in a manual bookkeeping system.

2. What are the basic types of information you must retain for each employee?

3. When would you record a change in an employee's withholding allowances?

4. Which government agencies have rules about retaining employee records?

Apply Your Knowledge Design an employee earnings record for a manual accounting system.

SUMMARY

Section 10.1

- Employers periodically deposit the taxes withheld from employees' earnings, as well as the employer's matching share of social security and Medicare tax.

- In the first calendar year of having employees, a company is on a monthly schedule; after the first year, a company is on either a monthly schedule or a semiweekly schedule, depending on the payroll taxes in the lookback period.

- If a company has accumulated $100,000 or more in taxes on any day during a deposit period, it must deposit those taxes on the next banking day.

- If a company on a monthly schedule has accumulated $100,000 or more in taxes during a deposit period, it must switch to the semiweekly schedule.

- Employers with annual tax payments of more than $200,000 must make their deposits electronically.

- When you record a tax deposit in your accounting records, you debit the liability accounts and credit the Cash account.

Section 10.2

- Employers file federal payroll tax returns quarterly (Form 941).

- Employers also file federal unemployment tax returns once a year (Form 940).

- The federal unemployment tax rate is 6.2 percent. The employer receives a credit for the amount paid according to the state rate (up to a maximum of 5.4 percent state rate).

- The annual earnings cap for federal unemployment tax is $7,000 per employee.

- States have different unemployment tax returns and you must check with your state for its requirements.

Section 10.3

- Employers must give W-2 forms to employees by January 31 and send copies to the Social

Security Administration by February 28. The February 28 deadline is extended to March 31 for employers who file W-2s electronically.

- Form W-3 is a cover sheet for the W-2 copies that are sent to the Social Security Administration.

Section 10.4

- All states except Texas require employers to purchase workers' compensation insurance.

- The workers' compensation premiums are determined by business classification and employee classifications.

Section 10.5

- Employers are required by law to maintain certain employee records. For more information, contact the IRS, the Department of Labor, and your state agencies.

ASSESS YOUR UNDERSTANDING

UNDERSTAND: WHAT HAVE YOU LEARNED?

 Go to **www.wiley.com/college/epstein** to assess your knowledge of the legal implications of employer payroll responsibilities.

PRACTICE: WHAT WOULD YOU DO?

1. The following payroll tax liabilities incurred during September:
   a. Income Tax Withholdings $2,300
   b. Medicare $256
   c. Social Security $2,193
   Give the entry to record theses liabilities.

2. Refer to question 1. Give the entry to pay these liabilities.

3. An employee earns $20,000 per year. Determine the maximum amount of federal unemployment taxation an employer would pay for this employee.

4. Determine the maximum amount, in the state of Nevada, of unemployment insurance a new employer must pay for an employee earning $20,000 per year if the federal government does not give a credit for the federa government unemployment taxes.

5. A new California employer has five employees. Each employee earns more than $7,000 per year. Determine the total amount of federal and state unemployment that must be paid given the federal government is allowing a 5.4 percent credit on the federal unemployment taxes.

6. Refer to question 5. Give the entry to record the total payroll unemployment taxes.

7. Refer to questions 5 and 6. Give the entry to pay the total payroll unemployment taxes.

8. What are the nine states that have no income tax?

9. What are the penalties that an employer can face for filing a late W-2 form?

10. Is there any penalty to the employer if he files fraudulent W-2 forms claiming wages paid that were actually not paid?

BE A SMALL BUSINESS ACCOUNTANT

Filing Late W-2 Forms

A new employer with approximately 20 employees decided to save money by doing his own payroll. This employer had received much advice from friends regarding outsourcing payroll, but since he had taken several accounting courses in college, he thought he could save money and handle the task. This employer actually did very well with the payroll calculations and check distributions, but he was not familiar with all the legalities regarding payroll and made what could be a costly error. His business was in full swing during the last and first quarters of every calendar year, so he did not take the time to complete the necessary steps to assure timely distribution of the W-2 forms. In fact, he was more than 60 days late distributing the forms. He is now told that he could possibly be fined a quite stiff penalty fee for this action. Is there anything he can possibly do to avoid the penalty?

Proper Recording of Payroll Taxes

A not-for-profit agency that is basically funded through grant money initially had one local office with five employees. This agency hired an onsite bookkeeper to do all of the daily financial work. An independent accountant was also kept on retainer to come in on a monthly basis to assure that the bookkeeper was on track with the records.

The bookkeeper kept excellent records and was able to do everything to the accountant's satisfaction. Over a period of time this agency grew to have six locations and 35 employees. As a result, the bookkeeper was keeping up with her daily tasks but was falling behind in the proper recording of the payroll taxes. While the taxes were taken out of the employees' checks and the tax amounts owed by the agency were reserved in a dedicated account, the actual disbursements of the payments were not happening out in a timely fashion. To save money, the agency decided to let go of the independent accountant because the bookkeeper had learned the job and was previously doing so well.

This agency has now been contacted at both the state and the federal levels regarding the late payment of the payroll taxes. What should be done to resolve this problem?

KEY TERMS

Deductible	The amount that must be paid before an insurance company pays anything.
Electronic Federal Tax Payment System (EFTPS)	The federal government's system to receive payroll tax payments by electronic funds transfer.
Federal Unemployment Tax Fund (FUTA)	The federal unemployment fund.
Form 940	Employer's Annual Federal Unemployment (FUTA) Tax Return, a form filed by employers at the end of the calendar year.
Form 941	Employer's Quarterly Federal Tax Return, a form filed by employers at the end of each calendar quarter.
Form 8109	Federal Tax Deposit Coupon, a preprinted coupon used to deposit various taxes including payroll taxes and unemployment taxes.
Form 8109-B	A Federal Tax Deposit Coupon that is not preprinted; you fill in your company information.
Form W-2	Wage and Tax Statement, a form prepared by employers and sent to employees and the federal government.
Form W-3	Transmittal of Wage and Tax Statements, a cover sheet for the W-2 forms that are sent to the federal government.
Lookback period	The 12-month period ending June 30 of the previous calendar year.
State Unemployment Insurance (SUI)	State unemployment funds.
Unemployment reserve account	A cumulative representation of its use by former employees that were laid off and paid unemployment.
Workers' compensation insurance	Insurance coverage for employees in case they are injured on the job.

REFERENCES

1. "Good Shepherd Nursing Home Works With OSHA On-site Consultation, Reduces Workers' Compensation Costs Over $800,000," U.S. Department of Labor Occupational Safety & Health Administration, www.osha.gov/dcsp/success_stories/sharp/ss_good_shepherd.html.
2. "Lowcountry Food Bank Increases Efficiency and Employee Satisfaction with Peachtree Direct Deposit." Sagesoftware.com, www.sagesoftware.com/pdf/pt/ss/pt_lowcountry-ss.pdf.

CHAPTER

11

SPECIAL JOURNALS: SALES AND CASH RECEIPTS

Revenue and Incoming Cash

Do You Already Know?

- How to save time journalizing and posting
- What are sales tax obligations and if you have them
- How to keep track of what people owe you

 For additional questions to assess your current knowledge of using special journals, go to **www.wiley.com/college/epstein.**

What You Will Find Out	What You Will Be Able To Do
11.1 The types of special journals and the purposes of the sales journal and the cash receipts journal	• Use a sales journal to organize transactions for merchandise sold on store credit; use a cash receipts journal to record cash received by your business
11.2 How to post from special journals to a general ledger	• Use special journals to save time posting; use subsidiary ledgers
11.3 How to post sales returns and allowances; how to journalize sales returns and allowances	• Manage paying and recording refunds to customers
11.4 The purpose of an accounts receivable aging summary	• Use an accounts receivable aging summary to manage customer accounts

INTRODUCTION

The general journal used in Chapters 4 through 10 can handle any type of transaction. However, it is not a practical way to record a large number of transactions. Companies with many transactions of specific types set up special journals.

In this chapter you will learn how companies use special journals to increase efficiency. You will also learn how to use subsidiary ledgers to keep track of individual customers.

11.1 SPECIAL JOURNALS

Special journal:
A journal used to record a certain type of transaction (i.e., sales, purchases, cash receipts).

A **special journal** is a journal used to record a certain type of transaction. For example, almost every company keeps one special journal for recording incoming cash and another special journal for outgoing cash.

This book uses four special journals:

- Sales journal.
- Cash receipts journal.
- Purchases journal.
- Cash disbursements journal.

The sales journal and the cash receipts journal are covered in this chapter. Chapter 12 discusses the purchases journal and the cash disbursements journal.

11.1.1 Sales Journal

Sales journal:
A special journal that records transactions for merchandise that your business sells on store credit.

Transactions for merchandise that your business sells on store credit first enter the books in the **sales journal.** Each entry in the sales journal must indicate the transaction date, customer name, invoice number, the price of the merchandise, and the sales tax charged. In the sales journal, the Accounts Receivable account is debited, which increases its value. The transaction also increases the value of the Sales account and the Sales Tax Payable account, which are credited.

Entries are made into the sales journal at the time the invoice is prepared. Some companies simply keep copies of the invoices in a binder, which serves as the sales journal.

Parts of a Sales Journal

Figure 11-1 shows a few days' worth of merchandise sales on store credit.

Figure 11-1

Sales Journal						Page 10
Date	**Inv. No.**	**Customer Account Debited**	**Post Ref.**	**Accounts Receivable Debit**	**Sales Tax Payable Credit**	**Sales Credit**
200X Mar. 1	243	Sandy Smith		212.00	12.00	200.00
1	244	Charlie's Garage		318.00	18.00	300.00
3	245	Padraig Perry		106.00	6.00	100.00
5	246	Jamie Jones		212.00	12.00	200.00

The sales journal is the first point of entry for merchandise sales made on store credit.

The sales journal has seven columns of information:

- **Date:** The date of the transaction.
- **Invoice Number:** The invoice number for the sale.
- **Customer Account Debited:** The name of the customer.
- **Post Ref. (Posting Reference):** A space to indicate that the transaction has been posted to the individual customer's account (as opposed to the general ledger account). The posting process is covered later in this chapter.

Small Business Accounting in Action ➡️
Use a sales journal to organize transactions for merchandise sold on store credit.

- **Accounts Receivable Debit:** The increase in the Accounts Receivable general ledger account.
- **Sales Tax Payable Credit:** The increase in the Sales Tax Payable general ledger account.
- **Sales Credit:** The increase in the Sales general ledger account.

Sales Tax

Wholesale business:
A merchandising business that generally sells products to other businesses.

Retail business:
A merchandising business that sells products directly to the consumer.

Sales tax:
A tax levied by state and local governments on retail sales.

Businesses that sell merchandise are wholesalers or retailers. A **wholesale business** generally sells products to other businesses. A **retail business** sells products directly to the consumer. State and local governments can levy **sales tax** on retail sales. The business making the retail sale must collect the sales tax from the customer and forward it to the government entity.

Sales tax collected from customers is a liability because the business doesn't pay it immediately to the government entity. A business usually collects sales tax throughout the month and then pays it to the government on a monthly basis.

Because tax rates vary from county to county, and even city to city in some states, managing sales taxes can be very time-consuming. Things get messy when you sell products in multiple locations. For each location, you must collect from customers the appropriate tax for that area, keep track of all taxes collected, and pay those taxes to the appropriate government entities when due. In many states, you have to collect and pay local (for the city or county government) as well as state taxes. An excellent Web site for data about state and local tax requirements is the Tax and Accounting Sites Directory at www.taxsites.com/state.html. This site has links for state and local tax information for every state.

States require you to file an application to collect and report taxes even before you start doing business in that state. Be sure that you contact the departments of revenue in the states you plan to operate stores before you start selling and collecting sales tax.

All sales taxes collected from your customers are paid when you send in the Sales and Use Tax Return for your state—you must have the cash available to pay this tax when the forms are due. Chapter 12 goes into detail about completing this form and paying the government.

11.1.2 Cash Receipts Journal

Cash receipts journal:
A special journal used to record all incoming cash.

The **cash receipts journal** is the first place you record cash received by your business. The majority of cash received each day comes from daily sales; other possible sources of cash include deposits of capital from the company owner, customer invoice payments, new loan proceeds, and interest from savings accounts.

In the cash receipts journal, the Cash account is always debited. The account that is credited will vary depending on why the cash is received. For example, cash taken in for sales is credited to the Sales account and the Sales Tax Payable account.

Parts of a Cash Receipts Journal

Figure 11-2 shows a series of transactions recorded in a cash receipts journal.

The cash receipts journal in Figure 11-2 has eight columns of information:

- **Date:** The date of the transaction.
- **Account Credited:** The name of the account credited. Depending on the type of transaction, the account name will be either a credit customer's name or a general ledger account that does not have its own column.
- **Post Ref. (Posting Reference):** A space to indicate where the transaction has been posted. The posting process is covered in Section 11.2.
- **General Credit:** The credit amount for transactions other than cash sales and customer payments on outstanding invoices (in other words, for transactions that are not so common and therefore don't have their own columns).
- **Sales Credit:** The increase in the Sales general ledger account.

Figure 11-2

		Cash Receipts Journal						Page 21
Date		Account Credited	Post Ref.	General Credit	Sales Credit	Sales Tax Payable Credit	Accounts Receivable Credit	Cash Debit
200X Mar.	1	Sales			80.00	4.80		84.80
	2	Sales			550.00	33.00		583.00
	3	Sandy Smith, Ck. 121					212.00	212.00
	3	Sales			150.00	9.00		159.00
	4	Hilary Green, Capital, Memo 25		1,500.00				1,500.00
	4	Sales			500.00	30.00		530.00
	5	Jamie Jones, Ck. 325					212.00	212.00
	5	Sales			600.00	36.00		636.00
	5	Short-term Loan Rec., Hart, Ck. 188		5,000.00				5,000.00
	5	Interest Income, Hart, Ck. 188		50.00				50.00
	5	Padraig Perry, Ck. 567					106.00	106.00

The cash receipts journal is the first point of entry for incoming cash.

- **Sales Tax Payable Credit:** The increase in the Sales Tax Payable general ledger account.
- **Accounts Receivable Credit:** The decrease in the Accounts Receivable general ledger account.
- **Cash Debit:** The increase in the Cash general ledger account.

You can set up your cash receipts journal with more columns if you have other accounts with frequent cash receipts. The big advantage to having individual columns for active accounts is that, when you total the columns at the end of the month, the total for the active accounts is the only thing you have to post to the general ledger accounts, which is a lot less work than posting every transaction individually to the general ledger. This approach saves a lot of time. (Transaction amounts entered in the General Credit column, however, do need to be posted to the general ledger individually.)

Small Business Accounting in Action ➡
Use a cash receipts journal to record cash received by your business.

IN THE REAL WORLD

Journaling the Profits of a Hobby

Adrienne loved to hunt through thrift stores to find unusual vintage jewelry and hats for herself and her friends. When she starting getting orders from other people for the items, Adrienne felt it was time to make her hobby

(continued)

IN THE REAL WORLD *(continued)*

an official business. To get started, she decided to rent some space in a friend's consignment antique shop, mostly to see how things would go. With four jewelry displays and three hat racks, Adrienne opened for business. Because she wanted to keep her finances simple, Adrienne went to an office supply store for some supplies, which included a cash receipts journal to record the business's transactions. The store had a number of different kinds to choose from, but Adrienne chose the one that had the column headings that most suited her needs.

Collecting on Cash Sales

You record most of your incoming cash daily because it's cash received by the cashier, called *cash register sales* or simply *sales* in the cash receipts journal. Most businesses collect some form of cash as payment for the goods or services they sell.

Cash receipts include more than just bills and coins; checks and credit cards also are considered cash sales. In fact, with electronic transaction processing (that's when a customer's credit card is swiped through a machine), a deposit is usually made to the business's checking account the same day (sometimes within just seconds of the transaction, depending on the type of system the business sets up with the bank). The only type of payment that doesn't fall under the umbrella of a cash payment is purchases made on store credit.

Sales slips:
Source documents for cash sales transactions.

Businesses create **sales slips** as source documents for cash sales. Sales slips are generated in one of three ways: by the cash register, by the credit-card machine, or by hand (written out by the salesperson). Whichever of these three methods you choose, the sales slip (also called *sales receipt*) serves two purposes:

- It gives the customer proof that the item was purchased on a particular day at a particular price in your store in case he or she needs to exchange or return the merchandise.
- It gives the store a receipt that can be used later to enter the transaction into the company's books. At the end of the day, the receipts also are used to prove out the cash register and ensure that the cashier has taken in the right amount of cash based on the sales made. (Chapter 8 discusses how cash receipts can be used as an internal control tool to manage your cash.)

You are probably already familiar with sales slips, but just to demonstrate how much useable information can be generated on a sales slip, here's a sample receipt from a sale at a bakery:

Sales Slip 2501			3/01/200X
Item	*Quantity*	*Price*	*Total*
White Serving Set	1	$40.00	$40.00
Cheesecake, Marble	1	20.00	20.00
Cheesecake, Blueberry	1	20.00	20.00
			$80.00
Sales Tax @ 6%			$ 4.80
Total			$84.80
Cash Paid			$90.00
Change			$ 5.20

Receipts contain a wealth of information that's collected for your company's accounting system. A look at a receipt tells you the amount of cash collected, the type of products sold, the quantity of products sold, and how much sales tax was collected.

Unless your company uses some type of computerized system at the point of sale (which is usually the cash register) that's integrated into the company's accounting system, sales information is collected throughout the day by the cash register and printed out in a summary form at the end of the day. At that point, you enter the summarized information about the cash received, total sales, and sales tax collected into the books.

Although in actuality you'd have many more sales and much higher numbers at the end of the day, here's what an entry in the cash receipts journal would look like for sales slip 2501:

Cash Receipts Journal							Page 21
Date	Account Credited	Post Ref.	General Credit	Sales Credit	Sales Tax Payable Credit	Accounts Receivable Credit	Cash Debit
200X Mar. 1	Sales			80.00	4.80		84.80

If you're using a computerized accounting system, you can enter more detail from the day's receipts and track inventory sold as well. Most of the computerized accounting systems include the ability to track the sale of inventory. Figure 11-3 shows you the QuickBooks Sales Receipt form that you can use to input data from each day's sales.

Figure 11-3

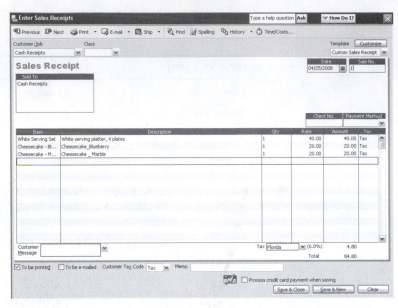

QuickBooks tracks inventory in the Sales Receipt window.

Collecting from Credit Customers

When you record a check received from a customer for outstanding invoices, you list the customer's name and check number as well as the amount. The total amount of Accounts Receivable is reduced by an entry in the Accounts Receivable Credit column:

		Cash Receipts Journal						Page 21
Date		Account Credited	Post Ref.	General Credit	Sales Credit	Sales Tax Payable Credit	Accounts Receivable Credit	Cash Debit
200X								
Mar.	3	Sandy Smith, Ck. 121					212.00	212.00

Recording Owner Investment

On March 4, Hilary Green put $1,500 of her own money into the business. The amount entered in the General Credit column will be posted to the Capital account at the end of the month:

Cash Receipts Journal							Page 21
Date	Account Credited	Post Ref.	General Credit	Sales Credit	Sales Tax Payable Credit	Accounts Receivable Credit	Cash Debit
200X							
Mar. 4	Hilary Green, Capital, Memo 25		1,500.00				1,500.00

Recording Interest Income

Interest:
The cost of borrowing money.

Interest is the cost of borrowing money. For example, when you buy a car using a car loan, you must pay not only the amount you borrowed but also additional money, or interest, based on a percent of the amount you borrowed.

Interest Income:
The general ledger account used to track any income earned in a company's savings account, certificate of deposit, or similar investment vehicle.

Interest Income is the general ledger account used to track any income earned in a company's savings account, certificate of deposit, or similar investment vehicle. If the company loans money to employees or to another company and earns interest on that money, that interest is recorded in this account as well. Because we are discussing incoming cash, this chapter deals with the Interest Income account. Chapter 12 covers accounting for interest expense.

There are two types of interest calculations:

Simple interest:
An amount of interest that is calculated by applying the rate to the principal only.

- **Simple interest** is calculated only on the principal amount of the loan.
- **Compound interest** is calculated on the principal and on interest earned.

Compound interest:
An amount of interest that is calculated by applying the rate to both the principal and any interest previously earned.

Simple interest is simple to calculate. Here's the formula for calculating simple interest:

Principal $\times$ interest rate per time period $\times$ time periods = interest

Assume that someone deposited $10,000 in the bank in a money market account earning three percent (0.03) interest per year. The interest earned over three years is $900:

$$\$10,000 \times 0.03 \times 3 \text{ years} = \$900$$

Unlike simple interest, compound interest is computed on both the principal and any interest earned. You must calculate the interest each year and add it to the balance before you can calculate the next year's interest payment, which will be based on both the principal and interest earned.

Here's how you would calculate compound interest:

$$\text{Principal} \times \text{Rate} = \text{Interest for Year 1}$$
$$(\text{Principal} + \text{Interest for Year 1}) \times \text{Rate} = \text{Interest for Year 2}$$
$$(\text{Principal} + \text{Interest for Years 1 and 2}) \times \text{Rate} = \text{Interest for Year 3}$$

You repeat this calculation for all years of the deposit or loan. The one exception could be with a loan. If you receive the total interest due each month or year (depending on when your payments are due), there would be no interest to compound.

The three-year deposit of $10,000 at three percent per year yields more earnings with compound interest than with simple interest:

$$\$10,000 \times 0.03 = \$300.00 \text{ Interest for Year 1}$$
$$(\$10,000 + \$300) \times 0.03 = \$309.00 \text{ Interest for Year 2}$$
$$(\$10,000 + \$300 + \$309) \times 0.03 = \$318.27 \text{ Interest for Year 3}$$
$$\text{Total Interest Earned} = \$927.27$$

You can see that you'd earn an extra $27.27 during the first three years of that deposit if the interest was compounded. When working with much larger sums or higher interest rates for longer periods of time, compound interest can make a big difference in how much you earn or how much you pay on a loan.

How do you account for loans and interest? Suppose a business makes a loan to another company. The principal is $5,000, the simple interest rate is 12 percent per year, and the term is one month:

$$\$5,000 \times 0.12 \times 1/12 \text{ year} = \$50 \text{ Interest}$$

The amount of the principal ($5,000) is recorded in a current asset account called Short-term Loan Receivable.

When the borrowing company repays the full amount of the principal ($5,000) and the total interest due ($50), the entry in the cash receipts journal will look like this:

		Cash Receipts Journal						Page 21
Date		Account Credited	Post Ref.	General Credit	Sales Credit	Sales Tax Payable Credit	Accounts Receivable Credit	Cash Debit
200X								
Mar.	5	Short-term Loan Rec., Hart, Ck. 188		5,000.00				5,000.00
	5	Interest income, Hart, Ck. 188		50.00				50.00

SELF-CHECK

1. What is the advantage of using a special journal?

2. List the columns that appear in a sales journal. Why doesn't a sales journal have a column for the Cash account?

3. List three transactions that might be recorded in the General Credit column of the cash receipts journal.

4. What is the difference between a sales slip and a customer invoice?

Apply Your Knowledge Your business was overcharged by the electric company for the month of April. You received a refund check in June. Which special journal would you use to record this refund? Identify (a) which general ledger accounts you would use and (b) which columns of the special journal you would use.

11.2 POSTING FROM SPECIAL JOURNALS

If you're working with a computerized accounting software package, you only have to enter a transaction once. The detail is automatically posted to the general ledger and to customer accounts, if needed. The examples in this chapter use a manual accounting system.

At the end of the month, you summarize each special journal by adding up the columns and then use that summary to post amounts to the general ledger. While the examples in this chapter don't list all the transactions for the month, which would of course be a much longer list, they do show how you post the journals at the end of the month.

Before posting the amounts, you "foot" the columns. That is, you add the totals to make sure the columns are in balance. You then post the column totals to the general ledger. This is less time-consuming than posting each individual transaction. Certain entries are also posted to a subsidiary ledger.

Accounts receivable ledger:
A subsidiary ledger that contains details about each customer's account.

Customer account:
A record of the amounts an individual customer has bought on credit as well as the payments received from that customer.

11.2.1 Subsidiary Ledgers

As defined in Chapter 3, a *subsidiary ledger* is a ledger that contains the details of the associated general ledger account. For example, the **accounts receivable ledger** contains details about each customer account. A **customer account** is a record of the amounts an individual customer has bought on credit as well as the payments received from that customer. If you add the totals of all the customer accounts, the sum will equal the balance of Accounts Receivable in the general ledger.

Table 11-1: Relationship Among the Ledgers

Name	Type	Content	Balance
General Ledger	General Ledger	All general ledger accounts	
Accounts Receivable	Subsidiary Ledger	Customers who buy on credit	Equal to the Accounts Receivable balance in the general ledger
Accounts Payable*	Subsidiary Ledger	Vendors from whom you buy on credit	Equal to the Accounts Payable balance in the general ledger

*Chapter 12 discusses the accounts payable ledger.

FOR EXAMPLE

See Figure 11-4 for an example of a customer account from the accounts receivable ledger.

Small Business Accounting in Action ➙ Use subsidiary ledgers.

This book uses two subsidiary ledgers:

• Accounts receivable ledger.

• Accounts payable ledger.

Table 11-1 shows the characteristics of three different ledgers: the general ledger, accounts subsidiary ledger, and accounts payable ledger.

Figure 11-4 shows a customer account from the accounts receivable ledger.

11.2.2 Posting from the Sales Journal

Sales journal transactions are posted to general ledger accounts and to customer accounts. Posting to the general ledger is done monthly—at the end

Figure 11-4

NAME	Sandy Smith				
ADDRESS	xxxx				
Date	**Description**	**Post Ref.**	**Debit**	**Credit**	**Balance**

The accounts receivable subsidiary ledger is organized by customer.

of each month. Posting to the subsidiary ledger is done right away (daily) to keep the subsidiary ledgers current.

Posting from the Sales Journal to the Accounts Receivable Ledger

Every entry in the sales journal affects a customer account and is therefore posted in the accounts receivable ledger. This posting process is shown in Figure 11-5.

1. In the accounts receivable ledger, find the customer account to be debited.
2. In the account, enter the date of the transaction in the Date column.
3. In the account, enter the invoice number in the Description column.
4. In the account, enter the amount in the Debit column.
5. In the account, calculate the balance and enter that amount in the Balance column.
6. In the account, enter the sales journal page number in the Post Ref. column.
7. In the sales journal, enter a check mark in the Post Ref. column.

Figure 11-5

Every sales journal entry is posted to the accounts receivable ledger.

Posting from the Sales Journal to the General Ledger

The totals of three columns are posted from the sales journal to the general accounts:

- Accounts Receivable Debit column.
- Sales Tax Payable Credit column.
- Sales Credit column.

The posting process for the Sales general ledger account is shown in Figure 11-6.

1. In the general ledger, find the Sales account.
2. In the Sales account, enter the date of the last sales journal transaction in the Date column.
3. In the Sales account, enter the total of the Sales Credit column from the sales journal.

Figure 11-6

					Accounts Receivable	Sales Tax Payable	
Date		Inv. No.	Customer Account Debited	Post Ref.	Debit	Credit	Sales Credit
200X Mar.	1	243	Sandy Smith	✓	212.00	12.00	200.00
	1	244	Charlie's Garage	✓	318.00	18.00	300.00
	3	245	Padraig Perry	✓	106.00	6.00	100.00
	5	246	Jamie Jones	✓	212.00	12.00	200.00
					848.00	48.00	800.00
					(115)	(255)	(415)

Sales Journal — Page 10

General Ledger

Sales — 415

Date		Description	Post Ref.	Debit	Credit	Balance Debit	Balance Credit
200X Feb.	28		S9		3,500.00		3,500.00
	28		CR20		9,000.00		12,500.00
	28	Closing	G8	12,500.00			
Mar.	5		S10		800.00		800.00

Sales journal column totals are posted to the general ledger account.

4. In the Sales account, calculate the balance and enter that amount in the Credit Balance column.

5. In the Sales account, enter the sales journal page number in the Post Ref. column.

6. In the sales journal, enter the Sales account number (in parentheses) below the column total.

Repeat the process for the Sales Tax Payable account and the Accounts Receivable account, using a debit for the latter account.

11.2.3 Posting from the Cash Receipts Journal

Transactions in the cash receipts journal are posted to general ledger accounts (at the end of the month) and, in some cases, to customer accounts.

Posting from the Cash Receipts Journal to the Accounts Receivable Ledger

The cash receipts journal is used to record all incoming cash. When the incoming cash is payment of a customer's outstanding invoice, that transaction must be posted to the accounts receivable ledger. This process is shown in Figure 11-7.

Figure 11-7

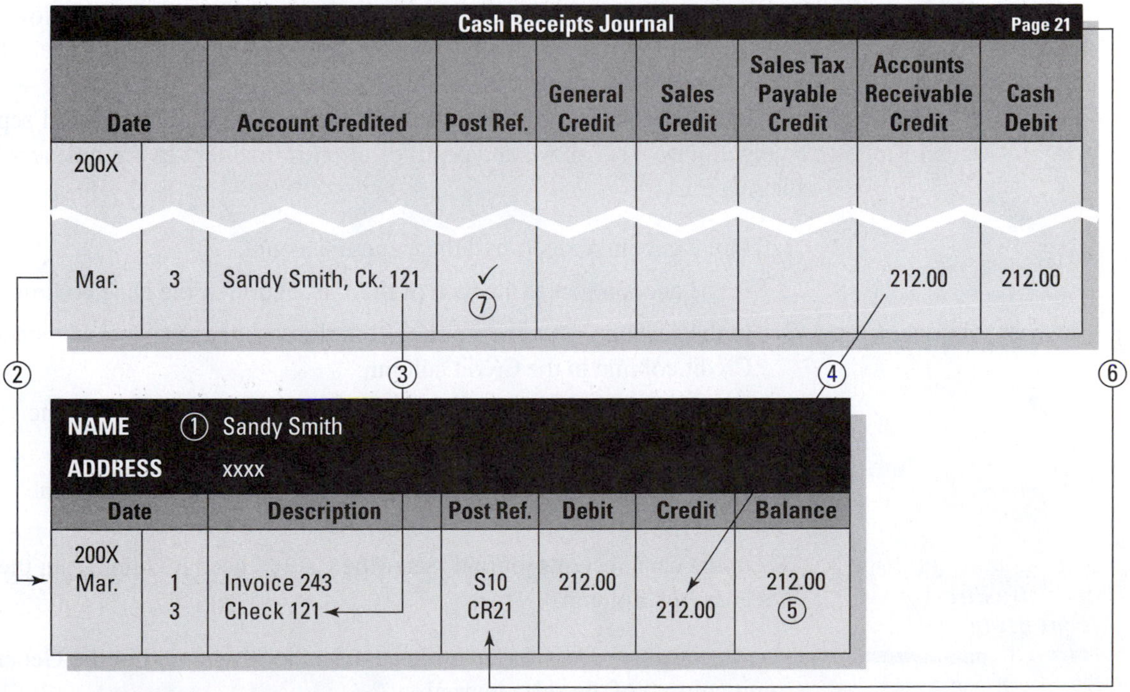

Customer payments are posted from the cash receipts journal to the accounts receivable ledger.

1. In the accounts receivable ledger, find the customer account to be credited.

2. In the account, enter the date of the transaction in the Date column.

3. In the account, enter the check number in the Description column.

4. In the account, enter the amount in the Credit column.

5. In the account, calculate the balance and enter that amount in the Balance column.

6. In the account, enter the cash receipts journal page number in the Post Ref. column.

7. In the sales journal, enter a check mark in the Post Ref. column.

Posting from the Cash Receipts Journal to the General Ledger

Transactions are posted from the cash receipts journal to the general ledger in two ways:

*   By column total.
*   By individual account (General Credit column).

The method for posting column totals is similar to that already described in "Posting from the Sales Journal to the General Ledger." The column totals in the cash receipts journal are used to post the following transactions: Sales credits, Sales Tax Payable credits, Accounts Receivable credits, and Cash debits.

Each transaction in the General Credit column must be posted separately. Figure 11-8 shows the posting for an investment in the business by the owner.

1. In the general ledger, find the Capital account.

2. In the account, enter the date of the transaction in the Date column.

3. In the account, enter the amount from the cash receipts journal General Credit column in the Credit column.

4. In the account, calculate the balance and enter that amount in the Balance column.

5. In the account, enter the cash receipts journal page number in the Post Ref. column.

6. In the cash receipts journal, enter the Capital account number in the Post Ref. column.

Small Business Accounting in Action ➡ Use special journals to save time posting.

Repeat the process for any other transactions recorded in the General Credit column of the sales journal.

Figure 11-9 shows the cash receipts journal after posting.

Figure 11-8

Cash Receipts Journal — Page 21

Date		Account Credited	Post Ref.	General Credit	Sales Credit	Sales Tax Payable Credit	Accounts Receivable Credit	Cash Debit
200X								
Mar.	4	Hilary Green, Capital, Memo 25	315	1,500.00				1,500.00

General Ledger

Hilary Green, Capital — 315

Date		Description	Post Ref.	Debit	Credit	Balance Debit	Balance Credit
200X							
Feb.	14	Balance forward					7,300.00
	20		CR20		2,000.00		9,300.00
Mar.	4		CR21		1,500.00		10,800.00

Sales journal column totals are posted to the general ledger account.

Figure 11-9

Cash Receipts Journal — Page 21

Date		Account Credited	Post Ref.	General Credit	Sales Credit	Sales Tax Payable Credit	Accounts Receivable Credit	Cash Debit
200X								
Mar.	1	Sales			80.00	4.80		84.80
	2	Sales			550.00	33.00		583.00
	3	Sandy Smith, Ck. 121	✓				212.00	212.00
	3	Sales			150.00	9.00		159.00
	4	Hilary Green, Capital, Memo 25	315	1,500.00				1,500.00
	4	Sales			500.00	30.00		530.00
	5	Jamie Jones, Ck. 325	✓				106.00	106.00
	5	Sales			600.00	36.00		636.00
	5	Short-term Loan Rec., Hart, Ck. 188	125	5,000.00				5,000.00
	5	Interest Income, Hart, Ck. 188	715	50.00				50.00
	5	Padraig Perry, Ck. 567	✓				212.00	212.00
				6,550.00	1,880.00	112.80	530.00	9,072.80
					(415)	(255)	(115)	(105)

A posted cash receipts journal.

SELF-CHECK

1. What is a subsidiary ledger? Give two examples.

2. Which is more time-consuming: posting a group of transactions from a special journal to a subsidiary ledger or posting a group of transactions from a special journal to the general ledger? Explain your answer.

3. True or False? Every transaction in the sales journal is posted to a subsidiary ledger. Explain your answer.

4. True or False? Every transaction in the cash receipts journal is posted to a subsidiary ledger. Explain your answer.

Apply Your Knowledge You are researching a customer's account in the accounts receivable ledger. Which journals might you see referenced on the ledger page?

11.3 SALES RETURNS AND ALLOWANCES

Sales return:
A company's acceptance of a return of merchandise from a customer.

A **sales return** is your company's acceptance of a return of merchandise from a customer. Most stores deal with sales returns on a regular basis. It's common for customers to return items they've purchased because the item is defective, they've changed their minds, or for any other reason. Instituting a no-return policy is guaranteed to produce unhappy customers, so to maintain good customer relations, you should allow sales returns.

Usually, a business posts a set of rules for returns that may include:

- Returns will only be allowed within 30 days of purchase.
- You must have a receipt to return an item.
- If you return an item without a receipt, you can receive only store credit.

You can set up whatever rules you want for returns. For internal control purposes, the key to returns is monitoring how your staff handles them. In most cases, you should require a manager's approval on returns. Also, be sure your staff pays close attention to how the customer originally paid for the item being returned. You certainly don't want to give a customer cash if he or she paid on store credit—that's just handing over your money! After a return is approved, the cashier returns the amount that was previously paid by cash or credit card.

Customers who bought the items on store credit don't get any money back. That's because they didn't pay anything when they purchased the item, but expected to be billed later. Instead, a form is filled out so that the amount of the original purchase can be subtracted from the customer's store credit account.

Sales allowance:
A reduction in the price originally charged for the merchandise.

Sales Returns and Allowances:
The contra revenue account used to track sales returns and sales allowances.

Contra revenue account:
A contra account with a normal debit balance.

Small Business Accounting in Action

Manage paying and recording sales refunds to customers.

A **sales allowance** is a reduction in the price originally charged for the merchandise. This situation occurs when something is wrong with the merchandise, but the customer chooses to keep it anyway.

11.3.1 Journalizing Sales Returns and Allowances

Sales returns and allowances are recorded in the **Sales Returns and Allowances** account. This is a contra revenue account. Chapter 6 defines a *contra account* as an account whose normal balance is the opposite of a related account's normal balance. A **contra revenue account** has a normal debit balance. The amount in Sales Returns and Allowances reduces the amount of sales reported on the income statement.

Sales returns and allowances are often recorded in the general journal. Companies with many sales returns and allowances might set up a special journal for this purpose.

11.3.2 Posting Sales Returns and Allowances

Like all transactions, sales returns and sales allowances are posted to the general ledger. If the original sale was on store credit, the return or allowance is also posted to a customer account. The process of posting a sales return or sales allowance is similar to that of posting any transaction from the general journal. (See Figure 5-2 in Chapter 5 for an illustration of posting from the general journal.)

There is one important difference if the return or allowance is for merchandise that the customer bought on store credit. In the general journal, you draw a diagonal line in the Post Ref. column for the Accounts Receivable account. Below the diagonal line, you enter a check mark as the posting reference

IN THE REAL WORLD

Putting a Sales Allowance to Good Use

Beverly and her husband build and sell custom-made playhouses in Connecticut. During a delivery to a customer who lived in a rural area, a mile down an unpaved road, the side of the playhouse was scratched by a broken tree branch. The customer called to complain right away. Instead of paying $250 to send a painter out to make the repair, Beverly offered to lower the price of the playhouse by $100, explaining that the customer would be able to paint it herself if Beverly were to send the paint color out. The customer agreed, and Beverly documented the transaction in the general journal as a sales allowance.

for the accounts receivable ledger. Above the line, you enter the Accounts Receivable account number as the posting reference for the general ledger.

General Journal					Page 9
Date		Description	Post Ref.	Debit	Credit
200X Mar.	5	Sales Returns and Allowances	485	100.00	
		Sales Tax Payable	255	6.00	
		Accounts Receivable/Charlie's Garage	115✓		106.00
		Return of merchandise			

CAREER CONNECTION

A love of art is the driving force behind a mural-painting partnership, but it's an appreciation for the numbers that keeps this business on track.

Danielle Acerra and Dawn Von Suskil are the creative team behind The Muralists Painting Studio (www.themuralists.com) in Bradley Beach, New Jersey. The two have been in business since May 2002, when they received an overwhelmingly positive response to the first mural they painted in an organic juice bar and café. These days, the two professional artists design and execute murals for both interior and exterior spaces in private, public, and commercial spaces.

Whether it's an uplifting mural in a neglected low-income neighborhood or a Tuscan landscape in an upscale restaurant, "We love connecting with the community through our art," says Acerra. Business has grown steadily since they founded the company, and the two spend about 75 percent of their time on the business—with 20 percent of that time spent on the financial aspects of operation. The two have worked out a system to balance all the components of the business: both paint, and Von Suskil concentrates on marketing and promotions while Acerra handles much of the day-to-day accounting.

Though she'd rather be painting than working on the computer, Acerra likes to keep up with the business's finances. "It is important to see in an organized way how much you are spending on supplies, gas, etc. so you know how to properly charge for a job." Using QuickBooks, Acerra enters information from bank statements and receipts to carefully track sales and expenses. "As a small business it is important to be responsible and remember to track all of your expenses and account for everything that comes in and goes out," she says.

The painting partners plan to expand the business to include a broader range of interior design services, sort of a one-stop design shop for businesses and restaurants.

Tips from the Professional

- Learn a computerized accounting program.
- Be organized about tracking expenses.
- Find time—a few hours a week or a couple of days a month—to keep up with the financial end of the business.

SELF-CHECK

1. What is a sales return? How is it different from a sales allowance?

2. What is a contra account? Why is the Sales Returns and Allowances account classified as a contra account?

3. How do you determine which general ledger account to credit when you journalize a sales return? What are the possible accounts you could credit?

4. True or False? Every sales allowance transaction is posted to a subsidiary ledger. Explain your answer.

Apply Your Knowledge Create a set of procedures for cashiers to follow when processing a sales return.

11.4 ACCOUNTS RECEIVABLE AGING SUMMARY

Accounts receivable aging summary:
A report that shows the money due from customers and how long it has been due.

The **accounts receivable aging summary** is a report detailing all outstanding customer accounts. It is usually prepared at the end of an accounting period. This report shows you what money is due from customers and how long it has been due.

For the purpose of proving out the books, the aging report is a quick summary that ensures that the customer accounts information matches what's in the Accounts Receivable general ledger account. Table 11-2 shows an aging summary. For purposes of managing accounts receivable, this report gives you a quick breakdown of which customer accounts are overdue.

FOR EXAMPLE

See Table 11-2 for an example of an aging summary.

Small Business Accounting in Action ➡
Use an accounts receivable aging summary to manage customer accounts.

Table 11-2: Aging Summary: Accounts Receivable as of March 31, 200X

Customer	Current	31–60 Days	61–90 Days	>90 Days
S. Smith	$300			
J. Doe	$100	$300	$200	
H. Harris	$500	$240		
M. Man	$400	$200		
Total	$1,300	$740	$200	

IN THE REAL WORLD

Keeping Tabs on Customer Accounts

Hilltop Liquors distributes a wide variety of beverages to dozens of clients—six of which have credit accounts with the business. Each month, the accountant for the company generates an aging schedule for the business's accounts receivable. This process helps Matt, the owner, keep track of how long customers have owed money on their accounts. The following illustrates the customer aging of those six accounts, giving the total due from each.

Customer Aging	0-30	31-60	61-90	Over 90	Total
Brick Tavern	780				780
Mixes	850	250			1,100
Red's			950		950
Joe's Pub				400	400
Dublin House	1,008				1,008
Bar A			750		750
Total	$2,638	$250	$1,700	$400	$4,988

At this point, the owner has invested $4,988 in accounts receivable, $2,350 of which is past the 30-day due date for payment. This month, Matt decides that he won't continue to sell on credit to Joe's Pub, because this is the fourth time in less than a year that its account is over 90 days late. He also decides to send payment policy reminders to Red's and Bar A, which are over 60 days late. Mixes, however, is Matt's biggest and longest-running client, so Matt feels comfortable about being flexible with that payment.

SELF-CHECK

1. What is the accounts receivable aging summary?
2. What specific items of information are provided in the accounts receivable aging summary?
3. According to the report shown in Table 11-2, during which period of time are outstanding accounts still considered current?
4. Describe the practical uses of the accounts receivable aging summary.

Apply Your Knowledge ▸ Create a policy for collecting past due accounts. In your policy, describe how you would use the accounts receivable aging summary.

SUMMARY

Section 11.1

- Special journals help to save time and increase efficiency in recording and posting transactions.
- Four examples of special journals are the sales journal, the cash receipts journal, the purchases journal, and the cash disbursements journal.
- Retailers must collect sales tax from customers, remit the tax to the government, and file sales tax returns.
- The cash receipts journal is used for all incoming cash, including infrequent transactions such as payment on a loan receivable.

Section 11.2

- When posting special journals, you only need to post the total of certain columns to the general ledger. For example, you post the total of the Sales Credit column instead of posting each individual transaction to the Sales account.

- A subsidiary ledger is a ledger that contains accounts of a single type that support a general ledger account.
- If a general ledger account has a subsidiary ledger (like Accounts Receivable has), then you must post individual transactions from the special journal to the subsidiary ledger. This is in addition to posting the special journal column total (such as Accounts Receivable Debit) to the general ledger account.

Section 11.3

- Sales returns and allowances are usually recorded in the general journal. If the original merchandise sale was on credit, then the transaction must be posted in the accounts receivable ledger as well as the general ledger.

Section 11.4

- The accounts receivable aging summary is a useful tool for managing customer accounts.

ASSESS YOUR UNDERSTANDING

UNDERSTAND: WHAT HAVE YOU LEARNED?

 Go to **www.wiley.com/college/epstein** to assess your knowledge of using special journals.

PRACTICE: WHAT WOULD YOU DO?

1. Calculate the sales tax in each of the independent situations.

	Sales Price	*Sales Tax Rate*	*Sales Tax*	*Total*
a.	$100	5.5%		
b.	$65	6%		
c.	$315	8.75%		
d.	$683	7%		

2. On April 23, 200X, an entity had a credit sale of $1,050 (excluding taxes) to customer Ransom Oaks. The tax rate for the sale is 7%. Ransom Oaks was billed with invoice #1305.

   a. What is the total dollar amount that the customer owes?

   b. Enter the sale in the Sales Journal (below).

Date	*Invoice Number*	*Customer Account Debit*	*PR*	*Accounts Receivable Debit*	*Sales Tax Payable*	*Sales Credit*

3. Complete the following table using simple interest.

	Principal	*Interest Rate per Time Period*	*Time Periods*	*Interest*	*Principal + Interest*
a.	2,000	6%	4		
b.	5,000	8%	3		
c.	1,100	7.5%	2		

4. Complete the following table using compound interest.

	Principal	Interest Rate per Time Period	Time Periods	Interest	Principal + Interest
a.	1,000	7.5%	2		
b.	1,500	8%	4		
c.	3,000	5%	3		

5. An entity borrowed $15,000 from a financing agency at a 6% interest rate for three years with interest compounded annually.

    a. Calculate the total amount of interest owed for the entire three-year period.

    b. What is the total repayment amount?

6. Refer to question 5. Suppose the initial loan of $15,000 was paid at the end of a two-year period. What is the total repayment amount if the loan is paid in two years?

7. Record the following transactions in the Sales Journal (below). The Sales Tax rate for all transactions is 6%.

    May 13   Invoice #1012, sold $5,000 of merchandise on account to Ray's Services.

           14   Invoice #1013, sold $950 of merchandise to Don Edwin on account.

           17   Invoice #1014, sold $1,520 of merchandise to Cal Development on account.

Date	Invoice Number	Customer Account Debit	PR	Accounts Receivable Debit	Sales Tax Payable	Sales Credit

8. Refer to question 7. Post the transactions in the Accounts Receivable Subsidiary Ledger (below).

Cal Development
Account #1210

Date	Description	Debit	Credit	PR	Debit	Credit

Don Edwin
Account #1220

Date	Description	Debit	Credit	PR	Debit	Credit

Ray's Services
Account #1230

Date	Description	Debit	Credit	PR	Debit	Credit

9. Refer to question 7. Post the information in the general ledger (below).

Accounts Receivable
Account #110

Date	Description	Debit	Credit	PR	Debit	Credit

Sales Tax Payable
Account #240

Date	Description	Debit	Credit	PR	Debit	Credit

Sales Credit
Account #410

Date	Description	Debit	Credit	PR	Debit	Credit

10. Prepare a schedule of the accounts receivable accounts. Does the sum of the accounts receivable subsidiary ledgers equal the Accounts Receivable account balance in the general ledger?

11. Record the following transactions in the Cash Receipts Journal (below).

June 1   Made a cash sale, $350. Sales tax rate is 7.5%.

   3   Received $1,055 payment from Hamilton Agency for an outstanding accounts receivable.

   7   Received $200 payment from Singletary Firm for an outstanding accounts receivable.

Date	Account Credited	PR	General Credit	Sales Credit	Sales Tax Payable Credit	Accounts Receivable Credit	Cash Debit

12. The following transactions occurred in the month of June at Jackson Blue Sales Inc. The tax rate is 6% for all transactions.

June 1   Credit sale of $500 to Jaylin Macon, invoice #3506.

   4   Sale to Andrea Collins, $650, invoice #3507.

   10   Sale to Justin & Craig Co., $2,750, invoice #3508.

a. Record the transactions in the Sales Journal (below).

Date	Invoice Number	Customer Account Debit	PR	Accounts Receivable Debit	Sales Tax Payable	Sales Credit

b. Post the information from the Sales Journal to the Account Subsidiary Ledger (below).

Andrea Collins
Account #1235

Date	Description	Debit	Credit	PR	Debit	Credit

Jaylin Macon
Account #1245

Date	Description	Debit	Credit	PR	Debit	Credit

Justin & Craig
Account #1255

Date	Description	Debit	Credit	PR	Debit	Credit

c. Post from the Sales Journal to the general ledger (below).

Accounts Receivable
Account #110

Date	Description	Debit	Credit	PR	Debit	Credit

Sales Tax Payable
Account #240

Date	Description	Debit	Credit	PR	Debit	Credit

Sales
Account #410

Date	Description	Debit	Credit	PR	Debit	Credit

13. The following transactions are to be recorded in the Cash Receipts Journal for Jackson Blue Sales Inc. Refer to question 12.

July 1   Received payment from Jaylin Macon for the June 1, invoice #3506 sale.

2   Cash sale, $500, excluding 6% sales tax.

12   Received full payment from Justin & Craig Co. for the June 4, invoice #3508, sale.

a. Record the transactions in the Cash Receipts Journal (below).

Date	Account Credited	PR	General Credit	Sales Credit	Sales Tax Payable Credit	Accounts Receivable Credit	Cash Debit

b. Using the completed Accounts Receivable Subsidiary Ledger from question 12, post the relevant information from the Cash Receipts Journal to the Accounts Receivable Subsidiary Ledger (below).

Andrea Collins
Account #1235

Date	Description	Debit	Credit	PR	Debit	Credit

Jaylin Macon
Account #1245

Date	Description	Debit	Credit	PR	Debit	Credit

Justin & Craig
Account #1255

Date	Description	Debit	Credit	PR	Debit	Credit

c. Using the completed general ledger from question 12, post the transactions from the Cash Receipts Journal to the appropriate general ledger (below) accounts. Cash has a $15,000 beginning balance.

Cash
Account #100

Date	Description	Debit	Credit	PR	Debit	Credit

Accounts Receivable
Account #110

Date	Description	Debit	Credit	PR	Debit	Credit

Sales Tax Payable
Account #240

Date	Description	Debit	Credit	PR	Debit	Credit

Sales
Account #410

Date	Description	Debit	Credit	PR	Debit	Credit

14. An entity made a $565 (including sales tax) sale on April 9, 200X. $115 (including $7 of sales tax) was returned on May 2. Give the General Journal entry to record the return.

BE A SMALL BUSINESS ACCOUNTANT

Aging of Accounts Reveals a Touchy Problem

After doing a detailed aging of the accounts receivable, a retailer was able to determine that his best customer was consistently late satisfying his debt. He also realized that the customer would make additional debt prior to satisfying his already existing debt. As a result of this customer consistently paying his debt late, the retailer is now experiencing a cash flow problem and is facing problems with his own debt. The retailer wants to resolve this issue in a manner that benefits both his customer and himself. He is perplexed as to exactly how to handle this problem.

Make suggestions as to how he can handle this problem in a very beneficial and tactful manner.

Credit or Cash Sales

A new business owner is wondering if he should allow credit sales or simply have cash sales. There is much more accounting work involved if the business allows credit sales. However, his sales volume would increase greatly with credit sales. What should he do to help him make the decision?

KEY TERMS

Accounts receivable aging summary	A report that shows the money due from customers and how long it has been due.
Accounts receivable ledger	A subsidiary ledger that contains details about each customer's account.
Cash receipts journal	A special journal used to record all incoming cash.
Compound interest	An amount of interest that is calculated by applying the rate to both the principal and any interest previously earned.
Contra revenue account	A contra account with a normal debit balance.
Customer account	A record of the amounts an individual customer has bought on store credit as well as the payments received from the customer.
Interest	The cost of borrowing money.
Interest Income	The general ledger account used to track any income earned in a company's savings account, certificate of deposit, or similar investment vehicle.
Retail business	A merchandising business that sells products directly to the consumer.
Sales allowance	A reduction in the price originally charged for merchandise.
Sales journal	A special journal used to record transactions on merchandise that your business sells on store credit.
Sales return	A company's acceptance of a return of merchandise from a customer.
Sales Returns and Allowances	The contra revenue account used to track sales returns and sales allowances.
Sales slips	Source documents for cash sales transactions.
Sales tax	A tax levied by state and local governments on retail sales.
Simple interest	An amount of interest that is calculated by applying the rate to the principal only.
Special journal	A journal used to record a certain type of transaction (i.e., sales, purchases, cash receipts).
Wholesale business	A merchandising business that generally sells products to other businesses.

12

SPECIAL JOURNALS: PURCHASES AND CASH DISBURSEMENTS

Purchases and Outgoing Cash

Do You Already Know?

- How to save time recording payments by check
- How to figure out principal and interest on monthly payments
- How to keep track of what you owe to vendors

 For additional questions to assess your current knowledge of using special journals, go to **www.wiley.com/college/epstein.**

What You Will Find Out	What You Will Be Able To Do
12.1 How to use special journals for merchandise credit purchases	• Use the purchases journal to record merchandise purchases on credit
12.2 How to use special journals for cash disbursements	• Record any type of cash payment in a special journal
12.3 The process for posting purchases and payments	• Update your vendor records and the general ledger
12.4 How to determine the aging of accounts payable	• Create a tool to manage vendor accounts

INTRODUCTION

This chapter introduces two special journals that are sometimes used in place of the general journal. The purchases journal is used by merchandising businesses. The cash disbursements journal is used by all types of businesses. In the following sections you will learn how to use these common special journals to save time and increase efficiency.

12.1 PURCHASES JOURNAL

All businesses must have something to sell, whether it is a service, a product they manufacture themselves, or a finished product purchased from some other company. This section discusses a special journal used by companies that sell merchandise. The term *merchandise* refers to goods that a business buys and then sells to customers.

Businesses usually buy merchandise on credit. Transactions for merchandise that your business buys on credit first enter the books in the **purchases journal,** one of the special journals used in a manual accounting system. Each entry in the purchases journal must indicate the transaction date, supplier name, supplier's invoice number, and the amount charged. In the purchases journal, the Accounts Payable account is credited, which increases its value. The transaction also increases the Purchases account.

12.1.1 Purchases Account

Purchases of merchandise for resale are not classified as expenses. Instead, they are referred to as *purchases.* The term has a limited, specific meaning. It refers only to the purchase of merchandise for resale. Tires for the company car and paper towels for the coffee room would not be considered purchases (unless you bought these items for resale). If you bought the tires and paper towels for use in your own business, they would be classified as expenses.

Merchandise purchases are recorded in the **Purchases** general ledger account, which is classified as a cost of goods sold account. **Cost of goods sold** is the actual cost of the merchandise you sell to customers in a single accounting period. The Purchases account is only one element used in computing cost of goods sold. Chapter 15 shows how to compute cost of goods sold.

Cost of goods sold accounts follow the same debit and credit rules as expense accounts. Therefore, the Purchases account has a normal debit balance.

Purchases journal:
A special journal used to record merchandise bought on credit.

Small Business Accounting in Action ➡
Use the purchase journal to record merchandise purchases.

Purchases:
The general ledger account that tracks purchases of merchandise for resale. It is classified as a cost of goods sold account.

Cost of goods sold:
The actual cost of the merchandise sold in a single accounting period. General ledger accounts classified as *cost of goods sold* have a normal debit balance.

12.1.2 Parts of a Purchases Journal

Figure 12-1 shows some store purchase transactions as they appear in a company's purchases journal.

Figure 12-1

			Purchases Journal			Page 7
Date	Inv. No.	Vendor Account Credited	Post Ref.	Purchases Debit	Accounts Payable Credit	
200X Mar. 1	210	Retro China		101.00	101.00	
3	166	Paradise Plates		240.00	240.00	
5	H-0903	Luxury Utensils Inc.		275.00	275.00	

The purchases journal is the first point of entry for merchandise bought on credit.

The purchases journal in Figure 12-1 has six columns of information:

- **Date:** The date of the transaction.
- **Invoice Number:** The vendor's invoice number for your purchase.
- **Vendor Account Credited:** The name of the vendor.
- **Post Ref. (Posting Reference):** A space to indicate that the transaction has been posted to the individual vendor's account (as opposed to the general ledger account).
- **Purchases Debit:** The increase in the Purchases general ledger account.
- **Accounts Payable Credit:** The increase in the Accounts Payable general ledger account.

IN THE REAL WORLD

Journaling Expenses and Purchases

Warner owns a small variety store in Seattle. Although he offers many specialty candy and toy items, most of what he sells is from one large supplier. In preparation for back-to-school season, Warner purchased, on account, items totaling $5,500 from his main supplier. Most of what he purchased is inventory for resale, but the order also included $100 of office supplies. To keep his books in order, he made the following entry in his purchases journal:

(continued)

IN THE REAL WORLD *(continued)*

	Debit	Credit
Purchases	5,400	
Office supplies expense	100	
Accounts payable		5,500

SELF-CHECK

1. What is meant by the term *purchases?*
2. What is meant by *cost of goods sold?*
3. What is the difference between *purchases* and *cost of goods sold?*
4. Are all purchases recorded in the purchases journal? Explain your answer.
5. Name two amount columns in a purchases journal.

Apply Your Knowledge How would you determine whether an item is classified as part of cost of goods sold?

12.2 CASH DISBURSEMENTS JOURNAL

Cash disbursements journal:
A special journal used to record outgoing cash.

The **cash disbursements journal** is the point of entry in your accounting records for all business cash paid out to others. In the cash disbursements journal, the Cash account is always credited. The account that is debited will vary depending on why the cash was paid out. Companies add columns to cash disbursements journals for their most frequent transactions.

12.2.1 Parts of a Cash Disbursements Journal

Small Business Accounting in Action
Record any type of cash payment in a special journal.

Figure 12-2 shows a series of transactions recorded in a cash disbursements journal.

The cash disbursements journal in Figure 12-2 has eight columns of information:

- **Date:** The date of the transaction.
- **Check Number.**

Figure 12-2

Cash Disbursements Journal							Page 12
Date	Account Debited	Check No.	Post Ref.	General Debit	Accounts Payable Debit	Laundry Debit	Cash Credit
200X Mar. 1	Retro China	1970			185.00		185.00
1	Laundry, C.C. Laundry Service Inc.	1971				65.00	65.00
1	Rent, Springfield Land Management	1972		400.00			400.00
3	Laundry, C.C. Laundry Service Inc.	1973				65.00	65.00
3	Credit Card Proc. Fees, American Bank	Bk. Stmt.		155.00			155.00
4	Bank Credit Line Payable, Amer. Bank	1974		150.00			150.00
4	Interest Expense, American Bank	1974		10.00			10.00
5	Note Payable—Truck, American Bank	1975		286.66			286.66
5	Interest Expense, American Bank	1975		100.00			100.00
5	Sales Tax Payable, Fl. Dept. of Revenue	1976		512.00			512.00
5	Paradise Plates	1977			101.00		101.00
5	Laundry, C.C. Laundry Service Inc.	1978				75.50	75.50
5	Specialty Mugs Company	1979			115.00		115.00

The cash disbursements journal is used to record all outgoing cash.

- **Account Debited:** The name of the general ledger account debited or the name of the vendor if the debit is to Accounts Payable. You can omit the general ledger account name if it has its own column (such as the Accounts Payable Debit column).

- **Post Ref. (Posting Reference):** A space to indicate where the transaction has been posted. The posting process is covered in Section 12.3.

- **General Debit:** The debit amount for transactions other than payment of vendor bills and laundry expense (in other words, for transactions that are not frequent and therefore don't have their own columns).

- **Accounts Payable Debit:** The decrease in the Accounts Payable general ledger account.

- **Laundry Debit:** The increase in the Laundry general ledger expense account.

- **Cash Credit:** The decrease in the Cash general ledger account.

This particular business uses a Laundry Debit column. You can set up your cash disbursements journal with different columns for accounts with frequent cash payments.

IN THE REAL WORLD

Keeping Track of Cash

Jake Miller was struggling to keep his Cleveland, Ohio, luncheonette in business. Food costs had risen dramatically, and new competition in the neighborhood was taking its toll. It became increasingly important for Miller to watch every dollar he spent, so he began taking a closer look at his business's finances. Instead of sending his bank statement to his accountant, he reconciled it himself. He carefully compared each cancelled check with his cash disbursements journal, looking for discrepancies. In doing so, he discovered new bank fees that he was not aware of; he made sure to record these fees both in his checkbook and cash disbursements journal.

12.2.2 Paying an Outstanding Bill

When you record checks issued for outstanding bills from vendors, you record the vendor's name and invoice number as well as the check amount. The total amount of Accounts Payable is reduced by an entry in the Accounts Payable Debit column, as shown in Figure 12-2. The name of the vendor should be recorded in the column titled "Account Debited."

12.2.3 Paying Expenses

A cash disbursements journal can have columns that are each devoted to a single type of expense. Payments for other expenses are recorded in the General Debit column.

Using Specific Expense Columns

The example in Figure 12-2 uses one specific expense column, which is titled "Laundry Debit." The total amount of the Laundry Debit column will be posted to the Laundry expense account in the general ledger at the end of the month.

Using the General Debit Column

Some expenses are not recorded frequently. For example, monthly rent payments are a regular cash outflow but not a frequent cash outflow. Cash outflows that do not occur frequently in an accounting period are recorded in the General Debit column. Figure 12-2 shows the monthly rent payment recorded in the General Debit column.

12.2.4 Paying Credit-Card Fees

Credit-card sales are considered cash sales. The cash is recorded immediately because there is no question about whether or not your business will receive it. The bank issuing the VISA or MasterCard assumes the risk of customer nonpayment. Your business always gets paid, unless the customer disputes a specific charge.

You must pay fees to the bank that processes your credit-card sales transactions, which is probably the same bank that handles all your business accounts. Monthly credit-card fees vary greatly depending on the bank you're using and the volume of your credit-card sales.

Each month, the bank that handles your credit-card sales will send you a statement with the following information:

- A list of your company's transactions for the month.
- The total amount your company sold through credit-card sales.
- The total credit-card processing fees charged to your account.

If you find a difference between what the bank reports was sold on credit cards and what the company's books show regarding credit-card sales, it's time to play detective and find the reason for the difference. In most cases, the error involves the charging back of one or more sales because a customer disputes the charge.

Credit-Card Processing Fees:

The general ledger expense account used to track the fees charged by the bank that processes a company's credit-card transactions.

Credit-card fees are deducted from your business bank account. In a computerized accounting system such as QuickBooks, the Reconciliation window allows you to enter the amount of the credit-card fees as you reconcile the bank account. In a manual system, the payment of credit-card fees is recorded in either the general journal or the cash disbursements journal. Whichever method you use, the expense is debited to an account titled **Credit-Card Processing Fees** or something similar. The entry in a cash disbursements journal uses the General Debit column, as shown in Figure 12-2.

12.2.5 Paying Loans and Interest

Interest Expense:

The general ledger account that tracks the expense you incur when you borrow money.

Chapter 11 discusses the concept of *interest* from the point of view of a lender. This section will discuss interest from the borrower's point of view. The **Interest Expense** general ledger account is used to track the amounts of interest you owe.

Businesses borrow money for both short-term periods (12 months or less) and long-term periods (more than 12 months). Short-term debt usually involves some form of credit-card debt or a line of credit. Long-term debt can include a five-year car loan, 20-year mortgage, or any other type of debt that is paid over more than one year.

Credit-Card Interest

When you get a credit-card bill at home, the various sections show you new charges, the amount to pay in full to avoid all interest, and the amount of interest charged during the current period on any money not paid from the previous bill. If you don't pay your credit-card bill in full, interest on most cards is calculated using a daily periodic rate of interest, which is compounded each day based on the unpaid balance.

On many credit cards, you start paying interest on new purchases immediately if you haven't paid your balance due in full the previous month. When opening a credit-card account for your business, be sure you understand how interest is calculated and when the bank starts charging interest on purchases. Some issuers give a grace period of 20 to 30 days before charging interest, while others don't give any type of grace period at all.

Lines of Credit

Line of credit:
The maximum amount you can borrow from the bank.

Bank Credit Line Payable:
The general ledger account that tracks the amount due on a line of credit.

As a business owner, you can usually get a better interest rate using a line of credit with a bank instead of a credit card. A **line of credit** is the maximum amount you can borrow from the bank. Typically, a business owner uses a credit card for purchases, but if he or she can't pay the bill in full, the owner draws money from the line of credit rather than carry over the credit-card balance. When you draw on a line of credit, you debit the Cash account and credit the liability account **Bank Credit Line Payable.**

When you make a payment for money borrowed on a line of credit, you must record the decrease in cash, the amount paid on the principal, and the amount paid in interest. Suppose you make a payment of $160 toward the outstanding amount on your line of credit ($150 principal and $10 interest). Here is the entry in the cash disbursements journal:

Cash Disbursements Journal								Page 12
Date		Account Debited	Check No.	Post Ref.	General Debit	Accounts Payable Debit	Laundry Debit	Cash Credit
200X Mar.	4	Bank Credit Line Payable, Amer. Bank	1974		150.00			150.00
	4	Interest Expense, American Bank	1974		10.00			10.00

Long-Term Liabilities

Promissory note:
A document in which you agree to repay a set amount of money at a specific point in the future at a particular interest rate (also known as note).

Most companies take on some form of long-term debt. This debt is often in the form of a promissory note. A **promissory note** is a document in which you agree to repay someone a set amount of money at a specific point in the future at a particular interest rate. Sometimes it is referred to simply as a *note*. Payments can be monthly, yearly, or some other schedule specified in the note. Most installment loans are types of promissory notes.

Amortization

When recording the payment on a long-term debt for which you have a set installment payment, you may not get a breakdown of interest and principal with every payment. For example, many times when you take out a car loan, you get a coupon book with just the total payment due each month.

Why is this a problem for recording payments? Each payment throughout the term of the loan assigns a different amount for interest and therefore a different amount for principal. No two payments have the same allocations of interest and principal. This is because of amortization. **Amortization** is a systematic plan in which part of each payment is for interest on the amount of principal still outstanding. The rest of the payment is applied to principal.

At the beginning of the loan, the principal is at its highest amount, so the amount of interest due is much higher than later in the loan payoff process when the principal balance is lower. Many times in the early years of notes payable on high-price items, such as buildings, you're paying more interest than principal.

In order to record long-term debt for which you don't receive a breakdown each month, you need to ask the bank that gave you the loan for an amortization schedule. An **amortization schedule** is a breakdown that shows the total payment amount, the amount of each payment that goes toward interest, the amount that goes toward principal, and the remaining principal after each payment. If your bank can't give you an amortization schedule, you can easily get one online using an amortization calculator. BankRate.com has a good one at www.bankrate.com/brm/amortization-calculator.asp.

Suppose a business purchases a truck for $25,000 by making a down payment of $5,000 and signing a 60-month note for $20,000 at an interest rate of 6 percent. Table 12-1 shows the amortization of the first six months of the note on the truck. You can see that the amount paid toward principal gradually increases, while the amount of interest paid gradually decreases.

Amortization:
A systematic plan in which part of each loan payment is for interest on the amount of the principal still outstanding.

FOR EXAMPLE

To view an example of an amortization schedule, go to www.bankrate.com/brm/amortization-calculator.asp.

Amortization schedule:
A breakdown that shows the total payment amount, the amount of each payment that goes toward interest, the amount that goes toward principal, and the remaining balance after each payment.

Table 12-1: Six-Month Amortization Schedule

Month	Payment	Principal	Interest	Remaining Note Balance
1	$386.66	$286.66	100.00	$19,713.34
2	$386.66	$288.09	98.57	$19,425.25
3	$386.66	$289.53	97.13	$19,135.72
4	$386.66	$290.98	95.68	$18,844.75
5	$386.66	$292.43	94.23	$18,552.32
6	$386.66	$293.89	92.77	$18,258.42

The first payment would be recorded in the cash disbursements journal as follows:

	Cash Disbursements Journal							Page 12
Date	Account Debited	Check No.	Post Ref.	General Debit	Accounts Payable Debit	Laundry Debit	Cash Credit
200X Mar. 5	Note Payable—Truck, American Bank	1975		286.66			286.66
5	Interest Expense, American Bank	1975		100.00			100.00

12.2.6 Paying Sales Tax

The concepts of *sales tax* and the *Sales Tax Payable account* are discussed in Chapter 11. Essentially, a business acts as a collection agent for state and local governments by collecting sales tax from customers and then remitting it to the government agencies with Sales and Use Tax Returns.

For example, the state of Florida requires you to file the tax return form monthly, between the 1st and 19th days of the following month. It's considered late on the 20th day of the month.

A payment of sales tax is recorded in the cash disbursements journal as follows:

	Cash Disbursements Journal							Page 12
Date	Account Debited	Check No.	Post Ref.	General Debit	Accounts Payable Debit	Laundry Debit	Cash Credit
200X Mar. 5	Sales Tax Payable, Fl. Dept. of Revenue	1976		512.00			512.00

SELF-CHECK

1. Which two columns appear in any cash disbursements journal?
2. Which special journal would you use to record a cash payment for merchandise?
3. Which account is used to record the interest you pay to lenders?
4. Describe how you would use an amortization schedule to determine the account coding for a monthly note payment.

Apply Your Knowledge Your business has a $20,000 line of credit with the bank. You drew $7,000 on the line of credit. One month later you paid $2,000 in principal and $60 in interest. What is the balance of your Bank Credit Line Payable account?

12.3 POSTING PURCHASES AND CASH DISBURSEMENTS

As discussed in Chapter 11, at month end you summarize each special journal by adding up the columns and then use that summary to post amounts to the general ledger. In other words, posting to the general ledger is done monthly while posting to the subsidiary ledgers is done daily. While the examples in this book don't list all the transactions for the month, which would be a much longer list, they do show how you post the journals at the end of the month.

12.3.1 Posting from the Purchases Journal

Accounts payable ledger:
A subsidiary ledger that contains details about each vendor's account.

Vendor account:
A record of the amounts you have purchased on store credit from an individual vendor as well as the payments made to reduce those amounts.

Transactions are posted to general ledger accounts and, in some cases, to vendor accounts in the accounts payable ledger. The **accounts payable ledger** is a subsidiary ledger that contains details about each vendor account. A **vendor account** is a record of the amounts you owe to an individual vendor as well as the payments you made to the vendor. The total of all the vendor accounts equals the balance of Accounts Payable in the general ledger.

Posting from the Purchases Journal to the Accounts Payable Ledger

Every entry in the purchases journal affects a vendor account and is therefore posted in the accounts payable ledger. The posting process is shown in Figure 12-3.

Small Business Accounting in Action ➤
Post purchases and payments.

1. In the accounts payable ledger, find the vendor account to be credited.
2. In the account, enter the date of the transaction in the Date column.
3. In the account, enter the vendor invoice number in the Description column.
4. In the account, enter the amount in the Credit column.
5. In the account, calculate the balance and enter that amount in the Balance column.
6. In the account, enter the purchases journal page number in the Post Ref. column.
7. In the purchases journal, enter a checkmark in the Post Ref. column.

Figure 12-3

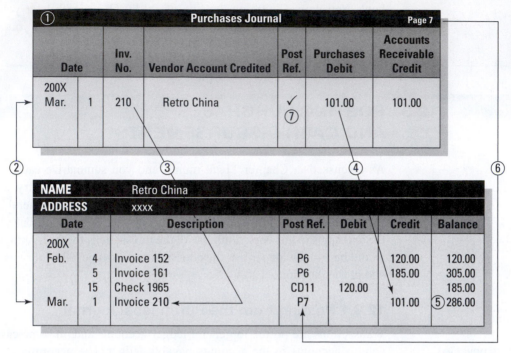

Every purchases journal entry is posted to the accounts payable ledger.

Posting from the Purchases Journal to the General Ledger

At this point it is worth stressing the importance of ensuring equality of debits and credits before posting column totals. The totals of two columns are posted from the purchases journal to the general ledger:

• Purchases Debit.

• Accounts Payable Credit.

The posting process for the Purchases general ledger account is shown in Figure 12-4.

1. In the general ledger, find the Purchases account.

2. In the Purchases account, enter the date of the last purchases transaction in the Date column.

3. In the Purchases account, enter the total of the Purchases Debit column from the purchases journal.

4. In the Purchases account, calculate the balance and enter that amount in the Debit Balance column.

5. In the Purchases account, enter the purchases journal page number in the Post Ref. column.

Figure 12-4

Purchases Journal					Page 7
Date	Inv. No.	Vendor Account Credited	Post Ref.	Purchases Debit	Accounts Receivable Credit
200X Mar. 1	210	Retro China	✓	101.00	101.00
3	166	Paradise Plates	✓	240.00	240.00
5	H-0903	Luxury Utensils Inc.	✓	275.00	275.00
				616.00	616.00
				(515)	(205)

② ⑥ ③ ⑤

① General Ledger							
Purchases							515
						Balance	
Date		Description	Post Ref.	Debit	Credit	Debit	Credit
200X Feb. 28			P6	5,400.00		5,400.00	
28		Closing	G8		5,400.00	–	
Mar. 5			P7	616.00		616.00 ④	

Every purchases journal entry is posted to the general ledger.

6. In the purchases journal, enter the Purchases account number (in parentheses) below the column total.

Repeat the process for the Accounts Payable account, using a credit instead of a debit.

IN THE REAL WORLD

Balancing the Books

Business is booming at Ruby's Roost, an educational toy store, and owner Maya Rogers has learned a lot about accounting since she opened her doors in 2005. To get the unique products her customers demand, Rogers deals with a number of suppliers, many of which are in Europe. Part of keeping her books in order means that she must maintain accurate accounts payable ledgers, which makes it easier for her to double-check the bills she gets from her suppliers. At the close of each month, Rogers reconciles her accounts payable ledger with her general ledger.

Over the years she has caught not only errors that she made in recording amounts in her ledgers, but errors in bills from her vendors.

12.3.2 Posting from the Cash Disbursements Journal

Transactions in the cash disbursements journal are posted to general ledger accounts and, in some cases, to vendor accounts.

Posting from the Cash Disbursements Journal to the Accounts Payable Ledger

The cash disbursements journal is used to record all outgoing cash. When the outgoing cash is payment for an outstanding vendor bill, that transaction must be posted in the accounts payable ledger. This process is shown in Figure 12-5.

1. In the accounts payable ledger, find the vendor account to be debited.
2. In the account, enter the date of the transaction in the Date column.
3. In the account, enter the check number in the Description column.
4. In the account, enter the amount in the Debit column.
5. In the account, calculate the balance and enter that amount in the Balance column.
6. In the account, enter the cash disbursements page number in the Post. Ref. column.
7. In the cash disbursements journal, enter a checkmark in the Post. Ref. column.

Figure 12-5

Payments to vendors are posted from the cash disbursements journal to the accounts payable ledger.

Posting from the Cash Disbursements Journal to the General Ledger

Transactions are posted from the cash disbursements journal to the general ledger in two ways:

- By column total.
- By individual account (General Debit column).

The method for posting column totals is similar to that already described in "Posting from the Purchases Journal to the General Ledger." The column totals in the cash disbursements journal are used to post the following transactions: Accounts Payable debits, Laundry debits, Cash credits.

Each transaction in the General Debit column must be posted separately. Figure 12-6 shows the posting for payment of rent.

1. In the general ledger, find the Rent account.

2. In the account, enter the date of the transaction in the Date column.

3. In the account, enter the amount from the cash disbursements journal General Debit column in the Debit column.

4. In the account, calculate the balance and enter that amount in the Debit Balance column.

Figure 12-6

			Check No.	Post Ref.	General Debit	Accounts Payable Debit	Laundry Debit	Cash Credit
Date		**Account Debited**						
200X Mar.	1	Rent, Springfield Land Management	1972	615	400.00			400.00

Cash Disbursements Journal — Page 12

					Debit	Credit	Balance Debit	Balance Credit
Date		**Description**	**Post Ref.**					
200X Feb.	1		CD11		400.00		400.00	
	28	Closing	G8			400.00	–	
Mar.	1		CD12		400.00		400.00	

General Ledger — Rent — 615

An amount from the General Debit column is posted to the general ledger account.

5. In the account, enter the cash disbursements journal page number in the Post Ref. column.

6. In the cash disbursements journal, enter the Rent account number in the Post Ref. column.

Repeat the process for any other transactions recorded in the General Debit column of the cash disbursements journal.

Figure 12-7 shows the cash disbursements journal after posting.

Figure 12-7

Cash Disbursements Journal							Page 12
Date	Account Debited	Check No.	Post Ref.	General Debit	Accounts Payable Debit	Laundry Debit	Cash Credit
200X Mar. 1	Retro China	1970	✓		185.00		185.00
1	Laundry, C.C. Laundry Service Inc.	1971				65.00	65.00
1	Rent, Springfield Land Management	1972	615	400.00			400.00
3	Laundry, C.C. Laundry Service Inc.	1973				65.00	65.00
3	Credit Card Proc. Fees, American Bank	Bk. Stmt.	620	155.00			155.00
4	Bank Credit Line Payable, Amer. Bank	1974	225	150.00			150.00
4	Interest Expense, American Bank	1974	635	10.00			10.00
5	Note Payable—Truck, American Bank	1975	285	286.66			286.66
5	Interest Expense, American Bank	1975	635	100.00			100.00
5	Sales Tax Payable, Fl. Dept. of Revenue	1976	255	512.00			512.00
5	Paradise Plates	1977	✓		101.00		101.00
5	Laundry, C.C. Laundry Service Inc.	1978				75.50	75.50
5	Specialty Mugs Company	1979	✓		115.00		115.00
				1,613.66	401.00	205.50	2,220.16
					(205)	(645)	(105)

A posted cash disbursements journal.

SELF-CHECK

1. What type of accounts are in the accounts payable ledger?

2. How do you determine the amount to post to the Accounts Payable account from a special journal?

3. True or False? Every transaction in the purchases journal is posted to a subsidiary ledger. Explain your answer.

4. True or False? Every transaction in the cash disbursements journal is posted to a subsidiary ledger. Explain your answer.

Apply Your Knowledge You are researching a vendor's account in the accounts payable ledger. Which journals might you see referenced in the ledger Post Ref. column?

12.4 MANAGING ACCOUNTS PAYABLE

No one likes to send money out of the business, buy you can ease the pain by tracking and paying bills in the Accounts Payable account. You don't want to pay anyone twice, but you also want to be sure you pay bills on time or else your company may no longer get the merchandise, supplies, or other things needed to operate the business.

12.4.1 Purchases Returns and Allowances

Purchase return:
A vendor's acceptance of a return of merchandise you previously purchased.

Purchase allowance:
A reduction in the price that you originally paid for merchandise.

Purchases Returns and Allowances:
The contra account for cost of goods sold account used to track purchases returns and purchases allowances.

Occasionally you will return unsatisfactory merchandise purchased from a supplier. A **purchase return** is a transaction in which your supplier accepts the merchandise and gives you a refund (if you paid cash) or a credit on your account (if you bought on store credit). A **purchase allowance** occurs when you keep the merchandise but the supplier reduces the price originally charged.

Purchases returns and allowances are recorded in the **Purchases Returns and Allowances** account. This is a contra account for cost of goods sold. Chapter 6 defines a *contra account* as an account whose normal balance is the opposite of a related account's normal balance. Since cost of goods sold accounts have normal debit balances, their contra accounts have normal credit balances. The Purchases Returns and Allowances account has a normal credit balance.

A company with many purchases returns and allowances might set up a special journal for this purpose. However, these transactions are usually recorded in the general journal:

General Journal					Page 9
Date		**Description**	**Post Ref.**	**Debit**	**Credit**
200X Mar.	7	Accounts Payable/Thanos Supplies	205 ✓	36.00	
		Purchases Returns and Allowances	535		36.00
		Return of merchandise			

Notice that, in the general journal, you draw a diagonal line in the Post Ref. column for the Accounts Payable account. Below the diagonal line, you enter a checkmark as the posting reference for the accounts receivable ledger. Above the line, you enter the Accounts Payable account number as the posting reference for the general ledger.

12.4.2 Accounts Payable Aging Summary

Accounts payable aging summary:
A report that shows the money owed to vendors and how long it has been due.

The **accounts payable aging summary** is a report detailing all outstanding vendor accounts. It is usually prepared at the end of an accounting period. The report shows you what money is owed to vendors and how long it has been due. Table 12-2 shows an aging summary.

For the purpose of proving out the books, the aging report is a quick summary that ensures that the vendor account information matches what's in the Accounts Payable general ledger account. For purposes of managing accounts payable, this report gives you a quick breakdown of which vendor accounts are overdue.

> **FOR EXAMPLE**
>
> See Table 12-2 for an example of an accounts payable aging summary.

Small Business Accounting in Action →
Create a tool to manage vendor accounts.

Table 12-2: Aging Summary: Accounts Payable as of March 31, 200X

Vendor	Current	31–60 Days	61–90 Days	>90 Days
Carol's Realty	$800			
Helen's Paper Goods		$250		
Henry's Bakery Supplies		$500		
Plates Unlimited	$400	$200		
Total	$1,200	$950		

CAREER CONNECTION

To cope with a big-name competitor, a neighborhood bookstore keeps a close eye on its accounts.

When a large book store chain opened in a nearby town, Rachel and Mark, the owners of a small neighborhood bookstore, were determined to stay the course. The chain's arrival would certainly affect their business, but they were sure they could adapt. While the couple considered ways of increasing sales (adding Internet service and offering music on weekends), they prepared for what they hoped would be a temporary slump in profit. More than ever, the couple used their accounting system's Accounts Aging Summary feature to help them manage the business's cash flow.

As business began to slow, the aging summary became an increasingly important tool for deciding who would get paid and who wouldn't, at least right away. Rather than just hoping for the best and fending off phone calls for payment, they could track which vendors and suppliers needed to be paid and when, and they kept a careful eye on what they considered their "A-list" vendors, which were those that they absolutely relied on to stay in business.

Tips from the Professional

- Take advantage of all the tools offered in your computerized accounting system.
- Look at your financial status as often as necessary, daily even, to stay on track.
- Base your financial decisions on the most current information possible.

SELF-CHECK

1. What is the account classification of Purchases Returns and Allowances?

2. What is the accounts payable aging summary?

3. What specific items of information are provided in the accounts payable aging summary?

4. Describe the practical uses of the accounts payable aging summary.

Apply Your Knowledge Create a policy for paying vendor bills. In your policy, describe how you would use the accounts payable aging summary.

SUMMARY

Section 12.1

- Merchandisers use the Purchases account to record the goods they purchase for resale.
- If the merchandise is bought on credit, the business uses a purchases journal to record the transaction.
- The purchases journal has a Purchases Debit column and an Accounts Payable column.

Section 12.2

- The cash disbursements journal is used for all outgoing cash.
- The cash disbursements journal has a Cash Credit column, a General Debit column, and additional debit columns for frequent transactions.
- Credit-card fees are a cost of doing business.
- Ways that businesses borrow money include credit cards, lines of credit, and promissory notes.
- Amortization causes the gradual shift in allocation of principal and interest in each payment over the term of a loan.

- An amortization schedule provides information about how much of each payment goes to principal and how much goes to interest.
- States require retailers to file Sales and Use Tax Returns within a specified time.

Section 12.3

- Because the Accounts Payable account has a subsidiary ledger, you must post individual transactions from a special journal to the subsidiary ledger. This is in addition to posting the special journal column total (such as Accounts Payable Credit) to the general ledger.

Section 12.4

- Purchases returns and allowances are usually recorded in the general journal. If the original merchandise purchase was on credit, then the transaction must be posted in the accounts payable ledger as well as in the general ledger.
- The accounts payable aging summary is useful for managing vendor accounts.

ASSESS YOUR UNDERSTANDING

UNDERSTAND: WHAT HAVE YOU LEARNED?

 Go to **www.wiley.com/college/epstein** to assess your knowledge of using special journals.

PRACTICE: WHAT WOULD YOU DO?

1. Record the following transactions in the purchases journal (below). All purchases are on account.

Aug   2   Purchased $2,000 of merchandise from McLaurin & Co., invoice #403.

        6   Purchased $2,375 of merchandise from Reed Wholesaler, invoice #721.

      10   Purchased $1.050 of merchandise from Williams Distributors, invoice #108.

Date	Invoice Number	Vendor Account Credited	PR	Purchases Debited	Accounts Receivable Credit

2. Refer to question 1. Post the transactions in the Accounts Payable Subsidiary Ledger (below).

McLaurin
Account #2210

Date	Description	Debit	Credit	PR	Debit	Credit

Reed Wholesaler
Account #2220

Date	Description	Debit	Credit	PR	Debit	Credit

Williams Distributors
Account #2230

Date	Description	Debit	Credit	PR	Debit	Credit

3. Refer to question 1. Post from the Purchases Journal to the General Ledger (below).

Accounts Payable
Account #210

Date	Description	Debit	Credit	PR	Debit	Credit

Purchases
Account #510

Date	Description	Debit	Credit	PR	Debit	Credit

4. a. Provide a schedule of accounts payable from the subsidiary ledger in question 2.

b. Does the sum of the Accounts Payable Subsidiary Ledger accounts equal the account balance of the Accounts Payable account in the General Ledger?

5. Record the following transactions in the Cash Disbursements Journal (below).

Sept.	4	Paid Rent for March, $1,500, check #2014.
	6	Paid McLaurin & Co., $2,000, check #2015.
	10	Paid William Distributors, $1,050, check #2016.

Date	Check Number	Account Debited	PR	General Debit	Accounts Payable Debit	Laundry Debit	Cash Credit

6. Using the completed Accounts Payable Subsidiary Ledger from question 2, post the transactions from the Cash Disbursements Journal in question 5 to the Accounts Payable Subsidiary Ledger (below).

McLaurin
Account #2210

Date	Description	Debit	Credit	PR	Debit	Credit

Reed Wholesaler
Account #2220

Date	Description	Debit	Credit	PR	Debit	Credit

Williams Distributors
Account #2230

Date	Description	Debit	Credit	PR	Debit	Credit

7. Refer to questions 3 and 5. Post the information from the Cash Disbursements Journal to the General Ledger (below). Cash has a $10,000 beginning balance. The Accounts Payable account has been updated to reflect the August transactions.

Cash
Account #100

Date	Description	Debit	Credit	PR	Debit	Credit
Sept.1	Beginning Balance				10,000	

Accounts Payable
Account #210

Date	Description	Debit	Credit	PR	Debit	Credit
Aug.10			5,425	PJ1		5,425

Rent
Account #560

Date	Description	Debit	Credit	PR	Debit	Credit

8. Why are credit-card sales considered cash sales? How does the seller receive the cash for a credit-card sale?

9. Define each of the following terms:
   a. Line of Credit
   b. Interest

10. What is a promissory note? Explain the amortization process in re-paying a promissory installment note.

11. Explain the difference between a purchase return and a purchase allowance.

BE A SMALL BUSINESS ACCOUNTANT

Business Debts on Personal Credit Cards

A young businessman had a home-based clothing business. He was doing well out of the home and decided to open a retail location. He knew that if he was going to actually open this location he would need to greatly increase his stock. As a result he decided to go to many of the clothing wholesalers and purchase additional stock. He used his personal credit cards to finance this venture. He has been at this location about six months and is now experiencing difficulty at the personal level because all of his credit cards are maxed out. His business is doing well and he knows that in a matter of time this problem will be resolved, but in the meantime what should he do?

No Sales Tax on Cash Sales

Joe Calibri is the owner of a small construction company. He has been approached on several occasions by family members and close friends about sales tax. They repeatedly ask that they be allowed to pay him for his work in cash. As a result of the cash sale he is told that he does not have to report it to the IRS and does not have to pay taxes on it. Joe is a hard-working honest businessman and does not want to involve himself in this illegal practice. However, he cares deeply for his friends and family and does not want to hurt them or make them angry. How should he handle this problem?

KEY TERMS

Accounts payable aging summary	A report that shows the money owed to vendors and how long it has been due.
Accounts payable ledger	A subsidiary ledger that contains details about each vendor's account.
Amortization	A systematic plan in which part of each loan payment is for interest on the amount of the principal still outstanding.
Amortization schedule	A breakdown that shows the total payment amount, the amount of each payment that goes toward interest, the amount that goes toward principal, and the remaining balance after each payment.
Bank Credit Line Payable	The general ledger account that tracks the amount due on a line of credit.
Cash disbursements journal	A special journal used to record outgoing cash.
Cost of goods sold	The actual cost of the merchandise sold in a single accounting period. General ledger accounts classified as *cost of goods sold* have a normal debit balance.
Credit-Card Processing Fees	The general ledger expense account used to track the fees charged by the bank that processes a company's credit-card transactions.
Interest Expense	The general ledger account that tracks the expenses you incur when you borrow money.
Line of credit	The maximum amount you can borrow from the bank.
Promissory note	A document in which you agree to repay a set amount of money at a specific point in the future at a particular interest rate. (Also called a note.)
Purchase allowance	A reduction in the price that you originally paid for merchandise.
Purchase return	A vendor's acceptance of a return of merchandise you previously purchased.
Purchases	The general ledger account that tracks purchases of merchandise for resale. It is classified as a cost of goods sold account.
Purchases journal	A special journal used to record merchandise bought on credit.
Purchases Returns and Allowances	The contra account for cost of goods sold used to track purchases returns and purchases allowances.
Vendor account	A record of the amounts you have purchased on store credit from an individual vendor as well as the payments made to reduce those amounts.

CHAPTER

13

MERCHANDISE INVENTORY
Knowing Your Costs

Do You Already Know?

- The two systems for keeping track of inventory
- How to determine inventory costs over a period of time
- How inventory affects net income

 For additional questions to assess your current knowledge of managing inventory, go to **www.wiley.com/college/epstein.**

What You Will Find Out	What You Will Be Able To Do
13.1 Parts of a merchandiser's income statement	• Compute gross profit; differentiate between the two systems of inventory; record initial cost using both systems of inventory
13.2 Different methods for attaching monetary value to inventory	• Evaluate costing methods for your business
13.3 The "lower of cost or market rule"	• Use an established accounting principle

INTRODUCTION

If your company keeps inventory on hand or in warehouses, keeping track of the products you sell is a critical component of asset management. Additionally, how you account for inventory affects your bottom line. While you can't manipulate costs to improve your reported profits, you can choose a costing method that best reflects your type of merchandising operation. In addition, for a merchandising business, keeping records is, perhaps, the most important part of the entire accounting system.

13.1 COST OF GOODS SOLD

As defined in Chapter 12, *cost of goods sold* is the actual cost of merchandise you sell to customers. When preparing your income statement at the end of an accounting period (whether that period is a month, a quarter, or a year), you need to determine the cost of goods sold in order to calculate your profit. "Cost of goods sold" is a line item on a merchandiser's income statement:

$$
\begin{array}{l}
\text{Net sales} \\
-\ \underline{\text{Cost of goods sold}} \\
\text{Gross profit} \\
-\ \underline{\text{Expenses}} \\
\text{Net income}
\end{array}
$$

Gross profit:
The result of net sales minus cost of goods sold.

Net sales:
Total sales reduced by returns, allowances, and discounts: Sales account − Sales Returns and Allowances account − Sales Discounts account.

Gross profit is the amount of profit before subtracting operating expenses. It is the difference between net sales and the cost of goods sold. **Net sales** is your total sales amount reduced by returns, allowances, and discounts.

Small Business Accounting in Action ➡
Compute gross profit.

Inventory:
A current asset account that tracks the merchandise on hand.

13.1.1 Perpetual and Periodic Inventory

Inventory is a current asset account that tracks the products you have on hand to sell to your customers. The balance of the Inventory account can vary depending on the way you decide to track the flow of inventory costs into and out of the business. Inventory cost flow is covered in Section 13.2.

Companies track the amount of physical inventory on hand using one of two systems:

- Periodic inventory.
- Perpetual inventory.

Periodic Inventory

Periodic inventory:
A system for tracking inventory that requires a physical count at certain times.

Physical count:
An actual count of the number of units of each type of good in inventory.

The **periodic inventory** system requires a physical count of the inventory in the stores and in the warehouse. A **physical count** is an actual count of the number of units of each type of good on hand. This count can be done daily, monthly, yearly, or for any other period that best matches your business needs. (Many stores close for all or part of a day when they count inventory.)

The cost of goods sold is determined by default, i.e., by subtraction. Therefore, any items lost to, for example, shoplifting, are automatically included in cost of goods sold because they are not in ending inventory. The formula for computing cost of goods sold under the periodic inventory system is:

$$
\begin{array}{ll}
& \text{Beginning inventory} \\
+ & \text{Net purchases} \\
\hline
& \text{Goods available for sale} \\
- & \text{Ending inventory} \\
\hline
& \text{Cost of goods sold}
\end{array}
$$

Perpetual Inventory

Perpetual inventory:
A system for tracking inventory that adjusts inventory levels as each purchase or sale is made.

Cost of Goods Sold account:
A general ledger account used in the perpetual inventory system.

The **perpetual inventory** system adjusts inventory levels as each purchase or sale is made. In order to use this method, you must manage your inventory using a computerized accounting system that's tied into your point of sale (usually cash registers).

The perpetual system provides more control than the periodic system. So even if you use a perpetual inventory system, it's a good idea to do a physical count of inventory at least once a year to be sure those numbers match what's in your computer system. Because theft, damage, and loss of inventory aren't automatically entered in your computer system, the losses don't show up until you do a physical count of the inventory you have on hand.

The perpetual inventory system uses a **Cost of Goods Sold account** to track the cost of merchandise actually sold to customers. The periodic inventory system does not use this account. Instead, in periodic inventory, the cost of goods sold is the result of the computation shown above. This book uses examples from both methods and will state which method is used in each instance.

Small Business Accounting in Action ➤ Differentiate between the two systems of inventory.

IN THE REAL WORLD

Trimming Time and Increasing Efficiency

As president of Just Moulding in Gaithersburg, Maryland, Kevin Wales appreciates a good inventory system. When he first started the company, which makes custom crown moulding, chair rails, and

(continued)

IN THE REAL WORLD *(continued)*

other decorative wood trim, each time he got a job he would go to the lumberyard and buy what he needed. When he realized that this system was not terribly efficient—he was buying the same material over and over—Wales purchased several thousand feet of lumber and stored it in his warehouse. Using QuickBooks, he entered the transaction and began to keep track of his stock. These days, when Wales gets a new job, he enters the data in QuickBooks, and the computer tells him whether he has enough material to do it. The computer even sends him a reminder to buy more when inventory gets low. Having the perpetual inventory management and accounting functions linked makes good business sense to Wales. "Otherwise I'd have to do the inventory first and then update the accounting system," he Wales. "If they can't talk to each other, you're doing double entry."[1]

13.1.2 Net Purchases

To compute cost of goods sold in a periodic inventory system, you use net purchases. As discussed in Chapter 12, the term *purchases* refers to merchandise that a company buys for resale.

Computing Net Purchases

Net purchases:
A component of cost of goods sold in the periodic inventory system; Net purchases = Purchases account − Purchases Sales and Allowances account − Purchases Discounts account + Freight In account.

The **net purchases** amount is your total purchases adjusted by returns and allowances, discounts, and freight charges. The formula to compute net purchases is:

> Purchases account
> − Purchases Returns and Allowances account
> − Purchases Discounts account
> + Freight In account
> ------------------------------
> Net purchases

These accounts are used only in a periodic inventory system. Chapter 12 covers the Purchases account and Purchases Returns and Allowances account. This section covers the remaining two components of net purchases:

- Purchases Discounts.
- Freight In.

Purchases Discounts

Purchases Discounts:
The contra cost of goods sold account used to track purchases discounts; it is used only in the periodic inventory system.

Cash discount
A discount offered to credit customers to encourage prompt payment of outstanding bills.

Purchases discount:
A cash discount taken by a buyer.

Sales discount:
A cash discount granted by a seller.

Freight In:
A cost of goods sold account that tracks the costs of shipping incoming merchandise; it is used only in the periodic inventory system.

The **Purchases Discounts** account tracks cash discounts granted to you by your merchandise suppliers. It is a contra cost of goods sold account and therefore has a normal credit balance.

Some businesses offer a **cash discount** to encourage prompt payment of outstanding invoices. You can tell whether or not your vendor offers a discount by looking at the invoice terms. If the terms read "n/30" then the total amount (the "net") is due within 30 days and there is no discount. However, if the terms read "2/10, n/30" then you can take a two percent discount if you pay the bill within 10 days, or you can pay the full amount within 30 days.

A cash discount offered by your supplier is a **purchases discount.** If you offer a cash discount to your own customers for prompt payment, it is a **sales discount.**

Freight In

The **Freight In** account tracks shipping charges for the merchandise you purchase. It is classified as a cost of goods sold account and therefore has a normal debit balance. This account is used only for shipping incoming merchandise, not for outgoing shipments of merchandise to customers. Shipping to customers is considered an operating expense, not a cost of goods sold expense.

13.1.3 Recording Initial Cost

The general ledger accounts you use to enter a new merchandise purchase are different for a periodic inventory system and a perpetual inventory system. Let's use the following series of transactions to demonstrate each system:

TRANSACTION
On April 27, 200X, your company received merchandise totaling $1,000 from Plates Unlimited, Invoice 885, terms 2/10, n/30. The shipping company, Fast Times, billed you $50, Invoice XY204, terms n/30.

TRANSACTION
On May 5, 200X, your company paid the bill from Plates Unlimited, Check 9221.

TRANSACTION
On May 25, 200X, your company paid the bill from Fast Times, Check 9265.

Initial Cost in a Periodic Inventory System

In a periodic system, the main purpose is to keep accurate records of the true cost of all of the merchandise purchased during an accounting period. The transactions for a periodic inventory system are shown below in general journal form:

General Journal					Page 12
Date		Description	Post Ref.	Debit	Credit
200X April	27	Purchases		1,000	
		Accounts Payable			1,000
		Plates Unlimited, Invoice 885			
	27	Freight In		50	
		Accounts Payable			50
		Fast Times, Invoice XY204			
May	5	Accounts Payable		1,000	
		Cash			980
		Purchases Discounts			20
		Check 9221, Plates Unlimited, Inv. 885			
	25	Accounts Payable		50	
		Cash			50
		Check 9265, Fast Times, Inv. XY204			

Notice that we never touch the Inventory account in these transactions. The Inventory account balance does not change during the accounting period. At the end of the accounting period, the Inventory account will be adjusted at the same time as certain other accounts.

During the accounting period, costs relating to inventory purchases are recorded in the cost of goods sold accounts:

• Purchases.

• Purchases Returns and Allowances.

• Purchases Discounts.

• Freight In.

Initial Cost in a Perpetual Inventory System

The perpetual inventory system uses one account to record inventory purchases:

• Inventory.

General Journal						Page 12	
Date		Description		Post Ref.	Debit	Credit	
200X April	27	Inventory			1,000		
		Accounts Payable				1,000	
		Plates Unlimited, Invoice 885					
	27	Inventory			50		
		Accounts Payable				50	
		Fast Times, Invoice XY204					
May	5	Accounts Payable			1,000		
		Cash				980	
		Inventory				20	
		Check 9221, Plates Unlimited, Inv. 885					
	25	Accounts Payable			50		
		Cash				50	
		Check 9265, Fast Times, Inv. XY204					

The perpetual inventory system does not use general ledger accounts for Purchases Returns and Allowances, Purchases Discounts, and Freight In. However, companies usually keep supplemental records of those cost elements.

In a perpetual inventory system, the cost of goods sold is recorded each time you sell inventory. It is a "piggyback" entry made at the same time as the entry to record the sale:

General Journal						Page 12	
Date		Description		Post Ref.	Debit	Credit	
200X June	2	Accounts Receivable			1,800		
		Sales				1,800	
	2	Cost of Goods Sold			1,030		
		Inventory				1,030	

Notice the general ledger account used to record the cost of goods sold in a perpetual inventory system:

• Cost of Goods Sold.

Small Business Accounting in Action ➡ Record initial cost using both systems of inventory.

Using Computerized Accounting to Record Initial Cost

When inventory enters your business, in addition to recording the actual costs, you need more detail about what was bought, how much of each item was bought, and what each item cost. You also need to track:

- How much inventory you have on hand.
- The value of the inventory you have on hand.
- When you need to order more inventory.

Accounting software can simplify the process of tracking inventory. Most computerized accounting systems give you the option of using a perpetual inventory system. Figure 13-1 shows the $1,000 merchandise purchase in QuickBooks using the perpetual inventory system.

Figure 13-1

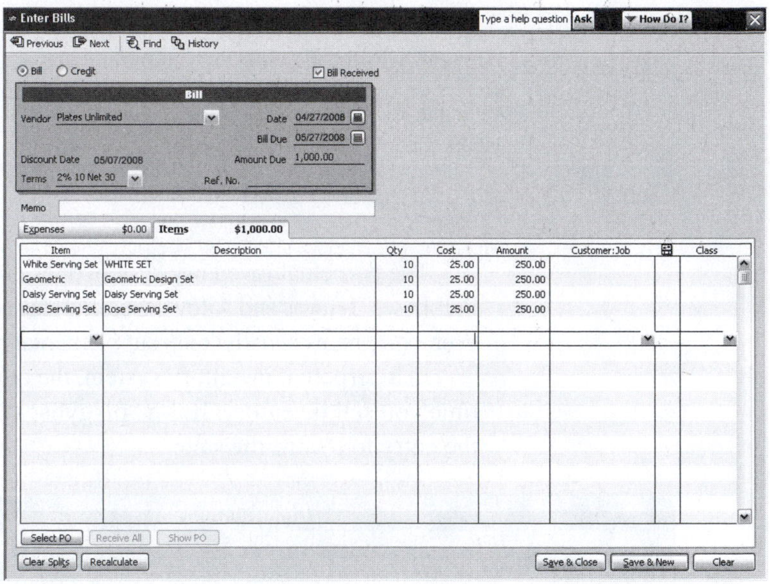

Recording an inventory purchase in QuickBooks.

Notice that on the form in Figure 13-1, in addition to recording the name of the vendor, date received, and payment amount, you also record details about the items bought, including the quantity and cost. By loading each item into the computerized accounting system, you can easily track the physical flow of inventory.

After you complete and save the form that records the receipt of inventory in QuickBooks, the software automatically adjusts the quantity of inventory you have in stock, increases the balance of the Inventory general ledger account, and increases the balance of Accounts Payable. (Remember, we are talking about the perpetual inventory system.)

Figure 13-2 shows how you initially set up an inventory item in QuickBooks. Note that in addition to the item name, two descriptions are added to the system: One is an abbreviated version you can use on purchase transactions, and the other is a longer description that shows on customer invoices (sales transactions). You can input a cost and sales price if you want, or you can leave them at zero and enter the cost and sales prices with each transaction. The first time you set up an inventory item, QuickBooks creates a Cost of Goods Sold account for your chart of accounts.

Figure 13-2

Setting up an inventory item in QuickBooks.

Notice in Figure 13-2 that information about inventory on hand and when inventory needs to be reordered can also be tracked using this form. To be sure your store shelves are never empty, for each item you can enter a number that indicates at what point you want to reorder inventory. In Figure 13-2, you can indicate the "Reorder Point" in the section called "Inventory Information." (A nice feature of QuickBooks is that it gives you a reminder when inventory reaches the reorder point.)

A limitation of using QuickBooks for perpetual inventory is the fact that you have only one option for inventory cost flow. QuickBooks uses the *average cost method*.

CAREER CONNECTION

The realities of business come knockin' on the door of one woman's creative business venture.

It takes more than a clever idea to make a business a success, and Jen Bilik knows more about that than most. In January 2002, Bilik founded Knock Knock, a gift and stationery company whose products typically represent one of the company's many philosophies: "Smartness is fun." Knock Knock, which is based in Venice, California, produces whimsical books, organizational kits, notepads, and an assortment of gifts and other items. Though the products are always fun, the work

(continued)

CAREER CONNECTION   *(continued)*

is not. "People who want to start this kind of company think: 'I'm going to get to be creative all the time,' and that's so not it," Bilik says.

Bilik, who says she spends about 80 percent of her 60-hour workweek on organization and operations, did not have much of a honeymoon period; trouble began in 2002 when the company released it first products. The items sold well enough that it quickly made sense to send the company's manufacturing operations to China. Orders poured in, which was great, but Bilik was left with little time to keep track of the fulfillment company that was supposed to unpack, inventory, and ship the orders. It eventually became clear to Bilik that the company, "just didn't know what they were doing." Inaccurate inventory counts meant serious problems for Knock Knock: The company ran out of stock of its most popular products during the holiday season.

Fortunately, a new fulfillment company has solved that problem, and Bilik is not likely to experience that level of inventory issue in the future.[2]

Tips from the Professional

- Be prepared for growth and change.
- Keep an eye on contractors.

SELF-CHECK

1. What is the formula for gross profit?

2. List the methods used to track the amount of inventory on hand.

3. In a periodic inventory system, which accounts are used to record the initial cost of inventory?

4. When would you use a general ledger account called Cost of Goods Sold?

Apply Your Knowledge   Use the following information to answer questions (a) and (b): You bought $18,000 worth of merchandise on credit. The vendor paid the shipping. Two days later you return $2,000 worth of merchandise to the vendor. Three days after that, you pay the vendor bill. The terms of the bill are 3/10, n/30.

a) Show the debits and credits using the periodic inventory system.

b) Show the debits and credits using the perpetual inventory system.

13.2 INVENTORY COST FLOW

Inventory is often a company's largest current asset. Your inventory system (periodic or perpetual) can tell you how many units of each item you have on hand at the end of an accounting period. But how do you determine the value of that ending inventory? The prices you pay for merchandise can vary throughout the year. Also, if you sell identical items, you don't know exactly which items have been sold and which ones are still in inventory.

In order to place a value on the remaining inventory, you have to make certain assumptions about the flow of inventory costs through your system. As you will learn, the flow of inventory costs doesn't always match the exact physical flow of inventory.

13.2.1 Determining the Value of Ending Inventory

The valuation of ending inventory is a two-step process:

1. Count the inventory.
2. Price the inventory, i.e., multiply the number of units by the price per unit.

A perpetual inventory system keeps a running total of the inventory on hand. The monetary value of the inventory items is determined by the cost flow assumption that you choose when you first set up your inventory system.

13.2.2 Inventory Valuation Methods

The value of ending inventory is arrived at by using one of four cost flow assumptions:

- Specific identification.
- First In, First Out (FIFO).
- Last In, First Out (LIFO).
- Average cost.

Specific Identification

Specific identification:
An inventory valuation method in which you maintain cost figures for each inventory item individually.

In the **specific identification** method, you maintain cost figures for each inventory item individually. Retail outlets that sell big-ticket items such as cars, which might come from the manufacturer with different features installed on each vehicle, use this type of inventory valuation method.

FIFO (First In, First Out)

First In, First Out (FIFO):
An inventory valuation method that assumes items are sold in the same order as they are purchased; that is, the oldest items are sold first.

With the **FIFO** method, you assume that the first items put on the shelves (the oldest items) are sold first. Stores that sell perishable goods, such as food stores, use this inventory valuation method most often. For example, when new milk arrives at a store, the person stocking the shelves puts the new milk at the back of the shelf and puts the older milk in front. Each carton of milk (or other perishable item) has a date indicating the last day it can be sold, so food stores always try to sell the oldest stuff first, while it's still sellable.

LIFO (Last In, First Out)

Last In, First Out (LIFO): An inventory valuation method that assumes items are sold in the reverse order of purchase; that is, the newest items are sold first.

In the **LIFO** method, you assume that the last items put on the shelves (the newest items) are the first items to be sold. Retail stores that sell non-perishable items, such as tools, are likely to use this type of system. For example, when a hardware store gets new hammers, workers probably don't unload what's on the shelves and put the newest items in the back. Instead, the new tools are just put in the front, so they're likely to be sold first.

Average Cost

Average cost: An inventory valuation method in which the cost of goods available for sale is averaged, and that average cost is applied to units in ending inventory and in cost of goods sold.

With the **average cost** method, you average the cost of goods received, so there's no reason to worry about which items are sold first or last. This method of inventory is used most often in any retail or services environment where prices are constantly fluctuating and the business owner finds that an average cost works best for determining the value of ending inventory.

IN THE REAL WORLD

FIFO's Tax Bite

Pittsburgh Paints had 5,000 cans of paint in inventory. The oldest of the paints cost $3.50 each. The next oldest 2,000 cost $3.75 each, and the last batch of 2,000 cost $4.00 each. The company, which is on the FIFO method of inventory accounting, filled a 1,000-can order at $4.50 a can. When it ordered 1,000 cans to replace those it sold, it had to pay $4.40 a can for them. The store's gross profits are determined by subtracting the cost of the oldest 1,000 cans, $3,500, from the gross sales, price of $4,500 for a total of $1,000. However, the store will have to use $4,400 of its gross receipts to replace the 1,000 cans that it sold, leaving only $100, which is not enough to pay the taxes on the $1,000 gross profit.

Changing Your Cost Flow Method

After you choose an inventory valuation method, you need to use the same method each year for your financial statements and when you file your taxes. If you decide you want to change the method, you need to explain the reasons for the change to both the IRS and to your financial backers. If you're running a company that's incorporated and has sold stock, you need to explain the change to your stockholders. You also have to go back and show how the change in inventory method impacts your prior financial reporting.

13.2.3 Choosing the Best Method

Why does it matter so much which inventory valuation method you use? The key to the choice is the impact on your bottom line as well as the taxes your business will pay. The following discussion assumes that the prices you pay for inventory increase over time.

FIFO, because it assumes that the oldest (and most likely the lowest priced) items are sold first, results in a low cost of goods sold number. Because cost of goods sold is subtracted from net sales to determine profit, a low cost of goods sold number produces a high profit.

The opposite is true for LIFO, which uses cost figures based on the last price paid for the inventory (and most likely the highest price). Using the LIFO method, the cost of goods sold number is high, which means a larger sum is subtracted from net sales to determine profit. Thus, the profit is lower with LIFO than with FIFO if your merchandise prices increase over time. The good news, however, is that the tax bill is lower, too.

The average cost method gives a business the best picture of what's happening with inventory costs and trends. Rather than constantly dealing with the ups and downs of inventory costs, this method smoothes out the numbers used to calculate a business's profits. Cost of goods sold, profit, and income tax expense for this method each fall between that of FIFO and LIFO.

With the QuickBooks inventory feature (shown in Figures 13-1 and 13-2), all inventory items are valued using the average cost method. If you use this method in your business, you can use QuickBooks and the financial reports it generates. However, if you choose to use one of the other three inventory valuation methods, you can't use the QuickBooks financial report numbers.

Check with your accountant to see which inventory method he or she thinks is best for you given the type of business you're operating.

13.2.4 Comparing the Methods

To demonstrate the impact that inventory valuation can have on profit, let's compare the three most common methods: FIFO, LIFO, and average cost. Suppose your company bought units of an inventory item at different prices on three different occasions. Before making these purchases, the company's beginning inventory on April 1 was valued at $500 (50 units $\times$ $10 per unit). During the month of April, the company purchased 500 units at three different prices and sold 475 units:

Beginning inventory:	50 units
Purchases	500 units
Units available for sale	550 units
Units sold	475 units
Ending inventory	75 units

The details of the inventory purchases are:

Date	Quantity	Unit Price
April 3	150	$10
April 15	150	$25
April 30	200	$30

Using FIFO

Here's an example of how you calculate the cost of goods sold using the FIFO method. With this method, you assume that the first items received are the first ones sold:

Sold from beginning inventory	50 × $10	$ 500
Next in – April 3	150 × $10	1,500
Then – April 15	150 × $25	3,750
Then – April 30	125 × $30	3,750
Cost of goods sold	475	$9,500
Ending inventory (from April 30):	75 × $30	$2,250

Notice that only 125 of the 200 units purchased on April 30 are used in the FIFO method. Because this method assumes that the first items into inventory are the first items sold (or taken out of inventory), the first items used are those in beginning inventory on April 1. Then the April 3 items are used, the April 15 items are used, and finally the remaining needed items are taken from those bought on April 30. Because 200 were bought on April 30 and only 125 were needed, 75 of the items bought on April 30 would be the ones left in ending inventory.

Using LIFO

With the LIFO method, you assume that the last items received are the first ones sold:

Sold from the April 30 purchase	200 × $30	$ 6,000
Next – April 15	150 × $25	3,750
Then – April 3	125 × $10	1,250
Cost of goods sold	475	$11,000
Left over from April 3	25 × $10	$ 250
Left over from beginning inventory	50 × $10	500
Ending inventory	75	$ 750

Because LIFO assumes the last items to arrive are sold first, the ending inventory includes the 25 remaining units from the April 3 purchase plus the 50 units that were in beginning inventory.

Using Average Cost

The average cost method produces results between FIFO and LIFO for both cost of goods sold and ending inventory value. This method requires two steps:

1. Compute average cost.

2. Apply average cost to units.

Step 1: Compute average cost.

Beginning inventory	50 × $10	$ 500
April 3 purchase	150 × $10	1,500
April 15 purchase	150 × $25	3,750
April 30 purchase	200 × $30	6,000
Goods available for sale	550	$11,750

Average inventory cost: $11,750 ÷ 550 = $21.364 per unit (rounded to one-tenth of a cent)

Step 2: Apply average cost to units.

Cost of goods sold	475 × $21.364 = $10,148
Ending inventory	75 × $21.364 = $ 1,602

Effect on Gross Profit

Assume the items are sold to customers for $40 per unit, which means total sales of $19,000 for the month ($40 × 475 units). Table 13-1 shows a comparison of gross profit for the three methods used in this example scenario.

Table 13-1: Effect of Inventory Valuation Method on Gross Profit

Income Statement Line Item	FIFO	LIFO	Average Cost
Sales	$19,000	$19,000	$19,000
Cost of goods sold	9,500	11,000	10,148
Gross profit	9,500	8,000	8,852

FOR EXAMPLE

See Table 13-1 for an illustration of the effects of inventory valuation method on gross profit.

Small Business Accounting in Action ➡️
Evaluate costing methods for your business.

Looking at the comparisons of gross profit, you can see that inventory valuation can have a major impact on your bottom line. In a period of rising prices, FIFO is likely to give you the highest gross profit because the first items bought are usually the cheapest. LIFO is likely to give you the lowest gross profit because the last inventory items bought are usually the most expensive. The gross profit produced by the average cost method is likely to fall somewhere between FIFO and LIFO.

SELF-CHECK

1. List the four inventory valuation methods.
2. Which method is most common for expensive, one-of-a-kind items?
3. In a period of rising prices, which method will result in the highest gross profit?
4. True or False? You can change the inventory valuation method to improve your financial results. Explain your answer.

Apply Your Knowledge Use the following information to compute cost of goods sold under the average cost method:

Beginning inventory:	200 units @ $13.50 per unit
July 2 purchase	100 units @ $14.00 per unit
July 15 purchase	300 units @ $14.25 per unit
Ending inventory	125 units

13.3 LOWER OF COST OR MARKET

Conservatism:
An accounting convention that requires assets and revenues to be understated instead of overstated if alternative measures exist.

Lower of Cost or Market rule (LCM):
The concept that inventory value should be recorded and reported at the lower of historical cost or current replacement cost.

Cost:
In LCM, *cost* is the historical cost of inventory.

Market:
In LCM, *market* is the current replacement cost of inventory.

Suppose you stocked up on inventory of a hot fad item. Months later, some of the inventory is still in your stockroom and consumer demand for the product has decreased. Your Inventory general ledger account shows the historical cost of the remaining inventory (say $2,500 in this example). But your suppliers are offering to sell more of the same items to their customers (including you) in the same quantity for $1,000.

In this case, your inventory value is overstated by $1,500 ($2,500−$1,000). This violates the accounting convention of **conservatism,** which requires that assets and revenues should be understated instead of overstated if alternative measures exist.

The **Lower of Cost or Market rule (LCM)** is a common application of the conservatism convention. Using LCM, you set inventory value to whichever is lower: Its cost on your books or the current market value. **Cost** is defined as the historical cost of the inventory as determined by whichever cost flow assumption you use. **Market** is the replacement cost for the inventory if you were to buy it today.

You would adjust your inventory value by crediting (decreasing) the Inventory account by $1,500. In a computerized accounting system using perpetual inventory, you can make the adjustment using the software's inventory module. For example, QuickBooks lets you change inventory value in Vendors>Inventory Activities>Adjust Quantity/Value on Hand>Value Adjustment. In a periodic inventory system, you would use a general journal entry.

IN THE REAL WORLD

Falling Prices and Profits

Christmas sales were slow, and at the end of December Jack's Music had 20 MP3 players left in inventory. Jack, who had bought the players from the manufacturer, paid $150 for each of them and had been selling them for a retail price of $200. On January 1, the manufacturer announced a permanent price reduction; now retailers can buy the players for $135 instead of $150. Within a week, Jack's competitors had restocked with these lower-priced MP3 players and were advertising them for $185 instead of $200. Jack was forced to drop the retail price; unfortunately, his gross profit will be just $35 each on the 20 players he already has in stock, instead of the $50 for each that he had planned on. This means his profits will be $300 less than projected ($15 less profit times 20 players). Jack reported this difference on the store's January income statement.

Small Business Accounting in Action
Use an established accounting principle.

The adjustment to reduce inventory value always involves a credit to the Inventory account. The account debited depends on how you choose to track this cost (and be aware that reducing the value of inventory *is a cost*). Some businesses use a cost of goods sold account called Inventory Adjustments to keep track of all the adjustments. A business using perpetual inventory might just debit the Cost of Goods Sold account directly. Whichever account you use, its balance is eventually rolled up into the Cost of Goods Sold line item on your income statement.

SELF-CHECK

1. Define *conservatism* in accounting.
2. Define the terms *cost* and *market* as they are used in the lower of cost or market rule.
3. Explain how the lower of cost or market rule adheres to the conservatism convention.
4. If the value of your inventory on hand has increased since you bought it, should you adjust your accounting records? Why or why not?

Apply Your Knowledge Suppose the balance in your Inventory account is $8,000, but if you bought the same inventory today it would cost $7,000. If you use the periodic inventory system, what journal entry would you make to observe the lower of cost or market rule?

SUMMARY

Section 13.1

- *Cost of goods sold* is your cost of the merchandise you sell to customers, and it appears as a line item on the income statement.

- The two-part formula for net income is: net sales − cost of goods sold = gross profit; then gross profit − expenses = net income.

- Companies track the number of inventory units on hand using either the periodic inventory system or the perpetual inventory system. A perpetual inventory system is difficult to maintain without accounting software.

- Even if you use the perpetual inventory system, you should do a physical count periodically to determine inventory losses from theft, damage, or other causes.

- In a periodic inventory system, the two-part formula for cost of goods sold is: beginning inventory + net purchases = goods available for sale; then goods available for sale − ending inventory = cost of goods sold.

- A periodic inventory system uses the following general ledger accounts to record initial inventory cost: Purchases, Purchases Returns and Allowances, Purchases Discounts, and Freight In. The Inventory account is never used to record inventory purchases.

- A perpetual inventory system uses the Inventory account to record all initial costs associated with inventory, and it uses a Cost of Goods Sold account to record the cost of inventory actually sold to customers. When the inventory is sold, two entries are made at the same time:

    Debit Accounts Receivable (or Cash)
        Credit Sales
    Debit Cost of Goods Sold
        Credit Inventory

Section 13.2

- The balance of the Inventory general ledger account can vary depending on how you track the flow of inventory costs. This means that an equal number of identical inventory units can have different values under different inventory valuation methods.

- The four inventory valuation methods are specific identification, FIFO, LIFO, and average cost.

- In a period of rising prices, FIFO results in lower cost of goods sold and higher gross profit. LIFO results in the opposite. The average cost method falls somewhere between the two.

- You must use the same inventory valuation method consistently. If you change methods, you must provide good reasons for the change to the IRS and your financial backers.

Section 13.3

- The Lower of Cost or Market rule is an example of conservatism in accounting.

ASSESS YOUR UNDERSTANDING

UNDERSTAND: WHAT HAVE YOU LEARNED?

 Go to **www.wiley.com/college/epstein** to assess your knowledge of managing inventory.

PRACTICE: WHAT WOULD YOU DO?

1. The following infomation is given:

Sales	$150,000
Sales Returns & Allowances	10,000
Sales Discounts	2,000

Calculate Net Sales.

2. The following information was provided for the month of July:

Inventory 07/01/0X__	$10,000
Inventory 07/31/0X__	8,000
Purchases	56,000

Calculate the Cost of Goods Sold using a periodic inventory system.

3. What is the difference between a periodic inventory system and a perpetual inventory system?

4. Using the information provided, determine the net purchases when a periodic inventory system is used.

Purchases	$60,000
Freight-In	1,700
Purchase Discounts	3,000
Purchase Returns & Allowances	2,500

5. What is a cash discount? When is a cash discount considered a purchase discount? When is a cash discount considered a sales discount?

6. The Martin Merchandise entity had the following transactions during the month of June:

June 2 Purchased $1,500 of merchandise from the Patae entity, invoice #6205, terms 2/10, n/30.

      5 Returned $150 of merchandise to the Patae entity from the June 2 purchase.

10 Received shipping bill from Quick Shipping for the June 2 Patae entity purchase, $75. The bill is to be paid later in the month.

12 Paid the Patae entity for June 2 purchase.

20 Paid Quick Shipping for the June 10 transaction.

Record the transactions using a periodic inventory system.

7. Refer to question 6. Record the June 2 transaction using a perpetual inventory system.

8. The following information is available for the Waterfront Merchandising Industry.

Sales	125,000	Purchase Returns & Allowances	1,500
Sales Returns & Allowances	3,000	Purchase Discounts	4,000
Sales Discounts	5,000	Ending Inventory	11,000
Beginning Inventory	12,000	Freight - In	2,000
Purchases	53,000		

a. Calculate Net Sales.

b. Calculate Cost of Goods Sold.

c. Calculate the Gross Profit.

9. Listed below are the inventory records of the Ellis entity.

	Units	Units Cost	Total Cost
Beginning Inventory	7,000	0.50	3,500
April Purchases	30,000	0.60	18,000
May Purchases	45,000	0.75	33,750
June Purchases	18,000	0.80	14,400
Totals	100,000		69,650

Calculate the cost of the ending inventory using the specific invoice method if the ending inventory consists of 20,000 units. 3,000 units are from the beginning inventory, 10,000 units are from the April purchase, and 7,000 units are from the June purchase.

10. Refer to question 9. The ending inventory consists of 20,000 units. Calculate the cost of the ending inventory using the average cost method.

11. Refer to question 9. With the ending inventory of 20,000 units, what is the ending inventory cost using the FIFO method?

12. Refer to question 9. What is the cost of the 20,000 ending inventory units using the LIFO method?

13. Farrah Fairway started up a new business selling Titanium putters over the Internet. She began by buying 45 putters for $22 each. During October—her first month of operations—she sold 28 putters for $42 each. Her only other expense for the month was advertising expense: $210. What was Farrah's net income (or loss) in her first month of operations?

14. What is the gross profit?

Sales	$ 14,000
Cost of Goods Sold	6,000
Administrative Expenses	1,400
Selling Expenses	3,500

15. What is the net sales?

Sales	$ 10,000
Sales Returns and Allowances	400
Sales Discounts	600

16. Find:
   a. Net Sales
   b. Gross Profit
   c. Operating Income

Sales	$ 20,000
Sales Returns and Allowances	300
Sales Discounts	900
Administrative Expenses	2,400
Selling Expenses	4,800
Cost of Goods Sold	9,000

17. Find:
   a. Gross Profit
   b. Operating Income
   c. Net income

Administrative Expenses	$ 9,000
Cost of Goods Sold	66,000
Interest Expense	3,000
Sales (Net)	110,000
Selling Expenses	19,000

BE A SMALL BUSINESS ACCOUNTANT

Periodic or Perpetual Inventory

The owner of a merchandising entity is attempting to determine if there is a need to invest in a periodic physical inventory. He feels as though he keeps adequate records with his perpetual system, and does not know if it is worth his company's time, effort, and expense to invest in having a periodic inventory done. He does have a large amount of cash invested in inventory and wants to do what is best for the company. What would you suggest?

LIFO or FIFO

A business merchandiser has heard much about costing inventory but does not quite understand how this is done. He has repeatedly heard the terms LIFO and FIFO, but doesn't understand what they mean. Someone has told him that one method is more beneficial in preparing his financial statements, but this all perplexes him. What should he do?

KEY TERMS

Average cost	An inventory valuation method in which the cost of goods available for sale is averaged, and that average cost is applied to units in ending inventory and in cost of goods sold.
Cash discount	A discount offered to credit customers to encourage prompt payment of outstanding bills.
Conservatism	An accounting convention that requires assets and revenues to be understated instead of overstated if alternative measures exist.
Cost	In LCM, *cost* is the historical cost of inventory.
Cost of Goods Sold	A general ledger account used in the perpetual inventory system.
First In, First Out (FIFO)	An inventory valuation method that assumes items are sold in the same order as they are purchased; that is, the oldest items are sold first.
Freight In	A cost of goods sold account that tracks the costs of shipping incoming merchandise; it is used only in the periodic inventory system.
Gross profit	The result of net sales minus cost of goods sold.
Inventory	A current asset account that tracks the merchandise on hand.
Last In, First Out (LIFO)	An inventory valuation method that assumes items are sold in the reverse order of purchase; that is, the newest items are sold first.
Lower of Cost or Market rule (LCM)	The concept that inventory value should be recorded and reported at the lower of historical cost or current replacement cost.
Market	In LCM, *market* is the current replacement cost of inventory.
Net purchases	A component of cost of goods sold in the periodic inventory system; net purchases = Purchases account − Purchases Sales and Allowances account − Purchases Discounts account + Freight In account.
Net sales	Total sales reduced by returns, allowances, and discounts: Sales account − Sales Returns and Allowances account − Sales Discounts account.
Periodic inventory	A system for tracking inventory that requires a physical count at certain times.
Perpetual inventory	A system for tracking inventory that adjusts inventory levels as each purchase or sale is made.
Physical count	An actual count of the number of units of each type of good in inventory.

Purchases discount A cash discount taken by a buyer.

Purchases Discounts The contra cost of goods sold account used to track purchases discounts; it is used only in the periodic inventory system.

Sales discount A cash discount granted by a seller.

Specific identification An inventory valuation method in which you maintain cost figures for each inventory item individually.

REFERENCES

1. Schreiber, Lynne Meredith, "Inventory Management: Keep It Clean," Startupnation.com, www.startupnation.com/articles/1532/1/inventory-management.asp.
2. Miller, Kerry. "The Mundane Realities of a Creative Biz," Businessweek.com, October 26, 2007, www.businessweek.com/smallbiz/content/oct2007/sb20071026_598416.htm?chan=search.

CHAPTER 14

ADJUSTMENTS AND THE WORKSHEET FOR A MERCHANDISING BUSINESS

Creating a True Picture of Assets and Liabilities

Do You Already Know?

- How to apply the matching principle
- How to use the Income Summary account in adjustments
- When you need to record accruals

For additional questions to assess your current knowledge of using adjustments and the worksheet for a merchandising business, go to **www.wiley.com/college/epstein.**

What You Will Find Out	What You Will Be Able To Do
14.1 The chart of accounts for a merchandising business	• Draw conclusions about a business by looking at its general ledger accounts
14.2 How to make an inventory adjustment	• Update the general ledger to reflect an ending inventory
14.3 How expense adjustments will affect assets and liabilities	• Estimate future bad debt and bring payroll expenses up to date

INTRODUCTION

This chapter explores the adjustments required for a merchandising business. Many of the adjustments are similar to those for a service business shown in Chapter 6. A big difference is the adjustment for inventory. You will learn how to make the adjustments required in a periodic inventory system. You will also learn how to set aside a reserve for future bad debts and how to record payroll expenses that have been incurred but not yet paid.

14.1 SETTING UP THE WORKSHEET FOR A MERCHANDISING BUSINESS

Take a look at Apparel Emporium's chart of accounts in Figure 14-1. You can learn the following information about a business just by looking at the general ledger accounts:

- This is a merchandising business (Inventory account).
- It uses the accrual basis of accounting (Accounts Payable account).
- It has at least some retail sales (Sales Tax Payable account).
- It is a sole proprietorship (Anna Rodriguez, Capital account).
- It uses the periodic inventory system (Purchases account).

You might also notice some new accounts that are introduced in this chapter:

- Allowance for Bad Debt.
- Accrued Salaries and Wages Payable.
- Accrued Payroll Taxes Payable.

These accounts are used for the adjustments. As defined in Chapter 6, an *adjustment* (or *adjusting entry*) is a journal entry that brings accounting balances up to date at the end of the accounting period.

Companies record adjustments to adhere to the matching principle, which is discussed in Chapter 6. A basic tenet of accrual accounting, the *matching principle* is the concept that revenue earned in an accounting period should be matched with expenses incurred to earn that revenue. While inventory is not an expense, it is a component of cost of goods sold (the actual cost of the merchandise sold in the accounting period). Cost of goods sold has the same effect as expenses on a company's net profit.

Figure 14-1

Apparel Emporium Chart of Accounts

Assets

1010	Cash in Bank
1020	Change Fund
1030	Petty Cash
1110	Accounts Receivable
1115	Allowance for Bad Debt
1210	Inventory
1310	Prepaid Insurance
1510	Store Equipment
1515	Accumulated Depreciation–Store Equipment
1610	Office Equipment
1615	Accumulated Depreciation–Office Equipment

Liabilities

2010	Accounts Payable
2110	Accrued Salaries and Wages Payable
2120	Accrued Payroll Taxes Payable
2151	Social Security Tax Payable
2152	Medicare Tax Payable
2153	Federal Withholding Payable
2154	State Withholding Payable
2210	Sales Tax Payable
2310	Bank Credit Line Payable
2510	Note Payable (Five-year)

Equity

3010	Anna Rodriguez, Capital
3020	Anna Rodriguez, Withdrawals
3030	Income Summary

Revenue

4010	Sales
4110	Sales Returns and Allowances
4210	Sales Discounts

Cost of Goods Sold

5010	Purchases
5110	Purchases Returns and Allowances
5210	Purchases Discounts
5310	Freight In

Expenses

Selling Expenses:

6010	Salaries and Wages–Store
6011	Payroll Taxes–Store
6110	Advertising
6210	Cash Over or Short
6310	Credit Card Processing Fees
6410	Supplies–Store
6510	Depreciation–Store Equipment
6910	Miscellaneous Expense–Store

General Expenses:

7010	Salaries and Wages–Office
7011	Payroll Taxes–Office
7110	Bad Debts
7210	Insurance
7310	Rent
7410	Supplies–Office
7510	Utilities
7610	Depreciation–Office Equipment
7910	Miscellaneous Expense–Office

Other Income

8010	Interest Income

Other Expenses

9010	Interest Expenses

A chart of accounts for a merchandising business.

Small Business Accounting in Action ➡ Draw conclusions about a business by looking at its general ledger accounts.

In a manual accounting system, the first step in preparing adjustments is to set up a worksheet. Information for the first three columns of the worksheet comes from the trial balance. Figure 14-2 shows a worksheet completed through the Trial Balance section.

Figure 14-2

	Apparel Emporium Worksheet For the Year Ended December 31, 200X										
		Trial Balance		Adjustments		Adjusted Trial Balance		Income Statement		Balance Sheet	
	Account	Debit	Credit	Debit	Credit	Debit	Credit	Debit	Credit	Debit	Credit
1010	Cash in Bank	31,000									
1030	Change Fund	500									
1040	Petty Cash	200									
1110	Accounts Receivable	83,979									
1115	Allowance for Bad Debts		425								
1210	Inventory	155,784									
1310	Prepaid Insurance	18,000									
1510	Store Equipment	60,000									
1515	Accumulated Depreciation—Store Equip.		14,303								
1610	Office Equipment	50,000									
1615	Accumulated Depreciation—Office Equip		9,750								
2010	Accounts Payable		114,537								
2110	Accrued Salaries and Wages Payable										
2120	Accrued Payroll Taxes Payable										
2151	Social Security Tax Payable										
2152	Medicare Tax Payable										
2153	Federal Withholding Payable										
2154	State Withholding Payable										
2210	Sales Tax Payable		2,750								
2310	Credit Line Payable		7,000								
2510	Note Payable (Five-year)		32,915								
3010	Anna Rodriguez, Capital		166,950								
3020	Anna Rodriguez, Withdrawals	60,000									
3030	Income Summary										
4010	Sales		601,200								
4110	Sales Returns and Allowances	38,500									
4210	Sales Discounts	2,000									
5010	Purchases	328,348									
5110	Purchases Returns and Allowances		19,000								
5210	Purchases Discounts		1,800								
5310	Freight In	4,000									
6010	Salaries and Wages—Store	29,423									
6011	Payroll Taxes—Store	3,174									
6110	Advertising	3,600									
6210	Cash Over or Short	92									
6310	Credit Card Processing Fees	1,860									
6410	Supplies—Store	6,000									
6510	Depreciation—Store Equipment										
6910	Miscellaneous Expense—Store	1,150									
7010	Salaries and Wages—Office	41,192									
7011	Payroll Taxes—Office	4,387									
7110	Bad Debt										
7210	Insurance	2,400									
7310	Rent	26,400									
7410	Supplies—Office	5,500									
7510	Utilities	12,100									
7610	Depreciation—Office Equipment										
7910	Miscellaneous Expense—Office	900									
8010	Interest Income		500								
8910	Interest Expense	641									
		971,130	971,130								

Account balances for a merchandising business.

SELF-CHECK

1. Which asset account would you always expect to see in a merchandising business's chart of accounts?
2. What is a common application of the matching principle?
3. How is cost of goods sold similar to expenses?
4. In a manual accounting system, what is the first step in preparing adjustments?

Apply Your Knowledge Review the chart of accounts and the worksheet in this section. List the contra accounts used by Apparel Emporium.

14.2 INVENTORY ADJUSTMENT

In a periodic inventory system, all purchases of inventory are recorded in the Purchases general ledger account (not the Inventory account). Unlike the perpetual inventory system in which the Inventory account is constantly updated, the periodic inventory system keeps the same Inventory balance throughout the accounting period.

Ending inventory is arrived at by making a physical count of inventory at the end of the accounting period. You then determine the value of the ending inventory by applying your particular inventory valuation method (Chapter 13). The balance of the Inventory general ledger account must be updated to match the value of the ending inventory. Changing the balance of the Inventory general ledger account requires two adjustments:

1. Remove the amount of beginning inventory.
2. Add the amount of ending inventory.

The effect of each adjustment on the Inventory account is as follows:

1. Beginning inventory − Beginning inventory = Zero balance
2. Zero balance 1 ending inventory = Ending inventory

Inventory is an asset account, so it is decreased with a credit and then increased with a debit. But which account is used to offset these entries? The offset account is Income Summary, first introduced in Chapter 7. The adjustments for inventory are shown in Figure 14-3:

(a) Debit Income Summary

    Credit Inventory

(b) Debit Inventory

    Credit Income Summary

Small Business Accounting in Action ➡
Update the general ledger to reflect an ending inventory.

IN THE REAL WORLD

Keeping Their Slice of the Pie

John and Anthony are the owners of Two Brothers, a pizza shop in upstate New York. Because the shop is close to a number of lakefront resorts, the summer season is especially busy. Fortunately, two nearby colleges provide Two Brothers with plenty of extra summer help. John and Anthony are mindful, however, that with the inexperienced help comes loss of inventory through food waste and mistakes—not to mention free slices for friends when no one is looking. The two pay extra attention to inventory, conducting more frequent periodic inventories. Though it's important to be well-stocked for business, John and Anthony feel that keeping too much inventory is an invitation to theft and waste. Every two weeks the two calculate the change in inventory by subtracting the ending inventory from the beginning inventory, with the goal of keeping the numbers on target.

SELF-CHECK

1. True or False? In a perpetual inventory system, you don't need to make an inventory adjustment. Explain your answer.

2. How do you determine the value of ending inventory in a periodic inventory system?

3. How many journal entries are required to update the balance of the Inventory account?

4. What offset account is used in the inventory adjustments?

Apply Your Knowledge   At the end of the accounting period, your general ledger shows the following balances (before adjustments):

Inventory	$ 38,000
Purchases	$109,000
Sales	$160,000

A physical count shows that your ending inventory is valued at $47,000. Prepare the journal entries required to adjust inventory.

14.3 ADJUSTMENTS TO RECORD EXPENSES

Apparel Emporium needs four types of adjustments to capture certain expenses in the accounting period:

- Bad debt.
- Accrued payroll expenses.
- Depreciation.
- Insurance.

14.3.1 Allowance for Bad Debt

It is a fact of business life that you are not guaranteed payment of all amounts due from all customers. "Bad debt" is a cost of doing business, and it must be recorded as an expense. Chapter 6 discusses the direct write-off method, in which you write off a specific customer's account after you determine you will never collect on it.

For the matching principle, the preferred method is the allowance method. In the *allowance method,* you compute an accounting period's bad debt expense by applying percentages to either the amount of your credit sales or the balances in your accounts receivable aging summary (see Table 11-2 in Chapter 11). You develop the percentages based on your company's experience with credit customers. If you are just starting a business, you base the percentage on the experience of other businesses in your industry.

Percentage of credit sales:
An allowance method of recording bad debt in which an estimated rate of bad debt is applied to credit sales made in the accounting period.

Apparel Emporium uses an allowance method called **percentage of credit sales** to compute bad debt. In this method, the estimated rate of bad debt is applied to the company's credit sales for the accounting period. Based on past experience, Apparel Emporium estimates that eight-tenths of one percent (0.8 percent) of credit sales will result in bad debts. Apparel Emporium had credit sales of $165,625 in the accounting period, so the estimated bad debt expense is $1,325 ($165,625 $\times$ 0.008).

The company must reduce the amount of accounts receivable reported on the balance sheet, but it does not touch the Accounts Receivable account. Instead, the adjustment is made in the Allowance for Bad Debts account.

Allowance for Bad Debt:
The contra asset account used to reduce the amount of accounts receivable reported on the balance sheet.

Allowance for Bad Debts is a contra asset account that is related to Accounts Receivable. The adjustment for estimated bad debt is shown in Figure 14-3:

(c) Debit Bad Debt

  Credit Allowance for Bad Debts

When you eventually identify a specific customer's account as uncollectible, you write off that account against the allowance. Think of the allowance as a reservoir that you dip into occasionally, and then refill at the end of the accounting period. (An allowance account is also called a *reserve account.*)

Suppose you determine that Jane Hobb's account is uncollectible. You already recognized the expense when you did the end-of-period adjustment debiting Bad Debt and crediting the allowance. Now it's time to dip into the reservoir:

Debit Allowance for Bad Debt

  Credit Accounts Receivable/Jane Hobb

Small Business Accounting in Action ➡️
Estimate future bad debt.

CAREER CONNECTION

No one wants to deal with the realities of uncollectibles, but an allowance for bad debts can help a business maintain its bottom line.

Like most businesses, Vincent's restaurant supply sells its goods on credit to customers, largely because it keeps the customers happy by giving them extra time to pay when they need it. Unfortunately, Vincent is occasionally stuck with a customer who does not pay, especially in tough financial times when many restaurants go out of business. Besides costing him money, these bad debts complicate Vincent's accounting.

Although Vincent must record the income at the time of sale, it may take a year or more of collection attempts to determine that the customer is not going to pay. Vincent's accounting solution is to make an allowance for bad debts; he puts money into the allowance as an expense of the company. When Vincent decides that a particular account is not collectable, he uses his Allowance for Bad Debts account to pay for the bad debt. Because he's already made the allowance, Vincent's financial statement is in order in the month that he writes off a bad debt.

At the end of each year, Vincent and his accountant meet to review the business's finances. The two evaluate the accounts receivable and make any necessary adjustments to his allowance for bad debts.

Tips from the Professional

- Use an accounts receivable aging schedule to monitor customers' payment activity.
- Work with an accountant to set a realistic allowance.

14.3.2 Accrued Payroll Expenses

Not all pay periods fall at the end of a month. If you pay your employees every two weeks, you may end up closing the books in the middle of a pay period, meaning that, for example, employees aren't paid for the last week of March until the end of the first week of April.

When your pay period hits before the end of the accounting period, you need to make an adjusting entry to record the payroll expense that has been incurred but not yet paid. An **accrual** is the entering into the records of an expense previously not recorded in the books. It can also refer to revenue earned but not yet recorded.

Consider the following scenario for Apparel Emporium, which issues paychecks every two weeks. On December 31 the company issued paychecks for the two-week period ending December 24. That means that employees worked one additional week between the end of the last payroll period (December 24) and the end of the accounting period (December 31). This payroll expense won't go on the books until payroll is processed in January. Apparel Emporium must accrue the payroll expense for that week (December 25–December 31).

Accrual:
An expense incurred in the current accounting period but not yet recorded in the books; also, revenue earned in the current accounting period but not yet recorded in the books.

Accrued Salaries and Wages Payable:
The current liability account used to record the obligation for wages earned but not yet paid.

The adjusting entry will increase Salaries and Wages with debits. Which general ledger account will be offset with a credit? The unpaid salaries and wages represent a liability, so the offset is a current liability account titled **Accrued Salaries and Wages Payable.** The adjustment to accrue unpaid salaries and wages is shown in Figure 14-3:

(d) Debit Salaries and Wages—Store

Debit Salaries and Wages—Office

Credit Accrued Salaries and Wages Payable

Notice that different accounts are used for store payroll and office payroll. Apparel Emporium reports store expenses and office expenses separately on the income statement (Chapter 15).

The company will also record the related employer payroll tax expense in the current liability account **Accrued Payroll Taxes Payable:**

Accrued Payroll Taxes Payable:
The current liability account used to record the obligation for employer payroll taxes on wages earned but not yet paid.

(e) Debit Payroll Taxes—Store

Debit Payroll Taxes—Office

Credit Accrued Payroll Taxes Payable

The Accrued Payroll Taxes Payable account is not the same as Social Security Tax Payable, Medicare Tax Payable, and so on. Those accounts are for liabilities on payrolls that are already processed. Apparel Emporium does not have any balances in these liability accounts because the company is current on its payroll tax deposits. Chapter 10 goes into detail about depositing payroll taxes.

In January, when the cash is actually paid out, Apparel Emporium will reverse the December accruals and then make a journal entry to record the payroll:

Step 1: Reverse the entry.

Debit Accrued Salaries and Wages Payable

Credit Salaries and Wages—Store

Credit Salaries and Wages—Office

Step 2: Record the payroll.

Debit Salaries and Wages—Store

Debit Salaries and Wages—Office

Credit Cash

Small Business Accounting in Action ➡
Bring payroll expenses up to date.

An alternative approach is to skip the reversing entry and simply debit the liability account when the payroll is processed in January:

Debit Accrued Salaries and Wages Payable

Credit Cash

IN THE REAL WORLD

To Accrue or Not to Accrue

The five employees of Kate's Kandy have been with the small retail shop since Kate opened it in 2005. From the beginning, Kate had avoided many of the accounting issues associated with accrued payroll expenses by paying all employees on the 15th and the last day of each month. Of course, she still has to accrue payroll taxes, which Kate manages through an Accrued Payroll Taxes Payable account.

14.3.3 Depreciation Adjustment

Apparel Emporium uses the straight-line method of depreciation (covered in Chapter 6). Because this company classifies each expense as either store expense or general expense, different accounts are used depending on the asset involved:

(f) Debit Depreciation—Store Equipment

   Credit Accumulated Depreciation—Store Equipment

(g) Debit Depreciation—Office Equipment

   Credit Accumulated Depreciation—Office Equipment

14.3.4 Adjustment for Prepaid Expenses

As discussed in Chapter 6, a *prepaid expense* is an asset that is paid up front and then allocated to each accounting period. Apparel Emporium's cash outlay for its commercial insurance policy during the year is shown below. Dissatisfied with its insurance company, Apparel Emporium went to a new company at the end of February. Apparel Emporium also beefed up its coverage for fidelity bonds and other potential liability protections. The new policy charged a higher premium ($1,500 per month) and required a year's premium in advance.

Date Paid	Length of Coverage	Month(s) Covered	Amount Paid
January 2	1 month	January	$ 1,200
February 1	1 month	February	1,200
February 28	12 months	March-February	18,000

The payments made January 2 and February 1 ($1,200 each) were charged directly to the Insurance expense account. However, charging the February 28 payment ($18,000) to expense would distort the amount of insurance expense by showing 14 months of premiums instead of 12 months. Instead, the $18,000 was charged to the current asset account titled Prepaid Insurance.

Figure 14-3

Apparel Emporium — Worksheet
For the Year Ended December 31, 200X

Code	Account	Trial Balance Debit	Trial Balance Credit	Adjustments Debit	Adjustments Credit	Adjusted Trial Balance Debit	Adjusted Trial Balance Credit	Income Statement Debit	Income Statement Credit	Balance Sheet Debit	Balance Sheet Credit
1010	Cash in Bank	31,000				31,000				31,000	
1030	Change Fund	500				500				500	
1040	Petty Cash	200				200				200	
1110	Accounts Receivable	83,979				83,979				83,979	
1115	Allowance for Bad Debts		425		(c) 1,325		1,750				1,750
1210	Inventory	155,784		(b) 133,972	(a) 155,784	133,972				133,972	
1310	Prepaid Insurance	18,000			(h) 15,000	3,000				3,000	
1510	Store Equipment	60,000				60,000				60,000	
1515	Accumulated Depreciation—Store Equip.		14,303		(f) 6,864		21,167				21,167
1610	Office Equipment	50,000				50,000				50,000	
1615	Accumulated Depreciation—Office Equip.		9,750		(g) 9,000		18,750				18,750
2010	Accounts Payable		114,537				114,537				114,537
2110	Accrued Salaries and Wages Payable				(d) 1,385		1,385				1,385
2120	Accrued Payroll Taxes Payable				(e) 149		149				149
2151	Social Security Tax Payable										
2152	Medicare Tax Payable										
2153	Federal Withholding Payable										
2154	State Withholding Payable										
2210	Sales Tax Payable		2,750				2,750				2,750
2310	Credit Line Payable		7,000				7,000				7,000
2510	Note Payable (Five-year)		32,915				32,915				32,915
3010	Anna Rodriguez, Capital		166,950				166,950				166,950
3020	Anna Rodriguez, Withdrawals	60,000				60,000				60,000	
3030	Income Summary			(a) 155,784	(b) 133,972	155,784	133,972	155,784	133,972		
4010	Sales		601,200				601,200		601,200		
4110	Sales Returns and Allowances	38,500				38,500		38,500			
4210	Sales Discounts	2,000				2,000		2,000			
5010	Purchases	328,348				328,348		328,348			
5110	Purchases Returns and Allowances		19,000				19,000		19,000		
5210	Purchases Discounts		1,800				1,800		1,800		
5310	Freight In	4,000				4,000		4,000			
6000	Salaries and Wages—Store	29,423		(d) 577		30,000		30,000			
6011	Payroll Taxes—Store	3,174		(e) 63		3,237		3,237			
6110	Advertising	3,600				3,600		3,600			
6210	Cash Over or Short	92				92		92			
6310	Credit Card Processing Fees	1,860				1,860		1,860			
6410	Supplies—Store	6,000				6,000		6,000			
6510	Depreciation—Store Equipment			(f) 6,864		6,864		6,864			
6910	Miscellaneous Expense—Store	1,150				1,150		1,150			
7001	Salaries and Wages—Office	41,192		(d) 808		42,000		42,000			
7010	Payroll Taxes—Office	4,387		(e) 86		4,473		4,473			
7110	Bad Debt			(c) 1,325		1,325		1,325			
7210	Insurance	2,400		(h) 15,000		17,400		17,400			
7310	Rent	26,400				26,400		26,400			
7410	Supplies—Office	5,500				5,500		5,500			
7510	Utilities	12,100				12,100		12,100			
7610	Depreciation—Office Equipment			(g) 9,000		9,000		9,000			
7910	Miscellaneous Expense—Office	900				900		900			
8010	Interest Income		500				500		500		
8910	Interest Expense	641				641		641			
		971,130	971,130	323,479	323,479	1,123,825	1,123,825	701,174	756,472	422,651	367,353
	Net Income							55,298			55,298
								756,472	756,472	422,651	422,651

A completed worksheet for a merchandising business.

The company needs to adjust the accounts for the insurance that was "consumed" from March through December ($1,500 × 10 months = $15,000):

(h) Debit Insurance
    Credit Prepaid Insurance

> **FOR EXAMPLE**
>
> See Figure 14-3 for a merchandising business's completed worksheet.

Keep in mind that the worksheet is an analysis tool. It is not part of the formal accounting records like journals and ledgers are. In order to bring the accounts up to date, you need to journalize and post the adjusting entries. This process is illustrated in detail in Chapter 6.

It's important to mention that although Apparel Emporium makes its adjusting entries on a yearly basis, the company would also monitor its performance and financial status throughout the year. Each time it reviews its financial position, the company would take into account any adjustments needed at that point. The worksheet allows the accountant to assess the accuracy and completeness of the adjusting entries before they are formally entered into the accounting records.

SELF-CHECK

1. What is the difference between the direct write-off method and the allowance method of writing off bad debts?
2. How do you determine the percentages to use in the allowance method?
3. What is an accrual?
4. Why do companies often accrue payroll expenses?

Apply Your Knowledge ▶ Use the percentage of credit sales method to determine bad debt, given the following scenario:

Cash Sales	$250,000
Credit Sales	150,000
Accounts Receivable	88,000
Rate used	1.5%

SUMMARY

Section 14.1

- The *matching principle* is the concept that revenue earned in an accounting period should be matched with expenses incurred to earn that revenue. Adjustments are used to apply the matching principle.

- An *adjustment* is a journal entry that brings accounting balances up to date at the end of the accounting period.

Section 14.2

- In a periodic inventory system, the inventory adjustment removes the beginning inventory balance and adds the ending inventory balance.

- The offsetting account for inventory adjustments is Income Summary.

- Adjustments to record expenses at the end of an accounting period include bad debt, accrued payroll expenses, depreciation, and allocation of prepaid expenses.

Section 14.3

- The allowance method for recording bad debt requires a debit to the Bad Debt expense account and a credit to a reserve account called Allowance for Bad Debt.

- When a customer's account is considered uncollectible, the entry requires a debit to Allowance for Bad Debt and a credit to Accounts Receivable. The Bad Debt account is not used because the expense was already recognized at the time of the adjustment.

- Expenses incurred but not yet paid are accrued at the end of the accounting period. One example is salaries earned but not yet paid. The entry requires a debit to the payroll expense account and a credit to Accrued Salaries and Wages Payable.

- A *prepaid expense* is an asset that is paid up front and then allocated to each accounting period as it is used up.

ASSESS YOUR UNDERSTANDING

UNDERSTAND: WHAT HAVE YOU LEARNED?

 Go to **www.wiley.com/college/epstein** to assess your knowledge of using adjustments and the worksheet for a merchandising business.

PRACTICE: WHAT WOULD YOU DO?

1. The Income Statement as well as Balance Sheet columns are shown below from a completed merchandiser's worksheet. The ending inventory is $12,000 and has been correctly placed in the appropriate columns. Prepare the necessary entries to adjust the inventory account.

Account Title	Income Statement	Balance Sheet		
Inventory	10,000	12,000	12,000	

2. An entity has credit sales in the amount of $75,000 at year-end. Based upon historical data, it has been determined that 2% of the accounts will prove to be bad debts. Make the adjusting entry to set up an allowance for the expected bad debts.

3. The Joshua Merchandising entity has weekly payroll as follows:

   Salaries & Wages – Store $10,000

   Salaries & Wages – Office $ 5,000

   March 31, the end of the accounting period, falls on Wednesday. Payroll is paid weekly on Fridays. Prepare the adjusting entry to accrue payroll.

4. Refer to question 3. There are associate payroll taxes for March 31 in the amount of:

   Payroll Taxes – Store $1,800

   Payroll Taxes – Office $3,500

   Accrue the payroll taxes.

5. Refer to question 3. Payday is Friday, April 2.

   a. Reverse the adjusting entry made on March 31.

   b. Record the April 2 payroll.

6. Refer to questions 3 and 5. Record the April 2 payroll without preparing a reversing entry.

7. An entity paid six months' rent in the amount of $9,000 on January 1. Statements are prepared monthly and an adjustment must be made on January 31 to update the Rent account.

   a. Prepare the entry to record the payment on January 1.

   b. Prepare the January 31 adjusting entry.

8. Depreciation calculations were completed and the depreciation amounts are as follows:

   Depreciation – Store Equipment $300

   Depreciation – Office Equipment $400

   a. Record the depreciation for the Store Equipment.
   b. Record the depreciation for the Office Equipment.

9. Explain the requirements of the Matching Principle.

10. Shown below is a partially completed worksheet for a merchandising entity.

	Merchandising Worksheet December 31, 200X										
	Trial Balance		Adjustment		Adj. Trial Balance		Income Statement		Balance Sheet		
Cash	25,000										
Accounts Receivable	150,000										
Allowance for Bad Debts		3,000									
Inventory	75,000										
Supplies	7,000										
Prepaid Insurance	2,000										
Store Equipment	15,000										
Acc. Depreciation, Store Equipment		5,000									
Accounts Payable		53,000									
M. Smith, Capital		93,000									
Sales		310,000									
Sales Discounts	3,000										
Sales Returns & Allowances	1,500										
Purchases	101,000	2,000									
Purchase Discounts											
Purchase Returns & Allowances		3,000									
Freight-in	2,500										
Salaries & Wages - Office	40,000										
Salaries & Wages - Store	19,000										
Bad Debt	28,000										
Totals	469,000	469,000									

Complete the worksheet using the following information:

a. 12/31/200X inventory is $70,000.

b. $1,500 of prepaid insurance has expired.

c. Depreciation on the Store Equipment is $1,000.

d. Accrued Office Salaries & Wages are $2,000 and accrued Store Salaries & Wages are $900.

e. Current credit sales dictate an increase in the Allowance for Bad Debt account of $5,000.

BE A SMALL BUSINESS ACCOUNTANT

Managing Bad Debts

The Ransom Merchandising entity has been in business for five years and has done quite well. However, there appears to be a problem developing with some of its accounts receivable. More and more accounts are becoming uncollectible. Ransom Merchandising employs all of the collection procedures to collect the debts, but many have proven simply to be uncollectible. The owner has noticed that the longer this problem goes on, the smaller the percentage of accounts receivable that are actually collectible. Is there a solution to this problem?

Necessity of Adequate Records

An owner was heard saying that he keeps his own books and he simply records what happens financially in his business. He continued to state that he really doesn't understand all the fancy accounting terminology but he has been doing all of his financial records for years and has not encountered a problem. When someone then asked him how much he actually incurred in certain expenses and how much inventory he had left, he replied, "I really don't know how to break it down like that. I just know that I bought a lot of merchandise, and I have quite a bit left over." When the person asked additional questions about his monthly expenses, the owner got annoyed and said, "I told you that I don't understand all of the fancy terminology, all my bills are paid." Is there any way this owner could be helped to maintain more adequate records?

KEY TERMS

Accrual	An expense incurred in the current accounting period but not yet recorded in the books; also, revenue earned in the current accounting period but not yet recorded in the books.
Accrued Payroll Taxes Payable	The current liability account used to record the obligation for employer payroll taxes on wages earned but not yet paid.
Accrued Salaries and Wages Payable	The current liability account used to record the obligation for wages earned but not yet paid.
Allowance for Bad Debt	The contra asset account used to reduce the amount of accounts receivable reported on the balance sheet.
Percentage of credit sales	An allowance method of recording bad debt in which an estimated rate of bad debt is applied to credit sales made in the accounting period.

15

FINANCIAL STATEMENTS AND THE CLOSING PROCESS FOR A MERCHANDISING BUSINESS

Completing the Cycle

Do You Already Know?

- How to compute the gross profit percentage
- What COGS is and how to zero it out
- The IRS paperwork you need if you hire independent contractors

 For additional questions to assess your current knowledge of the closing process for a merchandising business, go to **www.wiley.com/college/epstein.**

What You Will Find Out	What You Will Be Able To Do
15.1 How to read the classified financial statements for a merchandising business	• Organize information into meaningful subtotals using a classified income statement, statement of owner's equity, and classified balance sheet
15.2 Understand the closing entries for a merchandising business	• Close the books for cost of goods sold
15.3 Conduct year-end tasks after the books are closed	• Prepare required information returns for the IRS

INTRODUCTION

This chapter covers the financial statements and closing entries required for a merchandising business. In most ways, the financial statements and closing entries are similar to those for a service business shown in Chapter 7. A big difference is the use of a classified income statement instead of a single-step income statement. You will also learn about the year-end reporting required by the IRS for independent contractors.

15.1 FINANCIAL STATEMENTS FOR A MERCHANDISING BUSINESS

Classified financial statements:
Financial statements in which information is presented and summarized in specific categories (see *classified balance sheet* and *classified income statement*).

Classified income statement:
An income statement with sections for revenue, cost of goods sold, operating expenses, and other income or expense; also called a *multistep income statement.*

Single-step income statement:
An income statement that groups information into two categories. The first category is revenue, and the second category is cost of goods sold and expenses.

Net income from operations:
The financial result of regular, ongoing business operations; also called *net operating income.*

Apparel Emporium uses classified financial statements to communicate its results. In **classified financial statements,** information is presented and summarized in specific categories.

15.1.1 Income Statement

The **classified income statement,** also called the *multistep income statement,* has sections for revenue, cost of goods sold, operating expenses, and other income or expense. The operating expenses are further grouped into categories such as *selling* and *general.*

The income statement in Chapter 7 (Figure 7-1) used the single-step approach. The **single-step income statement** groups information into two categories: (1) revenue and (2) cost of goods sold and expenses. Figure 15-1 shows the multistep format for a merchandising company's income statement.

Subtotals

Notice that the multistep format presents subtotals for gross profit, net income from operations, and net nonoperating income (or expense). As defined in Chapter 13, *gross profit* is the subtotal of net sales minus cost of goods sold. **Net income from operations,** also called *net operating income,* refers to the financial result of your regular, ongoing business operations. **Net nonoperating income (or expense)** is the result of activities that are not directly related to your regular business operations; examples include interest income, loss from fire, gain on sale of investments, and loss on disposal of equipment.

The single-step format allows readers to calculate the same subtotals as appear in the multistep format, but those calculations mean more work

Figure 15-1

Apparel Emporium Income Statement For the Year Ended December 31, 200X			
Revenue			
Sales			$ 601,200
Sales Returns and Allowances	$ 38,500		
Sales Discounts	2,000		
Net Sales		40,500	$ 560,700
Cost of Goods Sold			
Inventory, Jan. 1, 200X		$ 155,784	
Purchases	$ 328,348		
Freight In	4,000		
Delivered Cost of Purchases	$ 332,348		
Purchases Returns and Allowances	$ 19,000		
Purchases Discounts	1,800	20,800	
Net Purchases		311,548	
Goods Available for Sale		$ 467,332	
Inventory, Dec. 31, 200X		133,972	
Cost of Goods Sold			333,360
Gross Profit			$ 227,340
Operating Expenses			
Selling Expenses			
Salaries and Wages—Store	$ 30,000		
Payroll Taxes—Store	3,237		
Advertising	3,600		
Cash Over or Short	92		
Credit Card Processing Fees	1,860		
Supplies—Store	6,000		
Depreciation—Store Equipment	6,864		
Miscellaneous Expense—Store	1,150		
Total Selling Expenses		$ 52,803	
General Expenses			
Salaries and Wages—Office	$ 42,000		
Payroll Taxes—Office	4,473		
Bad Debt	1,325		
Insurance	17,400		
Rent	26,400		
Supplies—Office	5,500		
Utilities	12,100		
Depreciation—Office Equipment	9,000		
Miscellaneous Expense—Office	900		
Total General Expenses		119,098	
Total Operating Expenses			$ 171,901
Income from Operations			$ 55,439
Other Income			
Interest Income		$ 500	
Other Expenses			
Interest Expense		641	
Net Nonoperating Expense			141
Net Income			$ 55,298

The classified income statement has more subtotals than the
single-step income statement.

Net nonoperating income or net nonoperating expense: The financial result of activities not directly related to the regular business operations.

FOR EXAMPLE

See Figure 15-2 for an example of a company's condensed income statement.

---

for the reader. Therefore, most businesses choose the multistep format to simplify income statement analysis for their external financial report readers.

External Users

The external income statement would not provide the same level of detail as the income statement used within the business. Figure 15-2 shows an example of a classified income statement released to the outside world.

Figure 15-2

Apparel Emporium Income Statement For the Year Ended December 31, 200X	
Net Sales	$ 560,700
Cost of Goods Sold	333,360
Gross Profit	$ 227,340
Operating Expenses	171,901
Net Income from Operations	$ 55,439
Net Nonoperating Expense	141
Net Income	**$ 55,298**

Most companies release condensed income statements to external readers.

Deciphering Gross Profit

Owners and managers use percentages to analyze the amounts on the financial statements. Chapter 7 covers measures of profitability such as *return on sales.* Another important profitability measure is the **gross profit percentage,** which calculates the amount of gross profit earned on each sales dollar:

Gross profit percentage: A measure of profitability that shows the amount of gross profit earned on each sales dollar (gross profit ÷ net sales).

$$\text{Gross profit} \div \text{Net sales} = \text{Gross profit percentage}$$
$$\$227{,}340 \div \$560{,}700 = 40.5\%$$

Business owners must carefully watch their gross profit trends on a monthly basis. Gross profit trends that appear lower from one month to the next can mean one of two things: sales revenue is down, or cost of goods sold is up.

If revenue is down month-to-month, you may need to quickly figure out why and fix the problem in order to meet your sales goals for the year. Or, by examining sales figures for the same month in previous years, you may determine that the drop is just a normal sales slowdown given the time of year and isn't cause to hit the panic button.

The other key element of gross profit, cost of goods sold, can also be a big factor in a downward profit trend. For example, if the amount you spend to purchase products for resale goes up, your gross profit goes down. As a business owner, you need to do one of five things if the cost of goods sold is reducing your gross profit:

- Find a new supplier who can provide the goods cheaper.
- Increase your prices as long as you won't lose sales because of the increase.
- Find a way to increase your volume of sales so that you can sell more products and meet your annual profit goals.
- Find a way to reduce operating expenses to offset the additional product costs.
- Accept the fact that your annual profit will be lower than expected.

Small Business Accounting in Action ➤ Organize information into meaningful subtotals using a classified income statement.

The sooner you find out that you have a problem with costs, the faster you can find a solution and minimize any reduction in your annual profit.

IN THE REAL WORLD

The Value of Numbers

Closing the books may seem like a chore, but it's a chance to take year-end numbers and put them to good use—and not just for Uncle Sam. "Use accounting for analytical purposes," says author and business consultant Linda Pinson. She suggests that business owners take their year-end numbers and compare them line by line with a business plan. The process will reveal areas of overspending or underperformance and help with decision making for the next year. Closing the books also gives owners another opportunity for detecting mistakes or fraud, a much more serious problem. This is especially true for owners who are too busy actually running their business to keep up with strict internal controls on a day-to-day basis.[1]

15.1.2 Statement of Owner's Equity

The statement of owner's equity shows the changes in the owner's financial interest during the accounting period. In computerized accounting systems, this statement is often incorporated into the balance sheet.

Two pieces of information required for this statement are not available on the worksheet and instead must come from the general ledger:

- Opening Capital balance.
- Investments by owner.

Small Business Accounting in Action ➡️
Organize information into meaningful subtotals using a statement of owner's equity.

On January 1, 200X, the opening balance of the Anna Rodriguez, Capital account was $146,950. Anna Rodriguez deposited $20,000 of her personal funds into the business checking account on February 1, 200X. The manually prepared statement of owner's equity for Apparel Emporium appears in Figure 15-3.

Figure 15-3

Apparel Emporium Statement of Owner's Equity For the Year Ended December 31, 200X		
Anna Rodriguez, Capital, January 1, 200X		$ 146,950
Investments by Anna Rodriguez	$ 20,000	
Net income	55,298	
Increase in Capital		75,298
		$ 222,248
Anna Rodriguez, Withdrawals		60,000
Anna Rodriguez, Capital, December 31, 200X		**$ 162,248**

The statement of owner's equity.

CAREER CONNECTION

In an effort to cut their losses and start a new chapter of their lives, a couple's small import business closes the books for good.

Adam and Tracy Wilson are not afraid of adventure. In their mid-twenties, the two embarked upon a three-month journey throughout Asia, visiting India, Nepal, Thailand, and Indonesia. Along the way, the two made contact with exporters in the hopes of raising enough money back home to import the exotic crafts, fabrics, and other native products. A year later, the two were the proud owners of two shipping containers and many thousands of dollars worth of imported goods, which they quickly began selling online and at festivals, craft fairs, and flea markets.

(continued)

CAREER CONNECTION *(continued)*

"We were able to make a good profit on the sales," says Tracy, "but our 'real lives' were getting in the way of our entrepreneurship." This became especially true after the couple, now in their thirties, had their first child. A series of moves throughout the Northeast in 2006 and 2007 left them with more expenses (transportation and storage) than income. It seemed the adventure was ending. The final straw came when the two discovered that mildew from a damp basement had ruined most of the remaining textiles and much of the wooden items. "It was time to liquidate," says Tracy, who did some research and found an online retailer who was willing to buy the undamaged metal goods from the stock that was left.

Though Adam, who had studied finance in college, had managed the bookkeeping along the way, the Wilsons hired an accountant to help them close the business's books and prepare their 2007 taxes. "I knew there'd be some tax tricks that would help us out with the losses from the past year," says Adam.

Tips from the Professional

- Decide ahead of time how long you're willing to accept financial losses.
- Keep track of expenses, even as your business comes to a close.
- Know when to call in experts for help.

15.1.3 Balance Sheet

Classified balance sheet:
A balance sheet that divides assets and liabilities into current and long-term categories.

Most of the balance sheet examples throughout this book use the classified format. The **classified balance sheet** divides assets and liabilities into current and long-term categories. Long-term assets will be used up in one year or more, and long-term liabilities will be paid off in one year or more. Long-term assets are further grouped into classes such as *fixed assets* (also called *property, plant, and equipment*) and long-term investments. Apparel Emporium has only one class of long-term assets.

The information for the balance sheet is picked up directly from the worksheet with one important exception. Long-term liabilities are analyzed to determine the amount of principal due in less than one year. The amount due in less than one year is reported as a current liability. The remaining amount is shown as a long-term liability. Apparel Emporium uses an amortization schedule (discussed in Chapter 12) to break down its five-year note payable into the current and long-term amounts shown in Figure 15-4. This breakdown is for balance sheet presentation purposes only. No journal entry is required.

Small Business Accounting in Action ➡
Organize information into meaningful subtotals using a balance sheet.

The external balance sheet would not provide the same level of detail as the balance sheet used within the business. Figure 15-5 shows an example of a classified balance sheet released to the outside world.

Figure 15-4

Apparel Emporium Balance Sheet As of December 31, 200X			
Assets			
Current Assets:			
Cash in Bank		$ 31,000	
Change Fund		500	
Petty Cash		200	
Accounts Receivable	$ 83,979		
Allowance for Bad Debts	1,750	82,229	
Inventory		133,972	
Prepaid Insurance		3,000	
Total Current Assets			$ 250,901
Property, Plant, and Equipment:			
Store Equipment	$ 60,000		
Accumulated Depreciation—Store Equipment	21,167	$ 38,833	
Office Equipment	50,000		
Accumulated Depreciation—Office Equipment	18,750	31,250	
Total Property, Plant, and Equipment			70,083
Total Assets			**$ 320,984**
Liabilities and Owner's Equity			
Current Liabilities:			
Accounts Payable		$ 114,537	
Accrued Salaries and Wages Payable		1,385	
Accrued Payroll Taxes Payable		149	
Sales Tax Payable		2,750	
Credit Line Payable		7,000	
Note Payable (Five-year), current portion		6,453	$ 132,274
Total Current Liabilities			
Long-term Liabilities:			
Note Payable (Five-year), long-term portion			26,462
Equity:			
Anna Rodriguez, Capital			162,248
Total Liabilities and Owner's Equity			**$ 320,984**

The classified balance sheet.

SELF-CHECK

1. Define classified income statement.
2. What is meant by nonoperating income?
3. How do you compute gross profit percentage?
4. Define classified balance sheet.

Apply Your Knowledge ▷ In one month, a company had net sales of $102,000 and cost of goods sold totaling $58,000. Compute the gross profit percentage.

Figure 15-5

Apparel Emporium
Balance Sheet
As of December 31, 200X

Assets

Current Assets:

Cash	$ 31,700
Accounts Receivable, net	82,229
Inventory	133,972
Prepaid Expenses	3,000
Total Current Assets	250,901
Property, Plant, and Equipment, net	70,083
Total Assets	**$ 320,984**

Liabilities and Owner's Equity

Current Liabilities:

Accounts Payable	$ 114,537
Accrued Expenses and Other Liabilities	17,737
Total Current Liabilities	132,274
Long-term Debt	26,462
Equity:	
Anna Rodriguez, Capital	162,248
Total Liabilities and Owner's Equity	**$ 320,984**

Most companies release condensed balance sheets to external readers.

15.2 CLOSING ENTRIES FOR A MERCHANDISING BUSINESS

As discussed in Chapter 7, *temporary accounts* are zeroed out after the financial statements are finalized. Temporary accounts are revenues, expenses, cost of goods sold (sometimes referred to as *COGS*) accounts, and the Withdrawals account. Figure 15-6 shows the following closing entries for Apparel Emporium:

- Revenue and other income accounts are closed to Income Summary.
- Cost of goods sold accounts are closed to Income Summary.
- Expense accounts are closed to Income Summary.
- Income Summary is closed to Capital.
- The Withdrawals account is closed to Capital.

FOR EXAMPLE

See Figure 15-6 for an example of a merchandising business's closing entries.

Figure 15-6

General Journal					Page 17
Date		**Description**	**Post Ref.**	**Debit**	**Credit**
200X Dec.	31	Sales		601,200	
		Interest Income		500	
		Sales Returns and Allowances			38,500
		Sales Discounts			2,000
		Income Summary			561,200
		To close revenue accounts for 12/31/200X			
	31	Income Summary		311,548	
		Purchases Returns and Allowances		19,000	
		Purchases Discounts		1,800	
		Purchases			328,348
		Freight In			4,000
		To close COGS accounts for 12/31/200X			
	31	Income Summary		172,542	
		Salaries and Wages—Store			30,000
		Payroll Taxes—Store			3,237
		Advertising			3,600
		Cash Over or Short			92
		Credit Card Processing Fees			1,860
		Supplies—Store			6,000
		Depreciation—Store Equipment			6,864
		Miscellaneous Expense—Store			1,150
		Salaries and Wages—Office			42,000
		Payroll Taxes—Office			4,473
		Bad Debt			1,325
		Insurance			17,400
		Rent			26,400
		Supplies—Office			5,500
		Utilities			12,100
		Depreciation—Office Equipment			9,000
		Miscellaneous Expense—Office			900
		Interest Expense			641
		To close expense accounts for 12/31/200X			
	31	Income Summary		55,298	
		Anna Rodriguez, Capital			55,298
		To close net income to capital, 12/31/200X			
	31	Anna Rodriguez, Capital		60,000	
		Anna Rodriguez, Withdrawals			60,000
		To close withdrawals to capital, 12/31/200X			

Closing entries for a merchandising business.

Small Business Accounting in Action

Close the books for cost of goods sold.

Unlike temporary accounts, *permanent accounts* are not zeroed out. Their balances are carried forward to the next accounting period. The permanent accounts are assets, liabilities, and the owner's Capital account. After the closing entries are journalized and posted, you prepare a postclosing trial balance if you are using a manual accounting system. Figure 15-7 shows the postclosing trial balance for Apparel Emporium.

Figure 15-7

Account Number	Account Name	Debit	Credit
	Apparel Emporium **Postclosing Trial Balance** **As of 12/31/200X**		
1010	Cash in Bank	31,000	
1020	Change Fund	500	
1030	Petty Cash	200	
1110	Accounts Receivable	83,979	
1115	Allowance for Bad Debt		1,750
1210	Inventory	133,972	
1310	Prepaid Insurance	3,000	
1510	Store Equipment	60,000	
1515	Accumulated Depreciation—Store Equipment		21,167
1610	Office Equipment	50,000	
1615	Accumulated Depreciation—Office Equipment		18,750
2010	Accounts Payable		114,537
2110	Accrued Salaries and Wages Payable		1,385
2120	Accrued Payroll Taxes Payable		149
2151	Social Security Tax Payable		-
2152	Medicare Tax Payable		-
2153	Federal Withholding Payable		-
2154	State Withholding Payable		-
2210	Sales Tax Payable		2,750
2310	Bank Credit Line Payable		7,000
2510	Note Payable (Five-year)		32,915
3010	Anna Rodriguez, Capital		162,248
Totals		362,651	362,651

A postclosing trial balance.

SELF-CHECK

1. Which temporary accounts are closed out in a merchandising business?
2. What does *COGS* stand for?
3. In closing entries, what is the offset account for COGS?
4. Do COGS accounts appear on the postclosing trial balance? Why or why not?

Apply Your Knowledge ▶ Journalize the closing entries for the following accounts:

Purchases, $55,000 debit balance
Purchases Returns and Allowances, $2,000 credit balance
Purchases Discounts, $1,000 credit balance

15.3 OTHER YEAR-END TASKS: FORM 1099

After the end of the year, you need to file certain reports with government agencies. Chapter 12 discusses state Sales and Use Tax Returns, and the following federal payroll reports are covered in Chapter 10:

- Form 941.
- Form 940.
- Form W-2.
- Form W-3.

Independent contractor:
A person who performs a specific task but determines the best method to do that task and is not under the direct control of you or your company.

Form W-9, Request for Taxpayer Identification Number and Certification:
A form in which an independent contractor provides a tax identification number and a statement about the legal form of business structure.

Just as you file Forms W-2 and W-3 for employees, you must file certain forms for independent contractors who provide services to your business. An **independent contractor** is a person who performs a specific task but determines the best method to do that task and is not under the direct control of you or your company. Examples of independent contractors are the outside accountant and outside attorney.

Be very careful when classifying a person as an independent contractor. The Internal Revenue Service has strict rules to prevent the misclassification of employees as independent contractors.

When you hire a new contractor, he or she should complete and turn in a **Form W-9, Request for Taxpayer Identification Number and Certification.** The purpose of the Form W-9 is somewhat similar to that of the Form W-4 filled out by employees (Chapter 9). The Form W-9, shown in Figure 15-8, asks the contractor for his or her tax

Figure 15-8

Form W-9
(Rev. November 2005)
Department of the Treasury
Internal Revenue Service

Request for Taxpayer Identification Number and Certification

Give form to the requester. Do not send to the IRS.

Print or type
See **Specific Instructions** on page 2.

Name (as shown on your income tax return)

Business name, if different from above

Check appropriate box: ☐ Individual/ Sole proprietor ☐ Corporation ☐ Partnership ☐ Other ▶ .... ☐ Exempt from backup withholding

Address (number, street, and apt. or suite no.)

Requester's name and address (optional)

City, state, and ZIP code

List account number(s) here (optional)

Part I Taxpayer Identification Number (TIN)

Enter your TIN in the appropriate box. The TIN provided must match the name given on Line 1 to avoid backup withholding. For individuals, this is your social security number (SSN). However, for a resident alien, sole proprietor, or disregarded entity, see the Part I instructions on page 3. For other entities, it is your employer identification number (EIN). If you do not have a number, see *How to get a TIN* on page 3.

Note. If the account is in more than one name, see the chart on page 4 for guidelines on whose number to enter.

Social security number

or

Employer identification number

Part II Certification

Under penalties of perjury, I certify that:

1. The number shown on this form is my correct taxpayer identification number (or I am waiting for a number to be issued to me), and

2. I am not subject to backup withholding because: (a) I am exempt from backup withholding, or (b) I have not been notified by the Internal Revenue Service (IRS) that I am subject to backup withholding as a result of a failure to report all interest or dividends, or (c) the IRS has notified me that I am no longer subject to backup withholding, and

3. I am a U.S. person (including a U.S. resident alien).

Certification instructions. You must cross out item 2 above if you have been notified by the IRS that you are currently subject to backup withholding because you have failed to report all interest and dividends on your tax return. For real estate transactions, item 2 does not apply. For mortgage interest paid, acquisition or abandonment of secured property, cancellation of debt, contributions to an individual retirement arrangement (IRA), and generally, payments other than interest and dividends, you are not required to sign the Certification, but you must provide your correct TIN. (See the instructions on page 4.)

Sign Here Signature of U.S. person ▶   Date ▶

Collect a Form W-9 from each independent contractor.

Form 1099:
The generic name for a group of IRS information returns used to report non-payroll payments.

identification number and a declaration of the contractor's legal form of business structure (sole proprietorship, corporation, partnership, or other legal form). This form should be kept in your files; it does not go to the IRS.

After year-end, you must complete an IRS information return **Form 1099** for certain payments you made in the previous year. Whether you need to send a Form 1099, and the type of Form 1099 you send, will depend on various factors:

Form 1099-MISC, Miscellaneous Income:
The Form 1099 used to report payments to an independent contractor for business services.

- The IRS has many different versions of Form 1099. For example, Form 1099-INT reports certain interest payments collected during the year. The Form 1099 version you are most likely to use for independent contractors who provide services to your business is **Form 1099-MISC, Miscellaneous Income.**

- If you paid a contractor less than $600 total for the year, you do not need to send a Form 1099-MISC to that contractor.

- If the contractor is a corporation, you usually don't have to send a Form 1099-MISC. However, there are exceptions. For example, you must send a Form 1099-MISC for legal services paid during the year even if the law office is organized as a corporation.

Figure 15-9 shows a blank Form 1099-MISC.

This book just touches on the topic of Form 1099. A comprehensive discussion of Form 1099 can be found in *General Instructions for Forms 1099, 1098, 5498, and W-2G* online at www.irs.gov/pub/irs-pdf/i1099gi.pdf.

You need to make three copies of your Form 1099:

FOR EXAMPLE

Go to www.irs.gov/pub/irs-pdf/i1099gi.pdf for more information on Form 1099.

- Send one copy to the contractor by January 31.

- Send one copy to the IRS by February 28.

- Keep one copy for your company files.

Form 1096, Annual Summary and Transmittal of U.S. Information Returns:
The cover sheet used to send Form 1099 to the IRS.

To transmit the Form 1099-MISC to the federal government, you use a cover sheet called **Form 1096, Annual Summary and Transmittal of U.S. Information Returns.** This form summarizes the information filed on the Form 1099.

Small Business Accounting in Action →
Prepare required information returns for the IRS.

For more information about independent contractors and reporting requirements, go to www.irs.gov. The Web site has a section titled "Small Business and Self-Employed One-Stop Resource" that contains a wealth of information about tax reporting and many other small-business topics.

Figure 15-9

9595	☐ VOID ☐ CORRECTED		

PAYER'S name, street address, city, state, ZIP code, and telephone no.	1 Rents $	OMB No. 1545-0115 **2007** Form **1099-MISC**	**Miscellaneous Income**
	2 Royalties $		**Copy A For Internal Revenue Service Center** File with Form 1096.
	3 Other income $	4 Federal income tax withheld $	
PAYER'S federal identification number	RECIPIENT'S identification number	5 Fishing boat proceeds $	6 Medical and health care payments $
RECIPIENT'S name		7 Nonemployee compensation $	8 Substitute payments in lieu of dividends or interest $
Street address (including apt. no.)		9 Payer made direct sales of $5,000 or more of consumer products to a buyer (recipient) for resale ▶ ☐	10 Crop insurance proceeds $
City, state, and ZIP code		11	12
Account number (see instructions)		2nd TIN not. ☐	13 Excess golden parachute payments $	14 Gross proceeds paid to an attorney $
15a Section 409A deferrals $	15b Section 409A income $	16 State tax withheld $ $	17 State/Payer's state no.	18 State income $ $

Form **1099-MISC**   Cat. No. 14425J   Department of the Treasury - Internal Revenue Service

Do Not Cut or Separate Forms on This Page — Do Not Cut or Separate Forms on This Page

Form 1099-MISC.

377

IN THE REAL WORLD

Taxed by Taxes

The growing complexity of the federal tax code is taking its toll on small business owners, forcing them to use the services of tax accountants and lawyers to stay on track. A Discover survey has shown that 77 percent of small business owners describe tax preparation and documentation as a "time-consuming process," and 74 percent said it "distracted them from the day-to-day operations of running their business." For many, the work of taxes is taking valuable time and resources away from growing a business. Despite the increasing use of tax and accounting software by small businesses, owners feel they must still rely on tax professionals, which can cost an average of $75 per hour. "It's costly, but it's a wise choice," said Barbara Weltman, a New York–based lawyer who specializes in small-business taxation issues. "Small business owners should be running their business and let the experts take care of their taxes."[2]

SELF-CHECK

1. Define independent contractor.
2. What is the purpose of Form W-9?
3. Which version of Form 1099 is a small-business owner most likely to use?
4. What is the purpose of Form 1096?

Apply Your Knowledge   Which of the following circumstances would trigger a Form 1099-MISC?

Your business paid a sole proprietor $550 in the calendar year for painting signs.

Your business paid $600 for attorney services from a law corporation in the calendar year.

Your business paid $650 to an accounting partnership for tax services in the calendar year.

Your business paid $700 in the calendar year to an interior design service organized as a corporation.

SUMMARY

Section 15.1

- Most businesses prepare classified financial statements.
- A reduction in gross profit percentage from one period to the next means sales decreased, cost of goods sold increased, or both.
- Long-term debt is divided into two categories for balance sheet purposes: the amount due in less than one year (current) and the remaining amount due (long-term).

Section 15.2

- Closing entries are made for revenues, expenses, cost of goods sold accounts, and the Withdrawals account.

Section 15.3

- You must be careful not to hire someone as an independent contractor when that person should really be classified as an employee.
- After the end of the calendar year, you need to send Form 1099-MISC to your contractors and to the federal government.

ASSESS YOUR UNDERSTANDING

UNDERSTAND: WHAT HAVE YOU LEARNED?

 Go to **www.wiley.com/college/epstein** to assess your knowledge of the closing process for a merchandising business.

PRACTICE: WHAT WOULD YOU DO?

1. What is the formula for the single-step Income Statement?
2. What is the formula used to prepare a multistep Income Statement?
3. What is the difference between Net Income from Operations and Nonoperating Income?
4. Explain Gross Profit Percentage. How is it beneficial to the owner?
5. The worksheet for the J. Eunice Merchandising entity appears below.

J. Eunice Merchandising						
Worksheet						
December 31, 200X						
	Adjusted Trial Balance		Income Statement		Balance Sheet	
Cash	35,000				35,000	
Accounts Receivable	20,000				20,000	
Inventory	47,000		47,000	50,000	50,000	
Supplies	3,000				3,000	
Prepaid Insurance	2,200				2,200	
Building	125,000				125,000	
Accumulated Depreciation, Building		30,000				30,000
Accounts Payable		40,000				40,000
Wages Payable		5,000				5,000
Sales Tax Payable		900				900
J. Eunice, Capital		105,000				105,000
J. Eunice, Withdrawals	3,000				3,000	
Sales		275,000		275,000		

Sales Returns & Allowances	5,000		5,000				
Sales Discounts	7,000		7,000				
Interest Income		6,000		6,000			
Purchases	79,000		79,000				
Purchase Returns & Allowances		2,000		2,000			
Purchase Discounts		4,000		4,000			
Freight-in	2,500		2,500				
Salaries & Wages - Office	80,000		80,000				
Salaries & Wages - Store	40,000		40,000				
Rent Expense	12,000		12,000				
Supplies Expense	1,500		1,500				
Insurance Expense	2,000		2,000				
Depreciation Expense, Building	3,000		3,000				
Miscellaneous Expense	700		700				
Totals	467,900	467,900	279,700	337,000	238,200	180,900
Net Income			57,300			57,300
			337,000	337,000	238,200	238,200

Prepare the Cost of Goods Sold section of a multistep Income Statement for the J. Eunice Merchandising entity.

6. Refer to question 5. Prepare a multistep Income Statement in good form for the J. Eunice Merchandising entity.

7. Refer to questions 5 and 6. J. Eunice had a beginning capital balance of $100,000. On July 2 of this current accounting year she invested an additional $5,000. Prepare the Statement of Owner's Equity for the J. Eunice Merchandising entity.

8. Refer to questions 5 and 7. Prepare a classified Balance Sheet for the J. Eunice Merchandising entity.

9. Using the information given in question 5, prepare the closing entries for the J. Eunice Merchandising entity.

10. Explain the need for the following forms:
   a. Form W-9
   b. Form 1099
   c. Form 1096

BE A SMALL BUSINESS ACCOUNTANT

No Closing Entries

The owner of the local merchandising firm has decided it is not necessary to prepare closing entries at the completion of the accounting cycle; he feels that it doesn't make much sense, so he is not going to adhere to that policy. Can you tell him why closing entries are needed?

Cost of Goods Sold

"I keep hearing this term 'cost of goods sold.' What does this mean and why is it any different than the other cost that I have?"

These are the words spoken by one curious business owner. How would you explain it to him?

KEY TERMS

Classified balance sheet	A balance sheet that divides assets and liabilities into current and long-term categories.
Classified financial statements	Financial statements in which information is presented and summarized in specific categories (see *classified balance sheet* and *classified income statement*).
Classified income statement	An income statement with sections for revenue, cost of goods sold, operating expenses, and other income or expense; also called a *multistep income statement.*
Form 1096	Annual Summary and Transmittal of U.S. Information Returns, the cover sheet used to send Form 1099 to the IRS.
Form 1099	The generic name for a group of IRS information returns used to report non-payroll payments.
Form 1099-MISC	Miscellaneous Income, the Form 1099 used to report payments to an independent contractor for business services.
Form W-9	Request for Taxpayer Identification Number and Certification, a form in which an independent contractor provides a tax identification number and a statement about the legal form of business structure.
Gross profit percentage	A measure of profitability that shows the amount of gross profit earned on each sales dollar (gross profit ÷ net sales).
Independent contractor	A person who performs a specific task but determines the best method to do that task and is not under the direct control of you or your company.
Net income from operations	The financial result of regular, ongoing business operations; also called *net operating income.*
Net nonoperating income or net nonoperating expense	The financial result of activities not directly related to the regular business operations.
Single-step income statement	An income statement that groups information into two categories. The first category is revenue, and the second category is cost of goods sold and expenses.

REFERENCES

1. Inc.com, "Closing the Books," Jonathan Sprague, December 2004, www. inc.com/magazine/20041201/accounting.html.
2. Inc.com, "For Small Businesses, an Annual Nightmare," Angus Loten, March 26, 2007, www.inc.com/news/articles/200703/tax.html.

APPENDIX A   DEPRECIATION

Imagine how bad your income statement would look if you wrote off the cost of a $100,000 piece of equipment in just one year. It would look as if your business wasn't doing well. Imagine the impact on a small business— $100,000 could eat up its entire profit or maybe even put it in the position of reporting a loss.

Instead of writing off the full amount of a fixed asset in one year, you use an accounting method called *depreciation* to write off the asset as it gets used up. Depreciation is covered in Chapter 6. This appendix supplements that discussion.

There are two types of depreciation:

• Depreciation for accounting purposes.
• Depreciation for income tax purposes.

A.1   DEPRECIATION FOR ACCOUNTING PURPOSES

Accountants use depreciation as a way to allocate the costs of a fixed asset over the period in which the asset is useable to the business. Some companies enter depreciation expenses into the books once a year just before preparing their annual reports. Others calculate depreciation expenses monthly or quarterly.

A.1.1 Knowing What You Can and Can't Depreciate

Businesses don't depreciate everything they buy. Low-cost items or items that aren't expected to last more than one year are recorded in expense accounts rather than asset accounts. For example, office supplies are an expense.

Lifespan isn't the deciding factor for depreciation, however. Some assets that last many years are never depreciated. For example, land doesn't depreciate. You can always make use of land. Unlike a vehicle or a building, land does not "wear out."

You can't depreciate any items that you use outside your business, such as your personal car or home computer, but if you use these assets for both personal needs and business needs, you can depreciate a portion of them based on the percentage of time or other measurement that proves how much you use the car or computer for business.

A.1.2 Figuring Out the Useful Life of a Fixed Asset

The IRS has created a chart that spells out the recovery periods allowed for business equipment for income tax purposes (see Table A-1). A recovery period is the anticipated useful lifespan of a fixed asset. For example, cars have a five-year recovery period because the IRS anticipates that they'll have a useful lifespan of five years. While the car will probably run longer than that, you're not likely to continue using that car for business purposes after the first five years.

Table A-1: Depreciation Recovery Periods for Business Equipment

Property Class Recovery Period	Business Equipment
3-year property	Tractor units and horses over two years old
5-year property	Cars, taxis, buses, trucks, computers, office machines (faxes, copiers, calculators, and so on), research equipment, and cattle
7-year property	Office furniture and fixtures
10-year property	Water transportation equipment, single-purpose agricultural or horticultural structures, and fruit- or nut-bearing vines and trees
15-year property	Land improvements, such as shrubbery, fences, roads, and bridges
20-year property	Farm buildings that are not agricultural or horticultural structures
27.5-year property	Residential rental property
39-year property	Nonresidential real estate, including a home office but not including the value of the land

You can use the IRS chart for accounting purposes, or you can develop a chart that makes more sense for your business. (Remember, we are now talking about accounting purposes, not income tax purposes.)

For example, if you run a trucking company, you may determine that your trucks get used up more quickly than those used by a business for occasional deliveries. Although the IRS says that five years is the normal useful life for a truck, you may determine that trucks in your business are only useable for three years. In that case, you would use a three-year life span for accounting purposes.

A.1.3 Delving into Cost Basis

In order to calculate depreciation for an asset, you need to know the cost basis of that asset. The formula for cost basis is:

Cost of the fixed asset + Sales tax + Shipping and delivery costs + Installation charges + Other costs = Cost basis

- Cost of the fixed asset: What you paid for the equipment, furniture, structure, vehicle, or other asset.
- Sales tax: What you were charged in sales tax to buy the fixed asset.
- Shipping and delivery: Any shipping or delivery charges you paid to get the fixed asset.
- Installation charges: Any charges you paid in order to have the equipment, furniture, or other fixed asset installed on your business's premises.
- Other costs: Any other charges you need to pay to make the fixed asset usable for your business. For example, if you buy a new computer and need to set up certain hardware in order to use that computer for your business, those setup costs can be added as part of the cost basis of the fixed asset (the computer).

A.1.4 Depreciation Methods

After you decide on the useful life of an asset and calculate its cost basis, you have to decide how to go about reducing the asset's value according to accounting standards. You have a choice of three methods:

- Straight-line.
- Double-declining balance.
- Units of production.

A fourth method called *sum-of-years-digits* is used infrequently in the business world and is therefore excluded from this discussion.

To illustrate the different methods, we will calculate the first year's depreciation expense for a truck purchased on January 1, 200X, with a cost basis of $25,000. We estimate that the truck can be sold in five years for $5,000.

Straight-Line

When depreciating assets using the straight-line method you spread the cost of the asset evenly over the number of years the asset will be used. The straight-line method is covered in Chapter 6. The annual depreciation expense using the straight-line method is:

$$(\$25,000 - \$5,000) \div 5 \text{ years} = \$4,000 \text{ per year}$$

Double-Declining Balance

The *double-declining balance* method of depreciation allows you to write off an asset more quickly than the straight-line method. This method is ideal for assets whose primary usefulness is in the early years of life.

You calculate the depreciation using the double-declining balance method with this formula:

$$2 \times (1 \div \text{Estimated useful life}) \times \text{Book value at the beginning of the}$$
$$\text{year} = \text{Depreciation expense}$$

The truck's depreciation expense using the double-declining balance method is:

$$2 \times (1 \div 5 \text{ years}) \times \$20,000 = \$10,000 \text{ per year}$$

As you can see, the depreciation expense for the first year of using the truck is $10,000. If you do the same calculation for the remaining years of useful life, you get the following results:

- Year 2: $6,000.
- Year 3: $3,600.
- Year 4: $400.
- Year 5: $0.

Eighty percent of the value of the truck is written off in the first two years.

Units of Production

The *units of production (UOP) method* works well primarily in a manufacturing environment because it calculates depreciation based on the number of units produced in a year. Companies whose machinery usage varies greatly each year depending on the market and the number of units needed for sale make use of this depreciation method.

The formula for calculating depreciation using the units of production method is a two-step process.

1. Find the UOP rate using this formula.

$$(\text{Cost} - \text{Salvage value}) \div \text{Estimated number of units to be produced}$$
$$\text{during estimated useful life} = \text{UOP rate}$$

2. Find the depreciation expense using this formula.

$$\text{Units produced during the year} \times \text{UOP rate} = \text{Depreciation expense}$$

You only need to use the units of production method if you're manufacturing products and if the usage of your equipment fluctuates widely from year to year.

A.1.5 Using QuickBooks to Calculate Depreciation

With different methods for depreciating your company's assets, you're probably wondering which method you should use. Your accountant is the best person to answer that question. He or she can look at the way your business operates and determine which method makes the most sense for you.

If you're using QuickBooks, the good news is that you don't have to manually calculate depreciation expense amounts. The Planning & Budgeting section of QuickBooks has a function called Decision Tools, and one of those tools helps you figure out your depreciation expense.

A.2 DEPRECIATION FOR INCOME TAX PURPOSES

One key reason to write off assets is to lower your tax bill, so the IRS gets involved in depreciation, too. As a business owner, you can't write off the cost of all major purchases in one year. Instead the IRS has strict rules about how you can write off assets as tax-deductible expenses.

Depreciation calculations for tax purposes are different from the calculations used for accounting purposes. You can use the straight-line method to calculate your depreciation expense for tax purposes, but most businesses prefer to write off the highest expense legally permissible and reduce their tax bills by the greatest amount. Two other acceptable IRS methods for writing off assets are:

- Section 179.
- Modified Accelerated Cost Recovery System (MACRS).

The big advantage of the Section 179 deduction is that you can write off up to 100 percent of the cost basis of qualifying property. If the property doesn't qualify, most businesses choose to use MACRS rather than straight-line depreciation.

A.2.1 Section 179

Section 179, which gets its name from a section of the tax code, is a great boon for companies. In 2007 businesses could write off up to $125,000 in newly purchased property that qualified for the deduction up to 100 percent of the cost basis of the property. In 2008, 2009, and 2010, the write-off amount will go up slightly depending upon the amount of a cost of living adjustment. Then, beginning in 2011, the Section 179 deduction drops back to $25,000 (unless Congress changes the tax law again).

The primary reason for this part of the tax code is to encourage businesses to buy new property in order to stimulate the economy. That's why only certain types of property are included, and there are limits on the amount that can be deducted for some types of property.

Basically, Section 179's qualifying property includes tangible property such as machines, equipment, and furniture. In addition, some storage facilities qualify, as do some single-purpose agricultural and horticultural structures. All cars, and any SUVs between 6,000 and 14,000 pounds, can't be fully written off under Section 179. You also can't write off property held for the production of income (such as rental property), most real estate, property acquired as a gift or inheritance, and property held outside the United States.

You can get full details about Section 179 by ordering a copy of IRS Publication 946, *How to Depreciate Property,* from the IRS or accessing it online at www.irs.gov. Be sure to work with your accountant to determine which equipment is eligible and how much of the cost basis is eligible for the Section 179 deduction.

A.2.2 MACRS

The most common type of depreciation write-off used by businesses is *modified accelerated cost recovery system,* or MACRS. The recovery period shown in Table A-1 is the basis for this depreciation method. After you know what type of property you have (three-year, five-year, and so on), you use the MACRS table in IRS Publication 946, *How to Depreciate Property,* to figure out the depreciation expense you can write off. Luckily, you can leave MACRS calculations for your accountant to do when he or she prepares your business income tax forms.

A.3 SETTING UP DEPRECIATION SCHEDULES

In order to keep good accounting records, you need to track how much you depreciate each of your assets in some form of a schedule. After all, your financial statements only include a total value for all your assets and a total accumulated depreciation amount. Most businesses maintain depreciation schedules in some type of spreadsheet program that exists outside their accounting systems. Usually, one person is responsible for managing assets and their depreciation. However, in a large company, these tasks can turn into full-time jobs for several people.

The best way to keep track of depreciation is to prepare a separate schedule for each asset account that you depreciate. For example, set up depreciation schedules for Buildings, Furniture and Fixtures, Office Equipment, and so on. Your depreciation schedule should include all the information you need to determine annual depreciation, such as the original purchase date, original cost basis, and recovery period. You can add columns to track the actual depreciation expenses and calculate the current value of each asset. Here's a sample depreciation schedule for vehicles:

Depreciation Schedule: Vehicles

Date Put in Service	Description	Cost	Recovery Period	Annual Depreciation
1/5/2007	Black car	$30,000	5 years	$5,000
1/1/2008	Blue truck	$25,000	5 years	$4,000

If you use a different method of depreciation for tax purposes, you should prepare schedules for tax purposes as well.

Depreciation can be more than just a mathematical exercise. Keeping track of depreciation is a good way to monitor the age of your assets and know when you should plan for their replacement. As your assets age, they'll incur greater repair costs, so keeping depreciation schedules can help you plan repair and maintenance budgets as well.

A.4 RECORDING DEPRECIATION EXPENSES

Recording a depreciation expense calls for a rather simple entry into your accounting system. No matter which method you used to calculate that expense, here is how you would record a depreciation expense of $4,000.

General Journal					Page 21
Date		Description	Post Ref.	Debit	Credit
200X Dec.	31	Depreciation—Vehicle	✓	4,000.00	
		Accumulated Depreciation—Vehicle			4,000.00
		To record depreciation for vehicle			

Most small businesses don't have to pay income tax. Instead, their profits are reported on the personal tax returns of the company owners. Whether or not the business itself pays taxes will depend on the legal form of business structure, which is covered in Chapter 1. From sole proprietorships to corporations and everything in between, this appendix briefly explains how taxes are handled for each form of business structure.

B.1 TAX REPORTING FOR SOLE PROPRIETOR

The federal government doesn't consider sole proprietorships to be individual legal entities, so they're not taxed as such. Instead, sole proprietors report any business earnings on their individual tax returns—that's the only financial reporting they must do.

Most sole proprietors file their business tax obligations as part of their *Form 1040, U.S. Individual Income Tax Return* using the additional two-page *Form 1040 (Schedule C), Profit or Loss from Business (Sole Proprietorship)*. Schedule C has line items for revenue, expenses, and cost of goods sold. Form 1040, Schedule C, and all other forms mentioned in this appendix can be found at www.irs.gov.

Sole proprietors must also pay social security and Medicare taxes. Social security and Medicare taxes are based on the net profit of the small business, not the gross profit, which means that you calculate the tax after you've subtracted all costs and expenses from your revenue. To help you figure out the tax amounts you owe on behalf of your business, use IRS form *Schedule SE, Self-Employment Tax*.

B.2 FILING TAX FORMS FOR PARTNERSHIPS

If your business is structured as a partnership, your business doesn't pay taxes. Instead, all money earned by the business is split up among the partners. The partnership files an information return, *Form 1065, U.S. Return of Partnership Income*. All profits and losses are passed on to the partners in *Form 1065 (Schedule K-1), Partner's Share of Income, Deductions, etc.*

Any partner receiving a Schedule K-1 must report the income on his or her personal tax return—Form 1040—by including an additional form called *Schedule E, Supplemental Income and Loss*. (Schedule E is used to report income from more than just partnership arrangements; it also has sections for real estate rental income, royalties, estates and trusts, and mortgage investments.) Partners must pay social security and Medicare taxes.

B.3 FILING TAX FORMS FOR CORPORATIONS

As discussed in Chapter 1, the two types of corporations are *S corporations* and *C corporations*. The different types of corporations have different income tax treatments.

B.3.1 Reporting for an S Corporation

An S corporation is treated the same as a partnership for tax purposes. The corporation files an information return called *Form 1120-S, U.S. Income Tax Return for an S Corporation*. All profits and losses are passed on to the owners in *Form 1120-S (Schedule K-1), Shareholder's Share of Current Year Income, Credits, Deductions, etc.* Each owner reports his or her share of the profit (or loss) on the Schedule E that goes with the Form 1040 individual tax return.

B.3.2 Reporting for a C Corporation

The C corporation is a legal entity separate from its owners. It pays tax on its earnings and files *Form 1120, U.S. Corporation Income Tax Return.*

B.4 TAX REPORTING FOR LIMITED LIABILITY COMPANIES

Limited liability companies (LLCs) do not pay taxes unless they filed a special form to be taxed as a corporation, but they do have to file information returns, which detail how much the company made and how much profit or loss was passed through to each owner. The rules for LLC taxes are complex and beyond the scope of this book.

B.5 PROFESSIONAL TAX SERVICES

Chances are you will have your outside accountant file your tax returns, or at least advise you if you choose to file yourself. You can find more information about income tax reporting requirements at www.irs.gov.

GLOSSARY

Account	A record that keeps track of increases and decreases in specific items.
Accounting	The total structure of records and procedures used to record, classify, and report information about a business's financial transactions.
Accounting cycle	A series of steps completed in an accounting period.
Accounting equation	The relationship among the balance sheet accounts: Assets = Liabilities + Equity.
Accounting period	The time for which financial information is being tracked.
Accounting period assumption	The concept that income is reported in regular time periods.
Accounts payable	The current liability account that tracks money the company owes to vendors, contractors, and others.
Accounts payable aging summary	A report that shows the money owed to vendors and how long it has been due.
Accounts payable ledger	A subsidiary ledger that contains details about each vendor's account.
Accounts receivable	The current asset account used to record money due from customers.
Accounts receivable aging summary	A report that shows the money due from customers and how long it has been due.
Accounts receivable ledger	A subsidiary ledger that contains details about each customer's account.
Accrual	An expense incurred in the current accounting period but not yet recorded in the books; also, revenue earned in the current accounting period but not yet recorded in the books.
Accrual accounting	A system in which transactions are recorded when completed, even if cash doesn't change hands.
Accrued Payroll Taxes Payable	The current liability account used to record the obligation for employer payroll taxes on wages earned but not yet paid.
Accrued Salaries and Wages Payable	The current liability account used to record the obligation for wages earned but not yet paid.
Accumulated depreciation	The contra asset account that tracks the cumulative amount of an asset's depreciation expense over its useful life span.

Acid test ratio	A measure of liquidity that uses only the most liquid assets ([cash + accounts receivable + marketable securities] ÷ current liabilities).
Adjusting journal entry	A journal entry that brings account balances up to date at the end of the accounting period. Also called an *adjustment*.
Allowance for Bad Debt	The contra asset account used to reduce the amount of accounts receivable reported on the balance sheet.
Allowance method	A method of determining bad debts by applying percentages to sales amounts or the Accounts Receivable general ledger balance.
Amortization	A systematic plan in which part of each loan payment is for interest on the amount of the principal still outstanding.
Amortization schedule	A breakdown that shows the total payment amount, the amount of each payment that goes toward interest, the amount that goes toward principal, and the remaining balance after each payment.
Annual report	A year-end summary of the company's activities and financial results.
Assets	All the things a company owns.
Audit trail	A chain of references that allows you to trace information back through the accounting system.
Average cost	An inventory valuation method in which the cost of goods available for sale is averaged, and that average cost is applied to units in ending inventory and in cost of goods sold.
Bad debt	The general ledger expenses account used to write off customer accounts that are determined to be uncollectible.
Balance sheet	The financial statement that presents a snapshot of the company's financial position as of a particular date in time.
Bank Credit Line Payable	The general ledger account that tracks the amount due on a line of credit.
Bank reconciliation	The process of explaining the differences between the bank statement balance and the general ledger Cash account balance.
Benchmarking	The process of comparing your results to industry trends for similar businesses.
Book value	The difference between the historical cost of an asset and its accumulated depreciation.
Bookkeeping	The methodical way in which businesses track their financial transactions.
Capital	The equity account that tracks owners' contributions to the business.
Cash disbursements journal	A special journal used to record outgoing cash.
Cash discount	A discount offered to credit customers to encourage prompt payment of outstanding bills.

Cash Over or Short	The general ledger account used to record discrepancies between cash sales recorded in the cash register and the amount of cash in the drawer.
Cash receipts journal	A special journal used to record all incoming cash.
Cash-basis accounting	A system in which transactions are recorded when cash changes hands.
Change fund	The money used to make change in cash transactions; also the name of the general ledger account used to establish this fund (Change Fund).
Chargeback	The reversal of a charge on a customer's credit card.
Chart of accounts	A list of all the accounts of a business.
Classified balance sheet	A balance sheet that divides assets and liabilities into current and long-term categories.
Classified financial statements	Financial statements in which information is presented and summarized in specific categories (see classified balance sheet and classified income statement).
Classified income statement	An income statement with sections for revenue, cost of goods sold, operating expenses, and other income or expense; also called a multistep income statement.
Cleared	The term describing a transaction that has been received and processed by the bank.
Compound interest	An amount of interest that is calculated by applying the rate to both the principal and any interest previously earned.
Compound journal entry	An entry that affects more than two accounts.
Conservatism	An accounting convention that requires assets and revenues to be understated instead of overstated if alternative measures exist.
Contra account	An account whose normal balance is the opposite of a related account's normal balance.
Contra asset account	A contra account with a normal credit balance.
Contra revenue account	A contra account with a normal debit balance.
Corporation	A separate legal entity, which protects an owner's personal assets from claims against the corporation.
Correcting entry	A journal entry that corrects a previous entry.
Cost	In LCM, cost is the historical cost of inventory.
Cost of goods sold	The actual cost of the merchandise sold in a single accounting period. General ledger accounts classified as cost of goods sold have a normal debit balance.
Cost of Goods Sold	A general ledger account used in the perpetual inventory system.
Credit	An entry on the right side of an account.
Credit card processing fees	The general ledger expense account used to track the fees charged by the bank that processes a company's credit-card transactions.

Current assets	Things the company owns and expects to use in the next 12 months.
Current liabilities	The debts the company must pay over the next 12 months.
Current ratio	A measure of liquidity that provides a quick glimpse of your company's ability to pay its bills (current assets ÷ current liabilities).
Customer account	A record of the amounts an individual customer has bought on store credit as well as the payments received from the customer.
Debit	An entry on the left side of an account.
Debt to equity ratio	A measure of financial strength that compares the proportion of the company that is financed by creditors to that proportion financed by the owner (total liabilities owner's equity).
Deductible	The amount that must be paid before an insurance company pays anything.
Deposit in transit	A deposit recorded in the Cash ledger account that has not yet cleared the bank.
Depreciation	The systematic allocation of the cost of an asset to expense over the asset's useful life. It is also the name of the general ledger account used to record this expense.
Direct write-off method	A method of determining bad debts by identifying specific customer accounts to be written off.
Double-entry accounting	A system in which you record all transactions twice, using debits and credits.
Earned income credit (EIC)	A tax credit that refunds some of the money an employee would otherwise pay in social security or Medicare taxes.
Electronic Federal Tax Payment System (EFTPS)	The federal government's system to receive payroll tax payments by electronic funds transfer.
Embezzlement	The illegal use of funds by a person who controls those funds.
Employee earnings record	A record that contains the payroll history for a single employee.
Employee Medical Insurance Payable	The general ledger account used to record the liability for amounts withheld from gross earnings for medical insurance premiums.
Employer identification number (EIN)	A number issued by the Internal Revenue Service to identify the tax account of a business that pays one or more employees.
Endorsement	A signature or stamp on the back of a check that transfers ownership of the check.
Equipment	The long-term assets account that is used to record equipment purchased for the business.
Equity	The claim the owners have on the assets of the company.
Exempt employees	Employees who are exempt from the FLSA; that is, they are not paid overtime.
Expenses	The cost of everything used to operate the company, excluding costs directly related to the sale of merchandise.

Fair Labor Standards Act (FLSA)	The federal law that sets rules for minimum wage and overtime pay, among other things.
Federal Unemployment Tax Fund (FUTA)	The federal unemployment fund.
Federal Withholding Payable	The general ledger account used to record the liability for amounts withheld from gross earnings for federal income taxes.
Fidelity bonds	Insurance to protect your business against theft and reduce your risk of loss.
Financial statements	Reports that summarize information about the financial performance and status of the business.
First In, First Out (FIFO)	An inventory valuation method that assumes items are sold in the same order as they are purchased; that is, the oldest items are sold first.
Fiscal year	A 12-month accounting period.
Fixed assets	Property used to generate revenue. Examples include buildings, factories, vehicles, equipment, and furniture.
Form 940	Employer's Annual Federal Unemployment (FUTA) Tax Return, a form filed by employers at the end of the calendar year.
Form 941	Employer's Quarterly Federal Tax Return, a form filed by employers at the end of each calendar quarter.
Form 1096	Annual Summary and Transmittal of U.S. Information Returns, the cover sheet used to send Forms 1099 to the IRS.
Form 1099	The generic name for a group of IRS information returns used to report non-payroll payments.
Form 1099-MISC	Miscellaneous Income, the Form 1099 used to report payments to an independent contractor for business services.
Form 8109	Federal Tax Deposit Coupon, a preprinted coupon used to deposit various taxes including payroll taxes and unemployment taxes.
Form 8109-B	A Federal Tax Deposit Coupon that is not preprinted; you fill in your company information.
Form I-9	Employee Eligibility Verification, a U.S. Citizenship and Immigration Services (USCIS) form used to verify an employee's eligibility to work in the United States.
Form SS-4	Application for Employer Identification Number, an IRS form used by employers to apply for an EIN.
Form W-2	Wage and Tax Statement, a form prepared by employers and sent to employees and the federal government.
Form W-3	Transmittal of Wage and Tax Statements, a cover sheet for the W-2 forms that are sent to the federal government.

Form W-4	Employee's Withholding Allowance Certificate, an IRS form on which employees provide information used to determine the amounts of income taxes withheld from their pay.
Form W-5	Earned Income Credit Advance Payment Certificate, an IRS form used by employees to request that the employer advance the EIC amount in paychecks.
Form W-9	Request for Taxpayer Identification Number and Certification, a form in which an independent contractor provides a tax identification number and a statement about the legal form of business structure.
Freight In	A cost of goods sold account that tracks the costs of shipping incoming merchandise; it is used only in the periodic inventory system.
General journal	A journal that can be used to record all types of transactions.
General ledger	A permanent record of all the accounts used in your business.
General partner	A partner who runs the day-to-day business in a partnership and has unlimited legal liability.
Gross earnings	The amount of an employee's earnings before any deductions.
Gross profit	The result of net sales minus cost of goods sold.
Gross profit percentage	A measure of profitability that shows the amount of gross profit earned on each sales dollar (gross profit ÷ net sales).
Income statement	The financial statement that presents a summary of the company's financial activity over a certain period of time.
Income Summary account	A temporary equity account that is used to close out revenue and expenses at the end of the accounting period.
Income tax	A tax based on the amount of earnings that are considered taxable.
Independent contractor	A person who performs a specific task but determines the best method to do that task and is not under the direct control of you or your company.
Interest	The cost of borrowing money.
Interest Expense	The general ledger account that tracks the expenses you incur when you borrow money.
Interest Income	The general ledger account used to track any income earned in a company's savings account, certificate of deposit, or similar investment vehicle.
Internal controls	Procedures that protect assets and provide reliable records.
Internal theft	Stealing of company assets (such as inventory) by employees.
Inventory	A current asset account that tracks the merchandise on hand.
Journal	A chronological record of daily company transactions.
Journalizing	The process of recording transactions in a journal.

Kickback	A payment made after the fact to an employee who provided a supplier with access to the company's business, often to the detriment of the employer.
Last In, First Out (LIFO)	An inventory valuation method that assumes items are sold in the reverse order of purchase; that is, the newest items are sold first.
Ledger	A collection of all a business's accounts.
Ledger account	An account in the general ledger.
Liabilities	All the debts the company owes.
Limited Liability Company (LLC)	A structure that provides a business owner with some protection from being held personally liable for their business's activities.
Limited partner	A partner who is a passive owner of a partnership and has limited liability.
Line of credit	The maximum amount you can borrow from the bank.
Liquidity	The ease with which an asset can be converted to cash.
Lock box	A place, run by a bank, that receives payments for businesses.
Long-term assets	Things that have a life span of more than 12 months.
Long-term liabilities	Debts the company must pay over a period of time longer than 12 months.
Lookback period	The 12-month period ending June 30 of the previous calendar year.
Lower of Cost or Market rule (LCM)	The concept that inventory value should be recorded and reported at the lower of historical cost or current replacement cost.
Manufacturing business	A business that sells goods it produces from raw materials.
Market	In LCM, market is the current replacement cost of inventory.
Matching principle	The concept that revenue earned in an accounting period is matched with expenses incurred in order to earn the revenue.
Medicare tax	A federal tax collected to provide some medical insurance to people who are on social security and meet other requirements.
Medicare Tax Payable	The general ledger account used to record the liability for both the Medicare tax withheld from gross earnings and the employer's matching portion.
Merchandising business	A business that buys inventory for resale.
Minimum wage	The lowest wage permitted under the FLSA.
Net income from operations	The financial result of regular, ongoing business operations; also called net operating income.
Net nonoperating income or net nonoperating expense	The financial result of activities not directly related to the regular business operations.
Net pay	The amount an employee is paid after subtracting all deductions.

Net purchases
A component of cost of goods sold in the periodic inventory system; Net purchases = Purchases account − Purchases Sales and Allowances account − Purchases Discounts account + Freight In account.

Net sales
Total sales reduced by returns, allowances, and discounts: Sales account − Sales Returns and Allowances account − Sales Discounts account.

Nonexempt employees
Employees who are covered by the FLSA; that is, they are paid overtime.

Normal balance
The increase side of an account.

Outstanding
The opposite of cleared; it means a transaction has *not* been processed by the bank yet.

Partnership
A business that is owned by more than one person and is not separate from its owners for legal purposes.

Payoffs
A payment made before the fact to an employee who will provide a supplier with access to the company's business, often to the detriment of the employer.

Payroll register
A record of the payroll activity for all employees in a specific payroll period.

Payroll Taxes
The general ledger account used to record the employer's payroll tax expenses.

Percentage of credit sales
An allowance method of recording bad debt in which an estimated rate of bad debt is applied to credit sales made in the accounting period.

Periodic inventory
A system for tracking inventory that requires a physical count at certain times.

Permanent accounts
Accounts whose balances are carried forward to the new accounting period (assets, liabilities, and Capital).

Perpetual inventory
A system for tracking inventory that adjusts inventory levels as each purchase or sale is made.

Petty cash
A small amount of cash kept on hand for unexpected expenses; also the name of the general ledger account used to establish this fund (Petty Cash).

Petty cash requisition
Required to replenish the petty cash fund; shows how the petty cash was spent.

Physical count
An actual count of the number of units of each type of good in inventory.

Postclosing trial balance
A list of all the permanent accounts and their balances; it is prepared after the end-of-period closing.

Posting
The process used to update accounts by transferring information from the journal to the ledger.

Prepaid expense
An asset that is paid up front and then allocated each month using an adjusting entry.

Promissory note
A document in which you agree to repay a set amount of money at a specific point in the future at a particular interest rate. (Also called a note.)

Proving out the cash register
The process of showing whether or not the cash register has the right amount of cash.

Purchase allowance
A reduction in the price that you originally paid for merchandise.

Purchase return	A vendor's acceptance of a return of merchandise you previously purchased.
Purchases	The general ledger account that tracks purchases of merchandise for resale. It is classified as a cost of goods sold account.
Purchases discount	A cash discount taken by a buyer.
Purchases Discounts	The contra cost of goods sold account used to track purchases discounts; it is used only in the periodic inventory system.
Purchases journal	A special journal used to record merchandise bought on credit.
Purchases Returns and Allowances	The contra account for cost of goods sold used to track purchases returns and purchases allowances.
Quick ratio	Another name for acid test ratio.
Reconciliation Summary	Report that includes the beginning balance, the balance after all cleared transactions have been recorded, a list of all transactions that have not cleared, and the ending balance.
Restrictive endorsement	An endorsement that transfers ownership of a check to a specific party for a specific purpose.
Retail business	A merchandising business that sells products directly to the consumer.
Return	The percentage you make on a base amount.
Return on assets (ROA)	A measure of profitability that tests how well you're using your company's assets to generate profits.
Return on equity (ROE)	A measure of profitability that tests how well the company earns money on owner investments.
Return on sales (ROS)	Ratio that indicates how efficiently a company runs its operations.
Revenue	The money earned in the process of selling the company's goods or services.
Salaries and Wages	The general ledger account used to record the employer's expense for employee gross earnings.
Sales allowance	A reduction in the price originally charged for merchandise.
Sales discount	A cash discount granted by a seller.
Sales journal	A special journal used to record transactions on merchandise that your business sells on store credit.
Sales return	A company's acceptance of a return of merchandise from a customer.
Sales Returns and Allowances	The contra revenue account used to track sales returns and sales allowances.
Sales slip	Proof of cash payment; also called a *receipt*.
Sales slips	Source documents for cash sales transactions.

Sales tax	A tax levied by state and local governments on retail sales.
Salvage value	An estimate of the amount that could be received by selling an asset at the end of its useful life.
Separate entity assumption	The concept that a business is an economic entity separate from its owner.
Service business	A business that sells services.
Simple interest	An amount of interest that is calculated by applying the rate to the principal only.
Single-step income statement	An income statement that groups information into two categories. The first category is revenue, and the second category is cost of goods sold and expenses.
Skimming	Taking money from customers and not recording revenue on the books.
Social security tax	A federal tax collected to provide retirement and disability benefits to workers.
Social Security Tax Payable	The general ledger account used to record the liability for both the social security tax withheld from gross earnings and the employer's matching portion.
Sole proprietorship	A business that is owned by one person and is not separate from its owner for legal purposes.
Source document	Evidence of a transaction.
Special journal	A journal used to record a certain type of transaction (i.e., sales, purchases, cash receipts).
Specific identification	An inventory valuation method in which you maintain cost figures for each inventory item individually.
State Unemployment Insurance (SUI)	State unemployment funds.
State Withholding Payable	The general ledger account used to record the liability for amounts withheld from gross earnings for state income taxes.
Statement of owner's equity	Statement that shows the changes to equity in an accounting period.
Straight-line method	Used to calculate an amount to be depreciated that will be equal to each accounting period based on the anticipated useful life of an asset.
Subsidiary ledger	A ledger that contains the details of a general ledger account.
T account	A visual tool used to represent actual accounts such as assets, liabilities, equity, revenue, and expenses.
Taxable benefits	Benefits on which the employee pays taxes.
Tax-exempt benefits	Benefits on which the employee does not pay taxes.
Temporary accounts	Accounts whose balances are closed—zeroed out—at the end of the accounting period (revenue, expenses, and Withdrawals).
Transaction	An economic event that causes changes in accounts.

Trial balance	A list of all the ledger accounts and their balances.
Unemployment reserve account	A cumulative representation of its use by form er employees that were laid off and received unemployment.
Vendor account	A record of the amounts you have purchased on store credit from an individual vendor as well as the payments made to reduce those amounts.
Wholesale business	A merchandising business that generally sells products to other businesses.
Withdrawals	The equity account that tracks money that owners take out of the business.
Workers' compensation insurance	Insurance coverage for employees in case they are injured on the job.
Working capital	A measure of liquidity that shows whether or not a company has the assets on hand to meet its obligations in the short-term (current assets − current liabilities).
Worksheet	An optional form used to gather the necessary information for the balance sheet and income statement.

INDEX